THE
LOST
LEADERS

EDWARD PEARCE

A *Little, Brown* Book

First published in Great Britain in 1997
by Little, Brown and Company

A CIP catalogue record for this book is
available from the British Library

ISBN 0 316 64178 2

Typeset in Sabon by Solidus (Bristol) Ltd
Printed and bound in Great Britain by
Creative Print & Design (Wales), Ebbw Vale

Little, Brown and Company (UK)
Brettenham House
Lancaster Place
London WC2E &EN

CONTENTS

ACKNOWLEDGMENTS

I list below the distinguished people, politicians, civil servants, academics and friends of the subjects who have made this book possible with detailed interviews. It should not be invidious, however, to make special mention among the many helpful people who have given time, information and entertainment of Lady Butler of Saffron Walden (Mollie Butler), and Lady Macleod of Borve (Eve Macleod). In addition, Mr Lars-Olof Lundberg, when Swedish press attaché in London, guided me to a monograph (written, happily, in English) by Thomas Munch-Petersen on Butler's controversial conversation with Björn Prytz of the Swedish Embassy in 1940. And Lord Cockfield, as well as being very generous with his time and cool judgment, made available the illuminating text of his unpublished book on taxation, which had to be abandoned when he was appointed to the Cabinet.

I am grateful to many more people: an inspiriting commissioning executive, Alan Samson; an infinitely painstaking editor, Caroline North, and everyone who helped by doing things for me or leaving me alone. To my wife, Deanna, who has lived with me living with this book, as well as reading the manuscript and proofs, my thanks are simply unlimited.

R. A. Butler Conversations and Letters
Lord Allen (Sir Phillip Allen)
Lord Alport
The late Lord Bancroft
Lady Butler

David Clarke
Lord Croham (Sir Douglas Allen)
Rt. Hon. Lord Denham
Rt. Hon. Lord Erroll (Frederick Erroll)
The late Lord Fraser (Sir Michael Fraser)
Sir Dennis Walters

Denis Healey Conversations and Letters
Rt. Hon. Kenneth Baker MP
Nicholas Comfort
Sir Frank Cooper
Tam Dalyell MP
Douglas Gabb
Rt. Hon. Denis Healey
Rt. Hon. Lord Howe
Sir Derek Mitchell
Sir Leo Pliatzky
Rt. Hon. George Robertson MP
Roger Stott MP
Sir Douglas Wass
Lady Williams (Shirley Williams)

Iain Macleod Conversations and Letters
Sir Reginald Bennett
Lord Carr
David Clarke
Lord Cockfield
Lord Deedes
Lord Gilmour
Lord Hayhoe
Sir Terence Higgins
Lord Jenkin
Lady Macleod
David Rogers
Sir Nicholas Scott
Lord Wakeham
Alan Watkins

INTRODUCTION

I never met R. A. Butler, though I saw him from far off. But when very young I tried with a group of school friends, who did this to candidates of all parties, to heckle Iain Macleod at the Hippodrome, Darlington. I forget, mercifully, what he said, but know that he took us sweetly apart.

I have been snubbed by Denis Healey when, as an undergraduate on the Oxford Labour Club Committee, I said something at dinner, also forgotten but (I know) misheard by him, and he replied in the best terminal Healey style, 'Lad, you don't know what you're talking about.' I only recall that all of us, many of whom had also been crushed, admired him at once and contrasted our guest with Harold Wilson who, trying to flatter us undergraduates, underrated our own self-scepticism. I have come to know and, I think, get by with Lord Healey rather better since that encounter.

When I started on this enterprise, the idea was to write perhaps 80,000 words, (possibly 100,000), on four figures. I had in mind the three set out here plus Herbert Morrison. Whatever the charm of contrasting the animus of Macmillan against Butler with the more wholesome hatred of Bevin for Morrison – 'Herbert's his own worst enemy.' 'Not while I'm alive he ain't.' – it was soon frustrated. Four times 20,000 or even 25,000 is an unsustainable notion when your first essay finally staggers out at 46,000.

Three it had to be, and the book is half as long again as first innocently proposed. Even so, these are essays not biographies. A life is set out with the basic narrative facts as a handrail. I have

aimed to produce critiques linked by the central common question, why did none of them become Prime Minister?

People will ask, they do ask me already, 'Why not John Smith
or Roy Jenkins?' or whoever. I have included no one whose
death kept him out of Number Ten, which rules out both Mr
Smith and Hugh Gaitskell. Death is sufficient reason where one
is looking for complexities. Why Roy Jenkins lost is clear
enough – a deep and early falling out. The question is answered.
I did not write about Kenneth Clarke in the faint and delusive
hope that, by some burst of sense, he might yet not qualify.

My function is that of journalist, not scholar, and I have
worked from secondary sources and from interviews with a
listed group of politicians, civil servants and acquaintances. No
scholastic apparatus sits at the back but very extensive reference
is handled in the text.

I have done what I can as a sympathetic critic to question and
amuse and can only commend what stands here.

PART
ONE

RICHARD
AUSTEN
BUTLER

CHAPTER ONE

Rab Butler was famous for 'Rabbisms', laconic, corner-of-the-mouth observations, invariably short, often ambiguous, very much better heard about others than suffered personally. Of Sir Anthony Eden he remarked, 'A great man, Anthony, and wonderfully gifted. But there is one thing which helps explain him. His mother, you see, was an outstandingly beautiful woman, while his father, a baronet in the north of England, was perhaps a little strange. And that is Anthony – part mad baronet, part beautiful woman.'

In the censorious cliché of our time, Rab Butler was 'judgmental'. The habit did not leave him when late in life he summed up a recently deceased younger politician. His cousin, David Butler, the Oxford psephologist, remembers his comments in 1977 on Peter Kirk, his successor in the Saffron Walden constituency who had just died at 49. He had, said Butler, been very unpopular and negligent as an MP and had wantonly killed himself by going on after his first heart attack. Such severity was, in part, a don's cool way of refusing to sentimentalise his sovereign judgment of merit. But it contrasts with the gaiety of his account of Eden, a cheeking of that great man, a sending-up of a vain, hysterical colleague which gains in credibility the more one knows about Eden. The second comment has about it some of the grimness of exile, also of ill-health. Butler had a skin complaint which made shaving painful and physically had rather let himself go, putting on weight and giving up on his appearance – not that the trim dapper look had ever applied to him.

As Master of Trinity he headed the most distinguished

academic foundation in Britain and had been nodded through to a second term, the nearest cool Cambridge can get to acclamation, with even a critic of his appointment, the radical social historian Dr Peter Laslett, observing that he had handled himself pretty well. David Butler also heard Rab doing minor business on the phone on university syndics affairs. 'He apologised very gracefully for interrupting our talk, took up the phone, offered a couple of quick suggestions, made a separate phone call himself, advised somebody else what to do and left you with the idea of a master politician without effort getting something useful done in this smaller sphere.' But small it was, and Butler remembered another sphere.

He was also at this time full of alert, astringent comment on the politics of the day. He did not admire Margaret Thatcher and would have liked, in 1978, to be rid of her as party leader – not an uncommon view then, less so after a few years, then, once again, not an uncommon view. Much of his scorn as a professional politician derived from her failure to understand Scotland, in 1978 as much a bubbling issue as it is now. He described being brought to meet her by his son Adam, at that time one of her parliamentary private secretaries. What advice had he to give the Conservatives then, rather than a memory? He took out a piece of chalk and wrote on the chest of his suit the word, 'Scotland' – Butler was never the dressiest of men – before saying 'Mary died with the word "Calais" written on her heart. You will die with the word "Scotland".'

David Butler describes him as thinking that Thatcher's whole behaviour over devolution and relations with the Scots was crazy. The Conservatives could not win without Scotland. Politics, he insisted, had made it necessary to build the Forth Bridge before the Severn Bridge, the link with England was quite short and Scottish institutions had stayed intact and strong. The thing to do was to guide her to the Treasury instead.

'Who then should be Prime Minister?' Butler giggled. 'Well that's the problem. Willie Whitelaw has some Baldwin-like qualities but he hasn't a tenth of Baldwin's intelligence.' Francis Pym, he added later, wasn't as stupid as he seemed: 'It is a pity he isn't a real Pym.' (Another witness, Lord Allen, former civil service head of the Home Office, recalls Butler's cheerful comment on Anthony Barber. 'Barber? The worst Chancellor in living memory.')

He turned from discussion of the Tory Cabinet and its lack of men in the mould of the leader of the puritan Long Parliament to a personal outburst. 'I would have been Prime Minister if it had not been for these people.' He went on to make it clear that by 'these people' he meant the squires, the stupid men of the backwoods. Advised that there were fewer squires in the parliamentary party now, he agreed. 'Yes. They have gone suburban.' (The party which accommodated David Evans and Vivian Bendall has surely gone rather further.)

The judgments made by Butler in these conversations are partial foundations for what we may come to think of him. He is here as unlike his image of benign indecisiveness as can be. The tone – on Whitelaw as on Kirk – is unforgiving of all human limitation. He is a true academic in his brutality as in the clearness with which he sees things. And Butler – Cambridge double first in History and Modern Languages and fellow of Corpus before he entered politics – *was* an academic. He might have been Prime Minister if he had not been.

The unkindness to Kirk begins to fall into place, not as spite, but as part of a general ruthlessness of vision (though perhaps, and to his disadvantage, only of vision). He speaks in the same conversation of his son Adam as the only worthwhile person in Mrs Thatcher's office entourage, something which echoes Lord Hailsham describing an electoral intake of Conservatives: 'They're none of them any good, apart from my son, Douglas.' But Butler's rating of Adam was only as 'nice, decent and straightforward'. And as one of Peacock's characters puts it, 'I would sooner die than be thought decent.'

His judgment of Mrs Thatcher was, as we have seen, the commonplace one of that time. She was a wretched leader of the Opposition – without impact and as unsure of herself as she later became exalted in self-delight. Her words during a mighty wobble before the 1979 election were: 'I shall be remembered as the woman who was allowed one go – to lead the Party to defeat.' And opinion about her in party and press was no higher.

All this would be revoked by conventional opinion in the face of crude success and cruder promotion. The *Sun* would shine on her, but she would live to be removed from office, as, more obliquely, Anthony Eden had been removed in Butler's prime days – and for manic qualities of single-minded insistence upon nonsense oddly reminiscent of Sir Anthony. The poll tax had, after all, many of the characteristics of a municipal Suez.

But Butler's judgment over Scotland is revelatory, for he was proved right in the long term, after the Conservatives had prospered for a decade and a half with ever less of Scotland at almost each election. And this reaction perfectly demonstrates his response to threats and conflicts generally.

Butler, as we all ought to know, had been an appeaser in the thirties and something of an appeaser *à outrance*. This is often given, without too much clear evidence, as the underlying reason for hostility to him when the question of the Prime Ministerial succession arose. He was also the negotiator who got the British out of the Central African Federation (something highly desirable to be out of), and the instinctive rejector of the Suez episode when Harold Macmillan, quite as much as Eden, was noisily for it. Equally, he was not quite resolute enough to make an open assault on the invasion as certain colleagues did.

It was the most natural thing for Butler to have taken a line over Scotland at one with *Guardian* and *Observer* opinion, if not to share their ardent empathy. It was natural, incidentally, for him to know a lot about the subject – he was inclined to be well informed – natural to avoid a stand-up quarrel with stroppy Scotsmen engaged in constitutional demands and resentful reminiscence. For Butler such people will have had a point of view which, if slighted or neglected, could turn into very bad politics indeed for a Conservative Party in London. His thinking on this issue over a twelvemonth had been constant. A year earlier in 1977 he had listened with pleased surprise to David Butler's view that the Scottish problem was overrated and that the Conservatives would win solidly. He himself at that date predicted a small Tory victory when James Callaghan went to the polls.

By now there had been a struggle inside the Tory Party between the accepters of devolution, notably Butler's own cousin Alick Buchanan-Smith, and resisters to any concession, notable among whom was Teddy Taylor. Essentially, Taylor would win the struggle, though he would subsequently lose his Glasgow Cathcart seat. Butler thought Taylor a nasty bit of work and cousin Alick ill done by, but acknowledged the future scourge of Europe as being by far the more effective politician. And given such disposition of forces, Butler simply did not think that devolution, that rational accommodation, could now come about under the Tories. His bleakness towards Thatcher derived from the conviction that failure to devolve would do lasting hurt to his party.

The Conservatives survived a Scottish ill-will which comes in cycles. But Butler's general judgment, that the Tories are fundamentally weaker without a Scottish element, that Scotland has an identity and an impetus towards autonomy and thus ought to be attended to, looked pretty good in the mid-nineties. After 1997 it looks unanswerable.

But one can see how the Butler instinct, one of response and consolidation, would be infuriating, not just to Mrs Thatcher in all her War Party afflatus, but twenty years earlier in the fifties, to squires and suburbanites wanting to make a stand, cut a figure or fulfil some similar heroic cliché of the emotions. Butler would never satisfy such yearnings but, as we shall see, he was remarkably equipped to provide Britain with good government. And most of the things he wanted to conciliate, including the Labour Party in its high creative phase, actually ought to have been conciliated.

The social peace and steady economics of the fifties he largely devised (better growth than we were to experience under Mrs Thatcher, by the way) were significant achievements. Naturally, they have lately been taken for granted as easy flowerings or deplored by the stern men of the revolutionary right for want of blood, crunch and resolution. They have been out of fashion in Westminster, but among the mere voters show signs of coming back into it.

The career under review is that of a man who held office almost continually between 1931 and 1964. He was out of ministerial office over that span only when his party was neither in sole command nor in coalition. He spent that period, 1945–51, as rethinker and drafter of Conservative policy and outlook, working from an office in Old Queen Street on the transformation of his party in ways quite as drastic, if more coherent, than the recent changes, under similar adverse pressure, made by Labour. In all this, he was again a conciliator, an abandoner of flags and of standards by which less complicated men expect to fight.

As a minister, which he became astonishingly early, he was to be involved at the very start of his career in Baldwin's plans for another sort of devolution – the India Bill, which would remove extensive powers from the hands of British administrators and place them into those of Indian politicians, notably accommodating the 'half-naked fakir' M. K. Gandhi. At the India Office, Butler would be a junior minister, but with a major bill to pass and his departmental head in the House of Lords matched against Winston Churchill in furiously resisting the whole legislation, he was hardly an obscure one.

He had enjoyed from the very start of his parliamentary life the patronage of a Cabinet minister, Samuel Hoare, and would enjoy that of a grander one, Lord Halifax. At the Foreign Office as Parliamentary Under-Secretary, he would, later in the decade, be a member of the team identified with appeasement, and was indeed a sturdy, unflinching believer that appeasement was right. He would use language about Churchill when he became Prime Minister, which makes his comments on Peter Kirk seem soft-spoken. And he did so as a 37-year-old junior caught on the losing side.

Surviving temerity and error because, ironically, he had impressed Churchill over the India debates, he would, as Minister of Education during the war, promote historic reforms granting universal secondary education via an examination ladder, making the select grammar schools open and free to all who passed up it. He was governing again – taking essential executive decisions (and selling them to a slowly responsive Churchill) – but also conciliating. In the era of Keynes, Beveridge and a great groundswell for Labour, Butler was acknowledging the spirit of the times and making terms with them. Liberal Conservative rhetoric likes to quote Disraeli on 'one nation'. There is also that phrase about finding the Whigs bathing and stealing their clothes.

Butler was not a flashy opportunist, but he was an assenter to progress (and perhaps to force). Significantly, very significantly indeed, he was one of the very few people who expected a bad result, probably a defeat, for the Tories in the 1945 election. Such a judgment may have involved some shrewdness, but it was of a piece with Butler's temperament, at once non-resistant and attuned to the evolution of things. The Tory Party created in Opposition, by way of the charters he devised, would be far removed from the narrow land-plus-business party of the twenties and thirties (or the illiberal market liberalism of recent years).

Although low party motives of sucking up to the *Zeitgeist* in order to get back into government flourished among Tories, the thinking he advanced would be kin with the instincts and unaccomplished wishes of his mentor, Stanley Baldwin. It would also be linked with the tempered Labour leadership of the fifties as 'Butskellism', though two outstanding politicians have rarely been less alike in human terms than Butler and the obdurate, prim, fiercely idealistic Hugh Gaitskell.

But Butler would give no solace to believers in hidden market hands, social Darwinism or the view that to obtain low inflation, unemployment was a price worth paying. At all times when he held office after the war, trade-union strength would vary from very great to enormous, and the central ideas of Labour would be a force to be amended or tempered, not overthrown and trampled on.

In all this Butler would be a representative figure. The Conservative Party became at that time remarkably indifferent to the notion of free markets. 'Free enterprise' would be a slogan in 1950 and 1951, and regulation had been easing even under the Attlee Government – witness the 'bonfire of controls' initiated by Harold Wilson at Trade. But the Tories generally accepted the need to compete with Labour in social matters, and Harold Macmillan, the builder of 300,000 houses on camera, stole Whig clothes every bit as effectively.

But as Chancellor for four years, Butler would be regarded as a very great success, able to cut tax and see general recovery, though his time would end sourly with contrary upbeat and salvaging budgets rapidly succeeding one another in spring and autumn of 1955. As I hope to show, the supposed electoral budget of spring 1955 had more complex roots and respectability behind its miscalculations. Butler was never a man for cheap tricks. Overall, his stewardship was a cheerful affair, fiscally firm, liberalising, lucky in some particulars like the terms of trade, but also, in the teeth of the eternal Conservative rhetoric, wisely scaling down Labour's over-commitment to defence! As a Chancellor, Butler is remembered with Roy Jenkins and Denis Healey as one of the great post-war holders of the job. That group would probably not now include Nigel Lawson, a measure of the depth of difference between Lawson's reflationary errors in 1988 and Butler's in 1955.

By contrast with the time of Lawson and Mrs Thatcher, the Conservative Governments of the fifties seem remote from what we think of as the contemporary right-wing norm. But words have complex meanings, and 'right-wing' during that decade had mostly to do with nationalism in a very late colonial form. The Suez Group of Julian Amery and his friends was created in 1954 to oppose British withdrawal from the zone around the canal where we had maintained a military presence. The actual invasion of that part of Egypt two years later, in response to the nationalisation of the canal by President Nasser, was a case of government accepting the sort of right-wing policy trundled about by noisy backbenchers. Bedded deep in contempt for 'native peoples' and derision at the notion of their governing themselves (though Amery himself was a gentler paternalist), it was also nostalgic for a time when we, the British, governed and that was how it should be. It was inexpressibly popular.

Butler, by every instinct, would be against the invasion and would be as surely right as in supporting pre-war appeasement he was wrong. But he would be against it cautiously and without revolt because the national and party mood chimed so perfectly with the severed bile duct and fragile personality of the Prime Minister. If Eden but slenderly knew himself, he knew horribly well what Britain wanted. As a good Government man, Butler would govern the country during Eden's absence after his collapse, and he would govern extraordinarily well, using a private channel through the US Treasury Secretary, George Humphrey, to restore normal relations and reconvene Britain in the eyes of allies as a sensible country behaving in normal ways.

When the office of Prime Minister fell open through Eden's unfitness – in all definitions of the word – Butler was universally proclaimed for the job and so much expected it himself that, to the dismay of his sister, he said at a family dinner-party, 'I wonder what I should say in my address to the nation.' The winner was Harold Macmillan, who had view-hallooed for war in the most satisfactorily patriotic and rabid way, before discovering, as Chancellor of the Exchequer, that sales of the pound as a vulnerable currency and the deadly and infuriated hostility of an awakened President Eisenhower and American opinion generally made his recent certainties perfect and demonstrable nonsense. At which point Macmillan had called halt, late but loud, in ways finally destructive of Eden.

Butler had been right, if not heroic; Macmillan wrong and disposed to panic. Butler had then calmly reassembled the pieces and performed all the best functions of diplomacy with the key ally. But at a meeting of Conservative backbenchers Macmillan made an effective speech and Butler an ineffective one. Macmillan's speech – lachrymose and self-serving in his best caramelised way – filled Enoch Powell with disgust, but it worked, and the finding of a new leader for the country was kept at a healthy arm's length from any consideration of merit.

Butler was to serve on in office, maintaining a complex relationship with Macmillan, not untinged with sadistic play of the most platonic and refined sort. Kept from the Foreign Office in the first of Macmillan's assertions of will (later deviously denied), he became Home Secretary, by consensus a very good one, reforming the law on prostitution and gaming, extensively building new prisons, introducing a major Criminal Justice Act and resisting a cry deep from the right-wing soul (and intestine) for the re-introduction of birch and cat-o'-nine-tails.

He would, in 1961, take up another duty and make a prolonged excursion to what was then the Central African Federation. Created in the lingering colonial spirit which had made the Suez invasion possible, this was effectively the tagging of a white-dominated self-governing state, Southern Rhodesia (lacking the forms and law of a state), together with two overwhelmingly black territories, Northern Rhodesia and Nyasaland, one of which, Northern Rhodesia, was rich in mineral deposits.

The object was to get Britain out of responsibility without power, escaping opprobrium from keeping rather primitive settler company under a general, open-ended, ulcerous obligation. This involved somehow standing up to the bullying and fierce-willed Southern Rhodesian politician, Roy Welensky, who had won all the rounds so far. This, almost to perfection, Butler did.

Continuously effective, shrewd and progressive in government, Butler would, in 1963, see his antagonist/colleague/oppressor, Macmillan, stumble under scandals and misfortunes, caused in small part by negligence, largely by ill-luck and the incautious libido of individuals. When misdiagnosed sickness persuaded the hale Prime Minister that he was dying, the place was again assumed to be Butler's almost by right. Making incredible exertions for incomprehensible purposes and conjuring up a popular, unsuitable mediocrity of some charm, the Earl of Home, using new legislation to make an eligible commoner of him, Macmillan barred from succession the outstanding member of his Government. A man publicly popular and perhaps alone equipped to win the oncoming election was thus frantically and furtively kept from doing so.

Butler failed to put up the fight his supporters, notably Iain Macleod and Enoch Powell, wished; a fight which would almost certainly have afforded him the premiership he had deeply desired in 1957 and still wanted but could not bring himself to take by justifiable aggression. It was open to him to resign – and three or four key colleagues were ready to follow – and deny Home a credible government. Why he should have held back is a key part of the whole Butler question.

Home became Prime Minister and the Conservatives lost the election. Butler, having been Foreign Secretary for the duration, rejected an Earldom in the resignation honours, but accepted from Harold Wilson (an Oxonian), showing characteristic thoughtfulness, the Crown appointment of Master of Trinity, Cambridge and that serviceable, unostentatious thing, a life peerage. He then returned to Cambridge, his happy second marriage, holidays on the Isle of Mull, his shrewd judgments of contemporary events and occasional bitter reflections that 'those people', the squires and stupid men, had kept him out.

A hint has been made of the reasons why such people and their less stupid allies should have done so. But the failure at the highest level of R. A. Butler is a complex matter into which policy and personality are interwoven. And his story cannot be told without the interaction of other people, Winston Churchill, Anthony Eden, Hugh Gaitskell and Harold Macmillan among them. Butler's failure was more brilliant than most politicians' success; how and why he failed are the questions which matter and which I shall try to answer.

CHAPTER TWO

Advantage takes many forms – social, intellectual, circumstantial. The child born near Attock in north-west India on 9 December 1902 took hold of a sheaf of them. His father, then a deputy commissioner who would rise to be a provincial governor, belonged to a clan. The Butlers, with the exception of Rab's Uncle Cyril, who accumulated cheerfully in the City, were not rich, but they were intellectually formidable and had constituted a collective force in education for more than a hundred years. If they had been teachers, they had not been ushers. Starting with George Butler, fellow of Sidney Sussex, Cambridge (1794), they had been headmasters of Harrow (twice) and Haileybury; fellows of Corpus Christi, Cambridge and Oriel, Oxford; Master of Trinity and Pembroke, Cambridge; Dean of Peterborough (twice); not to mention Canon of Winchester and Governor of the United Provinces and Burma. They were schoolmasters and university fellows dabbling a little in the Church, but finding highest reward in colonial administration. Rab's father, Sir Montague, had passed first in the Indian civil service examination, but his Uncle Harcourt, with lesser paper honours, got the United Provinces and Burma to govern. Rather bathetically Sir Montague ended his public career as Deputy Governor of the Isle of Man.

When Butlers married, they married with intellectual distinction. Francis Galton, the pioneer of genetics, was appropriately one connection; the Scottish Adam Smiths of Aberdeen, the Quaker Pease family of Darlington and railway entrepreneurship,[1] and the Cornish Kendalls, with their parliamentary tradition, yet others. The wife of the second Butler Dean of

Peterborough, Josephine, was one of the greatest Victorian pioneers of social work. Great-grandfather George, the ur-Butler, had tutored the sons of a Prime Minister, Spencer Perceval, and broke to them the news of their father's assassination in the Commons in 1810. Great-uncle Montague, the second Butler to rule Harrow, had flogged Stanley Baldwin for possession of a trifling piece of pornography and then seriously depressed the future Prime Minister's time at Cambridge by advancing to the first Butler mastership of Trinity just when Baldwin thought he had escaped the reproachful presence.

The inheritance was slightly oppressive: genetically endowed, striving, accustomed to authority, but not rich and both financially obliged and competitively driven to renew itself by exertion in every generation. Cerebral praetorians, the Butlers had done well out of competitive examinations for a hundred years before Richard Austen was born. Like the Russells and the Huxleys, they exemplified the recurringly gifted family. They had every imaginable connection and were advantageously wired, but generated most of their own power.

It seems enormously apt that Rab should have become the Minister of Education to exalt in 1944 a career made open to the talents by concentrated written recall of knowledge after intense study. He would suffer minor breakdowns in the course of his own Cambridge years. But the subsequent idea, general in Britain from the mid 1960s, that examinations are divisive and hurtful things is a measure of a difference between the latest generations and Rab and his strenuous ancestral kin. It is not a difference which flatters us.

His immediate background was the convention of his circumstances and day: Indian syces, Scottish nanny, return to the English south coast to a kinder than average prep school before Marlborough and Cambridge. But parents matter somewhat beyond convention or even genetics. Sir Monty Butler, despite his intellectual achievement – easy Cambridge first and Mastership of Pembroke after his public service – impresses in letters to Rab (and in his photograph – bald, bullet head with short back and sides, offset by small moustache and bow-tie), as a testy, censorious, little-affectionate figure. A believer, in response to native riot and disorder, that 'a cut to the buttocks' was efficacious, a sender of a ten-pound bank order when his son took firsts in each Cambridge tripos, he has the feel of the sort of Englishman to do substantial things abroad, chief among them the engendering of dislike in foreigners.

Rab's Scottish mother, Ann, seems quite different. She took time out to travel 12,000 miles in the days of laborious sea voyages so that the small boy's acclimatisation to prep-school education in Sussex after eight years at home in India was gently accomplished. She came again to see him into Marlborough and in the period following his university breakdown, and was on hand again to take him on holiday to Scotland immediately after his finals. Given the logistics and commitments to a large family, Ann Butler impresses as human and kindly in a fashion outside the pro-consular norm. Incidentally, her long-faced, heavy-nosed features are those Rab inherited.

Some of that affectionate concern would have been intensified by a formative event in Rab's childhood. At six he had a serious accident riding his pony. As he put it, with a laconic incisiveness prophetic of the adult Butler style: 'Prince went one way and I went another.' Three bones were broken in the wrist. It was subjected to blistering heat from a hot-water bottle, then wrongly set and a pound weight hung on to correct the curve in the arm. For the rest of his life his useless right hand hung immobile at his wrist. One aspect of his life was determined: he would never be a soldier, never see service in a great war. The event makes an odd parallel with Herbert Morrison, blind in one eye from a few days after birth as a result of another medical blunder, the defective hygiene of a midwife. The two reforming ministers who survived such childhood hurt might have agreed that progress is perhaps best measured in terms of things progressed from.

Academically, Butler would do what was expected of him but without any great dazzlement at school. He went on from The Wick, the pleasant prep school run by relations of the great Edward Thring, to Marlborough. Ann, again sensitive, supported his wish not to follow the elect family path (and some disliked cousins) to Harrow. To his own perplexity he did not pass the scholarship he took for Eton and Marlborough had to suffice.

It was wartime. He did the OTC thing and wrote ironically about visiting generals to his mother. He became a prefect in his last term and won a scholarship to Cambridge (to his father's old college, Pembroke), but there is no record of intellectual influence or stimulation. In his autobiography, *The Art of the Possible*, Butler ruefully quotes Charles Sorley, the poet (another cousin): 'And as public schools are run on the worn-out fallacy that there can't be progress without competition, games as well as everything degenerate into a means of giving fair play to the lower instincts of men.' Butler adds slyly that the crippled hand made him a competent blocking batsman, but barred the future Home Secretary from using corporal punishment 'even if I had wanted to'.

He found Marlborough's teaching of the classics – fast exercises with beatings for underperformance – contemptible: 'Although I reached the classical fifth before providentially changing, I never knew about the death of Socrates, never read Aristophanes or Euripides and never studied the oratory of Demosthenes or Pericles or the philosophy of Plato and Aristotle until much later in life.' Charles Sorley, who had been able to quote the *Iliad*, was shot dead at Loos in 1914 when he was 20 and Butler 11.

Instead the student developed an aptitude for languages which, with an eye to the diplomatic service, was deepened by half a year before university spent in France, first with a Protestant minister in Abbeville near Amiens, then, very importantly, as tutor in a Rothschild household, that of Baron Robert. Importantly because the opulent, liberal world of rich French Jews was entirely alien to, and much more enjoyable than, the boiled-mutton frugality of English public school and the nagging letters from his father on the all-importance of keeping within one's income. There had of course been Uncle Cyril living near to the school, Uncle Cyril whose wealth had been translated into Ming and Tang bowls and horses, Wilson Steer, Sickert and McEvoy, Tonks and Augustus John. 'How pleasant it is to have money' was something Butler learned early.

But the affection for life with the Rothschilds derived from serious cultural aspects and from perfect idyllic pleasure. In the pastor's family he had worked hard at Gautier (read every day for his large vocabulary), at La Bruyère and at Corneille, much of which was learned by heart. He had gone to the local college in highly democratic company, made friends with the son of the local signalman and from the signal box had watched the *grands expresses* with their great destinations go by. 'I was very lonely in the cramped small town surroundings of Abbeville, and the railway station seemed a point of contact with the wider world.'

The Rothschilds, by contrast, afforded summers in two successive years, first near Calvados, then at the Château de Laversine near Chantilly; talk of Greek legend and culture, rides in the woods and work on a study in French of the *Esprit Gaulois*. 'My knowledge of France and the French was electrically advanced in this friendly family atmosphere.'

The Cambridge to which Butler next passed on an exhibition seems to have been a liberating place. Strongly drawn to Oliver Prior who had taken over the department, he would take a first in French after two years. At the same time, with an eye on politics, he made for the Union. Cambridge undergraduate politics is less of a jungle than the Oxford Union, where each of the four offices is invariably contested. Get elected as Secretary at Cambridge and you are almost sure of progressing to the presidency. In a distinctly incestuous atmosphere, Butler intervened in his first debate to oppose a speech just made over the ever-active topic of troops in Northern Ireland by his cousin J. R. M. Butler: 'I leapt up just after Jim . . .' His political friends from the Union and the Conservative Association (not his only friends) included Patrick Devlin, later an outstanding judge; Geoffrey Lloyd, who would always be a close political ally; William Wolfson, a Russian–Jewish émigré; and Charles Smythe, later Canon of Westminster. Among the Liberal contingent were Selwyn Lloyd and Michael Ramsay, who would later make their respective best of the Conservative Party and the Church of England.

The presidency also brought him into contact with a Conservative then briefly leading the Opposition. Stanley Baldwin came, aptly, to speak against a motion extolling the art of rhetoric. Interestingly, in Butler's recollection, Baldwin, who spoke against, used the same metaphor that his cousin Rudyard Kipling would more grandly furnish for him in a great speech seven years later when he took on the press lords, conspiring then as now against merely elected Conservative leaders. He called rhetoric 'a harlot'. She has indeed entertained many gentlemen callers.

The vote was tied, and Butler took a chance with the fountain of Tory advancement by casting from the chair his decisive vote for the motion against the party leader. No offence was taken. Rab had been not a little stuffy in remarking that he had never read anything by P. G. Wodehouse, so Baldwin and the other guest speaker, Mitchell Banks KC, on departing, presented him at the station with a copy of *Something Fresh* and the observation that 'the sin of intellectualism is worse than death'. He was the gentlest Roland for the Oliver of H. M. Butler's whipping of the Harrow schoolboy Baldwin in the 1880s – 40 years on indeed.

The family influence of the great clan was not to be escaped, though the second in German and first in History that Butler added to his initial first in French owed nothing to his connection, except as Great-uncle Galton might have perceived things. But the Butlers were big, intrusively big, in Cambridge. Not only had Rab 'leapt up after Jim', but Uncle Will (Sorley – father of Charles) was Knightbridge Professor of Philosophy and fellow of Kings and the same Jim (J. R. M. Butler, Fellow of Trinity), an Independent and Rab's cousin, was defeated for one of the university Burgess seats in Parliament by Sir Geoffrey Butler, fellow of Corpus Christi – Uncle Geoffrey.

Geoffrey Butler would be intellectually important to Rab as well as sympathetic and accessible to the young generally. He was a specific kind of Tory, a social, humane and historically minded one. He had written an influential book, *The Tory Tradition*, suggesting that something more than the protection of property from its confiscators would inform a Toryism that looked for future influence. He had a relatively short life, dying in 1929, the year Rab entered Parliament, but he was to be a natural bridge for his nephew to Baldwin and temperate Conservatism.

After heavy study in his last year of a special subject, the last four years of the Peel Government, plus a paper in International Law in which he was also placed first, Butler took not only an individual last-year first, but was placed in the first division of the firsts in the whole tripos (an elect of the elect now discontinued). Significantly, his sympathies in the study of the Corn Laws campaign had been with Peel and against Disraeli, a prophetic preference for toiling reformer over dazzling spiv.

He had not done so much without pain. There had been illnesses both nervous and physical (jaundice) just before the exams. He was looked after by Prior and his wife, champagne and pills were taken, there was a panic in the middle of the International Law exam, but he still came top in it.

Illness and despatch were to be constants of Butler's life. He would always be able to do things. His father's characteristically discouraging and sour belief that he was not equipped for executive capacity would be answered in half a dozen ministries. But attendant anxiety, physical illness and a need to be cosseted and looked after would be part of the life-package. Finding a wife would matter beyond impulse and affection.

---

[1]The rich Quakers were, suitably, the prize of Cyril, the golden sheep of the family.

CHAPTER THREE

Impulse and affection were directed first towards Kathleen Smith, daughter of Butler's mother's brother in Aberdeen. Perhaps the greatest compliment to 'K.', as he called her, is that no mention of her name is made in his autobiography. But the letters which his biographer, Anthony Howard, quotes are quietly intense and at some distance from the fleering style with which Butler, young and older, dealt with the merely important.

'K. and I have got beyond the usual compromise and found something better. It is hard to make you understand on this bit of paper . . . We have come to a wonderful "*Parce que c'est toi, parce que c'est moi*" understanding . . .' The serious, rather grave love affair would seem to have been heavily discouraged by the family on grounds of conjugal affinity; Kathleen Smith was a cousin and, less importantly, two years older than Rab. The Butlers were a dynasty but a scientifically minded one, fearful of the blights falling upon grander dynasties breeding less carefully. And in Sydney Courtauld, he found someone, as they say, more suitable. Astonishingly suitable – she was the daughter of Samuel Courtauld, head of the textile company. They had known each other, affably but casually, in early Cambridge days – she had been an early Newnham student – and the friendship developed.

Shrewdly and disagreeably, Monty Butler approved in Sydney what he called 'astringent spurs'. The term 'spur' would stick in Rab's own mind and be mentioned by him to Susan Crosland as a metaphor for his first wife in an interview-for-profile 20 years after Sydney died.

She was nothing less than a great heiress and the indications are of Sydney rather than Rab deciding on the match. The laconic style returns in his references to the woman he would marry. The engagement was agreed to after a cruise of the Norwegian fjords with the Courtaulds on a boat called the *StaatsRad Ridderwold* (Ridderwold MP). Rab coolly hoped that his career might lead to a paddle steamer being named after him, too. The whole match was almost too well judged. He had outstanding academic credentials, political ambitions and excellent but unglittering connections and had already, through the Union, made impact. She had a modest degree and unexceptional gifts. But Sydney had energy and fierce drive, 'that ruthless, almost remorseless drive' which Ian Bancroft, Butler's private secretary, would see in her much later. Another close civil service colleague would in recollection long after her death speak of Rab as being 'a little afraid of Sydney'.

If she had the will and direction of her Huguenot-descended, vastly successful business family, she was also on their account set to be enormously wealthy. The £5,000 a year settled on Butler by his father-in-law positively shocked Sir Monty: 'I am amazed at the treatment you are to get.' And well he might have been: in 1926, when this marriage settlement was made, £1,000 a year was the goal of the highly successful professional man. Not yet 24 and seeking a seat in the Commons, Butler was paid the salary of a Cabinet minister – and at a time when Cabinet ministers were paid very much better than they are now. The spoon in his mouth at birth was of metal of a serviceable sort; the bonds of marriage would have the unostentatious distinction of platinum.

Butler was too serious a young man, for all his dry asides, to have married for money in the brutally understood sense of that phrase. But he had married to enormous advantage, with access to the world of industry, the funds for a concentrated political career and ease among all élites, and the cool assessment of 'how much a year?' natural to a Jane Austen parent was, if a little more discreetly, still part of the culture. A year or two earlier, another politically ambitious young man, already well enough to do through his family of publishers, had moved up in a different way in melancholy misalliance with the daughter of a Duke: that affectionate and unfaithful wife Lady Dorothy Macmillan.

It seemed sensible to everyone, including parents, that the young Butlers should complete Rab's education with a world cruise directed largely at the British Empire, one which he commenced with a certain laconic grandeur. 'Before leaving I called on L. S. Amery, then Secretary of State, to obtain introductions in Australia, New Zealand and Canada.' Even upon this jolly of super-deluxe jollies, some late-Victorian earnestness enters. Butler who had regretted the classical reading missed through the aridities of Marlborough, records catching up in translation. 'I was impressed with the lead Plato gives to education, but could make little progress with Aristotle. I travelled with Xenophon across Asia Minor and was easily absorbed in Herodotus.' Also reading Cicero and Demosthenes, 'for style', along with Macaulay, Froude and Stevenson, Rab had other privileges beside his lines to secretaries of state and useful new wealth.

Having accomplished Egypt, undivided India – Bombay, Nagpur (Christmas at Government House with his parents), Delhi and Lahore – then the anticlimax of Australia followed by New Zealand, the couple reached Canada, which impressed much more. The disposition of fate, with the Courtaulds in heavy attendance, to thrust upon Rab a bouquet of long straws was re-emphasised when the couple arrived gratefully in British Columbia to find a letter from Sydney's cousin, William Courtauld, advising that the sitting member for Saffron Walden in Essex, Foot Mitchell, was ready to resign and looked favourably upon Rab as a successor. He advised that the costs in subscriptions, the support of local good causes and the like would be around £1,000. To your average ambitious young man that was a ferocious sum, perhaps £30,000 nowadays. But to someone with £5,000 a year for life and the Courtaulds behind him, it would be an overhead. Another letter, from Sir Geoffrey Butler, confirmed William Courtauld's judgment of the present member's ripe and co-operative condition. (Mitchell would receive a knighthood before the end of that Parliament, but there is no evidence of the Courtaulds having arranged it.)

Anyone who has sweated blood to get onto the preliminary lists, kicked heels in anterooms, finally met, ingratiated himself with and taken impertinent questions from the selection committees of a major party before eventual selection for the pre-conditional losing seat recommended for candidates' experience and character may be excused spitting. Butler returned from a pleasant crossing of the Rocky Mountains and visits to Ottawa and Montreal, the local party accepted yokel status and the direction given by its betters, and he was duly selected, unopposed, to defend a majority of 5,949.

The casting of rose-petals underfoot for the young master was hardly in it. Margaret Thatcher had her Deptford (two goes), John Major his Holborn and St Pancras. Major at 24, hunched in his agent's car after a hard evening's canvassing, asked her if there was any possibility that someone with his background might conceivably get onto the list. But Butler was enjoying the fruits both of great (but respectable) wealth and meritocracy. He had been hired by the Courtaulds rather as the protectionists around Lord George Cavendish-Bentinck had signed up Disraeli and as the Rockingham Whigs had taken on Burke.

Patronage it truly was, but patronage employed with a discernment not often available. Butler had demonstrated the highest abilities to family and their connections, so he was being pushed. (When, more than 30 years later, another young man of great ability, Butler's own protégé, was being pushed, he encountered the first derisive cuckoo of by-election revolt. Such results are now a commonplace, but Orpington utterly destroyed Peter Goldman.)

The meritocrat in Butler set to work to learn the eighty villages and handful of small towns which made up the constituency. The Representation of the People Act existing in rudimentary and tolerant form at that time, he offered beer. Barrels of it were sent round to the branches to stress the need for import duties to protect British, and especially Essex, barley. In a tone of voice – perfect Rab in its flat surface and landmined substance and one to send professional feminists into Hyde Park – Butler guilelessly observes in his autobiography that his agent, a Mr Hunt, 'took great care of the women's association, with the most attractive of whose members he had discreet affairs. This greatly advanced the cause since women are the key to success.' The candidate also put on a touring film show, the cinematographic record he had taken during the world tour. It seems atrociously condescending to us, but with everyone finishing up afterwards at the pub, it established the idea that politics with Butler was meant for enjoyment. And, as Butler observes himself, 'The worst way to conduct a political meeting is with a Union Jack and a bottle of water.' He compared his work in the constituency with his intensive study of French in Abbeville. A little mechanistic, it was also quite characteristically thorough and professional. He was proud to know every by-road of every hamlet and quite as proud to have learned from Baldwin to avoid the sin of intellectualism. 'I spoke simply and directly at village meetings.'

The election, when it came, in May 1929, was a rough one for the Tories and MacDonald would form his second minority Government. Something of the mood of 1945 prevailed in parts of the country. Semi-rural seats like the Wrekin fell to Labour (and people were seen weeping with joy when that result was announced). But northern Essex was conservative enough to stay Conservative, and Butler had worked for his result with a minute care untypical of the times. He kept the majority above 5,000 and, at 26, entered Parliament, where he would serve until 1964.

CHAPTER FOUR

The events of 1929–31 – the second Labour Government, the world slump, the collapse of the underpinning to civil and elected government in Europe – are quite important, but this is an account of R. A. Butler. At this time, R. A. Butler was an Opposition backbencher concerning himself with the agriculture that interested Saffron Walden and with thoughtful observations about international co-operation on commodity prices and the gold standard. This is not to mock him; they were good, sensible things to be concerned about and, unlike another young backbencher, he felt no attraction at all to the doings of Sir Oswald Mosley. Mosley, originally a Tory, had passed noisily to Labour and become a minister in MacDonald's unlucky second Government. For a brief period in his unpleasant career, he was speaking sense. Charged with a reaction to the unemployment suddenly blowing through Britain, he accepted a broadly Keynesian line – public works and ready spending – and, not surprisingly, he had been rejected at the chaste and orthodox walls manned by the Chancellor, Philip Snowden, and the Governor of the Bank of England. He was right, but characteristically impatient, and responded by resigning both office and party allegiance and setting up what was briefly called the 'New Party'. The last word on Mosley had been uttered some years before by Beatrice Webb. Looking at the brilliant, eloquent, socially concerned and exciting young aristocrat, she observed in the style of a left-wing Lady Bracknell, 'Such perfection argues a rottenness somewhere.'

It would be absurd to suggest that Butler spotted the

rottenness or that Harold Macmillan was culpable in speaking up for Sir Oswald's daring but constructive thoughts before, over a matter of months, he invested in uniforms for marching paramilitaries who would give him stiff-armed salutes. Despite much indignation and unnecessary anxiety, all Mosley was good for thereafter was raw material for Wodehouse's Roderick Spode. But Macmillan wrote a letter to *The Times* sharing Mosley's indignation with Labour for abandoning its mandate and programme. 'Only, if these rules are to be permanently enforced, perhaps a good many of us will feel that it is hardly worth bothering to play at all. Sir Oswald Mosley thinks the rules should be altered. I hope some of my friends will have the courage to applaud and support his protest.'

A riposte signed by Butler and four Tory colleagues and with his fingerprints all over it referred to the remark about the game not being worth playing and observed: 'It is usually the player and not the game who is at fault. It is then usually advisable for the player to seek a new field for his recreation and a pastime more suited for his talents.' It was a brilliant thing to say and the accomplishment in tennis terms of a love game. But it was to be a long match.

The careers of the two men would accompany one another like honeysuckle and bindweed for three and a half decades more. Butler would be at all times, early and late, the Government man, the sustainer of the ministerial view; Macmillan would come to the front bench ten years behind him having been identified as a rebel and a leftist, better known as the author of a book, *The Middle Way*, preaching partial accommodation with democratic socialist ideas. Stanley Baldwin would once whimsically say to Butler, 'Try to avoid the extremes,' and – naming a ferocious imperial blowhard – advise him 'to steer between Harold Macmillan and Henry Page-Croft'. Macmillan and Butler were both witty, but Macmillan was as sensitive as Butler was wounding, and more guileful than Rab who, in the view of people who worked for him, maintained 'a peculiar innocence'. In that exchange something had been started.

But what had started for sure was the long Butler ministerial career. It helped to have connection through Geoffrey Butler with Samuel Hoare. It helped also to be a genuine Baldwin man, psychologically as well as by conviction. And the issue on which Butler would serve Baldwin had been mooted during the period of Labour Government. The Viceroy of India, Lord Irwin, later, by succession, Earl of Halifax, had been in that post since

appointment by Baldwin in 1926. MacDonald had left him
there, working to the Labour Secretary of State William
Wedgwood Benn. He would produce the Irwin Declaration that
'the natural issue of India's constitutional progress ... is the
attainment of Dominion Status'. His viceroyalty would also be
marked by the release of the leader of Indian Independence,
M. K. Gandhi, and the initiation of the Round Table Conference
directly involving Congress leaders.

The domestic effects were explosive. The Tory Right, with
Churchill at its head, proceeded to organise, hold public meetings and make war, not so much on the Government and only to
a degree against Irwin, but chiefly upon their own leader,
Stanley Baldwin. 'Let fulmination thrive' expressed it. And
though the word 'racist' was not in circulation, Churchill's scorn
at a Middle Temple lawyer posing as a type well known in the
East, 'striding half naked up the steps of the Viceregal Palace',
is instructive about one world we have lost and have done well
to lose.

The story of the attempt to destroy Baldwin as leader of his
party and the role in it of Beaverbrook's then dominant newspaper, the *Daily Express*, is well known. Its affinities with the
hatred heaped onto John Major by the Murdoch press and the
Daily Mail are real. And when in June 1995 Mr Major turned
upon his enemies and forced his own re-election, he was making
history repeat itself, as neither tragedy nor farce, but a bitter
little tragi-comedy. Butler had no problems with allegiance. Ten
years later, when Churchill was in the right, he would describe
him as an adventurer. When he was in the wrong Rab drew a
parallel between the great man and people who 'thought that
these niggers were slippery men who couldn't be trusted to
govern themselves'.

Rab, as a Baldwin loyalist with strong Indian Government
connections through his father and the approval of Sam Hoare,
was placed not just to be involved early in the National Government when it came in 1931, but to be involved in its Indian
concerns. That year did not merely see Baldwin in opposition
repulse his right-wing critics. World depression, accompanied
by the fatuousness of the Governor of the Bank of England, the
dull passivity of MacDonald and Snowden in the face of crisis
and the final farce of the May Committee calling for wage
reductions at a time of free-falling demand, made a present to
the recently beleagured leader of the Opposition of a National
Government gratefully sustained by 473 Conservative MPs.

A pattern would be shaped reflecting the nature of Stanley Baldwin, who commanded that Government without holding the premiership. George Orwell once called Baldwin 'a hole in the air'. William Connor, otherwise Cassandra of the *Daily Mirror*, gleefully told his wartime readers how he had climbed the wall of the retired Prime Minister's Worcestershire home and planted a poisonous plant which he enjoined to flourish in the soil of this hated man. A juster view of Baldwin would be that while over rearmament against Hitler – sharing the general horror engendered by the First World War and restrained by orthodox banking attitudes to defence expenditure – he showed a tragic slowness of response, he also saved the Conservative Party from becoming a citadel of stupid reaction.

If Fascism, which at the start of the thirties had expectations, came to nothing, this was partly the result of Baldwin's sane, honest character. Who, reading any account of the Tory Party during the crisis of the Parliament Act and the Lloyd George budget, or having seen the press campaign against a predecessor (the Balfour Must Go hate-fest) and the dabbling in treason over the Curragh Mutiny, would have imagined that the raw supporting forces of Conservatives, shown the example of continental Fascism, would have become and remained the stolidly decent constitutional party of the twenties and thirties?

Again, Baldwin's co-operation with MacDonald was not the spiderish entrapment of a betrayed Labour leadership beloved of tedious legend. Baldwin was ardently concerned that Labour, a new and unsure party, should be part of mainstream constitutional parliamentary politics (and quite as keen that his own party should resist the Fascist calls of Lord Northcliffe and stay in that mainstream). He had always encountered the Labour Party without virulent partisanship. His story of the industrialist who lectured him for an hour about the congenital idleness of the working class without himself stirring otherwise than to blow cigar smoke over greenfly on his roses, tells one more about Baldwin's social outlook than a body of heavy analysis.

He and MacDonald in 1931 were men standing in government at the bottom of a trade cycle, armed by conventional economic knowledge with no better weapons than an inapposite frugality. They can be compared with someone who took the example of Keynes – Franklin Roosevelt. But the numbers of the USA's slow recovery leave the American experiment, also very cautious, looking better psychology – 'being seen to do something' – than recovery. Both Roosevelt and the other experimenting and radical alternative, Swedish Social Democracy, owed something to war preparations and their effect on production. So, in the late thirties, did Britain; so, supremely, did Hitler.

Baldwin inherited a terrible hand and had no instincts either for experiment or for 'being seen to do something', but he kept the temperature down and politics decent. He can be faulted for inertia, for a low body temperature in politics, for lack of visionary hindsight in defiance of all received understanding on public spending and for sharing a near universal horror at rearmament. But sanity and decency have their uses. This is Rab Butler's mentor, the man on whom he modelled himself. The recollection of Baldwin always stayed with him. As mentioned at the outset of this essay, he would, towards the end of his life, judge by this benchmark William Whitelaw, a substantial and reputable politician, widely and rightly liked, and say that he hadn't a tenth of Baldwin's intelligence.

Within months of the formation of the National Government, Butler would be an auxiliary member of a Government which Baldwin, handling the humiliated MacDonald with gentle tact, controlled. Butler was made PPS to Samuel Hoare, Secretary of State for India. Within 11 months circumstances would push him, still not 30, into ministerial office. Resignations caused by Liberal departure from the Government over the Ottawa Trade Agreement left a hole in the form of the under-secretaryship for India; Rab filled it.

At the end of the 20th century we have evolved in Britain and elsewhere an expanded payroll. Promotion comes early and means less. Ministers, with the single monkish exception of the Minister of Agriculture, have become Secretaries of State and no Secretary of State is allowed to go unattended by fewer than three juniors. In monetary terms, ministers of state are small change, while Parliamentary under-secretaries are milk tokens. A government is never today less than 90 strong, if 'strong' is the word. As for PPSs, many of whom now serve junior ministers, they are a form of social plankton.

By contrast, in entering the National Government as Under-Secretary for India, Butler was taking up one of the few and prized real jobs in government. Its importance was seriously enhanced by the promotion of the Government of India Bill which, understudying Samuel Hoare, Butler would pilot through the Commons. In terms of controversy, the India Bill is best seen as a pre-echo to the Treaty of Maastricht which gave

Mr Major's government a foretaste of Hell across 11 months. It was actually an even larger affair of 473 clauses and 16 schedules and attracted 1,951 speeches, filling Hansard with 15,500,000 words over 4,000 pages, the whole process lasting 30 months. Butler quotes the numbers in his memoirs with a cheerful awe.

His promotion had involved him in drudgery, but not in routine, unremarked, backstairs drudgery. The stuffiest and most difficult senior colleague, something Sam Hoare worked at being, could not keep an able junior from heavy public exposure and gratifying debate at the highest level. And the highest level was Winston Churchill. Opposition to the India Bill, itself the culmination of round tables and direct consultations with the 'half-naked fakir' and his allies after the campaigns of civil disobedience, was opposed by those of traditional imperial opinion. They opposed it quite rightly given their own point of view. The vocabulary of democracy voiced by anti-imperialists was a tenuous thing in a vastly disparate population within what is properly called the subcontinent.

The bright, facile sentiments of a successful film like *Gandhi* have nothing to add to our understanding of a mightily complex historical development. Baldwin, MacDonald and their Government were engaged in a retreat from clear-cut imperial rule which had been largely honest and competent. They did so amid the great uncertainties engendered by personal charisma and organised disobedience, both riding upon the primitive certainties of religion. And as more than one religion was involved, they rode upon several fierce horses. Reform and conciliation were things undertaken by people who tentatively grasped the impossibility of maintaining the old order. It was all unheroic good sense laboriously pursued, in fact an intelligent and long thought-about form of appeasement. And, despite the bungling rush of the vain and preposterous Mountbatten, Viceroy at its 1947 cumulation, something which helped precipitate ferocious communal violence, it was sensible appeasement.

A highly imperfect form of government would ultimately emerge in the subcontinent, corrupt in parts, theocratic and/or crassly dictatorial in others. Overall, those tentative instincts of the mainstream Conservative and Labour politicians who began to move in the late twenties looks good with hindsight, the highest compliment to men scratching around in an ill-lit present tense.

But it looked abominable to Winston Churchill who threw against the India Bill quite as many resources of skewed intellect, rhetoric, reminiscence, dark warnings and rumbling eminence as he would at European appeasement. In the focus of the early thirties, this was the Churchill who had bungled Gallipoli, admired Mussolini and, as a calamitous Chancellor of the Exchequer, had in a fit of heroic incomprehension restored the Gold Standard. Grandiloquent, hectoring, leaving no horizon untoured, he set about full-scale resistance to 'betrayal of the British Empire'. He had newspaper support, the *Morning Post* and the *Daily Mail*, and he was his eloquent self in the Commons. Butler would compare himself, faced with Churchill, to the bullock traditionally tethered in tiger shoots as bait for the great beast of the jungle. The remark was, in the usual half-inadvertent Rabbish way, two-edged. The tiger devours the bullock only to be shot dead while repasting. Butler had shot a tiger.

He quotes Churchill's eloquence in his autobiography: 'These reforms have failed every test, moral and material . . . instead of contentment, these reforms have aroused agitation and dis-loyalty . . . they have awakened old passions which were slumbering under the long Pax Britannica.' The population of India had risen very sharply under British security, 100 million more people. Churchill visited Augustan periodic rhetoric upon them. 'The 100 million new human beings are here to greet the dawn, toil upon the plains, bow before the temples of inexorable gods. They are as much our children as any children could be.'

To read Butler as he recounts the thirties, the Government of India Bill and, to a degree, the struggle over appeasement, is to notice his polite exasperation with stuck-in-the-mud, reaction-ary, foot-dragging, contrary opinion. A Butler letter describes a woman from Bedford speaking at a Conservative women's regional conference who 'said it was wrong to give votes to naked men with bows and arrows instead of keeping all power in the hands of the British government'. The joint select com-mittee which considered the bill was addressed by 'Lord Lytton, a pro-consular type with a grace of sentient feeling which may not have given a dynamic impression, but which seemed to perpetuate British imperial standards'. Lord Derby, another participant, was noted for 'immense three-inch collars and cuffs, looking as though nothing would disturb him, including his own bulk which he carried without complaint'. Churchill's speech just quoted was 'fine, colourful and brilliant stuff, but the House was not carried away … Winston was entranced by his own imagery; he loved to hear himself as he knew others did, but whereas he was profoundly moved by his own words, others were not'.

If one were looking for the roots of Butler's ultimate high failure, an inkling of them might be found here and in other side-of-the-mouth remarks. All politicians worth talking to make bitchy remarks about one another. Cards are marked with enjoyment. Robert Boothby, talking to Hugh Gaitskell in the mid-fifties, described the Tory view of Butler as one of 'contemptuous derision', a ludicrous exaggeration of current irritation at that fumbled budget, expressed with characteristic florid bombast.

Such pronouncements matter little in themselves. But it is the voice behind Butler's comments which tells us most. It is clever; it is dismissive and speaks as an amused adult might speak of children – with a sort of tolerant contempt. Much of the contempt may be justified, as it was for the ignorant abhorrence of natives and abroad spoken at conference. Certainly, Butler would never have been able to make the atrocious appeal to the worst instincts of the party rabblement disgracing recent ministerial speeches in Bournemouth and Blackpool (speeches which Michael Heseltine has deliciously pushed into the Andes of parody). He was the least populist politician of an era not notably populist. But felt contempt easily becomes communicated contempt, and Butler's worst enemies never denied that he was the most candid and indiscreet of men. The mockery expressed in private letters for pompous important personages like Lytton and Derby would be quite as strongly felt for their minor equivalents in the parliamentary rank and file of Conservatism.

He inveighed to David Butler about 'the stupid men' who had prevented his final ascent, but it is rather likely that over time, many stupid men came to know that he thought them stupid. And on the joint select committee considering the India Bill sat Lord Salisbury, 'Bobetty', himself not intellectually distinguished, but who would later be charged with asking 'Who is it to be, Hawold or Wab?' Butler belonged by intelligence and affinity, even more than useful connection, to an élite. Elites, childishly disapproved of today, are essential for understanding things and doing them. But the non-élite sometimes have a voice, a voice which Butler, by small uncalculated condescensions over many years, alienated. One voice worth noting was that of Sir Nigel Ronald, who poured out to 'Jock' Colville a great chunter against Butler: 'a public danger, flabby in person, and morally and mentally as well; a young man whose whole influence was that of an old one, whose inclination was to put a brake on all initiative'. The last part is odd, but the comment on the old young man catches something which others would find attractive, a gravity tempered by hilarity.

But in the here and now of 1932–5 Butler was doing very well indeed. He was running under Hoare a gargantuan piece of legislation which preoccupied the political class. He was engaged in organisation and meetings outside Parliament to promote its thinking. He was serving the leader of his party and effective head of the Government for whom he had sincere and unreserved admiration. The cause itself was an enlightened one. And Baldwin's words at second reading quoted by Butler leave a good odour: '. . . let us welcome into our Commonwealth of Nations the Indian people, the majority of whom, I am confident, have no greater ambition than to see their country play a worthy part in the Commonwealth.' It is rhetoric of course, but the rhetoric of goodwill and enlightenment.

Having served the comfortable, cautious Baldwin with his own light touch, he would soon embark on a very different undertaking under the uncosy, assured Chamberlain, with whose certainties he would have an all too deadly affinity. Still a parliamentary under-secretary (he would be that for nine years in all), he would soon go fatefully to the Foreign Office.

However, for nine months only, he enjoyed a brief stopover at the Ministry of Labour, under the amiable, prolix former Liberal, Ernest Brown. Despite the short life of the job, it attracted Butler's most sympathetic qualities. It involved him in going vigorously about the country to see what unemployment was like. And having seen, he was firmly directed towards his subsequent determination, as Chancellor, not to endanger very high levels of employment, and as party reformer not to let the Tories revert to the ice-queen indifference of City of London men saying 'Too bad.' As he would later remark, 'Those who talk of creating pools of unemployment should be thrown into them and made to swim.' The experience was a part of his credentials for redrafting domestic policy in opposition; it also brought him into trade union and Labour company a good deal – quite deliberately so, since he made serious attempts to draw on the in-depth knowledge of Labour members with industrial constituencies. It was all admirably unThatcherian, and for the rest of his subsequent political life, he would enjoy very good relations with Labour people.

CHAPTER FIVE

It would have been a fine thing for Butler's record if he had been kept at the Ministry of Labour until the outbreak of war. Unfortunately, at this point Anthony Eden resigned. The youngest Foreign Secretary since the eighteenth century, debonair, graceful, talked about – in short, that most insubstantial of things, a star, Eden would by this act establish himself as an even more glamorous political property through an act of dazzling inadvertence.

Though not an appeaser, as Butler swiftly became, Eden was not remotely a full-dress Churchillian resister, either. His resignation had most to do with refined differences over the role of Italy – he was very hostile to Mussolini – and with pique at Chamberlain's independent breach of the Foreign Office closed shop by incursions into foreign policy. Thought-out opposition to the principle of appeasement came a poor second to affront. But it looked good and would help Eden look good for 20 years until he resigned again in rather different circumstances.

Unfortunately for Butler, Eden was replaced by Halifax, and Butler, a now expert Commons hand, was called in to conduct Foreign Office business in that House. Most unfortunately of all, Rab was not plunging into something he knew nothing about; he had been following events closely, and had become a convinced appeaser. 'War,' he would say in the Munich debate, 'settles nothing and I can see no alternative to the policy upon which the Prime Minister has so courageously set himself.'

In an interview given to the respectful Kenneth Harris not long after his retirement from politics, Butler advanced a general defence of appeasement. He emphasised the effects upon Baldwin of the vote for peace at the famous Fulham by-election and stressed the time bought for rearmament by Chamberlain's delaying action. In *The Art of the Possible*, written a few years later, in 1971, he quotes hard numbers: the single operational squadron of Spitfires with five in the pipeline available in September 1938, the 26 assembled by summer 1939 rising to 47 a year later.

He cites Sir John Wheeler-Bennett's defence of Munich, the more forceful for coming from a non-appeaser: 'Let us say of the Munich settlement that it was inescapable; that faced with the lack of unity at home and in the Commonwealth, with the collapse of French morale, and with the uncertainty of Russia to fight, Mr Chamberlain had no alternative to do other than he did; let us pay tribute to his persistence in carrying out a policy which he honestly believed to be right.'

Creditably, Butler quoted the whole of this paragraph from *Munich: Prelude to Tragedy*, which concludes, 'Let us not forget the shame and humiliation that were ours; let us not forget that, in order to save our own skins – because we were too weak to protect ourselves – we were forced to sacrifice a small power to slavery.'

At a time when muscular hindsight everywhere ripples its contempt for an uninstructible past, the views of that grown-up historian are very welcome. The only difficulty with a defence of the Chamberlain policy based upon the intelligent utilisation of the time bought, notably by Lord Swinton as Air Minister, is that one doubts if it was perfectly understood by Chamberlain or Halifax that time-buying was the main purpose of their actions.

Some measure of Halifax's cast of mind can be found in his reply in the House of Lords to the lucidly anti-Nazi Bishop of Durham, Hensley Henson. Henson had observed in dry terms, 'My Lords, really, as practical people looking coldly at the world and weighing facts calmly in the scales of reason, is it reasonable to trust the word of these dictators?' Genuinely shocked, it seems, Halifax rebuked the Bishop. 'I do not think that the statement which the Right Reverend Prelate made with great conviction this afternoon, that neither Signor Mussolini nor Herr Hitler was ever to be believed, is the kind of statement, coming from one in his position, that does assist the cause of peace.'

But then Britain hardly followed a coherent course in giving and then honouring the Polish guarantees. If that bluff were to be called, Britain would be forced into a war at a time not chosen and when only marginally more ready for it. In his Harris interview, Butler mentioned a belief in Government that war would not come until 1941 or 1942. The real historical irony lies in the absence of consistent devotion to either the heroic or the prudential. A hard-nosed policy based on staying out until more nearly threatened, meanwhile getting up to standard by hurried rearmament, is a logical whole. Contrariwise, going to war on moral principles and damning the arithmetic may be foolish, but it is majestically coherent.

Having self-interestedly avoided commitment but then, when nowhere near ready, to plunge into war because of moral pressure and public feeling is very slightly nonsensical. The commitment to Poland was surely the companion piece in passive leadership with Baldwin's response to the peace ballot and the Fulham by-election – a doing or not doing something because the public mood commanded it. Given the narrowness of the victorious margin in the Battle of Britain, that conflict, had it been joined a few months earlier, would very likely have been lost. A logical appeaser would have appeased longer.

Butler was to be anything but a trimmer in this matter. He signed up, as the Americans say, for the trip; and two years and a declaration of war later, was showing every sign of wanting to stay on the bus. When Munich had been followed by the invasion of the rest of Czechoslovakia, the Polish guarantees by the invasion of Poland, the British defence of northern Norway by the conquest of Norway, and that defeat by the parliamentary events which replaced Chamberlain with Churchill, Butler remained, logically enough, an appeaser, one convinced that early entry into the war had been a mistake.

Butler's own judgment of Chamberlain would be quietly recorded before his fall in an unpublished essay or memorandum dated November 1939 to be found among Butler's papers at Trinity, Cambridge.[1]

Having run through the Unitarian, progressive background of Chamberlain's father, Joseph, and his subsequent attachment to the idea of Empire, Butler observes of Neville Chamberlain that some people 'who have found difficulty in understanding his foreign policy, have attributed it to a latent sympathy with Fascism and a lively fear of Communism. Nothing could be further from the truth. He neither loves the one nor fears the other. Like most Englishmen he is not much interested in either theory, and he abhors the excesses and crimes of both.'

Chamberlain's training, says Butler, 'was liberal in a period of peace, when to the liberal mind war between civilised nations was becoming increasingly unthinkable . . . he had never worn uniform and all military and naval matters were to him extremely distasteful'. This is good sense and the thought occurs that as much might be said in defence of Butler himself.

However, in this memorandum, though he makes a defence of Chamberlain, Butler displays an ironic, indeed a Rabbish, tone. Chamberlain, he observes, 'had never met anybody in Birmingham who in the least resembled Adolf Hitler'. He was, moreover, 'the little boy who played with a wolf under the impression that it was a sheep – a pardonable zoological error, but apt to prove fatal to the player who makes it'.

Aware that Hitler had never kept his word to anyone else, he nevertheless expected him to keep 'this promise that had been made personally to him, from one gentleman to another. Nobody in Birmingham had ever broken his promise to the Mayor; surely nobody in Europe would break his promise to the Prime Minister of England.'

This is scornful stuff, made more so when he adds: 'A man so self-confident of himself and so confiding in others has as little chance in a Europe dominated by Stalin and Hitler as Little Lord Fauntleroy would have of concluding a satisfactory deal with Al Capone.'

But for all the ribbing, he does identify with Chamberlain's sort of man, whom he clearly sees as England's sort of man.

The English respect ability but they distrust brilliance. For them the very word 'genius' carries with it something derogatory. It connotes unconventional clothes and doubtful morals. They enjoy its manifestations, but they seldom give it their confidence. Now there is nothing brilliant and no suspicion of genius about Neville Chamberlain. The ordinary Englishman sees in him an ordinary Englishman like himself.

Fascinatingly, Chamberlain is then sharply faulted for his continued resistance to war-preparation and a standard defence of the entire policy is undermined.

'But a year ago [presumably November 1938] he resisted the demand which came from his own colleagues in the Cabinet for the setting up of a Ministry of Supply and introduction

of conscription. And he continued to resist it not only until, but after the rape of Prague [March] had proved the duplicity of Hitler. The further impetus of Italy's attack on Albania was required in order to shake his determination. Those who defend Munich on the ground that it gave Great Britain another year in which to complete her war preparations should reduce the period by more than half if they wish to estimate the amount of time that was actually spent on all-out preparations for war. For that long delay the Prime Minister is solely responsible. In Mr Baldwin's Cabinet Chamberlain has been as powerful; after he had got rid of one or two tiresome members, his was the only will that ever prevailed.

(Butler has added in ink above his typescript after 'has been as powerful' the words 'if not more powerful than his own chief'.) The memorandum ends rather sadly with an avowal that since Chamberlain had said that 'he is determined to destroy Hitlerism in Europe', and that 'firmness is a quality Chamberlain has never lacked, the world may rest assured that having taken up this task, he will not willingly lay it down until it is accomplished'.

Such whistling for posterity apart, Butler's November note on Chamberlain is that of an admirer grown exasperated. It was not offered for publication and can be excused charges of self-serving, if not of internal rationalisation. Essentially Butler the appeaser is saying of Chamberlain the chief appeaser that he got things wrong, that he was too narrow in outlook and too trusting and that such time as he gained he largely wasted because he went on believing in the error of judgment which had brought him where he was.

But in an earlier memo, dated September 1939, also among his Trinity papers,[2] Butler sounds more straightforwardly appeasing himself. Describing the last days of peace, he mentions his own contribution to a discussion on 5 August with Chamberlain, Halifax, Horace Wilson and Sir Alexander Cadogan: 'I pointed out to the Big Four that if they proceeded with the signing of the Polish Treaty on the afternoon of the 5th this would have a very bad psychological effect upon Hitler and would wreck the negotiations.'

He goes on in a very interesting vein to look back over earlier events: 'Nevertheless I still believe that Germany might have negotiated had we influenced the Poles earlier in the summer.

The Polish lot might thus have been better.' But Hitler would have 'got away with it again'. (For whatever reason everything quoted so far from the September memo has been deleted with three diagonal lines.) He then describes a walk in St James's Park with Halifax, who said with some banality, 'Well, it's going to come now. I wonder what we shall all feel like.' Halifax, minutes his deputy, 'has always adhered to the simple point that Hitler could not be allowed for reasons of our future "to get away with it".'

Ministers were reacting to pressure and popular feeling perhaps, rather than coolly sustaining a coherent policy. Butler quotes the League of Nations High Commissioner for Danzig, Burchardt, who had said that 'Polish diplomacy was not clever and that they had brought much of the trouble upon their own heads'. And, adds Butler, he had noticed that in the Foreign Office 'and in the upright mind of Alexander Cadogan, an absolute inhibition not to press the Poles to negotiate which lasted for all the weeks before the crisis. This inhibition in the Foreign Office, which was not shared by Nevile Henderson [the British Ambassador to Germany], was a result of the shame engendered in some breasts by Munich.'

Butler in these two papers is cool-headed enough not to believe that time has been won for the better conduct of war and censorious of Chamberlain for overconfidence that deals made with Hitler could hold as deals made on the Birmingham metal exchange held. In November, he almost seems to think the whole enterprise a mistake, and though he does not say 'we were wrong', he very powerfully implies it. Yet in late September, discussing the meeting of 5 August about the signing the same day of the Polish Treaty, he is a confident appeaser himself.

'Lean on the Polish Government' is the implication here. 'Don't let it stumble into a war and don't propel Hitler into feeling that he must make war by defying him.' A case can be made for such thinking, at least on grounds of down-the-line coherence: 'Do whatever has to be done to stop the war.' But it speaks the same misplaced confidence for which he gently mocks Chamberlain, without, of course, the provincial stigma. It would all end as the events of August 1914 had ended for Edward Grey, looking from his Foreign Office window at the lamplighter.

Butler had returned to Stansted. 'It was beautiful moonlight with a cool wind. Sydney and I walked out after dinner and stood in the long grass by the moat watching the reflections in the black water. We could hardly believe what had happened.'

When Chamberlain resigned in April 1940, Butler, urged on by Dunglass (Douglas-Home), had pleaded with Halifax to press for the prime ministership, much as his own circle would plead with him in 1963. There was nothing inexorable about Churchill's accession. A willing Halifax could have had the job. And after the shocks to come in France, he might have made more determined pursuit of a stand-off – followed presumably by an earlier, undistracted and more hopeful German invasion of Russia. But Halifax, troubled anyway by notions of Hitler 'getting away with it', wasn't willing.

Chamberlain's loss of support and the scenes which followed reminded Butler, recalling his Cambridge special subject, of 'certain aspects of the fall of Peel'. And Churchill's accession brought out peculiarly sour observations. His description of the new Prime Minister, 'half-breed adventurer', is not what is usually meant by a Rabbism. But he remained in government, asked by Churchill to stay and specifically to continue the stylishly uninformative replies to questions for which he was becoming known. He was flattered to find Churchill content with him and would not be disloyal. But understandably his ties were with Chamberlain, dying but still in government, and with Halifax. So inclined, he judged things very much as they judged them, doubting where Halifax in particular doubted.

Doubt was to find specific expression. On 17 June 1940 Butler took a stroll in St James's Park and met, he insisted by chance, Björn Prytz, Swedish Minister in London. They returned to the Foreign Office for a conversation which Prytz described in a telegram to Stockholm:

Britain's official attitude will for the present continue to be that the war must go on, but he assured me that no opportunities for reaching a compromise peace would be neglected if the possibility were offered on reasonable conditions and that no 'diehards' would be allowed to stand in the way in this connection. He thought that 'Britain had greater possibilities of negotiation [today] than she might have later on and that Russia would come to play a greater role than USA if conversations began.

During the conversation, Butler was called in to see Halifax who, says Prytz, 'sent me the message that "common sense, not bravado would dictate the British Government's policy".'

Halifax realised that such a message would be welcomed by the Swedish Minister, but that it should not be interpreted as 'peace at any price', a phrase quoted in English in Prytz's Swedish text.

That conversation took place at the direst moment of the war. Three days earlier, on 14 June 1940, German troops had entered Paris and on the 16th, the previous day, Paul Reynaud, the French Prime Minister, still disposed to fight the war, had resigned and had been replaced by Marshal Pétain.

The Prytz telegram would have immediate effect in Sweden, which was agonising over German demands, following the fall of Denmark in April, that it amend its neutrality to accommodate German military transports going to their war destination in Norway. Three Social-Democratic members of the all-party coalition were resisting a general Cabinet mood of acquiescence while the Prime Minister, Per Albin Hansson, hung back and waited for a tilt. The telegram was made much of by Christian Günther, the career diplomat Foreign Minister of the emergency coalition, who favoured the *realpolitik* of letting the Germans through. Given that Soviet troops had entered Lithuania on 15 June and Estonia and Latvia on the 17th, pressure on the Swedes all round was perfectly intolerable.

Prytz's account of his London conversation played its part in persuading the last stalwarts in the Swedish Cabinet that they could resist the requirements of Ribbentrop no longer. Ernst Wigforss, a Social-Democratic minister and of the three resisters the most dedicated, would say in his memoirs that uncertainty about British intentions tipped the scales on 18 June 1940 and 'took the last ounce of strength from the will to resist' (*tog . . . sista kraften ur motstondsviljan*). However, such was the mounting pressure that it may only have helped accomplish the inevitable.

Back in London eight days later, Churchill would inquire of Halifax what had been going on. For in the interim, heady assumptions had begun to be made. Günther had inquired through the British minister in Stockholm, Victor Mallet, if the message conveyed through the Prytz telegram was 'intended as a hint'. 'He had sent for me,' says Mallet to the Foreign Office, 'because he naturally did not intend to say or do anything which might embarrass His Majesty's Government.' In other words, Günther would make no moves to become an intermediary with the Germans to obtain a compromise peace until the British said so plainly.

The reply to Mallet, drafted by Butler and sent in Halifax's name, says:

> *In course of conversation, Parliamentary Under-Secretary remembers saying that the honourable end to hostilities, which neutral countries such as Sweden no doubt desired, would be best achieved by a policy governed by courage and wisdom. Conversation took this turn as a result of apparent anxiety of Swedish Minister lest war be perpetuated and extended. Minister however assented to view of Parliamentary Under-Secretary that force must be opposed to force. No special message from myself was intended, but Parliamentary Under-Secretary was called away to see me during his talk and Minister may have exaggerated the importance of this coincidence and of any polite message conveyed to him by way of explanation.*

Prytz would give it as his judgment that Butler was not speaking for the Government. His words were 'probably to be regarded as an expression of his and Halifax's private attitude and not intended to be conveyed further'. By this time, however, the *News Chronicle* correspondent in Stockholm had alerted Mallet to what two members of the foreign affairs committee in the Riksdag had told him – that 'Mr Butler had said that Britain would only continue the war if certain of ultimate victory'. This is a villainous garble of what Prytz reports and a neat demonstration of how rumour swells and twists. But, in all conscience, the real Prytz version contained quite enough. And the *News Chronicle* angle, not published on the street but buzzing through diplomatic channels, provoked a murky flow of clarification, bringing the matter to Winston Churchill's attention.

'It is quite clear to me,' wrote the Prime Minister to Halifax, 'that Butler held odd language [*sic*] to the Swedish minister and certainly the Swedes derived a strong impression of defeatism.' After touching upon a separate negotiation alarm, he added that 'any suspicion of lukewarmness in Butler will certainly subject us all to further annoyance of this kind', a notably mild way of putting it.

Butler's long letter in self-defence sent to Halifax the same day picks up the word 'lukewarmness'. He asked Halifax to look at the record of his dealings with foreign diplomatic ministers and 'ascertain from them whether any lukewarmness has been exhibited in my conversation'. This particular instance could only be judged by Prytz because he was the single other person involved. Then Butler added emphatically, 'I do not recognise myself or my conversation in the impression given.'

There was no record of this encounter, though Butler habitually kept Halifax informed with regular accounts of all diplomatic conversations, simply because of its casualness: 'I happened to meet him in the Park and he came into the office for only a few minutes; not being an arranged meeting, I did not keep a record.' He then recounted a subsequent comparison of notes with Prytz who

has since agreed with me that he opened the conversation by saying there was more need than ever for successful diplomacy now that Great Britain was left alone to continue the struggle. We ran over the many efforts to improve our position in the international field and M. Prytz was quite clear that it was in the interest of the neutrals to see an end to the war. I reminded him that if we were to negotiate, it must be from strength and that force must be met by force. From this he did not demur and he has since agreed with me that this account of our talk is correct.

Butler added that perhaps a conversation 'on the subject of an ultimate settlement' should not have taken place, but was certain he had 'said nothing definite or specific or that I now wish to withdraw'. Nevertheless, he apologised and placed himself in Halifax's hands. They were good hands to be in. Halifax exonerated Butler to Churchill with some warmth and, deftly alluding to a recent Foreign Office telegram sent to Victor Mallet, shifted responsibility onto certain Swedes. That telegram had told the British Ambassador in Sweden, 'For your private information, Mr Prytz told Mr Butler that he could not help thinking that certain interested parties in Sweden had mixed themselves up in this affair in an attempt to cause mischief.' In other words, 'Günther done it.'

As far as Churchill was concerned, the matter stopped there. It has to be remembered that Churchill may not have seen the Prytz telegram[3], merely a couple of phrases from it passed from the Swedish Foreign Minister, Günther, through Mallet to London: '... that common sense, not bravado would dictate HMG's policy. This would be of interest to the Swedish minister, but could not be interpreted as peace at any price.'

Happily, Churchill had many things to occupy him and, despite concern at lukewarmness from Butler, exacted no reprisals. But how he would have responded to talk of diehards not being allowed to stand in the way and no opportunity for reaching a compromise peace being neglected is hardly conjectural. Despite the quirky respect developed for the younger man during the India debates, it is difficult to see Butler surviving in office.

The full text would not be seen, even in Sweden, until the mid-fifties with the publication of two volumes of Swedish ministerial memoirs. As to its truth, Thomas Munch-Petersen in his learned monograph *Common Sense Not Bravado: The Butler–Prytz Interview of 17 June 1940* – the main source for this account – points out that Prytz was not the sort of foreigner easily confused by the sophistications of the English language. He had an English mother and was an Old Alleynian, damn it. Politically, like so many people, he personally had dithered between a soft and hard line, whose extremes in Swedish terms ran between seeking to play the mediator with German mastery implicit and wanting Sweden to go to war against the Nazis. But his reports before this one, far from making the most of British defeatist talk – which Günther at the Swedish Foreign Office doubtless wanted to hear – had recorded in Britain a near-universal resolution, excepting only a few City panickers, instances of what Orwell at about the same time had called 'disloyal rich men'. In a letter to Erik Boheman, permanent head of the Swedish Foreign Office, Prytz had written that the British will to fight on had grown and was now greater than at any time since the outbreak of the war.

Then again, when Butler's denials were made, they applied to limited parts of the telegram, those officially known to the Foreign Office only by way of what Günther had quoted to Mallet. The bits about no opportunity for reaching a compromise peace being neglected if reasonable terms were offered and no 'diehards' being allowed to get in the way were never the subject of debate or rebuttal by Butler or Halifax. The actual term, attributed by Prytz to Halifax, 'common sense not bravado', was not flatly denied by Butler. He merely says he does not recognise himself or his conversation in what has been quoted. He uses a rhetorical interrogative, 'You may inquire . . . why I was reported as saying that "common sense and not bravado would dictate our policy".' Oddly, he takes Halifax's supposed message and visits it upon his own head. But having done so, he does not answer the question he invites.

Finally, when the issue did surface in a private flurry towards the end of the war and in full public form in the mid-sixties, Butler's defence would be general. The Swede had raised the question of possible peace negotiations, so the topic was gone through subject to the unbending British line. As Butler put it in his memoirs in 1971, 'I certainly went no further than the official line at the time which was that peace could not be considered prior to the complete withdrawal of German troops from all conquered territories. This was common sense, not bravado.'

It is not easy to accept that if that phrase was used in 1940, and he never directly denied this, it was meant to be understood as he employed it 31 years later. Butler was never and would never be a disloyal rich man. But he was a good team player set in the way of thinking of the old captain rather than of the new manager. Appeasement was neither immoral nor traitorous, but it had always been an awful mistake, and the first apostle of that mistake was the Earl of Halifax with Butler his very loyal servant. Munch-Petersen argues that 'Taken as a whole, the evidence suggests that the Prytz telegram contains a substantially accurate account of what Butler said.'

It is hard to disagree with him, but perhaps the best gloss on the evidence involves recalling the notorious and much loved indiscretion of the man. A very possible sketch of events would be of Butler reciting the official view of the Churchill Government, but then slipping into the sort of murmured *obiter dicta* which belong in dubbin-brown italics: 'But then again, dear boy, another view might be that . . .' At the very highest levels, truth requires deniability.

Munch-Petersen again reminds us that the mood of the British Cabinet was fluid and evolving. Churchill did not enter office after the Norway debate fully armed and universally accepted. The possibility of reactivating appeasement was a serious one. Across 26, 27 and 28 May a debate took place in Cabinet following early and horrific German success on the Western Front, success vastly greater than equivalent developments at the start of the First World War. That debate concerned enquiries as to a possible compromise peace. Halifax was its chief protagonist, Churchill the absolute opponent. British troops were in full retreat. What was to become the Dunkirk evacuation and a quirkish, lopsided triumph, was at that moment the retreat *to* Dunkirk, the worst thing that had happened to a British army in historic memory.

Halifax was arguing that running a line through Mussolini, still heading a neutral country, could do no harm if only for the purpose of learning what the terms for peace might be. Britain had to face the fact, said Halifax, that 'it was not so much now a question of imposing a complete defeat upon Germany but of safeguarding the independence of our own Empire and that of France'. His view was not that Britain should accept *any* terms, ('peace at any price!'), but that, though the odds did not look good, Germany had internal problems (she did?) and Hitler might then offer a reasonable settlement. Churchill thought the chances of a deal which did not 'put us completely at his mercy' were 'a thousand to one against'. He was supported by Attlee and Arthur Greenwood, the Labour members of the War Cabinet – and by Neville Chamberlain, who came down against an enquiry as to terms. And with Labour and Chamberlain behind him, Churchill won.

Halifax's reaction as recorded in his diary is at least as scornful as anything reported by Prytz quoting Butler. 'I thought Winston spoke the most frightful rot, also Greenwood . . . I said exactly what I thought of them, adding if that was really their view, and if it came to the point, our ways would separate . . . It does drive me to despair when Churchill works himself up into a passion of emotion when he ought to make his brain think and reason.' That entry was made 30 days before Butler and Prytz took their stroll in the park. Paris was not yet occupied; Reynaud was still Prime Minister of France. But all events appeared to converge upon a choice between early abnegation and later conquest. In Sweden, by way of illustration, they moved from the struggle of the Wigforss group against accommodating Germany over Norway to anxious offers in July that the King of Sweden should negotiate with Hitler's Germany a peace for Britain.

But in Britain, things would get worse in order to get better. The Dunkirk evacuation may have been the salvaging of men after retreat from the theatre of battle – in textbook terms, 90 per cent of a defeat. But psychologically it was a fillip. The mood in Britain, alerted to war by the retreat and lifted by the successful evacuation in which all hands and so many human-sized little boats had been ardently thrust forward, was incompatible with making even the reasonable peace for which Halifax had argued in the War Cabinet. An odd mixture of heroic bloodymindedness and knowing exactly what was right swept over the country.

Orwell, writing at the time, caught it exactly when he said that Hitler's phrase about the Germans as 'a sleep-walking people' better described the British. They had been indifferently content, first to drift, then to let Chamberlain conduct the Munich submission. But not any longer. It was, said Orwell, like the passage in the Bible, 'Samson, the Philistines are upon thee'; as one the British people knew who they were and what they had to do. Churchill's words stopped being hopeful rhetoric against the tide and voiced what people wanted to hear, said out loud what they wanted to be.

Halifax, and Butler with him, came to represent the last line of dedicated, almost doctrinaire appeasement, and even Halifax was writing in his diary, 'I think he [Churchill] is right in feeling that if we can, with our resources concentrated, hold the devils for two or three months, there is quite a chance that the situation may turn in our favour. Anyhow for the present there is no alternative.' Though Alexander Cadogan noted as late as 2 July that the Pope was making 'tentative, half-baked suggestions' for a compromise peace and that 'silly old H. is hankering after them'.

The possibility that Butler and Halifax were jointly flying a kite via the Swedes cannot be ruled out, but as Munch-Petersen says, Butler's letter of justification to Halifax would have had to have been a complete charade and 'it seems too genuinely embarrassed and defensive for that'. Anyway, Butler might have been wrong and he might have wriggled, but he didn't run to such dishonesty. Common sense, if one may still use the phrase, suggests that Butler's conversation was a mixture of the official line, but advanced as a mechanical devotion uttered without too much conviction. It will have been spiced with indiscreet private observations expressing the genuine disbelief of the still credible appeasement party in a continued fight 'inspired by a passion of emotion instead of making the brain think and reason'. There was a market back at the Swedish Foreign Office for such a message, and, however intended, it was put to conclusive use inside the Swedish Cabinet. In Britain it was effectively the last rattle of appeasement.

Butler, however one likes and admires the whole man, however glad we are that he survived this extreme error to do so many sensible things sensibly, is seen throughout the episode to very great disadvantage. The appeasers had never been tentative or weak in their convictions. In what Halifax confided to his diary and Butler said about Churchill when he came to power, they showed an arrogance which does not improve in the light of their also being wrong. It is perfectly true that if Germany had not invaded Russia in 1941 and if she had treated British air defence as something which should suffer full and recurring assault until it gave way, a Britain then actually conquered, occupied and with a daily view of the swastika might have felt that a deal which sat out the early stages of the war, however humiliatingly, until greater world forces were joined would have been the wise course. Honourable men like Günther in Sweden appeased in the fear that conquest might last not for five years but 100.

Only fit for the very greatest occasions, Churchill had, after all, usually been wrong. He had long before sought, until dissuaded by civil servants at the Home Office, to dabble in the charmless practice of eugenics; he had espoused the calamity of Gallipoli; his understanding of the economy existed at the level of operetta. Had he been Prime Minister in 1926, Britain might well have had a civil war, workers shot and the country torn to unimaginably opposed poles of class and class, Right and Left. In India he was resisting incremental reform on the grounds that India was happiest in subordination. Always looking for a fight, he had many of the qualities of a stage Irishman whimsically translated to a ducal environment. But in 1940, as later, unknowable events would determine, he was superlatively and gloriously right. And for Butler to have been insistently against that judgment and careless of letting loose any denigrating words to fall upon foreign ears was the worst act of his largely admirable career.

But whether Churchill saw only the two phrases reported back by Mallet and was generous to Butler or saw the whole text and was astonishingly generous, generosity was what prevailed and what would leave him at the Foreign Office before some months later shifting him nonchalantly into a department, Education, for which he was magnificently suited. Churchill, who was, unlike all Butler's earlier patrons, a natural opposite in temperament and outlook – a man he had almost inadvertently charmed in conflict, had badmouthed in audible asides and to whom he had given grounds for dismissal – chose to keep, advance and put value upon him. It was astonishing, and speaks of an instinct, a fingertip feeling better accepted than analysed. But it existed and Butler was about to surge forward as the least likely of all Churchill's protégés.

[1]'Chamberlain: A Candid Portrait', RABF77 4 information sources, Norma Percy and Paul Stafford.
[2]RAB G1010, supplied by Mr Spencer via Ms Percy.
[3]Anthony Howard, in his biography (p.99), makes the assumption that Churchill would have seen the full text from intelligence code-breaking sources. Assumptions are all we *can* make, but the language recorded by Prytz, whether or not it fairly reports Butler, is explosive and carries a stronger than implicit slur upon Churchill as an obstacle to negotiation. Sneaking affection for Butler would have had to go a long way for the Premier to have rolled with a punch like that.

CHAPTER SIX

The great charm of the task which Butler would discreetly create for himself in the shadow of Churchill's benign indifference was that to get education right he had to understand the sheer extent of both problem and solution, and that done, he had to persuade difficult people to be sensible. It needed his mind and his fingertips and it got them.

This was the perfect subject for Butler. Since the graduation of George Butler at Cambridge in 1794, the family had been educationalists; headmastership was in their DNA. But if education was to be got right, it could hardly be too soon since so much of it was outrageously wrong. Attempts at reform existed largely on paper. The 11-plus examination had been recommended by the Hadow Report as far back as 1926, but inertia and the paralytic frugality of a banker's response to the depression had left any such expansion of grammar-school education systematically unaccomplished.

There existed, when Butler went to the Board of Education, the public schools, the part fee-paying grammar-school sector and a mass of elementary schools, many of them run by the churches, which Butler himself characterised later as suffering 'from the blight of poverty and inferiority associated with the traditions of the past'. Chief among the traditions of the past, all-preoccupying and daunting for reformers, were the church schools. The aborted purpose of the Hadow Report had been to break up the all-through 5–14 pattern of the elementary school and open up more places in grammar schools for abler pupils. But two things had sat on reform:

the instinct not to spend money and the churches.

The very first (and minute) state contributions to education had only begun in 1833 and much of that money then had gone to supplement schools provided by the Church of England. At the high point, there had been 12,000 of these, though the numbers were in decline. So was the quality; the inspectors, who remained busy during the era of economy, had compiled a blacklist of inadequate schools (about which nothing was done), and a high proportion of Anglican foundations sat firmly on it. Many of them were village schools operating in a catchment area where no alternative existed and, though there were a smaller number of nonconformist schools, education in such areas at a Church school staffed exclusively by members of the Church of England was a Hobson's choice.

The problem had its roots in a disappearing piously sectarian England, the Victorian rat-pit of inter-denominational uncharity in which the Church of England took its established place with unChristian pride. The arms of the House of Hanover occasionally still surviving on the tower arch of a parish church today had once been a universal requirement. The Church's privilege in education, largely run by the Church of England National Society, was an extension of this outlook and its schools represented what Christians would call works – works flatly proclaiming hegemony. The Roman Catholic schools were a separate problem and in Britain that Church's odd mixture of aggrandisement and self-pity would require separate and very delicate handling.

The radical notion of education favoured by the teaching unions was a secular, non-denominational system with any elements of religious teaching brought in as an extra, optional or otherwise. This would never be accepted by the churches in so direct a form. But the edge of the problem was being blunted by the existence of 'the Cambridgeshire syllabus', a sort of theological fix agreed to in that county by Anglicans, noncon-formists and teachers settling upon a controversy-avoiding core-Christian outline. Being sensible, it was much mocked, not least by the less than pious Churchill as 'the county-council creed', but it was being rapidly taken up around the country. For it meant that an agreed form of religious instruction could be guaranteed in return for the Anglicans leaving the burden of school funding and management to the local authorities.

It was, incidentally, no bad thing that Butler, with his Baldwinian good feeling for the Labour Party, had as his ministerial colleague a parliamentary under-secretary as useful as a couple of ministers of state, James Chuter Ede, a dour, unexciting Labour politician who had not merely been a teacher, but actually knew something about education. (A nonconformist, he observed that though he had been educated at an Anglican elementary school, there had been no chance of his teaching at one.) It is very odd that Anthony Crosland, who would later vitiate the Butler Act for reasons passing most intelligent understanding, remains an icon to students of Labour politics, while Ede, who helped create it, has the standing of an unregarded dowd. Butler would write to Home (then Dunglass), 'I find in Education that much of the drive towards a vaguely progressive future comes from Labour.' It would be Ede who, at a later stage, when the chance of a limited deal with the denominations might have seduced Butler away from a general Education Act, laid down the dictum 'No settlement without a general advance.' Butler accepted it.

Part of the difficulty was Churchill. Having been born in 1874, unsuccessfully educated at Harrow, eclectically cultivated, a cavalry officer with a touch of Cicero, a benign paternalist towards the lower classes, but without either focus or optimism, and taken up at that time with fighting a world war, his educational thinking, such as it was, amounted to vocationalism and uplift, trade-teaching and patriotism. 'Tell them about Wolfe at Quebec,' he said to Butler, though there were also startling bursts of imaginative generosity. What he did not want, however, was an Education Act, and when Butler, early in his stewardship, was unwisely daring enough to talk brightly of one, it was genially vetoed. For Churchill was familiar with the quarrels and political mires which had followed the attempts of Birrell and Fisher in 1906 and 1918 to make great reforms. He looked upon the churches rather as ministers of all parties would look upon the trade unions for nearly 40 years after the war. They were a drag upon efficiency, but taking them on meant trouble. The phrase 'divisive issue' existed to validate a simple flinching away from action. Butler's reaction to this was rather delicious.

He was deterred neither by his master nor the 'disappointingly compliant' tone of his Permanent Secretary, Maurice Holmes, who had concluded a defeatist memo with some self-comforting Sir Humphreyish generalities about longer-term prospects for the 'Promised Land'. Butler chuckles in his memoirs: 'Having viewed the milk and honey from the top of

Mount Pisgah, I was damned if I was going to live in the land of Moab. Basing myself on long experience of Churchill over the India Bill, I decided to disregard what he said and go straight ahead.'

What Butler knew about his master was that he didn't want a row with the churches and that public schools should be put on ice as too controversial, otherwise he could have what he wanted in bill form. 'I intended to have an Educational Bill and, three years after receiving his minute, I had placed such a bill on the Statute Book.' And what was more, Churchill sent him a telegram of congratulation.

To anyone who has lived through the decade of half-unhinged peremptory particularism which marked Margaret Thatcher's unhealthy reign, it is delightful to see how the incomparably greater figure whom she would confidingly refer to as 'Winston' actually behaved. This was grown-up politics. The great war leader laid down the law and drew a line. The intelligent minister with ideas of his own looked for the Prime Minister's real concerns, took care to keep out of them and followed the laid-down law in the most Pickwickian manner to the satisfaction of all parties.

It will not have been quite the smooth piece of Jeevesian insouciance that Butler implies. He did falter that once, edging towards a quick fix with the churches, but he had Chuter Ede to steady him. He also had the Labour Party and especially Ernest Bevin, who had left his village school at 11, vehemently at hand. For this would not be a bill which any mere Conservative Government enmeshed with the established Church could or would have enacted.

The business of winning over the Anglicans involved bringing them to give up the 'dual system' of Church of England school with inadequate subsidies, but their own instrument. Butler formulated an option. Schools might, he proposed, be 'controlled' or 'aided'. In a controlled school, the local authority would take on all expenses and appoint most of the teachers and governors while the religious syllabus would be the controversy-avoiding minimalism of the Cambridgeshire version (which Churchill had also called Zoroastrianism), or a local variant.

In an aided school, the Local Education Authority would still pay for salaries and running costs, but in return for making all appointments they would have to find half the cost of all improvements (50 per cent coming from the Exchequer). In a system of controlled schools the Anglicans would have to accept a system in which the predominant school would be allocated a measured amount of Cambridgeshire Christianity rather than have schools which were owned by and taught the doctrines of the Church of England. The second option was like giving up jam roly-poly for rice pudding with a spoonful of non-denominational marmalade. The Anglicans had 9,000 schools, more than they could afford and often not very good schools. When they were through they would have only 2,000. Some Anglican figures, like Headlam of Gloucester, Kirk of Oxford and, to a degree and later, Cyril Garbett, Archbishop of York, saw this. Headlam reacted with extreme language: 'This megalomaniacal Education Bill is a very evil thing.'

At that time there was a general mood for reform and one which might have produced an even more radical bill. The weave of change might nearly have snagged on the churches, yet the will was there to have readily produced a massive change in the status of the public schools. Even Churchill talked and wrote memos about filling 60–70 per cent of these elect places with bursaries: 'not by examination alone, but on the recommendation of the counties and the great cities'. Two things have to be remembered. The war years were a period of natural and surging radicalism. The Army Current Affairs Bureau was busy, the Soviet Union was a highly regarded ally. The intellectual tilt of the thirties had dumped a lot of intellectual bricks onto the political building site. 'The times,' to put it tediously, 'they were a-changin'.'

Change in the Church of England had its apostle in the stout, saintly and idealistically left-inclined William Temple, whose brief episcopate covered the key period of the bill's preparation. Neither an Establishment paladin like Lang before him nor his own successor, the authoritarian Fisher (the Church of England's counterpart to Lord Chief Justice Goddard), would have been beguiled by Butler. Neither of them, for that matter, would have been as worried about the neglect of children's education.

But in his handling of Temple, Rab was at once rational and serpentine. He put the utmost emphasis on the blacklist, the schools impotently damned by HM inspectors. The list contained 731 schools of which 543 were from the voluntary sector. Temple's socialist instincts and concern for the neglect of children were reached and touched.

At a meeting with the Archbishop, Butler played the card of inadequacy and spelt out the numbers on the list. Temple was shocked at something he ought to have known. But his concern was social rather than ecclesiastical. He wanted a school-leaving age of 16 – it was then 14 – and he wanted working-class children to get a proper education. The institutional selfishness of clergymen which had foiled the more ardent reformers for 70 years finally stalled. It would be a bad mistake to see Temple, for all that Butler worked skilfully upon him, as a naïve seller of the ecclesiastical pass. He minded about ragged children in poor schools. He wanted something better and, a little muddled, but with his own understanding of what counted, made a clerical sacrifice for high secular ends.

Other people had to be lined up and, in the case of Sir Robert Martin, a layman heavily involved in the National Society which ran Church education, Butler used a characteristic personal touch. He visited 'Brands', Sir Robert's home in Leicestershire, and dined before sitting late with him making the case. He had entertained Baldwin and Churchill at Stansted and impressed and pleased them both. He sought Sir Robert's hospitality to press home more confidingly his ministerial line. Today it would be called 'networking' and then, as now, it worked.

In practice, the Anglicans lacked the sectarian instinct to dig in and sustain a hermetic church, and with Temple persuaded to endorse the bill and look benignly on the controlled option, it could advance. The effect was good for education, injurious to the Church. Butler himself, a perfectly sincere Anglican, would write long afterwards that 'the perfunctory and uninspired nature of the religious instruction provided in all too many local authority and controlled schools had begun to imperil the Christian basis of our society'.

With the Roman Catholics he had much more trouble. The Catholics were both aggressive and defensive, a professional minority which expected nothing and asked for more. Their style owed something to Molotov, and in a dull leadership, the dominant figure could hardly have been a more perfect apparatchik than Monsignor William Godfrey, the apostolic delegate. The Cardinal-Archbishop, Hinsley, a man of serious quality and goodness, was dying and as Butler briskly notes, didn't seem to understand what was on offer. An early letter from Hinsley to *The Times* rejecting any freedom from denominational command seemed at one point to threaten the whole enterprise. The eventual successor, Griffin of Birmingham, is described by Father Adrian Hastings as 'the least important Archbishop of Westminster of the century, a nice hard-working nonentity ... also for much of the time a very sick man'. Godfrey 'one hundred per cent reliable in Roman eyes', was a drab bureaucrat whose own later term as Cardinal of Westminster would be known as 'the safe period'.

In fact, no one was properly in charge, Hinsley's death being followed by a long hiatus, and the higher Catholic clergy were not able to give Butler approval on a deal which did them any number of favours. Because they were wedded to spending money in a very unThatcherian manner upon schools, even not very good schools, which were their own, the Catholics would be beneficiaries of the 50 per cent subvention which Butler held out. They would build, collect, get into debt and build again. But in 1944, despite his best efforts, they never found the coherent voice (or grace) to say that they agreed. A visit to the Archbishop of Southwark and another to dine with a collective of northern Roman Catholic Bishops at Ushaw College only got him the individual assent of individual clerics. Immobility was consolidated in a collective leadership remarkable for dogged super-caution.

Temple was an incomparably more intelligent and imaginative figure than anyone the Catholics could offer, but their odd combination of resolution and irresolution – incoherence in discussion with the Minister and obdurate intention to go on running schools – worked in their context while Temple's idealistic affirmation in a church not geared for single-minded sectarian beavering unquestionably weakened Anglican influence.

However, there are more things in Heaven and Earth than God. With the controlled and aided option established, nothing stood in the way of creating a full secondary sector of education filtered by the 11-plus which Hadow had proposed 18 years before and which Crosland (and Williams *and* Thatcher) would destroy between 1965 and 1974. The house that Butler built probably represented the high point of British education. It came after the long, sterile combination of class distinction and economy and before the no less injurious practice of anti-educationalism spreading media studies and setting the novels of Frederick Forsyth for its watered-down A-levels. People did not start equal indeed, but the chance of the son of a manual labourer passing by examination to a curriculum of science, mathematics, ancient and modern languages and beyond that to a real university, now existed. Hardy's Jude could pass into Christminster.

To indulge a personal note, I remember the sourness of an elderly master in my northern grammar school saying that before the Butler Act, things were better because in those days 25 per cent of grammar school places could be bought, 'So we had more children from the nicer parts of the town.' The charm of rank endured. Life is not a naïve course of simple progress, a socialist hymn with lots of sunlight in it. And though the Butler deal could have been intelligently amended – notably by sophisticating selection into something less knifelike than a single examination and by equalising opportunity between different local authorities – he had made merit the test. The experience by this date of both privilege and paper equality suggest that it is a good one. This was a period of proper education available to talent and one in which no one could have imagined an airport novel being urged upon a sixth form by its teachers.

There was in the act one hint of the humbug to come. By splitting the elementary schools at 11 and making open the way to grammar-school education, Butler was offering the non-exam-passers continued elementary education, often in the same school (though much was done to develop specialised primaries). They would soon also get another year in school, but the term 'secondary modern' was coined and anointed as deserving 'parity of esteem' with grammar schools. At a secondary modern, you did no specialised science, no higher maths, no classics and only in a few cases the least scruple of a foreign language, while metalwork and woodwork came clumping into the curriculum. 'Parity of esteem' is a phrase which Mr Pecksniff could have rolled round his tongue.

In one area, Butler missed a radical opportunity. The public schools 50 years ago were at least as controversial as they are now and far more vulnerable to the hands of reformers. For an essential start in those days they were nothing like as good. They had their own blacklist, or at any rate a quadruple grading reminiscent of the one shown to Paul Pennyfeather in *Decline and Fall* when he contemplated taking a post with Dr Augustus Fagin at Llanabba: ' "Leading school", "First-rate school", "Good school" and "School". I should say that Llanabba is very much "School".' In the private assessments made by the Ministry, some very famous establishments – Harrow and Butler's own Marlborough among them – ranked no better than 'Good school'.

The idea of the great body of older public schools enjoying a

general excellence and being joined in their independent condition by the best of the former grammar schools with
Manchester at their head would have astounded the cool
reformers, never mind the visionaries of the Left, during the war
years. The existence of a dominant private sector, made strong
by furious exertion and money well spent, was unforeseeable. So
was their enrichment by able middle-class pupils rerouted from
crank-ridden mixed-ability comprehensives.

But the public schools, already recovering, got better and the
grammar schools would be wrecked, Circular 10/65 doing its
doctrinaire stupid bit. The Labour Government of 1964–70
didn't do much, but it did manage to cripple state secondary
education.

But if Butler had pushed at a door, partly ajar in 1943–4, the
public schools would have been transformed into forums for an
intellectual elect chosen by examination or local assessment
across country and class. Churchill's astonishing words have
already been quoted. The self-doubt of public-school headmasters was apparent. Robert Birley, headmaster of Charter-
house (later of Eton) was suggesting a 50–50 split between fee-
payers and won places. The issue was dumped on a committee
and the committee was also inflicted with a Scottish judge, Lord
Fleming, of exceptional negative enterprise. The remit was
vague, the committee large, the chairman a fool, the report
flaccid. Local authorities *might* offer bursaries; the public
schools *might* accept them. Co-operation was enjoined without
requirement upon two sets of people with quite independent and
very strong motives for not co-operating. Nothing happened.

The whole business is an odd reflection on Butler, and his
motives are not clear. He had said candidly and privately (often,
though not always, the same thing) that he carried no torch for
the principle of privileged education, though, in the historic way
of politicians, he took care to secure it for his own children. He
was preoccupied with other parts of the bill which were large
enough, in all conscience; and in the earliest days, he had feared
Churchill's expected opposition on this topic becoming a road
block to the whole bill. But Churchill stopped opposing the idea
and though Butler would visit elegant scorn upon Lord Fleming
in his memoirs, he accepted the committee's watery conclusions
when they came.

Butler was not a calculating or cynical man, but unlike Iain
Macleod, he was not inclined to wear his radicalism as an
escutcheon, and an element of the politic might be discerned

here. The Conservative Party could live with, might even take credit for, primary schools and 11-plus access to grammar schools for the merely able. But even in the pink-tinged forties, it would not thank the Conservative politician who threw Eton open to the talents. The Conservatives would for a considerable interim declare themselves in favour of reform while stressing their social concerns, even occasionally having them. But they were not likely to make Carnot Prime Minister.

And anyway, the age of formal coalition so comfortably suited to Rab was coming to an end, and he was one of the first to understand the fact. However, despite this, the influence of Labour thinking would actually intensify. The mood of 1945 took account of very many things: the long absence of two-fisted red and blue politics; the yet longer deprivations of working people, an important element of humane sympathy and radicalism within parts of the middle class and the work done over a decade and a half by Keynes and Beveridge. There was also a new executive confidence in the group around Attlee who had done good and respected work in coalition office. The cloud of muddle and resentment following 1931 had lifted.

Like men who had fallen from their horses and then got on again, they felt up to the ride. And the public wanted them in power. The Army Bureau of Current Affairs had done an agitprop job, a very model of the socialist schoolmaster of Conservative nightmares. Even Sherlock Holmes came out for the Left. In one of the wartime Basil Rathbone and Nigel Bruce series, the great detective concludes a Victorian yarn with a peroration on the need for egalitarian social change. And then, the Tories were stuffy and heavy hereditarians who had added new assumptions of superiority to old when the thirties crash gave them an extension of power. Finally, Churchill himself, believing his own legend, would invoke absurdities with talk of a Labour Gestapo (something which provoked the memoir-writing Butler to quote La Bruyère on Corneille, not altogether what we expect from Mrs Shephard).

The Tories were going to lose, though there were no opinion polls to break the news to them, but they made things worse for themselves by assuming firstly that they could continue the coalition after the war, secondly that their caretaker adminis-tration would be returned as a substantive Tory Government, and thirdly that Churchill, that most tangential and spasmodic of Conservatives, could helpfully be displayed for the encouragement of the multitude, like bunting. The voters were quite fond of Churchill, but not fond enough to elect a Conservative Government.

Butler never doubted that estimate. Characteristically, he had had his head down in the polite part of Essex, attentive to the electoral undergrowth as he never was to parliamentary low life. He said out loud what he learned so plainly, the only member of the Conservative leadership to expect a Labour triumph. Any element of defeatism in him was here justified ten times over. His 'opponent and friend' Stanley Wilson, pillar of the Saffron Walden Labour Party, would run him to a majority of 1,158. But while scheming politicians who yearn for a breath of opposition to asphyxiate their elders are usually disappointed, perhaps by a decade and a half of exile, the defeat Rab foresaw fitted his talents and perceptions admirably.

The times were exactly right for a man of his unflamboyant intelligence, pacific temperament and general executive stability of mind. But a shift of the Tory Party to a centrist position, accepting Keynes and Beveridge and even large measures of nationalisation, was made easier by the unpleasant view up the vertical cliff of one of the largest majorities ever won in an election.

The Conservative Party – in this different from Labour with its gloomy helot's instincts – is liable to move in a single lurch from oik-prodding triumphalism to snivelling melancholia. In fairness, a mood of creeping reformism had been affecting leading Conservatives for a long time. Harold Macmillan had, of course, always been a dangerous pinko, with an early career of Commons rebellions, alertness to deficit finance, wry notice by Baldwin and the publication of *The Middle Way*. Indeed, the younger Macmillan suggests an altogether brighter and vastly better informed version of Michael Mount, Galsworthy's uninteresting creation, the doe-eyed parliamentary son-in-law of Soames, who dimly cumbers the later volumes of *The Forsyte Saga*.

Macmillan was involved in 1946 in an attempt to abandon the name 'Conservative', a title informally in existence since it was casually coined by John Wilson Croker in 1831. Macmillan wanted it changed to the incandescently naff 'New Democratic Party' (a title to enjoy a mild and harmless existence in Canada later in the century). This was coolly received. As with Mr Blair's way of talking about something called 'New Labour', he created the impression of over-egging the pudding of moderation. But then, at that time, a shift to the Left was common. Anthony

Eden was influenced by a highly political civil servant, Oliver Harvey. Like a lot of silly clever men in 1945, Harvey thought that the Soviet Union was wonderful. Eden had been well treated by Stalin, who had poured quantities of spikenard on to that vain, unhappy soul. When Harvey spoke with admiration of the Soviet system of penal restraint which would later so excite Solzhenitsyn, Eden did not demur.

Then again, ideas of perfect markets which should not be interfered with seemed absurd to people who had lived through the mess which the free market had made of people's lives during the thirties. Such notions, reaffirmed at this time by F. A. von Hayek, had more takers among a doctrinaire element in what was left of the Liberal Party than among Tories, keener on class than competition and at all times an opportunistic and adaptable group.

Weak on issues, the Tories put great stress on personalities. For, to the mounting grief of Anthony Eden, they still had Churchill, vague and often seigneurially benign in what he remotely perceived of social matters. Though as deflater, troop-sender-in and latherer of unprofitable froths during the General Strike, he had a reputation in social matters that would frighten socialist children to bed. Churchill was 71 and had enjoyably abused tobacco and alcohol in ways to make social workers weep. He was moody and fractious, vague about home policy but, blessedly for Butler, disinclined to make way for anyone, especially 'dear Anthony'; indeed, he was already communicating his unease about Eden.

For this was a time when younger men looked interestedly about them. Oliver Stanley for one was a thinkable future prime minister in Harold Macmillan's eyes and, *a fortiori*, a future chancellor. Witty and good-natured, both as a natural grandee as a Derby, yet properly talented, he had superseded Macmillan, his old companion of reformist Tory politics, by becoming Colonial Secretary in 1942, provoking the Minister in Residence in West Africa into a letter of resignation which he had to be talked out of. In Butler's view Stanley was 'the most capable of us all ... the acutest brain on the Conservative front bench' and 'the keenest lance I have ever known in opposition'. He also thought him inclined to dither. If Stanley had not died at 54 in 1950, he would have had both the standing and the popularity to succeed Eden, and might imaginably have been preferred to him.

Oliver Lyttelton, also a force at this time, was a successful City businessman, intelligent, inclined to challenge assumptions, cool about Bank and Treasury, too successful and in too flaunting and grandiose a way for the sensibilities of the day. Altogether too flash, he would be thought of for the Treasury, then thought better of.

There also existed, out of all contention, but not known to be and certainly not knowing it himself, Robert Boothby. Boothby was to be extremely effective in opposition after the war and his booming voice and poster-paint personality made him better known than many in the ranks of the coolly ascending. Despite having been magnificently right on issues of some importance – the awfulness of unemployment and the merit of J. M. Keynes's proposals to handle it, plus Day One, 1933, recognition of Hitler as the Angel of Death – Boothby's carelessness in the lesser matters of adultery and declarations of financial interest barred him from public usefulness. The rueful, slightly coerced lover of Dorothy Macmillan and non-declarer of a minor promise of payment from a Czech businessman whose frozen assets he had attempted to have restored, he was probably also known to the very alert as bisexual. Even so, he was more fun than Selwyn Lloyd.

At this juncture, careers might usefully be brought up to date. Eden, after brief stopovers at the Dominions and the War Office, had resumed his near-perpetual foreign secretaryship in 1940 and stayed at it until 1945. When Stanley, born in 1896, had gone to the Colonial Office in 1942, he had already enjoyed an even more startling career than Butler. Minister of Transport in 1933 at the age of 37, he had advanced a year later to Labour, then in 1935 to Trade, and to the secretaryship for war in 1940. Macmillan, born in 1894, had only attained office, though he had leapt all junior posts, in 1942 when he was made Minister in Residence in north-west Africa. This post gave him responsibilities covering a multitude of sins, including General de Gaulle, whom the Americans, mindful of the Monroe Doctrine, were trying to remove from the leadership of France. He had become a minister at 48 against Butler's 38, Eden's and Stanley's 37. But this was a tortoise who would play rough.

Churchill, born in 1874 and Home Secretary when the oldest of this group, Macmillan, was still at prep school and when Butler was four, stood at a genial and improbable angle from the aspirants. As old men go, he was remarkably tolerant, inclined to overlook delinquencies, inflicting reminiscence and reflection rather than malice on the youngsters. But the game of Grandpa's Will gave him enormous innocent pleasure, such pleasure that he played it for six years of opposition and four of government through a paralytic stroke and onward to the upper slopes of senility.

All of these men, with the exception of Eden, enjoyed the House of Commons and were good at it. And they ventured into aggressive, if generalised opposition. In terms of policy, the Tories might have been acknowledging that the political spectrum was a leftward-leaning parallelogram which hauled them a good 30 degrees out of the vertical, very much a reverse-Blair situation. But at the same time, they conducted debate against Labour with an abandoned partisanship out of all keeping with their cautious intentions.

Interestingly, Butler, who to the stupid men seemed to be devious and whom not-stupid people like Macmillan chose to portray in that way – 'I always thought of him in a soutane . . . something of a Jesuit . . . He would have been marvellous in medieval politics, creeping about the Vatican; a tremendous intriguer, he always had some marvellous plan . . . and he loved the press . . .' – played next to no part in this charade. Rab thought that the Tory Party should accept the best of Labour's thinking on social security, employment and – with Ellen Wilkinson carrying out his proposal and raising the school leaving age to 15 – education. A great quality in Rab was distaste for the exultant cockerel mode of politics. Most liberal Tories, including Boothby then and Iain Macleod later, though unequivocal social reformers, would deliver speeches which for seamless vituperation would have done credit to the editor of the *Eatanswill Gazette*.

Butler was happiest then with a minimum of opposition duties in Parliament. At the same time he was laying up a vague, unvoiced resentment. Not actually more left-wing than most members of the young leadership group, he had been given the job by Churchill of co-ordinating and effectively drafting party policy for the future. That telescopes things slightly, but it is the effective truth. Butler, the non-combatant who had fought in neither war, was now sitting out the domestic struggle – war against rationing, physical controls, indicative planning and nationalisation – functioning as chief of staff, drafting measures of accommodation with the new status quo. It might be the only sensible approach, it might ensure that a boringly prudential Tory Party got boringly and prudentially back into power, but it did nothing for the red-blooded instincts. There was some parallel with Hugh Gaitskell's reputation among the Left as a dispassionate technician. Certainly 'Mr Butskell', the coining of Norman Macrae of the *Economist*, was in the making.

His work itself at this time was more significant than interesting. The writings of politicians, the books they and their research assistants compulsively produce are rarely compelling reading. The instinct of each of the four members of the SDP Gang of Four to put out a book over a twelvemonth is warning enough. And Butler's 'charters' are no exception. They serve a partisan purpose in a civil fashion rather than offer a reflection on society. They were designed also to pass committees of battered but suspicious politicians and, though they express respectable social concerns, they have a passionless tone, at once instructing and generalised. The wit associated with Butler's private comments is not much evident.

One senses here the influence of David Maxwell-Fyfe, Butler's lieutenant in all this. Not a naturally liberal-minded man, Maxwell-Fyfe had the misfortune to appear in the Butler memoirs, posthumously crucified by his former chief, who commended him for dedicated application work, 'not only pains-taking over every last detail, but immensely loyal'. If that were not damning enough to the practised political ear, which knows 'loyal' as a euphemism for 'stupid', Butler remarks, 'I never knew him spiky or difficult except in parts of his memoirs.' This sullen and resentful document had appeared two years earlier (in 1969) and was answered in half a sentence. Contemplating the vainglorious drudge, Butler speculates that 'he may have been living proof that Carlyle was wrong to define genius as a transcendent capacity for taking trouble'.

But the decision of Churchill to set him up in Old Queen Street as Grand Vizier (Ideas) involved, through a series of net-work groups working on the modernisation of policy, an extension of background positions Butler already had within the party organisation. A wise delegation by an old-fashioned cavalier to an up-to-date desk-worker of formulating what everyone should be thinking next year, the task rather set Butler up as an intellectual couturier.

CHAPTER SEVEN

When Churchill, coming to power in October 1951, showed Butler a Cabinet list with his name opposite the Exchequer, he continued the steady practice of elders and leaders – Hoare, Halifax, Baldwin, Chamberlain and his wartime self – who had regularly advanced Butler on his merits. (It might be argued that his political fortune lasted just as long as there were protective elders able to view ability untainted by competition.) But he was also indicating that Conservative economic policy would not be excessively remote from the pattern established over six and a half years by Dalton, Cripps and Gaitskell.

The economy would be production-led with purchasing power expanded to meet any prospective decline in employment, and instinctively the heads of the horses were turned towards expansion. As Butler made clear in retrospection, he was a firm statist, accepting a substantial Government role in cajoling and cudgelling the economy. The idea of the free market as a sort of gravity through which things and people might usefully fall had as much attraction in 1951 as those pools of unemployment in which he had invited right-wing businessmen to swim.

Economic policy would indeed be tramelled too much by a distinctly deferential approach to the trades unions, Churchill's requirement rather than Butler's. The old man had been burned too often by conflicts with the unions, and Labour had made great play during the election with the punitive horrors likely to emerge from a worker-bashing primitivist Churchill Government. The instrument of acquiescence was to be Walter

Monckton, Edward VIII's lawyer during the long crisis of his short reign. As politics, the soft line was to be a brilliant success, giving the lie to Labour atrocity propaganda, uttered ironically in good faith. Economically, however, this approach began to look even sicker as sporadic growth and militant unionism met in the later 1950s.

Butler was to spend the next four years in day-to-day argument with the man he had succeeded as Chancellor. Their names were to be not only linked, but joined in the notion of 'Butskellism'. The idea was of a Tweedledum-Tweedledee partnership of right-wing Socialist Party and left-wing Tory, each obnoxious to activists of his own party and thus by impli-cation the same sort of person. Since, despite Tony Benn, personalities matter quite as much as issues, it may be worth pursuing the comparison.

Both were Anglo-Indians from families of public servants and curiously, each had a Scottish, indeed an Aberdonian mother. Both had enjoyed outstanding academic careers, distinguishable as Cambridge and Oxford firsts may be distinguished and involving different subjects. Both had a cerebral view of politics, making the judgments they thought rational; both had a social conscience and a concern for the bottom of the heap; both came under fire from the fundamentalists of their own party who looked upon them as inclining to positions somewhere between dilution and treason. Both stood exceptionally high in the opinions of senior civil servants of the more intellectual sort. And they were, for the most part and with blips, on good terms with each other, showing considerable mutual respect.

But the affinities are less impressive than the differences. The single greatest of these was passion. No man was ever less aptly defined than Gaitskell as 'a desiccated calculating machine', a triumph of phrasing over truth if ever there was one. Gaitskell was a natural idealist with a degree of lightly concealed, but simmering fervour. The speeches of 1960 and 1961 against unilateralism and the Common Market are the best-known examples of this, speeches which no dispassionate technician could have made. Gaitskell's first biographer, Philip Williams, quotes a blazing statement, one far less well known, which came at the end of an otherwise technical speech, about his hatred of poverty and squalor, how it had made him a Socialist and how burning bright that commitment was. It would be acutely embarrassing to Mr Blair were he to read it.

Butler was a cool man, Gaitskell a hot one. If both could be indiscreet, Butler did indiscretion in a delicious, giggling way as gossip, Gaitskell invariably in a blast of indignation. His comment in the Commons during the Suez crisis about the triumph of an Israel to which he was sympathetic – that we had joined the burglar and shot the householder – is the sort of self-injurious thing only ever said in serious anger.

Then again, Gaitskell had lived in the real world. Nowhere was more real than the Vienna of 1934, where he had watched the evil little *putsch* of evil little Engelbert Dollfuss. Friends of Butler didn't risk execution or get taken off to jail by political policemen, and his view of abroad – art and scenery always excepted – remained distant, English and not desperately interested. Gaitskell, with his Russian–Jewish wife and close friends in the social–democratic parties was, by contrast, the complete cosmopolitan anti-Fascist. Butler was far more rational, far more detached, ultimately too much so. But he lived in a different party where he was doing good by stealth and to be a social Tory 'on the extreme left wing of the Tory Party', as Gaitskell himself put it, was the only realistic way to proceed.

While both provoked enmity, the sort visited upon the Labour leader's head was incomparably more vicious: the anonymous *New Statesman* profile which accused him quite falsely of nearly following MacDonald out of the Labour Party in 1931; the infantile painting by Richard Hamilton which showed the rejecter of unilateral nuclear disarmament with vampire carnivores; the petty procedural spite of Ian Mikardo trying in the Fabian Society to remove ex-officio members of the committee because Gaitskell was an ex-officio member; the expressions of simple hatred which marked the debate before and after the Scarborough Conference of 1960 couldn't have happened to Butler. Hatreds like that of Randolph Churchill for Rab were eccentric, the Conservative Party being in those days sensibly stuffy about expressions of violent feeling. The dislike was there all right, and was perhaps more dangerous for being constrained. Gaitskell would have needed to be wonderfully imperceptive not to have known who his enemies were. Labour were to do themselves enormous harm by their public quarrelling. The Tories did not hate less, but they were in those days more accomplished about the proper conduct of hatred.

But perhaps the most instructive difference between two civilised, intelligent politicians of a high and serious sort was that where Butler was cautious and prudential a little beyond the call of good sense, Gaitskell was pretty generally ready for a fight; answering moral imperatives, he could be morally imperious. It was a matter both of conviction and temperament. Almost certainly he liked a fight rather too much. The quarrel with Bevan was two-sided, and if it had been avoided, as Butler in his place would have avoided it, the Attlee Government would have been able to stick out the interim problems of 1951 and collect the economic rewards. A less passionately convinced politician than Gaitskell would have been well placed to see Labour through to the favourable terms of trade, improved supplies of consumer goods and the great Labour victory of 1954.

Butler's dispassion was part of his role as a good government man. He didn't do magnificent stands, but neither did he do ill-advised attacks like the Stalybridge speech in which Gaitskell bravely but indiscriminately laid into the whole left as a deutero-Communist enemy to be taken on. Those mistakes never did stop his ascent in the party, but they were an essential part of the cat-and-dog public image of a party devoting its talent to politics and its genius to war.

But the time would come when a moral imperative had its point. Conor Cruise O'Brien heard Gaitskell's televised broadcast answering Eden at the height of Suez in an Irish pub: 'A crowd accustomed to be cynical both about politicians and about Englishmen was deeply moved by Gaitskell's controlled and genuine passion ... A tram-driver lowered his pint. "You can't beat an Englishman," he said, "when he's straight." ' That is a perfectly wonderful thing to say – about Gaitskell, about Englishmen. Again, on this issue, it would have been good politics, much better politics for the long haul to the election, simply to have shut up. It would also have been entirely wrong.

But then over Suez, where Butler would comprehend the destructive, unreasoning folly in confected ultimatum, colluded operation and the war that dared not speak its name, but not move against them, resistance was unimaginably harder. Gaitskell had only to cut with the grain of his own party and of liberal, progressive *Manchester Guardian* Britain, and even so he was called a traitor to his face for his pains. Butler quite inevitably had to argue from inside and against the arterial nationalism of an enraged party.

In this and much more, he was a natural Conservative where his predecessor at the Treasury was a natural radical. Being a Conservative involved then no unnecessary excess of democracy. The Conservatives of the fifties, however willing to spend public money, conciliate unions and accept social welfare, were a social élite and one nimbly surviving, even if many members, like Maxwell-Fyfe and Macleod, had been co-opted into honorary membership. Gaitskell might not, like George Orwell, drink tea out of a saucer, but his sense of identity with working-class people was of a kind to infuriate Marxists by outreaching them. Gaitskell's friends were in the unions and categorically not just the bosses who gave him hard-handed backing. Both organised Labour, with its bloc votes, and working-class public opinion as polled, were steadily with him. Leeds was another home, never the constituency to be got away from. By contrast, Aneurin Bevan, annexed to the delights of London, had become an oddly metropolitan figure.

Gaitskell in Leeds and Butler in Saffron Walden are instructive. Both were devoted to their constituents and came to be loved by very many of them; both were conscious of using their gifts and good fortune in service. But Butler couldn't unbend, dance, make personal friendships and, as it were, step out of natural inequality in rural Essex as Gaitskell did in Hunslet.

Given the differences, it is interesting to read Gaitskell on Butler and to find him in conclusion employing the phrase used in this study throughout. 'Butler is on the extreme left of the Tory Party and is shrewd enough to understand that they have got to . . . live down the reputation . . . inherited from . . . the thirties . . . to be able to say to the electorate when the election comes, "no war, no unemployment, no cuts in social services, *just good Government*".' It is a description of a man getting things right and the implied criticism is of a lack of ardour, a getting of things right for reasons of too lucid good sense.

That judgment is perfectly reasonable. It acknowledges Rab's complete understanding of the transformed political map and the practical impossibility of restoring the full dress rig of British social injustice, though it misses the fact that Butler quietly *disliked* injustice. And the element in Gaitskell of simply having to say what he felt, an instinct never to leave a moral high point unoccupied, would later lead him into a denunciation of Butler after the mistakes of the 1955 budget that was plain wrong. Butler had been forced to impose taxes in the autumn of that year after inflation had been provoked by a pre-election 'give-away' budget. As I hope to show, the true reasons behind that error had little to do with cheap electioneering.

But Gaitskell's scorn was absolute. 'Now having bought his

votes with a bribe, the Chancellor is forced, as he knew he would be, to dishonour the cheque . . . He has behaved in a manner unworthy of his high office. He began in folly, continued in deceit, and he ended in reaction.' Nothing very desiccated about that. It is, in fact, a bad case of leaving the ethical pudding too long on top heat.

It was in any case an intolerant and self-righteous speech and Gaitskell, on a bad good day, was capable of doing justice to both adjectives. A good deal of puritanism flows through English radical politics, not the puritanism applying to sex or drink or enjoyment, but the price which has to be paid for the straight Englishman, a stiff-necked way of saying 'Your standards are not my standards.' John Bright expressed it when he churlishly returned Disraeli's compliment on the Angel of Death speech – 'I would have given anything to have made that speech' – with the words, 'You could have if you were honest.' Butler and Gaitskell shared problem-solving minds, but utterly different temperaments. Lack of partisanship was an aspect of Butler's pacific instinct suited to an intelligent adaptation to opponents' ideas which should be tempered and modified, but not rejected. Labour in those days had the ideological upper hand and the moral confidence that goes with it.

In spite of the budget outburst, the two men were on decent terms. Gaitskell's real division was with Macmillan, 'the great architect of complacency and the materialist outlook'. Visiting the US, Gaitskell compared the Democrats' view of Nixon – 'Tricky Dickie' distrusted far above all ordinary Republicans for his deviousness – with his own response to Macmillan. It was a mirror image of Macmillan's view of him as odious prig, the two opinions wrapped up a happy relationship of quietly simmering mutual scorn.

Ironically, the economic situation Butler inherited from his adversary involved massive commitments to military expenditure. A routine turn in all Conservative propaganda to this day has been to suggest that the 'Socialists' are unsound on defence, not really patriotic, unwilling to defend the country. Despite the brief interlude of Footery at the start of the eighties, this has always been shoddy nonsense, as much in Neil Kinnock's time as Clement Attlee's, and best answered with the figures.

As a proportion of gross national product (GNP, then the designated measurement), the share of expenditure given over to defence in 1952 (Butler's time, Gaitskell's budget) was 11.3 per cent. By 1957, a year after Rab's departure and reflecting his actions, it stood at 8.4 per cent. Part of Rab's inheritance from Gaitskell and the Labour administration was a fierce and furious commitment to Western defence, especially over the Korean War of 1950–3. Such devotion troubled the Treasury, always more unsound (and sensible) than the Labour Party on defence. The FO mandarin Roger Makins told Peter Hennessy that we had 'perhaps attempted too much', regretting that when asked by the Attlee Government whether we could afford the Korean undertaking, he had not answered with a simple 'no'. Britain could literally afford it, but only by accepting injurious diversion of financial resources. Douglas Allen, now Lord Croham, speaks a furious exasperation with Gaitskell for the unTreasury-like activity of actually urging the service ministries to spend more quickly. The programme undertaken in a rush in midsummer 1950, was to increase defence expenditure by 50 per cent to £3.4 billion at the hard values of that date. By December and after the antics of General MacArthur threatening invasion of China and China's consequent entry into the war, the price of British international responsibility had gone up to £4.7 billion.

We have hindsight and accuse from it. In 1950 the North Korean invasion, coming only two years after the Czech *putsch*, had concluded all the Eastern European swallowings, and less than a year after the Chinese Communists had accomplished control of the mainland, might fairly be viewed as a watershed. Communist advance was a fact; Communist disposition to open-ended conquest was very thinkable. As no one knew better than Rab, appeasement of any kind was violently discredited. But we were at the pattern-setting time of reconstruction, spending proportionally four times as much as now on defence. Germany, barred from any such contribution and humiliatingly obliged to concentrate on the unheroic likes of car manufacture, can today cite many causes for the years of economic triumph. Not spending money on defence was one of them.

Had Britain been internationally more perfunctory, sending nominal forces and heartfelt sympathy (and coolly acknowledging herself as less than a great power), had she been less responsible and less vain about her responsibility really mattering, an alternative future might have been accomplished. As it was, the Tories cut defence but not by enough, succeeding in diminishing Britain's military commitments by something like a quarter during Rab's time at the Treasury. But as Harold Wilson had said in the speech following his 1951 resignation from the presidency of the Board of Trade, 'the financial programme of rearmament was one which went beyond the physical resources which can be made available'. Many of the benefits of devaluation were blown. Long-term industrial developments were sacrificed to military priorities, inflation was quietly fed into the system and the foreigners' habit of buying elsewhere than from preoccupied Britain became entrenched. As Samuel Brittan remarks, the Bevanites, or at any rate, Harold Wilson, had been right. And the Tories, by the drollest of ironies, were caught up in the economic consequences of Labour's profligate spending on the military.

Butler's caution was never more aptly put to use. He was categorically not a technician, but he had a lot of sense and he rushed into nothing. He was assailed almost at the start by a mood of hysteria among advisers. There was a balance-of-payments deficit of £700 million (which was a lot of money; 13 years of jog-along inflation later, the £800 million left by Maudling would be electoral lamentation fodder to Labour politicians). The balance of payments was what mattered at that time, the gauge of health and concern. It had been looked after without recourse to interest rates, which had been static for 12 years. But available to any chancellor was a positive console of physical controls, a mighty Wurlitzer of regulation. Imported goods could be turned away by fiat, something elegantly illustrated by Churchill's winsome request that Butler help his French political friend, Daladier, retain his seat by rescinding the cruel bar on imports of the glacé cherries his constituency produced.

Rab's response to his overall problem was, except in one particular, that of an orthodox Labour chancellor of the times, to save money by means of austerity. There were, he announced, to be cuts in food and raw material imports and a cut in the overseas travel allowance, but very daringly, he reverted to use of bank rate, raising it half a point to $2^{1}/_{2}$ per cent! He would later push it to a screaming 4 per cent. His style at this time was suitably grave and stern. The deathbed language of his advisers, Edward Bridges and the young William Armstrong, who at a private Athenaeum lunch had talked of the blood draining away from the system, had communicated itself to the Chancellor. And he was to add a second dose of cuts including a measure out-Labouring Labour in its Roman austerity – a cut from 6oz to 4oz in the sweet ration.

Fortunately, the sense of humour and style were present as

well. The speech of that first budget was 'designed', he would later say, 'like a symphony of Mahler's with sharply contrasting movements. The first part (*Feierlich und gemessen*) talked darkly of the consequence of mightily falling trade reserves; the second movement (*Sturmisch bewegt*) contained the disagreeable parts of the budget' – that interest-rate rise, import restrictions and increased indirect taxes. But 'the third movement (*Heiter bedachtig*)' cheered everyone up by replacing the blanket handout of food subsidies with benefit and pension increases directed at poorer people.

What, however, he very sensibly did *not* do, despite advice and expectation, was increase income tax. In reality things were better (and more volatile) in the short term and the blood would flow agreeably back, giving Rab a degree of credit to which he had imperfect claims, just as the blame which marked the end of his chancellorship was misplaced. By his economies of expenditure he had done some substantive good and he had also made the right noises for calming the movers of money. Other things would be worse in the long term, away from the rabidness of markets; worse by way of overexpenditure on defence, lack of industrial investment and weakness towards the trades unions.

But in most of this, Butler was the prisoner of politics and of other people, one in particular. Winston Churchill had been determined in opposition to make the Conservative Party what cant calls 'caring'. He had addressed Butler in the maundering fashion of a roaring squire drawing breath for benevolence about 'not reducing cottagers to penury'. Churchill's own brutalist, send-in-the-yeomanry past, founded on a sketchy understanding of the economy, had now to be buried under a monument of social compassion informed by an understanding of the economy no less sketchy, but directed towards election.

The whole nonsense predated arrival in power. At Party Conference in Blackpool in 1950, the mood of the floor, ardent to do something big, had been caught by the platform. On the matter of council houses, the number 300,000 had been mentioned from below. Lord Woolton, Party Chairman, who was already Butler's steadiest jobbing enemy, now did him an entirely involuntary injury. 'Could we build 300,000?' he asked. Butler directed him to David Clarke, Conservative Research Director, who assented with reservation backstage. Woolton, a publicist before he was anything else – and he was very little else – hurried forward to embrace the uninstructed demand with an acceptance no better instructed and the fatuous words, 'This is magnificent.' With such little wisdom is the world governed.

Butler's own words before passing the matter to Clarke had been, 'Could we build them? The question is *should* we build them? And the answer is, it will make it that much more difficult to restore the economy.' But he then left the final word to Clarke the technician. Butler was at fault here. He was indeed subordinate and was not at this point Chancellor, only head of policy. But he did not take on the enthusiast determined to get things magnificently wrong. There is a certain melancholic analogy with Sir Robert Hall not telling Gaitskell in his teeth that we couldn't afford to fight an Asian war. As usual, he understood what should be done and as sometimes, was not obdurate or rugged enough to fight for it.

Conservative electioneering requirements, natural to Churchill, took over from economic strategy. They could be summed up in a sentence. Walter Monckton would buy off the unions and Macmillan would build 300,000 houses. To this grand misdesign, Butler was peripheral. He initiated neither folly and was uncomfortably placed to resist them. But they would constitute a far greater burden to a sensible running of the economy than the formal trammels Churchill fussily hung upon him on his appointment to the Treasury in 1951. These were an 'overlord', Sir Arthur Salter, sending disregarded memoranda in green ink; his old enemy, Lord Woolton, with a Treasury advisory committee, and the sham-omniscient Frederick Lindemann, Lord Cherwell, occupying the flat at Number 11 which the Butlers in Lord North Street didn't bother with.

Having meddled thoroughly injuriously with the broad objectives of policy, Churchill meddled irksomely with its day-to-day running. The single lesson, that he knew less than nothing about economics and should stay out of them, he did not learn.

The nonsense about which Butler was helpless and largely innocent was his cutting of the sweet ration and the amount of the citizen's own money to be taken on holiday, while other parts of the Government were autonomously building 300,000 council houses in a year and keeping the Glorious Gordons in Korea at around 11 per cent of GNP. At such a time, the notion of Treasury control with spending departments kept in a decent state of supplication would have been very handy.

Samuel Brittan, as good a guide as there is to this period, gives the Butler chancellorship good marks and makes the point that Conservative policy deteriorated as time passed, a deterioration marked by a shift from the expansionist instincts of Butler (and Gaitskell before him) to a fearful and defensive posture. Within the limits imposed on him, and successfully breaking out of some of them, Butler handled the Exchequer brief with the good sense of a non-specialist, the sort of intelligent generalist much admired in the higher civil service. Having been probably too bleak in his first budget and its follow-up measures, when he did get the glimmer of light to encourage expansion, he expanded.

Now all statesmen are politicians under the skin and, of course, Butler was happy, when a much better balance-of-payments figure appeared, to become in later budgets a tax-cutter, an abolisher of rationing and general bringer of good news. But none of his actions at that time were extravagances or political performances. They were liberating moves, tending towards greater freedom for the citizen and releasing purchasing power. After the good news came in, the Butler chancellorship was a much more sustainable course of economic dealing than spectacular acts of public spending or politically motivated sprees beyond the reach of Treasury prudence.

'We must not be frightened at a little more ease and happiness, or feel that what is pleasant must necessarily be evil.' The tone of a rather tentative Cheeryble brother contemplating a very small spoonful of whisky in the tea reflects the age. The fifties did not swing – sexual intercourse would not begin for another 11 years – but a pilot scheme for hedonism was thought to be in order. Behind the governess tones of the budget speech of 1954, expansion was being encouraged.

Earlier in 1952, still worried about all that blood draining away, advisers had wanted further cuts in personal spending, either tax increases or direct restrictions. Butler refused this and instinctively fought against a mentality wedded to suffering as a means of redemption. His move to reduce food subsidies and raise benefits and tax relief was not merely more equitable, it was aimed at keeping demand buoyant rather than punishing the high street further for all those soldiers, houses and lost exports. For a man who had no formal training in economics, he was sensing that what was good for activity was fundamentally right and to be helped wherever it could be.

There is in most chancellors a psychological factor. Temperamentally inclined to comfort and enjoyment, Rab was, subject to the numbers being right, a natural anti-Cripps. That statesman, who had been revered because of his personal austerity, pitched somewhere between St Francis and Alexei Stakhanov, was the perfect accompaniment to the penitential regime he imposed for our own good. But at least Stafford Cripps was eager to be fair, not something which could be said of finance ministers in the thirties. Butler was part of the political generation that lived through that period in lesser office and had been a marginal accessory to the taking of orthodox financial advice. Although Tory propaganda made play with escaping Labour severities, which it had at first intensified, the thirties mixture of Hobbes and inertia was being rejected far more decisively.

But of course, Butler enjoyed good fortune. In his memoirs he is remarkably candid. He quotes despatch-box banter between himself and Gaitskell and then says that such things are fine in debate, but you don't keep them up for the record. As Chancellor he had been, and proclaimed the fact, a beneficiary of a major turnaround in the terms of trade. 'Gaitskell,' he says, 'was Chancellor only for a short period, during which the terms of trade swung violently against us. I was Chancellor for more than four years, during most of which the management of the economy, though a perpetual headache, was helped by external circumstances.' That honesty was natural to Butler, part of his academic cast of mind and as unmistakably his as the unflinching and self-injurious way of marking down colleagues for their beta-query capacities.

Good luck and the good husbandry he reasonably takes credit for put Butler in a position to do subsequent popular things and make life easier. As the numbers improved and the advisers' enjoyable sense of tragedy was slowly dispelled, he was placed to liberate further. And some idea of his priorities is shown in the 20 per cent investment allowances he introduced in the 1954 budget. He was aware also of the harm being done by Churchill's extraordinary appeasement of the unions. He had fierce language from the Treasury economic survey to guide him. Wages had risen by $7^{1}/_{2}$ per cent in 1953–4 against a $2^{1}/_{2}$ per cent increase in per-man output and by a further three points by March 1955.

Incomes policy, attempted by Cripps in 1948–50, would return and would steadily fail after invariable early success. Butler, meanwhile, talked laconically of 'voluntary moderation'. But Churchill's political pre-emption of an intelligent approach to the unions (not at all the same thing as making war on them) by raising expectations and union morale helped to make an incomes policy unlikely to succeed when it was tried. The

contrast with the German experience of *Mitbestimmung* with
the hard numbers confronted by unions and employers together
is altogether too bitter.

One event (or long drawn-out episode) rather stands out
from everything else in Butler's time as a self-contained unity. It
was called perhaps as an anagram of the names of civil servants,
'Robot' and it represented an attempt at a partial floating of the
pound. It was an attractive idea aimed at counteracting the
stop-go tendency, the drag on expansion, which occurred with
every move of the balance of payments, and in those heavy-
handed days, it was an extremely daring one. Oddly enough,
Churchill, groping around and knowing that he was groping
around, instinctively favoured it. He 'felt in his bones that it was
right to free the pound', said Butler. It seemed like a response to
murderous runs on the pound then just experienced and
seemingly ever-threatening.

Churchill himself mused to Oliver Lyttelton, 'In the worst of
the war I could always see how to do it . . . Today's problems are
elusive and intangible, and it would be a bold man who could
look forward to certain success.' (The thought occurs that the
combination of a floating rate and Sir Walter Monckton was a
very dodgy one.) Opposition came from those who feared risks
and gambles and those, like Gaitskell and some Treasury figures,
who disliked the *laissez-faire* implications. The idea was
opposed by the fussing duo of Cherwell and Salter, whom Butler
dismisses with a startling mixture of Cambridge aplomb and
New York Jewish idiom as 'peripheral kibitzers'.

More serious to him personally were the reservations of Lord
Swinton (Cunliffe-Lister the Spitfire-building Air Minister), for
whom he had serious respect and affection. Swinton wanted the
Sterling Area Commonwealth countries to equalise their own
balance of payments down first if there was to be confidence.
Oliver Lyttelton was, as fervently, in favour, and he and Butler
fought for Robot some way beyond the wire, causing the 1952
budget to be postponed. They lost, not to the kibitzers but to
Treasury and Cabinet instincts for keeping hold on Nurse, even
a nurse liable to go off on a periodic bender. Butler is savaged for
his part in this episode by Edmund Dell in his book *The
Chancellors*, but then at the hands of Mr Dell no chancellor goes
unsavaged.

The late Ian Bancroft who worked directly with him gives an
admirable account of Butler's style. He was good at making up
his mind, though it was his way with an idea to try it on like a

suit and walk about for a day or so before rejecting or buying it. He was, says Lord Bancroft, reasonably good at communicating with and informing civil service colleagues, though no one was as good at this as Stafford Cripps. On the other hand, Butler never felt that he saw enough of the head of the civil service, the genial, overworked Edward Bridges. 'I never *see* Edward,' he grumbled.

Butler was inclined to complain about small things and indulge in a certain small-time self-pity, though not about big things. As a speechwriter he had, says Bancroft, infuriating habits, composing pieces like music then shredding them to change the order for the purposes of impact. Once, talking to William Armstrong about information as rhetoric, he said, 'Show the whiskers of the rabbit, then pop it back in the hat for later.'

Very much like Michael Heseltine in more recent times, Butler liked to work departmentally, by way of the large meeting. He was also much relied on by particular colleagues: 'Buck' De La Warr, Thomas Dugdale and the President of the National Farmers' Union, Jim Turner, all regularly came to him for help and continued to do so after he left the Treasury. He was generally gregarious, but could never be prevailed upon to extend this to the House of Commons. His PPS, the much loved Hubert Ashton, cricketer and brother-in-law of Gaitskell, was always trying to have him spend more time at the Commons and would drag him to the smoking-room once a session, but he was never at home there and would regularly refer to 'the private member' as in 'private soldier'. Lord Alport, who knew Butler and Sydney very well, recalls telling him to pull himself together and cultivate the backbenchers. 'He just shrugged and said, "You know me. It's just not in my nature."'

Politically, through all of this, Butler stood very high indeed. Newspapers fêted him; more than once he was named man of the year. Significantly, even the Tory-eating *Daily Mirror* saluted him in this way. He had first done the unpopular things, establishing a name for courage, but luck and management had not kept him too long at that thankless task. He was cutting tax, getting rid of regulations, ending rationing. His public style, courteous but assured and slightly directoral, went down well in deferential Britain, which likes gentlemanliness and is grateful for gentlemen who are competent, as he was, at the highest level. Other chancellors Lloyd and Heathcoat Amory would be hirelings; Butler was a great officer of state.

When Winston Churchill, entertaining Alcide de Gasperi, the Italian Prime Minister, in Downing Street, felt his leg go numb, the symptom of a major stroke, occasioning a state crisis to be conducted in camera, it was to Butler that the role of head of Government and acting Prime Minister would go. Anthony Eden, the approved heir to Churchill, was himself incapacitated – both ill and abroad – in a Boston, Massachusetts hospital.

There is a school of thought which believes that Butler might, given ruthless will, have used this position to make himself Prime Minister. One can imagine Harold Macmillan so positioned, first squaring party high-ups and the dullards at the Palace, before informing the nation through manly tears that tragedy, the great sufferings of a revered leader and a dearly beloved comrade in arms, compelled him, an old man and unwilling, to take up an intolerable burden for a very little while, in all of which reluctant service he begged for the prayers and love of a Christian nation. Macmillan might have done this, especially if armed like Butler with inside information from a niece, Jane Portal, working in the Prime Minister's office. But for all that Churchill was past it and Eden not up to it, an honest politician, which Butler essentially was, could do no such thing. Churchill was a great man to whom he owed gratitude; Eden had seniority and would have had to have been assailed behind his back when ill.

No doubt timidity played a part along with propriety, but good sense did too. The reverbations of a sick-room coup, the flaw of illegitimacy running through the new ministry, the inflamed outrage of Anthony Eden and what would have been his personal party would have been a formidable undertaking, however long a week may be in politics.

It should be said that the form among politicians, despite ardent disagreements, had not been altogether ruthless for some time. Baldwin, the guiding spirit of shrewd decency, had encouraged MacDonald to hold office when he could have commanded it for himself. Chamberlain had succeeded Baldwin by consent and without conflict. The struggle which had ended in Churchill's accession had manifestly been waged for a high, urgent principle. Attlee, despite adverse appearances, had been backed through the nadir of 1947, and Morrison's manoeuvres and resentments against him had done Morrison no good. The Bevan–Gaitskell struggle was bitter indeed, but belief and conviction ran through it.

For really dirty politics one had to go back to the age before and after the First War, to the rat-pit where Lloyd George gouged Asquith; where Balfour, wounded from the earlier Balfour Must Go campaign, saw off Curzon and the dying Bonar Law was used like an offensive weapon by his friends against their enemies. Not for nothing did Harold Macmillan look nostalgically back to the Edwardian era.

Charges against Butler of weakness in the 1953 crisis are seen through a filter coloured by the Portillo style. The instinct of the angels round the throne at that time – Norman Brook, Cabinet Secretary, and John Colville, Prime Minister's Private Secretary – was to be immensely Establishment, correct and untruthful. The Prime Minister had been overworking and had been commanded to take a complete rest by doctors. Taken in the context of a relatively well-conducted period, such charges won't wash.

Senior and informed people to whom I have talked in preparing this essay, Michael Fraser, Ian Bancroft and Douglas Allen, all concur that Eden should never have been Prime Minister; that on grounds of his erratic, explosive temperament alone, he was unfit for the job. The political class knew it and Churchill demonstrated his fear of it. Like his radio contemporary, Mrs Dale and her Jim, he 'worried about Anthony' right through his correspondence. But images and soundbites existed before they were given names, and the public perception of Eden at this time was of a *preux chevalier* with beautiful manners and the natural aptitudes of a gentleman with added intelligence. The Eden who wrestled with Evelyn Shuckburgh of the Foreign Office to get at the dividing window of an official car to vent blind rage at a lost driver was not part of the public's understanding. The ministerial class knew better and the idea of getting rid of him must have had great charm, but it was unrealistic. His reputation towered above him.

Meanwhile, Butler's friend the Chief Whip James Stuart warned him that he was doing two and a half jobs – Prime Minister, Chancellor and foreign affairs spokesman in the Commons – and that he should heed the example of Stafford Cripps, broken by overwork. It was fair warning, despite Rab's lucid and swift despatch of business, to someone so clearly intended, as Tony Howard puts it, to play Martha.

It was almost Butler's doom to stand in as Premier for the first of a dozen times, and to do the job extremely well. But perhaps he needed the work, for by this time he knew that his wife of nearly 30 years was very ill. Sydney was dying hideously of cancer of the mouth. (She would steadily deteriorate and die in

December of 1954.) Butler's splendid run of luck stood at its apogee and had begun to turn.

But across 1954, at any rate in economic terms, no one would have thought so. The economic weather, as Wilde's Cecily puts it, 'continued charming'. He produced a sensible, neutral budget, but he rightly claimed credit for the fact that in that year 'for the British trader and consumer, the war ended'. Controls on allocation of materials, on foodstuffs and on a good part of what was imported, indeed on most prices, had gone. Butler, delighted at the derationing of meat, stopped his car en route to his Essex home in a village called Aythorpe Roding, went through the papers from his red box and proudly signed the order. The authoritarian virtue which had touched the public-school team spirit as much as the socialist sense of coercive social justice was finally being put aside.

The caveat might perhaps be made that Butler should have retained, by way of Butskellism, a government care and concern for the individual performance of industry, for training, standards of after-service and for what were already becoming the German industrial virtues. Even so, the whole mood was expansionary and optimistic, and it was at this time that the famous forecast that the standard of living would be doubled in 25 years was made. Roughly and readily, he was proved correct, though we have not enjoyed the 4 per cent annual growth which would have made for deepest content. The significance of the remark, which caused a stir at the time, was the new way of looking at commonplace information and the fact that, as generally with Butler, he was being positive and encouraging.

Sam Brittan makes the point that Butler's optimism extended to international contagions. If America went into recession, as was feared in 1954, national and international steps would have to be taken to correct the effects. Four years later Heathcoat Amory, Macmillan's first Chancellor, was talking a deflationary despair. The strength of sterling was all that mattered 'and we must conduct our finances with a special caution in difficult times'. This was the voice of a new defeatism and national loneliness, but it came after reversals which began in Rab's chancellorship and which need to be understood.

The orthodox view of Butler's spring budget of 1955, neces-sarily so called because its mistakes provoked an autumn one, are that, with an election in prospect and for low electioneering purposes, the Chancellor engineered a give-away budget, took sixpence (2^1/$_2$ contemporary melancholy pence) off income tax and distributed £135 million of reliefs in the middle of a boom, overheating the economy. This saw the Tories to an increased majority before Butler had to come back in the autumn with a desperate parcel of emergency measures including chunks of purchase tax, the so-called 'pots and pans' budget, earning enormous contempt for letting shoddy politics override the stewardship of the economy. This is the burden of Hugh Gaitskell's savage rhetoric quoted earlier.

A mistake certainly, a major wrong move after three and more years of prudence and well-judged expansion. But an electioneering budget, a cheap trick played for party advantage at the expense of prudential conduct of the long-term economy, was something unimaginably unButler-like. Despite his amiable rhetorical jokes about 'showing a whisker of the rabbit', there was little of the showman and nothing of the trickster about R. A. Butler. And lest that sound like a sentimental prejudice, evidence is offered by people present in the Treasury and competent to judge matters that he intended no such thing.

The account of Lord Bancroft, given to me in conversation and later supported by another high-ranking civil servant of the time, Alan Lord, is that both the injurious aspects of the year's budgets, the minor but politically embarrassing imposition of purchase tax on household goods in autumn and the grave error of cutting income tax by sixpence in spring, derived from official advice tendered by civil servants in good faith.

It is a tradition in Britain, though Mrs Thatcher never seemed happy with it, that politicians must never blame civil servants for what goes wrong. And Butler never did blame them. Though apparently furious, he adhered to the old maxim, 'If you get it wrong we take the blame, if you get it right we take the credit.' But Ian Bancroft says simply that the Chancellor's two immediately relevant advisers, Edward Bridges, head of the civil service, and Bernard Gilbert, the economic adviser, pressed upon Butler the dangers that Labour, if elected, might feel that it could raise income tax yet further. Without taking sides against Labour, they very much desired that it should not regard the current level as a floor.

This was a time when direct tax was coming perilously close to standard rate at 50 per cent and political parties had none of the present effete inhibition about raising it. One might ask what reflection Bridges and Gilbert had given to the effect of tax cuts on an economy warming up, something not contingent on a change of government. One might say that Butler might have seen this himself, but misjudgment is not chicanery.

It was still Butler's decision; he took it and got all possible blame for it. But if events are looked at historically, a chancellor can be, at the very least, understood if, when his immediate most senior civil servants – the force for everything staid and prudential – tell him that what would be most agreeable in political terms is actually a public good, he seizes it. In a minor key Bancroft adds something politically important: that Customs and Excise, asked in the autumn to indicate what goods would fall under a particular band of purchase tax, failed to list all those involved and thus presented the Opposition and the headline-writers with an extra twist of derision – the 'pots and pans' budget. A little ironic additional force is lent to Lord Bancroft's allocation of error, when he takes back as credit for the civil servants that broadly correct and impactive prophecy of a doubling of the standard of living in 25 years. '*That*,' he says, 'was got up by Edward Bridges and me!'

History should make its adjustments, but Butler's experiences in 1955, falling on him, remember, after the two-fisted punch of his wife's death in December 1954, were miserable. There was a new Prime Minister, Anthony Eden, vividly unstable, a contemporary, not an elder, amenable to the malicious whispering of Lord Woolton against the Chancellor, ignorant of the economy and home matters, but determined, with the resolution of the weak, to make a mark on them. 'He was,' said the late Michael Fraser, 'someone who should never have been Prime Minister.' Fraser, the Conservative Party's own principal civil servant, describes Eden to me as 'two people, one of whom could be immensely courteous, showing beautiful manners, and another who was simply enraged'.

Eden, arriving at Downing Street in April, wanted Butler away from the Treasury quickly. Oddly for someone who would show so much compliance, he dragged his feet successfully, though hardly to his advantage, having to endure the public humiliation of the autumn assembly of broken pieces. On top of that, his successor would be Harold Macmillan, who had, over the previous 15 months, moved sweetly from Defence to the Foreign Office, a fleeting encounter before the Treasury, rather like the passage of John Major in 1989 and with a similar conclusion. But Macmillan, who had confided to his diary a cynical interest in 'how long Anthony manages to stay in the saddle', did not move gratefully and delightedly into the Treasury.

Understanding the rewards of being difficult, he played up and made a scene. As he had created one when Oliver Stanley was put over him during the war, as he had demanded at every point that *his* housing programme should have protection, he now insisted on first place on the home front and exclusion of Rab from the honorific title of Deputy Prime Minister. Chutzpah hardly describes it. For a man who made enormous play of a gentlemanly and gracious style in politics, Macmillan matched it with a hunched, obdurate and untrusting substance. He was being enormously advanced and demanded the full price of accepting advancement.

Butler made no effective demands that autumn. He could and should have insisted upon the Foreign Office; he had the seniority and knowledge of its ways. Eden, who knew little else, was bent on putting a subordinate there, Selwyn Lloyd, a man who, had he but known it, was on the brink of indestructibility. Failing that, anything less than the Home Office represented demotion. James Callaghan, a man with a touch of Macmillan's heroic insolence, requested, required and got that place after his own far greater humiliation, the devaluation of 1967.

There is a final little irony here. Butler had lost standing and delighted enemies with his budget problems. But one day's atrocity is often the routine of the next. Autumn budgets were to become a commonplace; and from Heathcoat Amory and Maudling, Macmillan as Prime Minister would positively *require* electioneering budgets. Selwyn Lloyd, stuffily responsible, would be sacked as Chancellor to make one possible, and when the time came for Roy Jenkins under Labour to practise a firm rectitude (and much good it did him), non-electioneering budgets had become a matter of public remark. At the end of 1995 the sillier sort of right-wing Conservative was screaming at Kenneth Clarke for another such bundle of improvidence.

Yet Eden was not a strong character. Macmillan knew how to squeeze concessions out of him. If Butler had had a touch of sullen unwillingness and had dug his toes in, he could surely have had one of the two jobs. Instead, he settled unhappily for the leadership of the House and the lesser ceremonial rank of Lord Privy Seal, a vague post combining house management under a parliamentary system compliant, not to say servile at that time, with assorted odds and ends, bits of Home Office business and atomic energy. He had eminence without impact, seniority without command – much like an archdeacon. He was Lord High Nothing Very Much. For the first time, he was without a supportive senior and dependent upon the goodwill of contemporaries, the rather older contemporaries who had watched his meritocratic ascent under Baldwin, Chamberlain and Churchill. They now formed a tight circle and kept him out of it.

It was at this time that Francis Boyd, the very shrewd political correspondent of the *Manchester Guardian*, wrote a monograph on Butler. It was friendly and admiring, as might have been expected, but the goodwill contained a deadly suggestion to which Butler gave chuckling assent. If called upon like Peel to split his party, Boyd doubted if he would do it. 'We sat together,' says Bancroft, 'each with a copy of Francis Boyd's little book, flicking through the pages. Rab came to that bit and giggled: "It's so true, you know." ' In the middle of 1956 Butler compounded things by being taken ill. There is much vagueness about its nature. Lord Croham (Douglas Allen) calls it, rather Victorianly, a *crise de nerfs*. The symptoms, including a loss of balance, suggest something more physiological, akin perhaps to Ménière's disease, but nervous illness had afflicted him since childhood, notably at Cambridge, and one can only speculate about the role of career anxiety of the kind affecting his last university year.

But Britain was moving into a period of political volatility. The famous *Daily Telegraph* leader demanding 'the smack of firm government' spoke many things, a desire by the right-wing of those days for undefined satisfactions, the recognition by informed opinion of Eden's frailty and of Churchill's unofficial want of confidence in him, perhaps also an itchy intuition that this was a Prime Minister whose position was not unassailable and against whom discontents could be enjoyably mobilised. And Eden, vain, self-doubting, explosive, was perfect baiting material. Butler's observation about the beautiful woman and the mad baronet had been a devastating thing to say, but given that all ill-speaking is gravitationally attached to its victim, it must have assured bitter resentment from the Prime Minister. He did not, after all, react sensibly to the *Telegraph* leader, nor to the further expounding of it by Donald Maclachlan, who had written it. He took affront, but also issued denials. Saying, 'No, it's not true, I'm not weak,' is a fair demonstration of weakness. In fact, attacks were not confined to a single piece. The right-wing Suez Group were a presence, the *Mail* and the *Telegraph* were then, as ever, impatient for the equestrian qualities of leadership and the bloodshot personality of Randolph Churchill worked off its animus in Beaverbrook's *Evening Standard*. Meanwhile, within the Cabinet, Macmillan, understanding that bullying works, bullied.

His immediate objective, that he should be free to end food subsidies which, after all, futilely benefit the well-to-do, was sensible enough and Eden's resistance was based as much on fear of unpopularity as on economic ignorance. But Macmillan's method, the threat to resign, which won him in his own estimate 'four fifths of my demands', illustrated most of what needs to be understood about both Eden and Macmillan – that strength finding weakness will know what to do. As Brendan Bracken said in a letter to Beaverbrook, who concurred:

> Your prophecy that [Macmillan] would make trouble for Eden has been swiftly proved. He sent in his resignation yesterday on a cunningly contrived issue which would have gravely embarrassed his boss and would have given [him] the credit for being the only virtuous and strong man in the Government . . . Unfortunately he [Eden] has given this man a job which puts him plumb in the middle of the political stage and we may be sure he will make fullest use of his nuisance value.

Eden was, into the bargain, the victim of the incompetent surgeon who had severed his bile duct. Taken with the doctors who respectively told Macmillan that he had cancer when he didn't and Rab that he did not when he had, the record of the medical profession in tending politicians is more intriguing than reassuring. The Suez expedition, marked by a stupendous mis-calculation of Britain's interests, the tolerance of her allies, the markets and her own strength, a hysterical conjuring up of Hitlerian evil in the irksome but ultimately decent Nasser, and an undertaking adorned with more, worse lies to Parliament than Mr Profumo would ever tell, could only have been under-taken by a man as sick and unstable as Eden. And it was more ardently popular than any merely useful, civilised undertaking of Conservative or Labour governments since the war. Sending our boys to kill inferior foreigners was and is a notion of limitless appeal to press and nation.

It is not the function of this book to chronicle the shifts, evasions, lies and aborted violence of high policy at this time. What happened from the American withdrawal of investment for the Aswan Dam through the Egyptian nationalisation of the canal, the wrangling at the UN, the visit of General Challe and M. Gazier and the Sèvres deal by which a pretext for war was confected, constitute a self-contained, if blowsy epic. But Butler's role in the affair, or not in it, matters very much in assessing his ultimate career frustration.

Eden formed an Egypt committee with Selwyn Lloyd, Macmillan, Salisbury, Home and Walter Monckton. This indicated prior hostility to Butler, officially third man in the Government. He had thus no early opportunity in the July–August phase of a crisis which came to war in late October of playing a major restraining role. Perhaps Eden made the exclusion because he already thought Butler untrustworthy. 'I only set down that I wish Butler were a man I could respect. Lloyd George once called him "the artful dodger", but if this is important in politics it is not enough.' This was said in 1963 at the time of the second succession crisis. It is evidence of Eden's view (and personality), not of objective conduct.

A year or two later, Butler, talking to Nicholas Henderson of the Foreign Office, said of his own role in Suez, 'I was not disloyal to Eden. I was critical because I thought it mismanaged. Being the son of a civil servant, I thought it wrong to treat officials as Eden did over Suez. I didn't like the collusion either. *I should have resigned, shouldn't I?*'

Butler made a couple of supportive speeches on the broad conduct of events about which his biographer, Anthony Howard, makes heavy weather. A speech to Party Conference saying that he had never known the qualities of courage, integrity and flair more clearly represented than in the Prime Minister, suggests that, at Party Conference, Dr Johnson's rules for lapidary inscriptions also apply. When the fighting was over, the troops stalled and the pound running, he told the Commons on 13 November that he had never wavered in support of the Suez policy. This also was not true, but both statements fall into the category of incantatory avowal, witnessed by the fact that they were linked with the proclamation of pride in membership of 'a united Government and a united Party'.

The point of an incantatory avowal is that it says something known to be untrue but without the least intention to deceive. Certainly such remarks are not meant to deceive colleagues or even members of opposition parties. 'The Prime Minister is a splendid chap with all the qualities of Wolfe at Quebec and Charlie Brown, and unlike the other lot, we are a united party.'

Bancroft says that he never heard Butler so unconvincing, and

Butler's question to the civil servants present in their box was not the usual 'Was I any good?' but 'Did I sound sincere?' The truth is that before he was finished, Eden had not just done for himself and inflicted unimaginable damage on Britain, he had locked his colleagues into a pillory of incredible assertion. Ministerial statements on the subject for decades afterwards, especially those denying collusion, had the quality of masses said for the repose of Eden's soul.

In the hedgerows of the real world, Butler seems to have had two views of Suez: that military action should not be pursued at all without UN approval or, alternatively, that Britain should go for 'the straight bash', taking action without any humbug about separating combatants or stopping forest fires. His taking of the first line and then the second is cited by critics as devious and disloyal. It might indeed be seen as weakness, a deferring to the mood of the war party, but what he proposed neither injured, nor should be seen as having tried to injure, Eden. Had either piece of advice been taken when offered, that statesman would have come out of the conflict intact, still Prime Minister and untainted by duplicity.

Butler's most immediate civil service colleague, Ian Bancroft, who, with Burke Trend had gone with him from the Treasury to the Privy Seal Office, was a fervent opponent of the whole operation and told Butler so. Ready to resign himself, he wanted Butler to pull out and for his pains had the one furious row of their fond relationship during which Butler, he said cheerfully, 'threw a telephone at me'.

In fact, resigning, though it would have been morally cathartic and would in the greater perspective have been the proper thing to do, would have had only incrementally more effect than the move from the Ministry of Defence upon which the pacific Walter Monckton insisted, or the resignation of Edward Boyle from his junior post. And Butler was not, unlike these three, against the *Ding an sich* of bashing Nasser. He 'thought it mismanaged' and was 'against the collusion'. He didn't have the moral impetus for resigning of those who were flatly against invasion, though members of the Cabinet knew enough about the collusion to have grounds for going. But then it has been clear throughout this study of his career that Butler was not a resigning man. He was neither temperamental, nor given to perceiving intolerable affronts, nor did he ever, like Macmillan, use the threat of departure as an offensive weapon. In Bancroft's judgment, 'His heart wasn't in it, but he wasn't willing to resign.'

The jog-along man of government jogs along. And in Butler's case, after Suez, he spent the time picking up pieces, righting the economy, assuaging the enraged Americans and governing the country in an unshowy normal way. It was essential that he should be there. But for much of the time, he and Macmillan were in contact with the Americans. David Carlton, one of Eden's two principal biographers, who is rather more anti-American than he is anti-Eden, is as hostile to Butler over this as was Eden himself. It fits with his view of the Eisenhower Administration wanting to replace the Prime Minister with 'a Janos Kadar figure' to do their bidding. (Kadar had been established at this time, after the Soviet invasion of Hungary, as a Soviet puppet, something he did not altogether remain.)

But American hostility (and strength to make hostility hurt) were facts of life which Eden had brought on his own head. It was one thing to be scornful of the entity that liberal rhetoric calls 'world opinion', but that part of world opinion which can sell sterling and wave on others selling it is not rhetorical. Denied Carlton's dreams of a siege economy, US assets frozen and a rugged Gaullism before the letter (a two-headed Anglo-French Gaullism against the markets at that), acceptance of an American veto was part of the package.

It is more instructive to note Macmillan's part in events. The man who had wondered at the outset 'if Anthony could stay in the saddle', had, as Foreign Secretary and before the crisis ever began, taken an initiative, in December 1955. At this time, Eden had been no enemy of the Egyptians. He was not, after all, the saboteur of the Aswan Dam project (that was the US Secretary of State, Foster Dulles). Nor was it a concern of Eden's to use the pro-Western Baghdad pact as a means of encirclement against Egypt as Nasser feared. Carlton quotes Humphrey Trevelyan, British Ambassador in Cairo, as saying that, in return for an end of the propaganda coming from Radio Cairo, the British would not seek to draw any more Arab states into the pact.

At which sensible point, Macmillan sent to Amman Sir Gerald Templer, a plain, very plain, soldier much given to the straight bash, precisely to persuade the Jordanians to join. Trevelyan was then told to inform the Egyptians 'that Templer's mission had not been to press Jordan to join the pact'. This was a lie folded over a betrayal of a promise and gave Egypt no reason ever to expect honest dealing from the British. As this was done when Eden was inclined to *avoid* a quarrel with Nasser, such brutality, amended by cavalier untruth, constituted at best dreadful crassness. And there is nothing extravagant about Carlton's view that perhaps already Macmillan was playing up to the anti-Eden Suez group of right-wing nationalists. He would do so not in some detailed, long-laid plot, but as a self-serving promotional overture played to a particular gallery.

Certainly, once the crisis started in August 1956, Macmillan appointed himself, as it were, chief extremist. On 30 July he informed Robert Murphy, Eisenhower's emissary, that military action was inevitable and that 'Britain would not become another Netherlands', writing with satisfaction that 'we have succeeded in thoroughly alarming Murphy'. He also rejoiced at having stirred up Dulles who, alerted by Murphy, came to London himself to seek and get a much more conciliatory line from Eden. What stemmed from Dulles's descent on London was postponement of action in return for a flurry of supportive American rhetoric, what John Prescott calls 'warm words'.

Maybe something would happen which would justify bashing Nasser; maybe by getting a collective of canal-users in conference against him, he might be pushed diplomatically into retreat. But for Dulles, the seizure of the canal simply wasn't reason enough for doing something which would reinforce the paranoia of Asian governments, like that of Nehru, by giving them valid reasons for anger against the white West. Eden accepted the Dulles line and tried to read into it as much tacit support for later use of force as he could. Christian Pineau, the French Foreign Minister, present at the time, believed no such thing and tried to persuade Eden to expect no help. When the moment came to use force, it would have to be covert and exercised in the forlorn hope of US endorsement.

Ironically, Macmillan's trumpeting had worked against the hard line by publicising it and helping to create circumstances in which it could only be followed by cheating.

But Macmillan continued as underwriter of that hard line. When Gaitskell wrote an open querying letter to *The Times*, worrying aloud about Eden's ambiguity over force, Macmillan told him that he felt 'relieved that Mr G. should take this line, as it entirely destroyed the argument that [the] PM had climbed down'. Then, after a visit to the US, Macmillan returned even more inclined to make war. Carlton quotes, but does not identify, a report:

He [Macmillan] was anxious for action. He may have noticed on his return from the US a certain weakening of Eden's

resolve, a new predisposition for negotiation. Eden prob-
ably missed his strong personality ... It was now,
apparently, that Macmillan took the bellicose French line
very strongly and threatened to resign unless, if the UN
failed to accept British demands, force were used. He had,
he said, almost menacingly, 'taken soundings' in the
Conservative Party – the Conservative conference was a
week off – which led him to think that at least his own
friends ... would not stand for a negotiated settlement.

Quoted beside this are the milder but quietly damning words of William Clark, Eden's publicity adviser, who subsequently resigned:

Towards the end of October, he [Macmillan] intervened in a
cabinet meeting (at which I was not present but which
many of us heard about) to say that he did not see how,
having gone to so much preparation of a military sort, he
could continue to support a Government which did not
make use of that military preparation. This was a fairly clear,
though reasonably polite, threat to resign if there wasn't
military action.

Macmillan, as he records himself, also assured Eden 'of my strong feeling that the President was really determined to stand up to Nasser. When I explained to him the economic difficulties in "playing it long", he seemed to understand. He accepted that by one means or another, we must achieve a clear victory.'

The economic difficulties of playing it short (and violent) would be embodied in the moment when, a couple of weeks later, Macmillan heard of prospective US moves against Britain: 'Oil sanctions! Then that's it.' (The same Macmillan would later coin a phrase about 'unflappability'.) For the President and Dulles were determined upon no such thing as a 'standing up to Nasser' which involved bombing Egypt. Dulles, annoyingly, was much given at this time to sermonising about 'colonialism' (British: the evils of). It was pious humbug, but it was the pious humbug of an indispensable, veto-wielding ally. And Macmillan, who had been noted by Eisenhower for his conciliatory tone, should have known it, perhaps may have known it.

When the crisis came and the Americans proved to be incandescent, convinced that they had been tricked and lied to and that a proper expression of such dancing outrage would be their withdrawal of IMF supporting funds against a run on the pound, it would be Macmillan as Chancellor who fluttered the white flag. As his sympathetic biographer, Alistair Horne, puts it:

> *But it was Macmillan who decided the issue. He told the Cabinet that there had been a serious run on the pound, viciously orchestrated in Washington. Britain's gold reserves had fallen by 100 million over the past week – or by one eighth of their remaining total . . . Telephoning Washington and then New York, Macmillan was told that only a cease-fire by midnight would secure US support for an IMF loan to prop up the pound. Secretary of the Treasury, Humphrey, whom he had found so amiable in Washington, was leading the pack against Britain.*

A phrase Macmillan later denied stating, but which is repeated by Horne, was that 'unless there were a ceasefire, he could no longer be responsible for Her Majesty's Government'. And a ceasefire there was. If the allegations are correct, Macmillan had threatened resignation unless fighting began and threatened it unless fighting stopped.

Butler can be faulted over Suez. His first wish, not to take military action without United Nations approval, made sense. His shift to a candid act of war without collusion was a weakening in the direction of so much trumpeted aggression. There was a lot to be said for resigning, everything to be said for offering sustained clear opposition, for being as plain in his hostility as Walter Monckton had been. Butler managed also to give a bad impression. The friendly Reggie Maudling spoke of a skirt being lifted to avoid the dirt, the anti-Suez resigner, Edward Boyle, very much Butler's protégé, wrote sadly of 'the way Rab has trimmed and turned'. But Butler's faults are those of passivity, bewilderment at all this rage, of half seeing what was wrong and not fighting it, perhaps at worst of letting Eden stew in his own virulent juice. And defences may be cited: early exclusion from inner-circle activity and the effects of his illness in midsummer.

What Butler did *not* do, however, was to stoke up Nasser's distrust by first intriguing against him with Arab neighbours and then ordaining a flagrant lie to be told about this misconduct. He did not threaten his resignation if a war so long prepared for were not fought. He did not reassure a wavering Prime Minister of the American President's (non-existent) determination to stand up to Nasser. He was not the Chancellor who was told about the preparatory steps against a run on the pound which could be taken – a heavy pre-emptive drawing on the IMF before a run and before it was stopped – and who flatly ignored this advice, leaving Treasury officials to state as late as 31 October that a drawing should be delayed as long as possible 'to give tempers time to cool all round'.

Leaving aside for the moment all theories of entrapment followed by profit-taking, and confining opinion to simple departmental competence, Macmillan had, over 15 months, first as Foreign Secretary, then as Chancellor, and at all times as Eden's trusted Cabinet colleague, been systematically and in working detail, incompetent, flawed in judgment and wrong. It is difficult to imagine the Suez catastrophe happening if the gratuitous errors listed above had been avoided. A performance of dull objective neutrality on all those counts would have left the vacillating Eden still dithering without reaching a conclusion. Given the actual conclusions – sterling crisis, breakdown of Anglo–American relations and retreat from military engagement on orders from a foreign power – dithering had much to recommend it.

So far from succeeding to the prime ministership, Macmillan might, on simple merit, have properly been retired from public life. Brendan Bracken, the casual chronicler of Macmillan's conduct, summed up his whole performance before ending with a quotation from another Irishman, Sean O'Casey:

'Until a week ago Macmillan, whose bellicosity was beyond description, was wanting to tear Nasser's scalp off with his own fingernails. He is like that character in O'Casey's play:

Let me like a hero fall
My breast expanding to the ball

Today he is the leader of the bolters.'

And if he had been worse than incompetent, charges might be laid that, with a predator's knowledge of Eden's febrile character – fearful of seeming fearful, absurdly defensive towards newspaper vituperators and wrong-footed by false parallels with Munich – Macmillan could manipulate the Prime Minister at will. He fully understood Eden's weakness and his own main acts worked upon that weakness. When after the collapse – the flight to Jamaica and Eden's pathetic return before exiting via Harley Street opinion – the two figures met for farewells, the account given by Macmillan demands bad music played by the violins of a hotel orchestra.

*I could hardly believe that this was the end of the public life
of a man so comparatively young, and with so much still to
give.*

*We sat for some little time together. We spoke a few
words about the First War, in which we had both served and
suffered, and of how we had entered Parliament together
at the same time ... I can see him now on that winter
afternoon, still looking so youthful, so gay, so debonair –
the representative of all that was best of the youth that had
served in the 1914–18 war.*

In New Testament terms, Eden should have counted himself
lucky not to have been kissed.

In the intervening time, Butler had enjoyed a harsh but lucidly
rational intermezzo as, yet again, acting Prime Minister. Having
offered limp politics during the events of Suez, he was confronted with the problems of government, spilt milk and
quadratic equations, and went about them with quiet,
methodical despatch. But this included following the direction
of his friend George Humphrey, US Treasury Secretary, to accept
the UN resolution on withdrawal before IMF payments could
resume. Rab not only had to fulfil the degrading requirement, he
had to go to the Commons and say that Britain was withdrawing troops from the canal and allowing them to be replaced
by a UN emergency force, intolerable Swedes and Norwegians
in pale blue helmets burnished with United States approval.
Payments did resume, the pound was relieved, normality
resumed in the day-to-day world. But the Conservative Party in
the Commons, having eaten crow, struggled to digest it.

A hundred signatures were put to a resolution accusing the
US of gravely threatening the Anglo–American alliance. Butler
went to the 1922 Committee – all Tory MPs – to explain.
Calamitously, he took with him Macmillan, who, he tells us in
his autobiography, 'had stood shoulder to shoulder with me' in
the crisis. Butler made a low-key, rather dark-textured speech of
no great impact. Macmillan spoke for 35 minutes, impressing
upon Enoch Powell 'one of the most horrible things that I
remember in politics . . . seeing the way Harold Macmillan, with
all the skill of the old actor–manager, succeeded in false-footing
Rab. The sheer devilry of it verged upon the disgusting.'

CHAPTER EIGHT

Success – on this occasion, 35 minutes of reminiscence, patriotism, and the nice old man act – helped make Macmillan Prime Minister. His tendency to play up his age – he was 62, but did a very decent 76 – was noted on another occasion by a senior civil servant, Sir Philip Allen (now Lord Allen, former Permanent Secretary at the Home Office). He did his old man act, says Lord Allen, switching into it just before going onstage to speak and then abruptly switching out of it afterwards. But Macmillan knew what pleased his back-benchers. They were emotionally shocked; they had been humiliated; their rampant nationalism had been followed by a brute humbling from the Americans, to whom such Englishmen had wanted to attach themselves. The loss and the hurt were unbearable. The message they sought was 'Say it ain't so.' Macmillan managed to give the impression that as far as rhetoric, making 'em laugh and making 'em cry, plus blaming everyone else could make it, then perhaps it might not be altogether so.

If Macmillan, however meretriciously, sounded right, he also looked right. Often in politics, people are guided by appearances. The non-candidacy for the premiership of Robin Cook, probably the most talented member of the present Labour front bench, was largely attributable to the fact that nothing has ever given him occasion to work up much physical vanity. It is an odd fact and not at all trivial that Macmillan had physically changed. He had been a good-looking young man in the dreamy romantic mode who, in early middle age, with his bad teeth, brushed-back hair and wire spectacles, looked silly and eager, a little like a pedantic leveret. But by his late fifties, the thick hair flowing, the teeth amended and modern glasses used more often in gesture like a power-lorgnette, not to mention full exploitation of his height (less than Butler's, but with a guardsman's flamboyant erectness), he looked like people's idea of a statesman. Stooped, near-scruffy, baldish but not *coherently* bald and rather sack-shaped, Butler also had a lopsided, rather saurian face which enemies could see as conveying his 'oriental cunning'. In the depressing contest of looking right, Butler lost hands down to most people.

Bracken has it that Macmillan was telling people that he wouldn't serve under Butler. In a speech to the Commons, he made a reference, commonplace in the misjudgment of the time, but handily pointed for Butler, explaining Suez in terms of Munich. As delusive comparisons go, this recurring nonsense deserves to be regarded as an analogy on the banks of the Nile. But when the time came for Rab to be rejected on the famous shimmer through the Cabinet of Lord Salisbury – 'Who is it to be, Wab or Hawold?' – the false heroics of a conflict which had been lost because all diplomatic, military and economic sense was against ever trying it on rose up and demanded their own false hero.

Butler later wrote of being 'aware that frequent talks and re-unions took place in the study at Number 11'. And no friend of Macmillan would be a loser and none of Butler's a winner when jobs came to be distributed in mid-January. Butler seems to have acted on the assumption that Eden would at least last through to the end of the session in July 1957. The oriental cunning and Jesuitical intrigue of Macmillan's banter, which never were a great feature of Butler's real career, played no part now. Rather there was a simple failure of precautionary domestic diplomacy.

Macmillan and his people understood that the earlier a change of prime minister came, the better his chances. They had almost certainly, in view of the earlier and later hostility of Eden to Butler, the voice of the outgoing Prime Minister. Churchill, when canvassed, described Macmillan as the more decisive character. All the newspapers were to proclaim Butler, a reflection that they, like Butler, were governed by seniority in major office and a body of achievement. The Cabinet which decided things was, with a handful of exceptions, for Macmillan.

In one sense he deserved the premiership. He had perceived

Eden's vulnerability very early and he had understood the implications of his recurringly grim health and broken political position in the immediate present. Accordingly, he had chased the job. His speeches to the Commons and to the 1922 committee had been election speeches. He had solicited colleagues. His 'standing shoulder to shoulder' with Rab (a remark on Butler's part more naïve than ironical) had been part of a performance. And from the failure of Suez in the early days of November until Eden threw in his hand ten weeks later, he had given a performance, well judged, handsome and serving his purposes.

He had deserved to win, but deserving to win is not the same thing as deserving to govern. Politics had triumphed over government and in the six years of the Macmillan administration, that enjoyable but ephemeral floor show, politics, usually *did* triumph over government.

Behind Butler's failure at this point stood several influences. As argued earlier, politics, despite its momentousness, had been peculiarly orderly as to succession since the fall of Lloyd George. Baldwin, himself the beneficiary of a vicious manoeuvre run by men more devious than himself, proceeded, once established, to live life as a cricketing metaphor. And all the changes of leadership in both parties for upwards of 30 years were to be regular, either obvious crown princes like Chamberlain or supposed Bugginses like Attlee. Alternatively, they would, like Churchill, be the products of great events and as great debate. Perhaps the only exceptions to this lay in Herbert Morrison's yearnings and murmurings and Attlee's later retributive determination to do down Herbert. Across 20 years, Morrison's resentful ambition did him no good.

Butler had flourished in this time and his temperament was happy with a meritocracy arranged by good manners. He was not geared to intrigue. His energies were engaged by business and problems, never more so than over these two months in restoring the economy and relations with the United Nations and America. He had worked exceptionally hard and effectively, but not at politics. In the scramble for advancement, he had neither alertness nor avidity. He had not stooped and did not conquer.

Part of the problem was naïvety. Essentially, he expected to be appointed, as in the past, because he had done well and deserved the office. He was to be quite shattered by not getting what he could not understand he must take. And in an outburst of bitterness, alien to his usual comfortable, giggling style, he said savage things on the record to Derek Marks, correspondent of the *Express* and later its Editor, who judged it kindest to tear up his notes, a chivalry and sensibility unimaginable in the age of Rupert Murdoch.

But Macmillan's skilful self-promotion apart, why did the Cabinet reject Butler? He was never, for a start, all that popular. Walter Monckton who did in fact signal support on this occasion, had grumbled years before about not wanting to work under a cold fish like Butler. The inability to suffer fools gladly has its effects on the membership of a government as much as on any social group, and Butler only ever charmed at the level of intelligent dispassion (he was at his most popular with senior civil servants for exactly this reason). The dry snidery which delighted them and us, could seem like sneering contempt to (and for) them. He truly wasn't Godolphin Horne, not being like Belloc's character 'nobly born'. But a colleague singed by a Rabbish epigram might well feel that this man held the human race in scorn. Godolphin, remember, 'never took your hand or smiled, but merely smirked and nodded'. Enough people adored Butler, but there was always a bonhomie deficit, something which could start a run on a minister.

But beyond personality conflicts, he had come through a congeries of injurious developments. He was burdened with the 1955 supposed 'electioneering budget'. The death of his wife, Sydney, in December 1954 had certainly affected him and had taken away that combative and aggressive influence. He had had the bout of illness with the consequent loss of balance which had affected him during the middle of 1956 and may have contributed to his lassitude over Suez. He occupied no hard departmental job in which he could ostentatiously shine, and finally, over Suez, he had been half-heartedly right without the nerve or moral energy to engage.

There were great achievements behind him and others to come. But the replacement of Eden, which Macmillan, with the instincts of a barn owl, had seen coming and was ready for, occurred when Butler had made no plans and was caught in a hiatus between the great tasks which would make his overall reputation. He was liable now to be judged short term, always a risk where the Conservative Party is concerned. And in the short term he was out of focus and fashion. Actually, the work in which he was involved between the collapse of the invasion and the succession was as important as anything else he did, but it was damage limitation, acceptance of defeat, the making of a humbled accord with the world, not something for which thanks fly up.

The rest would not be silence. Butler was too much in love with the ministerial function to go away. But Macmillan, once elevated, handled him with a graceless assertion of will later deceitfully memorialised. In his memoirs the former Prime Minister wrote: 'It was therefore a great relief to me when Butler chose the Home Office.' Butler had chosen the Foreign Office.

All reason and a quiet life were for granting it. But Macmillan pleaded that he wanted no more heads on chargers and stayed with the off-dazzle of Selwyn Lloyd. Flat and platitudinous, though not a fool, Selwyn Lloyd was to make an ironic lifelong career – MoD, Foreign Office, Treasury, House leadership and speakership – upon the low esteem in which superiors professed to hold him. Ironically, he was only ever sacked from a post for having been one of our better chancellors, being brave and unpopular in ways not acceptable politically to his boss, Harold Macmillan.

Butler's reasonable wishes were resisted, a test of strength of will which Macmillan won, and he went to the Home Office he would have liked in 1955. Articles were written about Butler now setting his mind upon becoming 'a great reforming Home Secretary', a poignant comment on a man just passed over twice. But in many ways he did, and a scatter of reforms and social adjustments over his four and half years show the good sense, practicality and essential liberalism of the man. He was, however, also custodian of capital punishment in the form of the ritual degradation of hanging. He would say in the Harris interview eight years later that capital punishment had worked itself out. One doesn't doubt what Butler himself, Lord Allen and Butler's second wife Mollie all attest: that decisions on executions distressed him and were treated specially, with a couple of days set aside to read everything and think about nothing else. However, among the cases where the law took its disgusting course, there are decisions which could only have been made when faith in the essential rightness of all policemen and the truth of their verbal statements was commoner than it is now.

One doesn't reproach Butler for the execution of James Hanratty. Though this last case was the most contentious of his time, most of the evidence indicating doubt was assembled post-humously. But one wonders how he approved the execution of Gunther Podola, widely believed to have been beaten up in the cells after arrest, something which today would destroy a prosecution. George Riley was hanged, made subject to the new capital murder definition which required only a verbal statement from the police that he had *said* he wanted some money when there was no evidence he had taken any. Ronald Marwood was hanged for the stabbing of a policeman on the strength of statements to the police questionably obtained. Like other home secretaries, Butler grew fairly sick of the death penalty, but he lived in his own time and among Conservatives. Actual Conservative opposition to the death penalty was a very extreme position, taken up by the likes of Edward Boyle, who had also resigned over Suez.

Then again, it would not be until 1963 that Superintendent Harold Challoner would demonstrate the possibility of a crazed senior officer committing perjury and planting evidence. The trials of the pornography squad for bribery and the case of the head of the Flying Squad, Kenneth Drury, all lay in the future. All policemen in the period of Rab's home secretaryship – 1957– 62 – were still seen in the fictional glow of PC George Dixon. To be fair to Butler, he never was a cause-committed liberal in the way that Edward Boyle was. But he was as liberal as office, party and circumstance permitted and skilful enough usually to get further than that.

One way to begin a reformist reign was to make himself master of the department. He did this with a startling display of ruthlessness, by sacking Sir Frank Newsam, who had dominated the office, and the mediocre ministers, like Maxwell-Fyfe and Gwilym Lloyd George, who had occupied it. Newsam was over age, but everyone was frightened of him. Butler gave him an order – what Macmillan liked to call 'a little something to wear under your tie' – and replaced him with a Scottish civil servant, Charles Cunningham, who worked with him very well. But had Rab been anything like as brisk as this in purely political circles a few months earlier, he would not have been at the Home Office.

His touch was not always masterful. He took in as a key junior David Renton, an uncomplicatedly strong-minded opponent of anything that looked like sympathy for immigrants, homosexuals or other riff-raff, and one who had some impact, especially on immigration – though a really tough line on black people getting off ships had to wait for a Labour Government and the avuncular James Callaghan. To his credit, Butler never did give the Tory Right much cause for satisfaction.

They wanted flogging back and went on about it with a

disagreeable rapture suggesting ambiguity of motive. But the rod and staff which should comfort them were ever and again smoothly denied. Butler rather specialised in handling party conferences maddened at the tingling thought of physical retribution and sending them away unfulfilled, but making no trouble. 'I am to answer 28 bloodthirsty resolutions at the Conservative Party Conference at Blackpool. With great difficulty we have chosen one out of the 28 which is at least moderate. On this at least I can make a reasonably calming speech.' Not for nothing had Churchill retained him for his gifts of silken non-compliance.

The Right will not have liked his fitting in of what became the Obscene Publications Act of Roy Jenkins with the ministerial goodwill private members' legislation always needs. Quite how the enlightened thinking of 1960, with its focus upon rescuing James Joyce and Henry Miller, looks in the longer perspective of explicitly choreographed beatings to death on film and so much else that we now hold dear, is dubious. It is probably as pointless to damn as to smirk approval. Some evil seems to be as much oceanic as inevitable.

But the central merit of Butler at the Home Office was that he built prisons. And he was experienced enough and strong enough to get the money for them, getting Macmillan on side with a letter spelling out just how serious his intentions were. He was, however, to be hindered during this period by an assumption of Macmillan and everybody else that he was such a crisp despatcher of work, such a useful chap in the office, that other jobs, like the chairmanship of the Conservative Party, might be piled onto the leadership of the Commons, which he still held with the Home Office. Tony Howard's image of an umpire sinking under the weight of bowlers' and fielders' sweaters catches things very nicely. He was of course also, on and off, acting Prime Minister. But Butler lacked the defects of character necessary in a successful party chairman, who should display tedious virulence in equal part with noisy rapture and be burdened by no ill-considered good taste.

As Home Secretary he would reform the status of charities, legalise off-course betting, penalise soliciting for prostitution rather than prostitution itself, introduce a measure of immigration control, avoid legalising homosexuality, avoid restoring corporal punishment, and put up £20 million in the values of the early sixties to build new prisons, with some emphasis on accommodation for young criminals.

As to all this, you pays your money and you takes your choice. To the pre-feminists of the day, the Street Offences Act was against the girls rather than the customers. Sense would say that taking them off the street and putting their advertisements in telephone boxes, the inadvertent consequence, rationalised business methods.

The people who enjoy the idea of corporal punishment and the people who think it wrong to lock up offenders are more nearly allies than they might care to acknowledge, and both disliked what Butler did in their sphere. People who lack the ferocity of one group and the utopianism of the other would reckon that he got the balance more or less right. Making betting shops available makes sense to most people, though the serious consequences of addictive widespread gambling are not to be sneered at.

Broadly, Tories have a problem over pleasure. A minority, in the pattern of the late Sir Cyril Black, are straightforward puritans. But more often, Tories feel themselves the descendants of the Cavaliers with an over-the-shoulder glance at Charles II, that ur-Tory and someone who, in a friendly light, might piously be called a libertarian. If you believe in free markets in widgets, it isn't easy to deny a free market in more enjoyable, less mentionable things. Still, even supposing that, like Dr Johnson, you think that no man is more innocently employed than in making money (a very dubious assertion), there are problems about saying what he shall make it from.

They quite like the idea of not being against sex, drink, betting and smoking. But they are troubled by the people who look up to politicians and demand a moral lead. Just as most Tories like to swear the Commons oath on the Bible, so, despite the roistering and whoring tendency, the same Conservative politicians are usually good for a short burst of moralising. The Labour Party, with its chapel inheritance and authoritarian instincts, is caught up in similar ways.

Butler, taking the Home Office at precisely the time when hedonism was trembling on the edge of going public, when the idea of central command virtue was beginning to look silly, behaved cautiously but managed to go rather a long way and, as far as possible, geared the law to facilitate what people wanted to do, not least by arranging for them to do it indoors. Betting shops and tarts' basements were part of the same approach, one of not frightening (or annoying) the horses, but otherwise shimmering away from the enforcement of subjective standards.

Philip Allen, a close Home Office witness, describes him at work as someone 'who would sinuously glide round things. In contrast,' he adds, 'to Henry Brooke, who would charge at everything.'

He also remembers Butler putting a lot of time into sweetening the political doubters of his measures by 'doing the rounds of the smoking-room'. This contradicts almost everyone else's recollection of Rab's unwillingness to seek out and affect camaraderie with the Conservative underclass. But these excursions, says Lord Allen, were strictly on behalf of business to be got through. He also has memories of the Rab style. A telephone conversation would start, he says, with Butler exercising the utmost prudence, his remarks so guarded and cryptic as to be almost incomprehensible to a colleague in the same room. Then, as he warmed to gossip and opinion, the reputation of a senior Tory politician would be cheerfully dismissed as calamitous. 'No one,' he says, 'who has worked with Butler will ever forget that giggle.'

As Home Secretary, Butler cut cautiously with the grain, but he did act and act substantially after six years during which Tory conduct of the Home Office had made it a Department of Inertia. Skilful as his operations had to be, the movement to liberalisation was very nigh inevitable. Sexual and moral tolerance would prove surprisingly popular and Roy Jenkins, building upon Rab's steady start, would carve a niche for himself as the grandest facilitator of all, a wuffian on the stair, perhaps. But then, perhaps the real hero of sixties freedoms was neither Butler nor Jenkins, but John Profumo. The Minister for War, caught out in love, did not so much frighten the horses as make them bolt.

The six and a half years which made up the Macmillan Government saw Butler do many jobs, not least, recurringly, the one for which he had been thought too indecisive, soft, aloof, and generally unsuitable, the prime ministership. But this did not ensure the loyalty of Macmillan. The Prime Minister had little aptitude for courage in defence of unpopular policies which his ministers thought were right and for which he would take extensive credit. The hue and cry for corporal punishment, which tends to be mentioned today as a minor piece of tiresomeness, unnerved him. He seriously contemplated replacing Butler at the Home Office with Reginald Manningham-Buller, the overpromoted Attorney-General, a loud-mannered man with right-wing sympathies and, if not Caligula's horse, then certainly his groom. At the same time, Macmillan would be agitated and worried about the excessive radicalism of Reginald Maudling, 'so out-and-out' as Butler reported him 'for changing the constitution of Northern Rhodesia'; changing it, that is, so as to prevent settler domination of a territory notably African.

At one stage, Macmillan told Rab that he had been piling too many offices upon him and observed the 'frictions between my Home Office views and record and the party's wishes to see flogging restored'. The implication that Macmillan was tempted to gratify Sir Cyril Osborne and other flagellatory dervishes with a touch of judicial whipping does not fit the long-cultivated Macmillan image. But he always had a streak of panic under fire, why else contemplate sending Manningham-Buller to the Home Office? However, that horse passed his threshold unmounted, for Macmillan was after something else from Rab and his tone was calculated to depress and insult. He wanted him out of the party chairmanship (no loss) as he had found someone with more fire, Hailsham. He might also now relinquish the leadership of the House. Had Rab, by the way, ever thought of taking a peerage?

It was arguably the low point of Butler's career. The great office had passed by, his position was under fire from the rabblement, the Prime Minister was at once windy and disloyal, the excuse existed to strip him of two jobs and he had caught a glimpse of the Valley of the Peers, splendid interment British-style. In fact, at a bound, Rab was to be free. He made an outstanding speech to Party Conference, the sinuous, gliding-round, Jeevesian sort of speech civil servants admired, and perfectly routed the floggers (and the extenders of the death penalty) and indicated, interestingly, the rewards of keeping one's nerve where Macmillan had partly lost his. The job which did shortly come up for him would be the product of another Macmillan anxiety.

He was to be sent by Macmillan on a specific overseas mission: adjudication on the future of the Central African Federation. The undertaking was a sort of backhanded compliment. A massive three-handed piece of diplomacy was to be involved. Government was split by the question between, on the one hand, the Commonwealth Secretary, Duncan Sandys, and on the other, successively Iain Macleod and Reginald Maudling. Sandys, of whose dull but inveterate mind Butler remarked, 'He makes you want to drink whisky at ten in the morning,' favoured the federation. To be only a little crude, he saw the settlers' point of view. At the Colonial Office, first Macleod, furiously, then Maudling, with startling resolution, saw the point of view of the blacks. The two departments shared a problem, but nothing else. Butler was being hired, because of his seniority and because he was extremely good at problem-solving, to take it out of all their hands. Even though he would soon afterwards leave the Home Office, he was so manifestly engaged on a historic rescue that status didn't matter. Aptitude was being acknowledged. He was delightfully in his rational element, the briar patch of knotty substantial business where he was born and raised.

One cannot obtain a better notion of the quality of Rab Butler, his mind and his spirit, than to quote from his memoir, *The Art of the Possible*, on this assignment.

Although I remained at the Home Office until July 1962, I had already in March [1962] taken on responsibility for Central African affairs. Sir Charles Cunningham, the head of the office, regarded it as quite natural for the Home Secretary to be given this 'residual' problem. I found his view rather touching, even inspiring. The problem involved the livelihood and liberty, the expectations and emotions, of nine million people governed under what was at one and the same time, the most ambitious and the most anomalous of the constitutional arrangements of our rapidly evolving Commonwealth.

This is the all-accomplishing civil service mind mocking the all-accomplishing civil service mind for the hubris of thinking that so much could so lightly be accomplished.

And in the perspective of the last 40 years, there are reasons for humility. The Central African Federation had been created by Alan Lennox-Boyd at a time when white settlers, though never quite the social equals of the London political class, were thought of as all right. The notion that they were buyers into privilege with an ugly contempt for Africans was not strong in 1953 and the contempt not thought objectionable. As for independent states in Africa being governed by black Africans, that was seen even in official Labour circles as a very long-term notion, something for which Fabian tactics of gradualism had especial application.

The tone of Arthur Creech-Jones' (appropriately) Fabian pamphlet on the subject was far on the prudential side of the policy which was actually to be embarked on by Iain Macleod with Macmillan's cynical support. Looking at the execution of Ken Saro-Wiwa as a single act exemplifying the record of the federal Nigerian Government; looking at the quality of rule in Malawi (Nyasaland), Tanzania (Tanganyika plus Zanzibar), not to mention various unpleasantnesses in Uganda, the view taken by the Fabians had something to be said for it. The oddest of all ironies was to be the fact that, though the British Government rightly developed acute concern for black men being governed by white settlers through a federal fix, it was (and remains) bleakly enthusiastic for the idea of Ibos and Ongani being governed by Hausa through another federal fix.

But Butler was charged with reaching a conclusion (and selling it) about the Central African Federation, an arrangement which had very little to be said for it. Essentially, Southern Rhodesia – later Rhodesia, now Zimbabwe – with its 250,000 white settlers, at this time had been put together with Northern Rhodesia, with its few thousand and large reserves of profitable copper, with Nyasaland (no whites and no reserves) a sort of orphan making weight. By this fix the settlers got wealth and took on authority. The Colonial Office still stood in reserve behind them, but de facto power was substantial and dominion status – parity with Australia or more aptly, South Africa – was a latent possibility; certainly in the light of 1953 thinking, the logical progression. The implication of such freeing of the masters would be the departure of fusspotting Colonial Office officials worrying about the 'blecks'. *They* would thenceforth be handled in the short *sjambok* way that settlers knew they understood.

The discontents among the African population and the strength of official and political unease with the settler mentality would make it a long, long way from 1953 to 1962, when Rab was asked to deal with a 'residual' problem, the irony of which was not lost on him. Still for a few months Home Secretary, he set off on a pro-consular visit. Initially, he had come to find out if the federation or an amended version of it could still work. In fact, there already existed the report of the commission headed by Walter Monckton which said pretty plainly that it could not. Butler would meet all parties, the governors of the territories, the African leaders and those of the whites.

The most important of these was Roy Welensky, a coarse-grained colonial, but one whose rough ways never let him seriously break the rules. As with most of his generation of

Commonwealth politicians, grumbles at toffish theory-instructed London were undermined by a profound unacknowledged deference. And Welensky, the ex-boxer, was anyway an innately more moderate man than the shrill imitation Transvaalers who would come to power shortly in Southern Rhodesia. He had a common-sense view that Africans were all right if you didn't burden them with things they didn't understand and if, like a regular bloke, you treated them right. A share in government was something for a rain check.

The rising view in Southern Rhodesia, one soon to sweep into power there in the form of the Rhodesia Front, was less sophisticated. Black men were inferiors from whom any absurdly conceded rights should be taken away. Tory politicians were traitors and Labour politicians Communists, and Monty Butler's 'cut to the buttocks' was the natural medium of communication with restless natives.

Rab's journeys told him that Nyasaland, wholly black and federated against all popular will, was unsustainable as a part of the federation. Nobody valued Nyasaland except as psychology. It wasn't useful, but if it went, Northern Rhodesia and its copper would have the impetus to follow. And the existence of the copper belt was the main reason for the existence of the federation.

Inexorably, the view taken by Macleod and Maulding was being reached by their mentor. And in his hands, it would go through. The visits themselves as well as the conclusions were important. Butler was good at diplomacy, entirely at home with the administrators like Glyn Jones, who governed Nyasaland, and Evelyn Hone in Northern Rhodesia; they were, after all, civil servants. He got on immensely well with Africans, rank and file as well as leaders. Alan Lord, the civil servant who accompanied him, recalls Butler saying quietly: 'This is a black man's country isn't it?' And the odd patrician anxiety to care which never left him in Saffron Walden had every application above the Limpopo. Africans called him 'Big Elephant', which he genially interpreted as a compliment to a sage and senior beast, and he enjoyed a series of rapturous receptions. Guided by Jones, whom he seems to have admired very seriously, he coped with Dr Hastings Banda, even then a quite old and bad-tempered autocrat very liable to walk out if rubbed up the wrong way.

Butler, as Lord sees him, was a fastidious man, most at ease with the best minds and not happy with the dull. He was at home with grammar-school meritocrats, like Lord himself and Glyn Jones, with first-class degrees and wrong accents, and was curiously benign to the people at the bottom. On the other hand, distaste for the rapidly assumed masterfulness of the local white settlers, very much Croydon on horseback, would follow naturally.

Beyond having these instincts, he was able to follow them without serious upsets because he knew how to handle Welensky, which is more than his Prime Minister did. Lord is certain that Welensky, who could bluster and intimate no end of slightly vaporous menace, had frightened Macmillan. Self-evidently he did not frighten Butler, who was enormously polite to him (and about him in the memoirs), but explained with perfect courtesy in stages over his rolling programme why first Nyasaland and then Northern Rhodesia could not be retained within the federation. He refers to Welensky at times with an injurious affection which he clearly showed to him.

But the resolution of events – the separation of Nyasaland to be followed by that of Northern Rhodesia, the loss of copper-belt revenues to the Salisbury interest – was part of a retreat in Africa characterised either as enlightened wisdom or scuttle. It came at the end of a ten-year transformation of British Government attitudes from the underlining of the federation into the notion 'It is a black man's country, isn't it?' It was a shift from Lennox-Boyd to the shared view of Macleod, Maudling and Butler. It was followed, not surprisingly, by the Unilateral Declaration of Independence of (Southern) Rhodesia, by sanctions, guerrilla warfare, defeat of the whites and a shift of pressure onto South Africa.

Short term, Butler's withdrawal couldn't have been done better, long term it couldn't have been done any other way. But it is worth reflecting that the aspect of Butler which did the approved liberal thing in Africa was the same aspect that he showed over India (also approved) and Munich (deplored). It is a sort of creative passivity on the part of someone bent upon taking an illusionless view of events.

CHAPTER NINE

Being away was a very good thing to be. It had been a perfectly dreadful time for the Macmillan Government. In July 1962, the Prime Minister had staged what was instantly called the 'Night of the Long Knives', something which earned, a year in advance, Nigel Birch's later bitter comment from Browning:

Let him never come back to us . . .
. . . Never glad confident morning again!

He sacked an armful of ministers, some reasonably, some not, and altogether too many, giving overall the impression of a boyar in a *droshky* throwing footmen into the permafrost to lighten the journey. It was decisive all right, terminally decisive and best seen as a glimpse of Macmillan's innermost and worst character, self-interest lit by panic.

In January 1963, General de Gaulle vetoed Britain's membership of the EEC for which with unwise trumpets she had applied. For once, Macmillan's poor old gentleman ploy, never far from threatening tears, received brutal and pertinent dismissal. '*Ne pleurez pas Monsieur,*' said his old wartime acquaintance from Africa. The motives – well-founded distrust of Anglo–American affinities and a certain cockerel malice – were less important than the effect, which was to knock the stuffing out of the Macmillan Government and batter the Prime Minister's confidence. The central direction of policy was gone and the Government was left aimless in midstream.

The death of Hugh Gaitskell in the same month was to prove

a neutral factor given that this highly regarded opponent was now replaced by Harold Wilson, a leader of the Opposition with outstanding talents for that job. But when Gaitskell lay dying, Macmillan observed that the illness was perhaps playing into his hands, a remark that Anthony Howard temperately ascribes to 'perhaps an unappetising side to his character'.

The Government suffered at about this time the first of its sex scandals, the odd, never quite resolved affair of the spy, Vassall, and the letters from a junior minister, Thomas Galbraith, which at any rate conveyed a hand-on-knee feeling. This age, more nagged by homosexuals than persecuting them, can look at both the charges and denials with relief that we don't go on like that any more. Except that in politics, for all sexual excursions, homosexual or heterosexual, we *do* go on, interminably.

By March, with Rab back in England and giving sensible advice, the next scandal commenced its jolting course. The whole business of John Profumo was an affair which by mid-summer would be an *affaire*. It would place in the more readable pages of history the Secretary for War, Stephen Ward, Christine Keeler and Mandy Rice-Davies and the assorted bit-part players from Lucky Gordon, the West Indian heavy, to the louche Lord Astor. There was also an array of shadows – unnamed politicians, nobility and royal connections who may or may not have been Bill Astor's guests, worn masks, been slaves at the swimming-pool or otherwise played the fool. And it pre-occupied the nation the way nothing had preoccupied it since VE Day.

Butler's instinct was not to get excited. 'Not on a Friday morning, surely!' was his grown-up and low-temperature response to Macmillan's urgent requirement of his comforting presence while a cajoled and done-over Profumo made a state-ment to the Commons asserting a perfect and incredible innocence. According to William Deedes, present at the early-morning inquisition, Profumo was half drugged, having been hauled out of bed after taking a couple of sleeping pills. He didn't precisely tell a lie under duress, but he told the lie the Government wanted to be true and wanted him to say. The issue was multiplied tenfold.

The Butler option had been to encourage Profumo to ask for an inquiry, one which would have stayed well away from the judiciary, and to step down from office in the interim. The story would have been off the heat and, even if an affair had been disclosed, there would have been no deception of the Commons.

A love affair conceded through the filter of a Westminster enquiry would have been a bump, not a thunderbolt – no deception, no trial or suicide of Ward, no Denning Report and the Government, with an eyebrow up, would have remained coolly distanced. But Macmillan, in defiance of his image, was flapping. He was emotional, reactive, and exactly playing the game of opportunistic Opposition backbenchers.

The episode rather makes the Butler case in terms of what prime ministers are for. Macmillan was better theatre, often more fun and he could display to advantage anything that could be displayed. But the decisiveness he claimed did not exclude a tendency to run in small frantic circles. He could lurch from insouciance into apocalypse in one easy move. Butler's inability to be stirred implied a disinclination to get excited.

By June, Macmillan (in Scotland) was having to be told, ironically by Butler, that things were much worse than he supposed and that the Profumo cauldron, left on the low heat of an official denial, was about to boil over and scald anyone in reach. By this time the central question of the Prime Minister remaining in office began to be generally asked.

There was a period after midsummer when a rougher politician than Butler might have carved briskly for himself. He was himself engaged in valuable work, his African missions culminating in the very satisfactory Victoria Falls Conference – all of which kept him at arm's length from the misjudgments that had transformed Profumo's dalliance into a wide-screen crucifixion. Macmillan was emotionally stricken; the press had turned on him and were shuffling the metaphors of quittance. They went on in that vein to give a reception to Lord Denning's unworldly little romance which disregarded the soothing conclusions of the Master of the Rolls and damned the Prime Minister.

But it was all beyond Butler's nature. His defects – irresolution and comfort with continuity – and the most dangerous of his virtues – a sort of derisive loyalty – were against a clear preparation for succession. Yet he was in many ways very well placed to succeed. These were not the circumstances of 1957. He was touched by nothing that had gone wrong. He had not just completed a highly controversial budget or been limply right about a popular little war. He was now the well-accredited reforming Home Secretary widely admired for his work, the returning diplomat who had smoothly got us out of horrid entanglements in Africa. He was Proficiency Butler, the doer of the jobs that had to be done while other people were, in every imaginable way, screwing up.

In a sense, his own fatal lack of hungry will to take office *ought* not to have been an impediment. His own civil service-cum-meritocratic instinct that, as the best man, he ought to get the job, would have obtained in most successions.

For we cannot grasp Butler's defeat without understanding the role of Macmillan's enmity. Rab's failure to kick the ball or use the revolver, metaphors bestowed on events by Iain Macleod and Enoch Powell respectively, were a disqualification for *getting* the job, not for doing it. But they were a disqualification because Macmillan had chosen to make the job obtainable only if Butler was willing to pull the house down – ready to resign and take colleagues with him.

For Macmillan had entered into a succession of conversations across the later months of his reign. He had told Lord Hailsham in June 1963 (Profumo time) that he had originally thought of Lord Home for the succession and that he had asked him if he was ready to renounce his earldom to that end, a manoeuvre being innocently facilitated by Tony Benn in his struggle against inherited encumbrance. As Dennis Walters, Hailsham's personal assistant at this time (not yet an MP), relates matters, Macmillan told Hailsham that Home had been 'far from enthusiastic . . . he lacked the ambition and the steel necessary to get the job as well as the economic expertise to compete with Harold Wilson'.

Macmillan, so Hailsham told his assistant, had decided that Hailsham was the right man, citing his academic qualifications and popularity with the Party. Hailsham then said: 'But what about Rab? Surely he is the most obvious successor.' 'On no account,' said Macmillan. 'Rab simply doesn't have it in him to be Prime Minister.' Very understandably, Sir Dennis prints his own key response to Hailsham at what he had been told, 'Harold Macmillan may let you down when it comes to the point.'

So, between June and October, it was the view of Hailsham that he was the chosen heir of the Prime Minister. Quite when Macmillan would go was not then clear. It had seemed at one time as events crackled around him, that he might go in midsummer. Butler, self-comfortingly and put off by talk against his own chances from the unloved and unreliable Major Morrison, Chairman of the 1922 Committee, waited on a later date. What nobody expected was a crisis that would occur in the middle of a Party Conference, a shoot-out on Blackpool north shore.

But this was not the only conversation Macmillan had had. In January 1962 he had said to Butler: 'Either I shall decide to go before the election, in which case it all falls on you, or it will be a year or two after an election, in which case it will not be so certain.' In February 1963, before Profumo broke for the first time, he had said to Butler that 'the combination of the Kennedy image plus Harold Wilson at 46 is a potent force in favour of a younger man'. Nigel Fisher, the first biographer of Iain Macleod, reckons that the advancement of Macleod and Maudling and even Heath arose from more than their abilities. 'In order to avoid the possibility that Butler might be chosen, Macmillan had brought forward three younger men who were of sufficient experience and seniority to be considered.'

Maudling was made Chancellor, Macleod Leader of the House and Heath was given the Common Market negotiations. According to Fisher:

Each of them had been given opportunities, but none of them had emerged decisively at that time as generally acceptable to the party. Macmillan did not consider that any other member of his Cabinet in the House of Commons was even a possibility. Given his determination to stop Butler at any price, the Prime Minister had to consider a candidate from the House of Lords, now made conceivable by the passing of the Peerage Act that summer.

That text resonates. Few people were less malicious than Nigel Fisher and he wrote with an excellent knowledge of Iain Macleod's own judgment. He also quotes Kenneth Younger's life of Lord Home: 'It was widely known that Macmillan would never countenance Butler as his heir . . . it was appropriate that the postal address of Chequers was Butler's Cross.'

All three candidates advanced were men of ability and would have risen on merit, indeed risen under Butler, but they were hurried forward and given assignments intended to show them to advantage. In the same way, Hailsham, once the aura of favour descended upon him, was sent to Moscow, ironically at the expense of Alec Home, the Foreign Secretary, to collect credit with signature of the Test Ban Treaty, something largely to be topped and tailed, but a very good way of laying on instant statesmanship.

Macleod's own view was very sympathetic to Butler, not only because of natural sympathy on all the broad issues, domestic and African, with only Rab's uncertainty about Europe making any difference of opinion, but on grounds of intelligent and perfectly decent self-interest. Butler had risen under patrons, he would be a natural and happy patron to Macleod for the future and his own failure would indeed help keep Macleod from the top. But Macleod also acknowledged one sensible central thing which, by the end, seems not to have mattered very much to Harold Macmillan. Butler was, of all prospective leaders, the one best placed to win the next election.

He had seniority, not the null Buggins sort, but general success in two of the three great offices of state, plus accomplished conduct of the Central African business. He was the least partisan Tory, in marked contrast to Hailsham's teeth-on-edge-setting bombast, something very important when the Tories had been losing by-elections from Orpington onwards in an unprecedented way. All this when polls, just beginning to haunt the political mind, pointed to extreme annoyance with the Tories. Here Rab was Old Tried and Trusted, possessor of exactly the old-shoe qualities which the small 'c' conservatism of the voters readily falls back on in general elections.

The very idea of considering Hailsham was slightly manic. He had extensive intelligence on paper – there were people of calibre like the young Ian Gilmour, who were devoted to him – but someone who dresses in a hooped Victorian bathing-costume, rings a bell at Conference, dandles his new baby in public, denounces a woman as being 'of easy virtue and a proven liar', then goes on about adultery among unnamed colleagues and does all of this in a loud and carrying voice to the accompaniment of assertions of his Christian convictions, leaves behind a certain impression. It is an impression which lingers yet: of a slight derangement of temperament forever barring a clever man from being taken altogether seriously.

So we have a Prime Minister, in Fisher's words 'implacably opposed' to Butler's succession, advancing new men, sounding out older men and finally ransacking the House of Lords, all for one purpose: to stop the man best placed to rescue the Conservative Party from a prospective defeat which reflected public displeasure with a state of affairs for which this same Prime Minister was responsible.

The failings which Butler showed in 1963, the disinclination to use the revolver of Enoch Powell's violent metaphor, is well enough known. He was to spend long hours with his wife and a supportive editor, John Junor, being begged to act and not acting. When Hailsham finally learned that Macmillan had let him down and transferred his support to Lord Home, he rang Butler and begged him to 'Don your armour, dear Rab!' among similar baroque entreaties. Butler, according to Dennis Walters, replied, 'I was just dozing off,' then, 'I take note of your remarks, but now I really must doze off.'

This may exaggerate the degree of debility and inertia shown by Butler but, as his former Private Secretary, Bancroft, argues, there was an element of fatalism about him. Far from being, as in Macmillan's fantasy, a Jesuit compulsively intriguing in some 17th-century Vatican corridor, Butler was bad at recognising how much Macmillan essentially *hated* him. He was bad at organising the team of his own men which existed in willing numbers. He was bad at catching Macmillan, down and humili- ated that summer, and stamping. He was entirely incapable of saying, as Alan Lord puts it, 'Well, my dear Alec, I'm delighted for you, my dear fellow. But as I shan't be able to serve and four or five of my friends won't serve either, I do hope that when you catch 22 sheep and hang blue ribbons round their necks, you have every possible success against Mr Wilson.'

He had known, since Home told him that he was having a medical check-up against the prospect of the job, how he was placed. It was open to him to rally support, to threaten Macmillan with withdrawal and to use the press where he had good ties and friendships.

The events of the last days are broadly known and are summed up in the words of Martin Redmayne, generally thought of as the least of post-war Tory chief whips. 'It's too late. It's all been arranged.' These days were marked also by the activities of Maurice, Macmillan's son, and Julian Amery, his right-wing son-in-law, both of whom moved around waverers and potential opposers making a market for the final choice, Alec Douglas-Home. Harold Macmillan put his genius into intrigue. By 1963, it was one of the few things he still believed in. And as he secluded himself in that ana- chronistically named King Edward VII Hospital for Officers, the final pantomime began.

He sent out his son and son-in-law, informed the Queen of an interpretation of opinion which filtered through his own prejudices, and sent the foolish Lord Dilhorne (Manningham- Buller) on a mission about opinion to which the answer was required in advance. Essentially he echoed the lines of Belloc on Lord Lundy:

The stocks were sold; the Press was squared
The Middle Class was quite prepared.

Home, unlike Lord Lundy, was quite avid enough for the top job and the machine did its stuff as Maurice and Redmayne went to work. The Queen, as Ben Pimlott now tells us, was delighted to have a congenial fellow owner of Scottish land, a measure, as Pimlott does not say, of Her Majesty's torpor and lack of political alertness. Butler made no moves, despite the efforts of his allies. Macleod, Powell, Aldington, and, slightly behind, Maudling, all urged resistance. But they were hardly up with events either. Surprise was part of the advantage; Macleod had laughed scornfully only days before at certain dark reports on Home. 'Don't be bloody ridiculous. Alec told us in Cabinet he wasn't a runner.'

Hailsham had a similar response, 'I simply don't believe it. Alec has told me that he is not a candidate, and we have agreed that we could not possibly leave the House of Lords simultaneously.' Lord Home was a nice man and had every right to pursue his own career, but the notion of his being the Scottish landowner's answer to the Christian life is overdone.

The final days themselves took the absurd pier-end form they did because of Macmillan's own precipitate and sub-heroic response to finding himself unable to pass water. Encouraged by yet another doctor working for that sinister medical conspiracy against the Conservative Party, he was persuaded that he had cancer of the prostate and was dying. If Butler moaned about physical discomfort and frequently felt sorry for himself, Macmillan translated the panic shown in the July massacre and the Profumo crisis into a medical condition which he would survive for another 23 years. If Butler is to be reproached, as he is, for passivity in the face of hostile circumstances, it is worth noting that Macmillan was running away from his own political crisis. He would, after all, have been better placed himself to have won an election in late 1964 than the matchstick-fancier he now advanced to Downing Street.

CHAPTER TEN

If Butler was fatalistic about his own career, Macmillan had a streak of wider despair. The phrase 'things will last for our time' was used about his outlook and embodied many of his opinions. One of these was a gross exaggeration of the appeal and prospects of Soviet Communism and the Left generally. Then again, for a statesman with some claim to taste and literacy, his time in office was marked by a brutal efflorescence of what is called development: egg-box concretisation of the landscape coupled with the knocking down of anything old and handsome which might be standing in the way.

The backlash against such developments came after his time, but Gavin Stamp, the architectural critic, tells the gloomy story of a delegation he joined to protest at the impending demolition of the Euston Arch. Macmillan expressed his uttermost sympathy, deplored what was to be done, spread his hands and said, 'But my dear fellows, what can I *do*?' As Stamp observed, he could have done anything. He was Prime Minister, he could invoke old laws and pass new ones. He could use the weight of his office.

In much the same spirit, Macmillan expected the worst for himself and his party. If he was ill, he panicked and thought he was dying. If his party was going through a rotten patch, it was on the way to annihilation. Clearly the hard knocks of Profumo, by-elections like Orpington, what then passed for unemployment, rejection by De Gaulle and the rest of it represented the End. We know more about polls and swings of opinion than Macmillan did, and he can be excused some anxiety on hitting a new, unprecedented switchback condition of public opinion. It would give stomach-turning rides to a succession of prime ministers, but his own bump of despair played its part. Macmillan was a first-rate taker of opportunities, a splendid public presence, an endearing wit – as when he asked for Khruschev's shoe-banging at the United Nations to be translated. But for someone who recycled his military experiences to such advantage, he was not exactly steady under fire.

Having little sense of perspective, he was drawn ever and again to apocalyptic options. The common-sense hardihood of a belief that he himself could right the Tory Party's fortunes did not exist. Accordingly, his end, like so much of his time in office, became a succession of contradictory manoeuvres, little spasms of purpose directed to distract attention if they didn't get the boiler to fire. To play up the younger men in 1962 and start making overtures, first to Home, then to Hailsham, before finally reverting to Home, parodies what he did in government. But the moves are cognate.

Macmillan went on world tours and to summit meetings, he favoured expansionist budgets without much thought to consequences, he sacked a third of his Cabinet, he made a dramatic bid to enter Europe. There was always about his Government an atmosphere of ardent, but not perfectly considered, doing, and always a faint hint of Prince Ptomkin. To be thrashing about for a successor while believing that, fundamentally, it was all hopeless was the pattern of the man, for all his grace and presence, and indeed for all his flicker of Chicago.

But behind the panic and gloom, he was clear about one thing: that he should not be succeeded by Butler. One looks for reasons without finding good ones. At the worst reading of Rab, taking into account his lack of fight on this occasion, pursuit of any alternative to him – first by way of major constitutional adjustment to the slightly preposterous Quintin Hogg, then to the 14th Earl of Home – was obsessional hostility tumbling into farce. Rab, all of a private dither and not much good in a party fight, had done too much hard, creative work in too many spheres, much of it quite recent, to be compared with the eccentric lawyer with his rattling mannerisms or with Home, a one-subject technician garlanded with an Oxford fourth, ignorant of economics, social policy or an atom of home policy, and sitting for the previous 13 years in the House of Lords.

We are looking for real reasons and many are offered. Macmillan, as he occasionally remarked, had fought in the First

War. Rab had not. But Butler with his frozen and useless right hand and wrist was C3 in anybody's book. And on 11 November 1918, he had been a full month short of his 16th birthday. Incidentally, Alec Home, a polio victim, had not seen military service either. Butler had been a Municher while Macmillan was creditably against it. But Alec Home had been Chamberlain's PPS. He had flown from Heston to Munich with the Prime Minister and had no later reservation about the rightness of the policy. Quintin Hogg, as he was that time round, had fought the famous Oxford by-election against the Master of Balliol as a specifically pro-Munich Conservative and a very silly one.

Butler and Macmillan had been on opposite sides during the thirties, Butler adhering to Baldwin and Chamberlain, while a left-inclining Macmillan went through his radical phase. Butler seems to have believed in the importance of this himself and mentioned it. But, exactly as with Munich, both Home and the later-entering Hailsham were identified with the old Establishment.

Then there was the exchange of 1930 in *The Times* when Butler had mocked Macmillan for his sympathy with the pre-Fascist Mosley, suggesting that people not playing by the rules should find themselves another game. It would be astonishing if so slight a blow bruised so deep as to ache after 33 years. Butler's gift for the clever catty remark which, while pleasing everyone else, never much endeared the victim, would continue to be seen. For instance, the Prime Minister, who liked to advertise his Latinity, once had a book in his hand when Butler called into the office. Butler took it up and looked. 'Ah, Livy,' he said with puzzlement. 'But I always thought of Livy as a fourth-form text.'

The Mosley episode was an early example of Macmillan's end-of-the-world instincts, his tendency to see climax and catastrophe in things that Butler expected to roll by. More pertinently, Butler enjoyed a richer, busier, early career, holding office for nine years while Macmillan was kept back. That is something, but surely not enough. It is a reason for hating him at the time, not for a grudge nursed across a generation.

One factor which is underplayed in analysis is the extent to which dislike grew with ill-treatment. Macmillan knew he had pushed Butler aside in 1957, knew that he had denied him the next job he wanted, the Foreign Office, and said untruthful things about the exchanges in the diary. But he continued to torment Butler with here a prospect of advancement, there a dashing of hopes, the suggestion of the Colonial Office as demotion at one stage, then the question, 'Have you ever thought of taking a peerage?' Between successful Tories, for whom titles are casual currency, that last was deeply insulting, like trying to bribe somebody with bottletops.

Butler had no answer to personal hostility except, rather sadly, to pretend to himself that it wasn't serious. Poignantly, he said more than once that he thought Macmillan liked him really. But the Prime Minister who spoke of 'a willing camel' and had established his own Mary–Martha regime, knew just how badly he could treat Butler without provoking either rage or resignation or yet political trouble. The limpness begat contempt and perhaps also an urge to do yet more to hurt, combined with the ill-will we commonly have for people we have treated badly.

Temperamentally, all the leaders of the Tory Party after 1945 are fascinating subjects as fascinatingly involved with one another. Eden is neurotic and suspicious, his suspicions much fed by Macmillan. Churchill, for all his fits and starts of moods, is essentially pretty sane and tolerant. The one incontestably great man in that gallery was without long-burning resentments and quite liked other people.

Butler had risen by merit aided by in-laws' money, had been hired by the Courtaulds, brought forward by Hoare, Halifax, Baldwin, Chamberlain and Churchill, proof not just of ability but of temperamental easiness. But on that route, he learnt no street-fighting strengths; he could seem terribly aloof and superior despite the constituency benignity and the happy private life spoiled only by Sydney's death (and Sydney had been the street-fighter). He didn't mix, despite Hubert Ashton's best efforts, with the Tory underclass at Westminster – something very understandable but not good politics.

He gained a name for intrigue without intriguing and he couldn't keep his mouth shut when he had something clever to say. He was a grandee, but a grandee without armour. He was a practical working talent, but no politician and, as more than one of his civil servants has said about him, he had a streak of naïvety, of unworldliness.

Macmillan, by contrast, was a modest ministerial success, something of Dryden's Zimri – 'everything by turns and nothing long'. But everything he did on the way up – 300,000 unaffordably expensive houses and encouragement of a despicable and ruinous little war – was done to get higher yet. He had a spot of

religion, nearly turning Catholic under the absurd influence of
Father 'Ronnie' Knox at Oxford. He dramatised everything:
cannibalising Stockton, the Somme and his remote Scottish
ancestors, the crofters, as so much painted scenery for the
character he was inventing. He had nerve and courage, but no
loyalty to colleagues, a deficiency shared with Margaret
Thatcher. And like her, he ended with both a bang and a chorus
of whimpers. As for intrigue, he couldn't see a thread without
pulling it. He looked for low motives in other men, expecting to
find them there.

For the most part, Butler in office knew what to do and
became happy talking problems and optional solutions with the
intelligent, exam-passing men who run the civil service.
Macmillan knew how to get office and would very nigh kill for
it. He had, after all, left things late: he was 55 when he entered
Churchill's peacetime Cabinet near the bottom. But career
boosts apart, he was not at all sure what he wanted to do with it.
Like Iago, he never quite had the motive for what he did, but it
was obviously what he was always meant to do. Butler,
meanwhile, was like Macbeth trapped in Act I:

Art not without ambition . . .
. . . What thou wouldst highly,
That thou wouldst holily . . .
Letting 'I dare not' wait upon 'I would',
Like the poor cat i' the adage

Macmillan's perception of Butler told him that in contests of
personality, he would always win. And an element of cruelty
made him insist on winning when all sense was for not having a
contest. The question should be asked of Butler, as it will be of
all the figures discussed in this book, what if he *had* been Prime
Minister?

The faults are acknowledged. Butler had no stomach for
personality clashes and great efforts of will. He lacked Humpty
Dumpty's preoccupation with who shall be master. But
considering Education, the Treasury, the Home Office and
Africa (his last, no-account, supernumary year at the FO really
doesn't arise here), he was probably the most successful
departmental minister of the age. He enjoyed work and did it at
an impressive, untired speed. He took his time on decisions, but
didn't dither here. 'The wearing of a suit before deciding about
purchase', is how both Nicholas Henderson and Ian Bancroft
describe his decision-making process. But, supremely, he had

none of the faults which led to so much trouble across the Conservative fifties and early sixties.

It is unimaginable that Butler would have been panicked, as Eden was, by the jeering words of a journalist into trying to prove himself as an international arm-wrestler in the bar parlour of the world. Under Butler there would have been no Suez invasion, no break with America, no run on the pound, no Tory nervous breakdown, no 'finding a role', no hang-ups, though doubtless any amount of press fulmination.

Having been caught out once with what eyewitnesses believe to have been an inadvertent electioneering budget, he would, ironically, have been the very last prime minister to countenance another. Macmillan took Butler's budget stumble, which had advanced him, and turned it into standard practice. Given rejection of such moves, Butler would never have authorised Maudling to make his 'dash for growth', a piece of gambling plus expansionism natural to Macmillan.

Now assuming for a moment that he had won the 1964 election, Butler would not necessarily have been quicker to devalue than Harold Wilson. (Only George Brown and Donald MacDougall at the Treasury grasped *that*.) But not having made a dash for growth, not being Labour leader, attracting no prejudice and paranoia and being a reassuring figure to markets, he might never have been faced with the question.

Neither so panicky nor so disloyal to colleagues as Macmillan, he would not have sacked them wholesale, like the Little Tailor of Bremen, killing 'seven at a blow', and never therefore reaped the prolonged misery of Government demoralisation and destabilisation which followed. He would have been slow to turn to Europe, being full of anxious Essex fears, not the taxi-driver prejudices perceived of that county today, but the worry of so many farmers that the EEC would not make them rich. But he wasn't a Europhobe. Had Britain, after initial refusal to enter, delayed and then sought entry without the zealotry of Edward Heath, doing so coolly as a useful option, we might have signed a better deal. Macmillan's Europe was another firework display, Heath's a single-minded crusade. Not hurrying might have made sense.

Overall, he would have been non-charismatic, uninspiring to the tabloids, which mattered less then, but infinitely competent and comforting, an old shoe, even an old boot, but blessedly short of febrile compulsion. He would also have kept politics better humoured. The way he was edged out and then again denied initiated a period of distinctly nastier politics. Heath would help Home on his way. Thatcher would overthrow Heath in a ballot, an exhausted Cabinet and party would turn Thatcher out of office. Major lived with the speculative malice of half a dozen newspapers and an element in his party bent on his destruction. Clarke, as obviously the choice of merit as Butler, has been stopped with a not-Clarke junior. For all the ambitions everyone held, it simply wasn't like this from Baldwin through to Eden's succession. (In the Labour Party hatred is usually a more disinterested, ideological matter.)

Butler had ahead of him, when the stocks were sold and the middle class prepared at Blackpool, another year weakly or dutifully serving on under Home as Foreign Secretary; another touch of indiscretion telling a journalist of his pessimism during the election and being roundly damned for it; an offer of an earldom from Home (refused); and an offer to be Master of Trinity, Cambridge with that Morris Minor among armigerous vehicles, a life peerage from Wilson, both of which he took.

There were to be 19 years of life before he died of cancer in 1982. He was imperfectly happy at what he had not been and might have been, but he painted, read, chaired a committee on mental health (to please his old secretary, Bancroft) and wrote its report. He wrote stylishly terse memoirs, helped by Peter Goldman, the protégé whose defeat at Orpington had been his political extinction. He moaned to his young cousin David. But he had often moaned, and physical pain, especially his untreatable skin complaint, gave him a bad time.

At the end of writing about it, one sees that his had been a formidable life, something he must have seen also and been comforted by. He was not equipped to *become* Prime Minister, rather he was the opposite of Tacitus's Galba, '*Capax imperare nisi imperasset*' – Fit to govern if only he hadn't. He didn't govern, but we know enough about him to be decently sure that he would have governed rather well.

PART
TWO

DENIS
WINSTON
HEALEY

CHAPTER ONE

The story is told of three journalists clubbing together to entertain politicians.

> We took Roy Jenkins to lunch and he talked about Jamaican cigars being as good as Cuban cigars, so he smoked a Jamaican cigar. When we got the bill it was £105, which in 1980 was impressive. Then a week or two later, we took Denis Healey out, and when we got the bill it was £115. One of us mentioned the comparison to him, which was terribly infra dig. But Denis didn't mind at all, and we heard later from one of the research assistants that he'd gone along the Shadow Cabinet corridor banging on doors and shouting, 'I'm more expensive to lunch than Jenkins.'

The same Denis Healey, in the beautiful, but less noticed *My Secret Planet* (a sort of intellectual and cultural autobiography which appeared after the great hit of his political self-account, *The Time of My Life*), cites Heinrich Heine on the parallel achievements of Robespierre and Kant.

First of all, Healey sets out Kant's philosophical argument. 'The heart of the *Critique* lies in a passage where Kant echoes Pascal by showing that reason can be used to prove contradictory propositions on some of the most important issues which challenge our minds ... "antinomies of pure reason". Our reason,' says Healey, 'operates through structures of logic which do not exist outside our mind ... By putting the nature and limitations of the human mind at the centre of knowledge, Kant made it impossible to prove the existence of God by argument. Metaphysics is no longer a rational activity.'

He then quotes from Heine the last cool word on Kant and Robespierre: 'But both presented in the highest degree the type of the narrow-minded citizen. Nature had destined them for weighing out coffee and sugar, but fate decided that they should weigh out other things, and into the scales of the one it laid a king, into the scales of the other a god . . . And they both gave true measure!'

The contrast between Kant and Robespierre, god and kings, is not weightier than the contrast which may be made between Healey and Healey.

There are probably more than two Healeys, but the roistering, noisy, sometimes bullying Healey and the man of acute sensibility who takes on not just Kant and Heine, but adores Yeats, Dickinson and Blake and can cite the little-known American writer on nature, John Muir, make up a lot of him. The first is capable of leaning over Dennis Canavan, a loud, null Scottish left-winger not readily acquainted with the antinomies of pure reason, and saying over and again, 'You fucker. You fucker.' As friend and enemy alike say, 'Denis doesn't have dignity.' The commonest epithet, often used affectionately, was 'thug'.

Yet in the same breath, the complaint from similar critics on his own right wing of the old Labour Party was that he wouldn't join the fight.

The second Healey might quote Yeats, as he does in another context, and say, 'We are but weasels fighting in a hole.' Throughout a long life and one of the most interesting of all political careers this century, Denis Healey has run a profound culture and a sensibility to numinous things in tandem with heavy workaday politics where problems were often solved by strength of will. The reasons for his not being good in that fight, *the* fight, when a section of the Labour Right defected from the party and formed the SDP under the leadership of Roy Jenkins, are horribly complex. Despite lack of what school prefects call 'keenness' on Europe, Healey did not differ from that faction much on ideas and objectives. But he was never going to be one of them.

One can give credible low and personal reasons for his absence. The SDP, though it had other strands, could not have existed without Roy Jenkins, a rival, also an equivalent talent and a different kind of man. And although one could imagine either serving under the other in the ordinary circumstances of politics, Healey would not kill the Labour Party to make Jenkins king. But more subtly and more essentially, Healey would not try to kill the Labour Party (or sweep it aside as irrelevant) in any circumstances whatsoever; and Jenkins and Jenkins' following, perfectly honourably, would. After his baroque and bloodshot fashion, Healey is a good party man.

He might treat Labour as he treated the wretched Canavan. He would certainly, as a politician, frequently fail in grace towards individuals and, through superfluous brutalities towards party colleagues, accumulate enemies among neutrals and even the like-minded, enemies whose votes would weigh against him on the day. Where Rab Butler was politely aloof and glazed over in the company of an obscure colleague, Healey might, if irked, produce a devastating slap-down. But he was institutionally loyal, emotionally loyal, too. Hugh Gaitskell's phrase in the great Scarborough speech of 1960 was 'the party we love'. Sounding high flown, it was nonetheless perfect truth from Gaitskell, and Healey, who made a memorable short contribution on that occasion, felt the same emotion.

There is no merit in drawing 'odorous comparisons' between Healey and Jenkins, though the counterpart between their careers will prove irresistible later on – indeed, one must be quietly grateful that Jeffrey Archer has not turned them into a novel. Neither course taken was dishonourable; each was close to being programmed to go the way he went. But a fight against the Labour Party, even at its most stupid and self-destructive, in the melancholy time when Arthur Scargill, Moss Evans, Clive Jenkins and Tony Benn commanded so much of it, and when Healey's own career had just been crippled, was a fight for which Denis Healey was constitutionally unfit. The man who had been offered the secretary-generalship of NATO not long after his wounding leadership defeat at the hands of Michael Foot turned it down without serious hesitation. Yet his own argument, that he wanted to be in politics rather than administration, is hardly enough.

Like Butler, Healey was a Government man; like him, he won the admiration and affection of mandarins as a doer of the job. And since the secretary-generalship of NATO isn't a sinecure and has generally gone to serious working politicians, he would have been suited to it. The truth is partly that Healey would have missed the fights. During the bleak late years in which his party burned in the pit it had dug, this former Government minister, with no previous great compulsions towards debate, suddenly flowered in the chamber.

This is his dead sheep period – dead and golden. As a Commons sketchwriter I sat through all of it and recollect with some fondness what pleasure the man gave and how the appearance of his name on the enunciator would bring us instantly out of the press tea-room. Yet this wit and battler, taking on the ungrateful business of frontbench drudgery against the ascendant Thatcher, was the veteran of 11 years of senior ministerial work in two departments, Defence and the Treasury. He really didn't have to stay. Admittedly the chances of return were worse than they looked, delusions of hope were still about. But by late 1980, Labour were so slashed to the gut in their unpleasing act of ritual suicide that all calculation of self-interest argued against staying on.

Healey was 62 in 1979, old enough to pull out altogether, not so old that he could not take highly paid and suitably grand work outside. The mastership of an Oxford College, the directorships, perfectly apt for a former Chancellor who might threaten to make pips squeak, but who had turned the economy round, were not pursued. He did not arrange to be driven in a Rolls–Royce car on behalf of the Royal Fine Arts Commission.

Denis Healey, ironically enough, formed a relationship with the new leader, Michael Foot, in the dust of Labour's decline, a touching relationship between two men who stood at opposite ends of their party – rhetorician with runner of armies and currencies, pious man with profane – but both straight, both devoted by their lights to that party, both, in the time of its collective breakdown and collapse, trying to save it.

The other irony which touches Healey – and it is not widely taken up – is that at one and the same time, he failed utterly, indeed did not try, to create a personal following for himself. An identifiable faction of Healeyites might have burrowed and run for Healey personally; he managed to become, on available poll showings, astonishingly popular in the country – with Labour supporters for sure – but very much also with the broad public. He had exactly that personal appeal – part trust, part ability to amuse, part admired robustness – which, in electoral terms, gives any party essential extra support when directed through a popular leader. Labour led by Healey in 1983 or 1987 would have heavily outperformed Labour led calamitously by Foot or greenly and tentatively by Kinnock.

And a final absurdity is that when discussing Healey today or indeed on doing so in the mid-eighties, I have found the comment of those who voted against him, including left-wingers, to be melancholy, wistful, often strongly admiring and, above all, regretful. Most Labour MPs about at the time *know* that they should have chosen Denis Healey. If that is poor consolation, it is still an uncommon historical compliment and, anyway, it is all the consolation there is.

Healey is a child of selection and merit, of the north of England, though born in Kent and of part-Irish extraction. He is an old-school highbrow of a kind fashionable academics detest: well-stocked mind, inclined to quote poetry, given to donnish argument by knock-me-down assertion, someone who remembers his sixth form with love. His politics were typical of the age he lived through: left-wing to the point of actual membership of the Communist Party. But he would be a classicist, a Latin and Greek specialist, a thing which the age abhors but which makes a bridge between intellectually disciplined thought and sensibility.

He was to become a soldier, not an administrator in uniform but a soldier under cannon fire: that he was a beachmaster at Anzio for the Italian landings is a permanent fact about him. He was running something important and being shot at. 'Every man thinks the worse of himself for not having been a soldier,' said Dr Johnson, who said much the same thing about going to Italy. Healey briskly combined the two. Major Healey, like Colonel Heath and Brigadier Powell, came into politics with, as it were, further education.

His time at Transport House, Labour headquarters, as International Secretary of the Labour Party, would be specifically in the service of Ernest Bevin. He would devil for Bevin, write for Bevin and pamphleteer for him at a time when the politics of the British Left accommodated a large faction which perceived the Soviet Union as broadly a good thing and Josef Stalin as broadly a good man. Hindsight and a tidal river of evidence have made those unimaginable opinions. The despotism of the one and the criminal malevolence of the other are historic commonplaces. When Stalingrad was a vivid contemporary event, when *Animal Farm* had been turned down by a succession of publishers headed by T. S. Eliot at Faber – and at his prissiest, finding it 'inappropriate at this time' – opinion was quite otherwise.

To be attached to Ernest Bevin was a statement of commitment: it involved fights from embattled positions. The soldier's habits would be reinforced.

The battle which would be fought when Healey entered the Commons – though he was not at this stage heavily parliamentarian in his activities – followed the same pattern. The Campaign for Nuclear Disarmament was *not* a Soviet front organisation, however benignly the Russians viewed it. CND was as British as tea on the deanery lawn and indeed rather well received at clerical addresses. It hung upon a hope that our being decent would be reciprocated by someone being decent back. In long perspective, it looks neither sinister nor angelic, just irrelevant. The British involvement in nuclear defence, instigated by Attlee with minimal consultation, had become the keystone of British policy.

Whether it seriously defended us when United States self-interest would have decreed guarantees and when the Soviet Union was as negative and cautious as it became after the great forward roll of 1945 is doubtful. *Amour propre*, in the form of a place at the conference table, probably counted for most and it is hard to see how a Dutch foreign policy of loyal minimalism would actually have affected the country's security, at any rate after the death of Stalin. But Government didn't have hindsight at that time and the stand taken – firm commitment with the US, foundation of NATO and general rejection of soft lines – not only made sense given what we knew, it was prudential and existed to be stronger than it needed to be.

Temperamentally, Healey did what he was certain to do, but in his relationship with Hugh Gaitskell he never adopted the leader's moral and imperious tone. He was developing as a technician of foreign affairs and, to a growing degree, defence; he was unequivocally on the right in this whole long dispute, but the streak of moral intensity in Gaitskell and later in certain SDP people, one which pushed things *à outrance*, wasn't there.

The placing of Healey between Hugh Gaitskell and Harold Wilson is important about him. If he found Gaitskell too sure and evangelistic, he seems to have had a cheerful contempt for Wilson. This was another Yorkshireman come through Oxford, and one who had also come from nowhere. Wilson's career in the thirties had demanded a hard slog at his modern go-ahead subject, PPE and only titular politics – he was a Liberal. In 1945, it had meant attachment to Labour, but moderate Labour – the bonfire of controls – good sense, actually, as was Wilson's disbelief in spending that 11 per cent plus on defence for the Korean War. But with good judgment of numbers also went a furtive (and unnecessary) career alertness which involved playing along with the Left when they swelled to a big following in 1951, and to a deft diminuendo across the decade as they declined.

Wilson's politics were, at best, good judgments of situations, at worst body swerves. There were decencies, humane instincts and an absence of all prejudice, but no convictions of any sort; the no convictions filled out by a rhetoric of morality. It was his misfortune, not far short of tragedy, to have been made a leader having no objectives, when he was designer-made for all-proficient deputy. Arguably, Healey would become Harold Wilson's Harold Wilson, while not being like him in anything except grasp, despatch – and aloneness.

The failure of the two Wilson Governments – and despite the intelligent arguments of Ben Pimlott, his biographer, they did fail – affected the character of the men and women serving under him. The Left had thought with incredible naïvety that Harold Wilson was with them, if not of them, and lived to grow embittered, resentful and ready to quarrel. The ideological Gaitskellites had to live with blur after insistent, dogmatic clarity and with simple all-dividing personal mistrust between themselves and the Prime Minister. They lived with a running analysis of the chemistry of reshuffled cabinets: is the new man ours or theirs? That happens with the Tory Right today and much good it is doing that party.

Wilson learned to live by the cuttlefish ink of institutionalised reshuffle. The only people in that Government who enjoyed much comfort were the performers of functions: Michael Stewart, ironically carrying out Wilson's very Gaitskellite foreign policy through the years of Vietnam, and Healey, reorganising the structure of the Ministry of Defence. There are theories of Wilson distrusting and fearing Healey, but tentative, never-pushed suggestions of other posts hardly bear this out. Not becoming Foreign Secretary during the Vietnam War was a favour, however intended. On the whole, he stayed where he wanted to be for six years, got on (more or less) with his military commanders while hacking their position back, and accomplished a complex necessary exercise – more than most ministers in that Government could claim. Despite Wilson's reliable paranoia, Healey's contempt for him probably outran any prime ministerial anxiety about the Secretary of Defence.

But Healey, much more markedly than in his difference from Gaitskell, was at a distance from the Jenkins group. Personality came into that, and ambition – obviously they did. Jenkins had been promoted from marginal Aviation to the Home Office and the Treasury. It would be humbug in the most Kant-conditioned politician not to have a subjective judgment about that. They were the two ablest men in Wilson's cabinets and warm sympathy between them would have been an unreasonable requirement, though Healey himself is insistent on both his respect for and decent relations with Jenkins.

But it is also true that Healey's opinions were not the group's, that he saw Europe and its integration with neither grief nor rapture. He was, after all, probably better acquainted and in closer co-operation with more European politicians, certainly of the Left, from his apparatchik days and the Ministry of Defence, and he knew more about European culture from Dante to Ibsen than a historian of Edwardian and Victorian Britain like Jenkins. There is nothing Asquithian about Denis Healey. Again, the social graph of the Chancellor – friends with the Devonshires and Violet Bonham Carter, rather mannered, a good deal of social field-placing – indicated an alienation from the Labour Party Hugh Gaitskell knew and loved: working class and educated idealist alike, often wrong-headed, oftener thick-headed, but itself and not undeserving of love.

When Jenkins walked away in the mid-seventies, putting him quite off course in pure Labour terms, Healey had no occasion to grieve. Without adjusting any opinion he automatically moved up the succession field. So when Wilson again took up Government, not, I think, wanting it and perfectly awake to the economic consequences of a union movement which had got out of hand and now controlled too many switches in a system it didn't understand, Healey had to do the job Jenkins had done. After early euphoria and optimism, always a Healey weakness, he proceeded to heavy cutbacks just in time for the markets to panic too late. He went on to accept what the market seemed to have given him, most of which had come from bad statistics – wrong figures on the Public Spending Borrowing Requirement (PSBR) and so on, but with all of which he was stuck. The process of reform was already advanced when the money markets showed a fall, and the fall precipitated resort to the International Monetary Fund, which asked for things the Labour Party, already in a nervous state, violently did not want.

Conservative legend has the IMF involvement as rescue by wise outsiders, not that party's current football supporter-like stance on obscene foreigners. The Treasury instinct, that the whole exercise was late and ambiguously useful, except in the quasi-mystical field of confidence, is more persuasive. Whatever the measures, Healey would leave the economy recovered and strong (just as Kenneth Clarke did). His problems and Labour's were purely political. The price of cuts and freezes had been resentment among the lower paid. Intelligently facing it with flat-rate figures not percentages, he had just about got out of that one when James Callaghan, trying for normality, named a projected figure, 5 per cent, on the question of pay rises, which affronted the troublesome and excitable leadership of unskilled unions.

The electoral defeat which followed the consequent winter strikes was something which Healey could only watch. The shrewdest, least theoretical politician of the day, Callaghan, had dabbled in a projection and got it wrong. Unlike 'Crisis, what crisis?' which he never said, 'Five per cent,' which he certainly did say about pay rises, did for them all.

In the party struggles which would follow, Healey, who had been strongly fancied for the succession, paid many bills. He had been rough with backbenchers, had stroked no hair and bought few beers in his 28 years in Parliament. He was either the right man or he wasn't; he hadn't the silken touch for getting on side. He had governed the country in what mattered most, the economy. But governing it well and getting it right was to be no excuse with those outraged at the bunch-fisted way it had all been done. Finally, in a close contest, there were fervent right-wingers and very silly people who wanted worse to achieve their own better. A very few of these voted for Michael Foot in the contest. Rather more of the not at all silly, but irked and brushed-off people like Tam Dalyell, who should never have been brushed off, did likewise. It was enough to elect narrowly over Healey's head a nice old gentleman regarded in the country as a manifest nonsense, and to set Labour on a path of constructive self-annihilation.

What remained for Healey after this was an after-battle. The Labour Party had lost morale and structure like a ship with shattered steering. The means to Labour becoming a truly left-wing party through the rise of its own Governor Moonbeam, Tony Benn, was to be the removal of Healey from the position of deputy leader, where he was faithfully working with a sobered if unhappy Foot. Healey was much associated in his handling of the IMF with the phrase 'Sod off.' The Jenkinsites were about to do their own cosmic sodding off by way of group defection. Healey did everything he could to stop this though he had neither hopes for nor inclinations towards that undertaking, but the temptation to walk away alone would have seduced many after a major career.

Fighting, contrary to what certain SDP critics said, was very much in the Irish blood. He did stay. The victory to retain the symbolic deputyship was a dreadfully close thing finally determined by one union, NUPE (National Union of Public Employees), being persuaded to hold a democratic poll of its membership. That poll's heavy bias to Healey says everything that needs to be said about his fortunes under any honest party system. That burst of unrigged opinion and personal popularity inside the union whose national and local leadership had conjured up the 'Winter of Discontent' demonstrated the real state of union membership opinion generally. But it was a victory for other people, for Kinnock, Smith and for the handsome vacancies of Tony Blair.

Gaitskell's phrase had been: 'We will fight, fight and fight again to save the party we love.' That is what Healey did, and his fighting at that juncture, when the interior of large cars beckoned him, saved that party from further fall. He had been a Good Party Man indeed. But his combination of driving practical intelligence, comfortable internationalism, refined sensibilities just out of sight, and a bedrock of political things he was clear-minded about would have made him a leader broader-ranging than Callaghan, better balanced in judgment than Gaitskell, more honest and coherent than Wilson. The whole story must be followed, but it is a leadership one would have liked to experience as there are others it would have been pleasant to have avoided.

CHAPTER TWO

Denis Healey's father, Will, was born in Northern Ireland near Enniskillen, the son of a tailor, John William, who soon after came to England to practise his trade. Denis's mother, Winnie Powell, came from Gloucestershire, the daughter of a railway stationmaster. South Wales is full of English names like Heseltine and Howe, and the western marches of England with Welsh ones. For what it is worth, not very much, the Healey inheritance was Celtic and Will Healey was a sentimental Irish Nationalist. He was given to talk of Shan van Vocht and the iniquities of Tim Healy (no relation) who had turned on Parnell along with the Catholic bishops – shades of John Joyce and Simon Dedalus, a thought which might please Denis.

The Healeys were not Roman Catholic, though. John William Healey had given up that adherence, something which the Church bureaucracy kept on record and with which the Cabinet minister was to be confronted, date and all, half a century later by the future Cardinal Heenan, then Bishop of Leeds.

Both parents were teachers and thus travellers. Denis was born in Kent, but Will Healey, rising to be principal of Keighley Technical College, would take his family to Yorkshire. In Rab Butler's family the mother was benign and the father hard. Denis Healey writes lovingly about both parents, but the clear indication is that Winnie, not hard but strong, was the chief influence. Will was an engineer, but one with a charming vein of physical impracticality: melting down tents with paraffin and killing off canaries he was trying to disinfect. Winnie, who had less education but the one gift which matters most, that of intense interest, was the reader and prompter of reading, someone who went to Workers' Educational Association lectures and listened to serious talks on the BBC Home Service. There is a nice parallel with Butler's elect family tree of public-school heads and masters of Cambridge colleges. Nothing like so grand, it was still privileged. This was the sort of home into which books came, from which theatres were visited, in which ideas were welcomed and where argument rolled on. It turns up, also Yorkshire-based, in J. B. Priestley's *Bright Day*.

A place at the early age of eight at Bradford Grammar School meant another kind of privilege, the sort of education his colleague, Anthony Crosland of Highgate School, would seek to eradicate: the large, super-selective, direct-grant, northern grammar school in which, however socially divisively, you learnt about advanced physics and Plato. Healey was born for this sort of thing and writes about school, as later about Oxford, with fervour. Alan Bullock and Maurice Hodgson, later chairman of ICI, were contemporaries. There was Thucydides to study, there was Chesterton as an enthusiasm, followed by Virginia Woolf and the historical novels of the then well-known Merejkowski. Then came the necessary sixth-form preciousness when *Scrutiny* and T. S. Eliot commanded the universe, followed by Empson and I. A. Richards. By a chance of his own free-ranging reading quite outside the prescriptions of thirties fashion, Denis stumbled upon Samuel Beckett, another decade's buzz-writer. He did so by way of the early novel *Murphy*, the one which begins, 'The sun shone, having no alternative, on the nothing new.' He got it, of course, out of Bradford Public Library.

Healey then did what clever boys had to do, despite Crosland: he took a scholarship to an élite university, to an élite college for that matter. In 1936 he would go up to Balliol to read Greats. But before Balliol, he undertook a journey through Germany. He went across that country by bicycle, slept in barns and youth hostels at a penny a night, ate black bread with strawberry jam and salad and potatoes, accomplishing a five-week trip for five pounds. He was already left-wing, but reckons that he visited Germany less to see the monster of Nazism close-up than to visit the Salzburg Festival for Reinhardt's production of *Faust*. He queued up in the rain, got a standing place and speaks reverently of the experience. But however much the famous Healey hinterland of museums, art, music and theatre was being laid here with internationalist enthusiasm, it wasn't possible to visit Hitler's Germany, even wearing its polite Olympic-year face for visitors, without drawing political conclusions. He observed that the most Nazi people he met were the Austrians, that many German working people insisted self-delusively that they submitted to Nazism rather than endorsed it – they used the metaphor of the beefsteak, brown on the outside, red within – and that the Czechs he met were mostly Socialists or Communists.

He got into arguments, but not into so much as a hint of violence, simply noting the drilling at youth hostels and the wooden models of bombs used to collect money for the Air Force. He liked the Germans themselves well enough and did not let political preoccupation take away the pleasures of an enterprising mind-and-body holiday. The Healey energy and the devouring urge to intelligent enjoyment was at work. If his classical training prompted him by way of Lucretius and the Epicureans to take much from intense enjoyment of little, there has always been in Denis Healey a compulsion to take his much from much.

The Balliol he entered on his return for the four years of Oxford Greats, the classical degree, offered him a culture oddly more modern than the one taken in by Butler 15 years before at Cambridge as a modern languages student. The classical courses taught by E. R. Dodds and Russell Meiggs were high quality. Dodds, teaching Greek poetry, brought in Louis MacNeice (another classicist) to talk; the links with modernism, then in its high and hopeful time, were extensive and Healey conceived a devotion to Eliot, wrote an essay on 'Burnt Norton' and found *Murder in the Cathedral* worthy of the Greek dramatists.

His concern with philosophy continued, involving the Kant already quoted, Hume, whose brisk lucidity delighted him, and the dialectical materialists. But in spite of becoming a member of the Communist Party at Oxford, the importance of which in his mental outlook can be debated, he despised the party's official philosophy. Dialectical materialism, he tells us, seemed even then 'a superficial triviality quite unworthy of Hume and Hegel, from whom it was confected'. Healey's intellectual briskness is already recognisable.

All around were the intellectual and artistic enthusiasms (and chic) of the day: Donne and Hopkins, those great archeological unearthings and honorary modernists, the GPO film unit, the surrealists, some jazz, Paul Nash, Betjeman before the market rush. The ardent things of the thirties stand up pretty well today.

It was a radical time and innovation had not turned into the charlatanry and barrel-scraping of recent times. Picasso and Magritte were a better cause for defying the elder generation than vivisected sheep. (Healey and his Art Club friends, in touch with Roland Penrose, had a hand in a surrealist exhibition featuring Magritte's frisson-inducing *Le Viol*). It was what the Nazis called '*Kultur Bolshevismus*', no matter how much real Bolshevik taste in art was pure Paris salon *circa* 1875. Being young at the hour when the credible, exciting new was in flood was an exhilaration not to be had again.

But Healey stresses older Oxford influences. The Master of Balliol, Sandy Lindsay, not a dominant or an innovative mind, was a great spirit naturally attractive to the young. He was also interested in metaphysical and Christian thinking outside the cool lines of the 18th century and after. Healey read Berdyaev, Shestov and Kierkegaard under his influence and reckons that reading to have contributed most to his Socialist convictions: 'It appealed to something in my nature.' Lindsay's own Christian Socialism was honourable and decent rather than the latest required thing, but it joined academic studies to the political world. Lindsay brought in continental scholars as refugees. He was to stand as the Popular Front candidate against the pro-Munich Conservative, one Quintin Hogg, in the 1938 Oxford by-election. He lost, but the great issues of the day coalesced around the contest and, if perceptions of the good and the not good were ever to be set ostentatiously against one another, antinomies of pure prejudice, Oxford was surely the place for doing it.

The politics of Oxford at this time were, at least for those who avowed politics and engaged in it, Left and again Left. The only non-Communist on the Labour Club committee, according to both Healey and the then Liberal Harold Wilson, was the Scot, Thomas Wilson, later a distinguished economist. The leading figure in Tory politics was Edward Heath ('Teddy', as Healey mischievously remembers him), a fervent anti-Munichite who at the Oxford Union described the Chamberlain Government at Munich as turning all four cheeks at once.

For Healey to become a Communist Party member in this atmosphere is not remarkable, though it has fascinated some commentators and misled others. Almost certainly it would, in the longer term, colour his specifically anti-Communist opinions within the Labour Party – not least a contempt for fringe left vagrant Marxism, something upon which ex-Communists, whatever the distance they have since travelled, generally agree.

The differences between the outlooks of Healey and another Balliol contemporary, Roy Jenkins, were something else. By chance, Edward Heath, Healey and a significant American Democrat figure, Phil Kaiser, succeeded one another as Chairman of the Balliol Junior Common Room at this time. Of notable contemporaries, only Christopher Mayhew would put up much of a fight in specifically rejecting Communism, in which he would be joined later by Roy Jenkins. Tony Crosland, according to Healey, called himself a Marxist at this time, but couldn't steel himself to join 'the Party'.

Healey makes a refining point about two sorts of Communists at this time, those caught up in the enthusiasms of the late thirties and those who had joined earlier and belonged to a slightly senior age group. He was recruited by Peter Hewitt, a friend of Philip Toynbee, both elder brethren. Toynbee was no more than a slightly silly man of unimpactive talent, but he belonged to the group which was middle class and public school. Healey pinpoints this group's outlook by noting that it took John Cornford and his thoroughly Stalinist and bullyingly unpleasant verse seriously. It was a triumphalist approach and dated from the time of open Stalinism before the party line changed in Moscow to making overtures to idealists by way of the Popular Front and anti-Fascism. It was from their initial ranks of serious (and often socially dislocated) Communists that the Cambridge agents would come. Healey would be pushed for Chairman of the Labour Club by the CP apparatus, ironically against someone who would stay in that party all his life, Tom McWhinnie.

But his actions in 1939 make clear how unsound he was from an objective party point of view. Back at home in Keighley in the long vac before the start of his fourth year, reading Kant on 'the transcendental synthetic unity of aperception', he was interrupted by his mother coming upstairs to say: 'Put away your books. War has been declared.' The Communist line had shifted after Ribbentrop and Molotov's agreement, and to the good party men this was now an imperialist war to be regarded with detachment. Healey volunteered for the Army.

The whole picture of Healey's education is of a confluence of best circumstances. He was in an élite place among star contemporaries at a time of world crisis, cultural flux and an urgency intense to any even half-alert mind. One has listened to other children of that time attempting ever and again over the succeeding decades – at Suez or over Vietnam or other ultimately incidental and middle-rank crises – to recreate the mood of the late thirties. This showed in the invocation on the Left of the word 'Fascism' to characterise anything from amendment of trade-union privileges to museum charges. And of course, Tories have been no better. The notion of Nasser as Hitler in the febrile mind of Anthony Eden spoke as much nostalgia as derangement. (Professor John Ramsden has argued that an excellent PhD might be done on the historic misuse of the word 'Munich'.)

By the time Healey actually became a soldier, the long delays of the phoney war which kept him away from Oxford waiting for a non-materialising call-up until November, had given him time to finish his degree, a First in Greats. He had been educated in the old approved way to the best of Oxford's ability and in the newest, most exhilarating one by the interesting times in which he lived. For another five years of military service that education would continue. But though 'interesting times' are viewed by the Chinese as a curse, Healey cheerfully acknowledges that the Army, like so many other undertakings, was something he enjoyed.

Most of the civilised world now knows that Healey was a beachmaster at Anzio, a fact that enabled him to look admirals of the blue in the eye when slashing their budgets 20 years later. Not so many people know that he was also officer counting service arrivals and departures on Swindon Station, making up the numbers he didn't have and squaring his totals with a friendly ticket-collector.

He went on to do similarly exciting work as Rail Traffic Officer at Hull, Halifax, Leeds and Sheffield. It was the sort of tedium about which memoirs of the early years of the last war often complain, though it involved the sort of timetabling and organisational grasp which would be put to great use on grander occasions, as was his experience as passenger/observer when an American cargo boat made an uncontested landing in Algeria. What might be called the sexy part of his military work did not begin until April 1943 when, after his training in Scotland as Landing Officer, his ship left the Clyde for Algiers and then Tunis and inspection by an unadmired General Montgomery, 'a sharp, ferret-like face and pale green eyes, wearing his vanity like a foulard'.

That group was now part of Division 78 for the invasion of Sicily. Healey was not employed as beachmaster for Sicily itself as his group disembarked at Avola three days behind the taking of the bridgehead. He expected to go into action at Salerno, having been called and recalled three times to and from Tripoli from where that assault would begin. He may well have lived because finally he wasn't sent. Healey had been transferred to 231 Landing Brigade, commanded by General Urquhart, as Landing Officer for an assault aiming at a point north of Reggio Calabria. The officer who replaced him for the Salerno landing was killed within hours.

The actual invasion, which shifted again, from the original Pizzo to the sweetly and paganly named Porto San Venere, was not itself what in those days was called 'a piece of cake'. The change of location was brought about by a storm which destroyed several landing craft. The Germans were emplaced and the commandos had landed three miles off target. The troops who came onshore ran into bombardment from 88mm mortars and assaults by dive bombers. There were heavy casualties to be taken back to Sicily. But the bridgehead was established in Salerno with the Porto San Venere access as a support to it.

There would then be for Healey, as happens in wars, a lull, in this case a south Italian lull, first in Bari, where he was sent on a staff posting, then Naples. The Italophile and the name-dropper in Healey both enjoyed themselves. He worked with Marcus Sieff, then a colonel, usually head of Marks and Spencer, and Val Duncan, future head of Rio Tinto Zinc, and he made friends with the son-in-law of Lord Gort, former Commander-in-Chief. John Donaldson, later Arts Minister under Callaghan, was also the husband of Frances Donaldson, whose life of her father, the playwright Frederick Lonsdale, is something of a classic.

Together Donaldson and Healey saw opera and in the finger-clicking way of liberators stirred out music from stray orchestral players. Healey also speaks of reading Croce in Italian (in defiance of the civil servants who would say affectionately years later 'He thinks he speaks Italian'). There was also a love affair – something parenthetically taken in and spoken of later with affection – with an upper-class woman from the nursing yeomanry. Poetry was read and weekends were later discerningly spent together in Positano and San Gimignano as the army advanced.

The Anzio raid, in which Healey's part is well known, he rather plays down. It went well and according to plan as the Calabrian landing certainly had not, and British casualties were lower than American. But in military terms, he sees it was a mistake trumped by a bigger German mistake. Too few troops being invested in it, the operation was made strategically successful by German over-investment on other fronts.

At one point, Healey came close to being beachmaster for another landing, on the island of Krk off Yugoslavia to pre-empt Tito taking Fiume (otherwise Rijeka). He was not sorry to be saved this rough undertaking when Tito pre-empted his pre-emptors and took Fiume anyway. Healey was now a trusted specialist officer with a formidable military group, the Seventh Armoured Division, and taking part in victory.

In that atmosphere private excursions were possible and Healey, based in Florence, with the assistance of a driver, made his own outing to Austria and the edge of Yugoslavia. Travelling through Bologna, Sirmione, Verona and Udine, he went into Austria through Villach to Klagenfurt, and in Gorizia and Trieste saw the partisan takeover all around. He was witness all the way to German retreat and desertion. Another of his new friends, Brigadier Jack Profumo, was flying the British Commander to Switzerland to negotiate German surrender throughout Italy. The show, as some soldiers liked to call it with artful nonchalance, was coming to an end.

The phrase 'a good war' makes military men of any sensibility flinch. But, objectively, Healey did have a good war. The rank of major was nothing startling in 1945 – Profumo, as noted, was a brigadier, as was Enoch Powell, and 'Teddy' Heath was a colonel – but Healey had been a decidedly unornamental major. Landing officers are seriously important people whose competence affects lives, and Healey had successfully run one quite important landing and one very important one and been tee-ed up for another before Tito played spoilsport. The time spent at Swindon and Halifax had been the beginning of qualification as a technician in a field where technicians were respected. To be a first-class transport officer functioning with the staff was itself recognition. And the whole of his career, until the last unsuccessful bit, would turn on a succession of people – Hugh Dalton, Ernest Bevin, then two leaders, Gaitskell and Wilson – acknowledging that Healey went straight into the team because of what he knew and what he could do.

Another aspect of war is that no one really has a good one. Much of it, as Healey says himself, was spent 'in paralysing boredom'; even in a 'show' run vastly better than were the First War trenches, it is still about killing people and there are bodies to clear away. 'There never was a good war yet nor a bad peace,' Healey quotes Benjamin Franklin, but it was a war he and most soldiers had believed in, the more educated the more belief, as a war against Fascism and one which invalidated the assumptions of pacifism.

He was a Day One volunteer, no longer a Communist but still hotly left-wing, a practical soldier employed to solve problems, also five years older and educated by the boredom and the mistakes as well as the danger and killing. He quotes Clough's *Amours de Voyage* to demonstrate the smart/silly kind of one-up sixth-form pacifism he had toyed with and put aside:

. . . and no man
Finds quite distinct the assurance that he of all others is
called on,
Or would be justified, even, in taking away from the World
that
Precious creature himself.

He was to spend a great deal of his time contradicting the assumptions of all forms of pacifism, especially unilateral disarmament. He was going to be the Labour politician who said direct, unflinching things which so offended colleagues drawn to pacifism, a cause naturally popular to any sort of Left. This being so, the leadership of the Labour Party in Wilson's time and after never liked to say them. Defence policy would be conducted by stealth. But all that lay years ahead; in the short and medium term, lines of argument were to be sharp and hard-edged and Healey's combination of technician and bloody shovel-caller were exactly what would be wanted.

The transition from soldier to politician would be routed through the office, not that Healey is thought of as a bureaucrat. But with the war concluding, a first taste of politics would offer itself. He had had a political invitation from the Labour member for Keighley, Ivor Thomas, to have his name put on the candidates list. He had other offers becoming a high flyer: participation (in some comfort) in the team writing the history of the Italian campaign, postgraduate scholarship at Merton pursuing that study of the philosophy of art which, like Miss Havisham's wedding dress, would stand long in his attic. But Labour offered him Pudsey, a seat remote from prospects of victory, and he took it. Still a soldier, he appeared at Blackpool in uniform, as many did, and made a rather bad speech.

'The upper classes in every country are selfish, depraved,

dissolute and decadent . . . The struggle for Socialism in Europe has been hard, cruel, merciless and bloody.' It wasn't untrue, and his shock at the blind greed of the upper classes in Greece – seen during a hiking holiday – and Naples, observed towards the end of the war, was quite genuine. But such rafter-ringing was the Spanish Tragedy aspect of Healey. Quick as he was to see a refinement, he would always be hard pressed in debate to work up a nuance. Sincere certainly, true in many ways, this was still rant, but it was also an indication of the direct, uncrablike nature of Healey, the public figure. No one would hand him their hat and there would be no ambiguity whatever.

For the moment he would be outside the public arena. Pudsey narrowly rejected him, though with the sort of drastically diminished margin – 1,600 votes in the Ruislip of the West Riding – which reflected the mood and shattered assumptions. It was time to do several things: to get a job, leave the Army and marry.

It was a measure of Healey's standing at a time when he had written nothing, been out of the country at war and was known only through word of mouth, in albeit in highly political circles of fast-rising clever young soldiers, that Harold Laski, Hugh Dalton and Aneurin Bevan all backed him for International Secretary of the Labour Party. He was well out of Parliament at this stage, not just because sensational marginals are invariably lost at the next election, something which would have thrown a controversial figure on the market at the start of Labour's 13-year exile, but because he was to become even more of a technician over six years travelling and meeting Socialist leaders worldwide and working to the Foreign Secretary, Ernest Bevin. As the junior Foreign Office Minister he might otherwise have become, he could not have been more active. Of Bevin's deputies, Hector McNeil died early and Christopher Mayhew would function increasingly as a semi-independent figure. Healey got for himself, as was his wont, another burst of education, an international one this time.

He also busied himself accumulating the thing he would talk about 35 years later in defeat, the hinterland. Whatever names are dropped or cultural jack-handles wielded, Healey's desire to see as many good performances of serious plays, concerts of music and exhibitions of art, is real, vigorous and takes the form of appetite. The Olivier/Richardson season at the Old Vic, Myra Hess's late National Gallery concerts, friendships in the arts – with the dancer William Chappel and a British Museum curator beginning to write short stories, Angus Wilson – and the restaurants of Soho were important as more than patina to a busy life. But culture has always been cheerful with Healey, he doesn't do books and art penitentially or as a requirement. The hinterland was acquired by enjoyment in a boy-and-sweetshop kind of way.

It was shared with his new wife, and girlfriend of some standing. Edna Edmunds was to become, as Edna Healey, one of the political wives about whom nothing spiteful or injurious is said. The only stories in later years are cheerful ones like her injunction to Elspeth Howe after the Tories won the 1979 election, 'You'll have to do something about the kitchen boiler at Number 11.' She has made a comprehensively autonomous career for herself after raising three children, in writing a life of Angela Burdett-Coutts and the recent account of Buckingham Palace. Edna, from the Forest of Dean, exam-routed through Oxford, sympathetic and loyal but entirely capable of answering back, seems to have adjusted herself to Healey's imperious instincts with the sort of skill and fleeting comment which left him ruefully appreciative of her quality.

John Biffen tells a story from the eighties which gives a good idea of Edna Healey's satirical and affectionate measure of Denis. A dinner-party had been given for the two politicians – both prized by the brighter end of the press as Commons performers – by some parliamentary journalists, of whom, says Biffen, he himself was wary and in awe, anxious not to give offence or open himself up to later ironies. Awe not being a Healey characteristic, the former Chancellor was in the mood for pre-emptive strikes and blazed cheerfully away at sketch-writers and other potentially injurious persons, explaining to them where (most places) they had been hopelessly and pathetically wrong. Biffen, having enjoyed this over the evening, finally made a move to leave and said his thanks. Edna turned to her husband and said lightly, 'I think we can go now as well, Denis. I don't *think* there's anyone you haven't insulted.'

I have, as it happens, a memory of my own. When, at Labour Party Conference in 1981 the horribly tight final result of the Benn challenge on the deputy leadership came through, I was standing very near the Healeys. Someone attempted to ask Edna a question. She said simply, 'Denis has won. Nothing else matters,' and put an arm round him. Healey talks of happy marriages being preconditional to successful political careers and does so with authority.

Demobbed, married, hired, he was now, in 1945, to commence a career of pure Labour Party politics, which, from Transport House officer to life peer, was at the time of writing 52 years long. He was to become a sort of apparatchik, though few men have ever been less like the dull, insistent, carnivorous plankton who provide your natural apparatchiks. But in 1946 he was going into a Soviet-assailed world in which such creatures counted. The ex-Communist was about to work closely with Ernest Bevin, to argue strenuously in print for NATO and the American alliance, to form personal ties with senior American politicians (admittedly Democrats) and to come unequivocally down on one side of the line which divided all those in left-wing politics with the courage to make up their minds. The side he came down on was that of commitment to a Cold War struggle against the power and potential aggrandisement of the Soviet Union. He would do this as the quickly valued and heavily used junior colleague of Ernest Bevin, with whom there were mighty affinities.

'There was a great deal of the emperor in Mr Bevin's outlook,' wrote a senior FO official, Sir Ivone Kirkpatrick. A left-wing MP, Ernest Millington, would respond to the National Service Bill of 1947 with the fear that 'the real purpose of it was to put an iron glove on the fist of the Foreign Secretary which he is so fond of shaking at the leaders of the USSR'.

A year after that superabundantly fatuous remark, the body of Jan Masaryk, Foreign Minister of Czechoslovakia and son of the founder of the state, was found in the courtyard of Hradcany Castle. Whether the death was murder or suicide induced by despair scarcely matters in any moral sense. This was a final step in the process, completed by *putsch*, of a Communist takeover of that country. It was a process in which the left-wing faction of the Czech Socialist Party, led by Zdenek Fierlinger, had played a straightforwardly treasonable part. By the time NATO was formally created in 1949, the point and purpose of Bevin's resolution against the Soviets and reliance on American alliance had been generally understood as common reason. But the early days after the war were something else.

It is difficult in this era, when the Soviet Union has been consigned to that dustbin of history of which its spokesmen spoke so fondly, and when Tony Blair's watered thinking dominates the Labour Party, to comprehend the mood of 1945. A number of facts combined with a leap of the imagination is necessary. The thirties had been a period when the manifest enemy had been Nazi Germany. This was not, to be honest, on account of the anti-Jewish persecutions now seen as its essence, but as what was generically called 'Fascism', a drive by the authoritarian Right everywhere to eliminate opposition and specifically to lock up, kill and generally suppress Socialists and anyone who looked like a Socialist.

This was a truth, but only one of two truths. It was the great *donnée* of the day and it had made up the minds of a great tranche of a generation that the totalitarian threat was on the Right. By extension and dubious logic, the forces of the Left were its enemy and thus our friends. The fact of Stalin's rule having been despotic and murderous in degrees equal to, possibly greater than Hitler's did not register, except with individuals like George Orwell, who had eccentric perception of a reality available but intolerable.

The show trials of Moscow in 1936 and 1937 were known and reported, if the waves of imprisonment set out later by Solzhenitsyn and Shalamov were only vaguely murmured about, and some faint idea of the slaughter at the White Sea Canal, built to kill the men building it, was on the record though making no stir.

An extensive perversion of understanding was widespread. It would be evidenced in Kingsley Martin's treatment of the Moscow trials in the *New Statesman*, a piece of pitiful dither, chalice-passing and moral vacancy worthy of a curate torn between doubts and a snug living. The period of maximum support for the Communist Party coincided with a high point on the graph of Stalin's murderous paranoia. A young man like Denis Healey could be excused for not taking in the full panorama in his late teens and early twenties. But the Healey who had grown out of such adolescent delusion would find himself arguing against the Ernest Millingtons who had not grasped it by 1947.

In that last year appeared a pamphlet, 'Keep Left', with 12 signatures on it, written by Ian Mikardo, Richard Crossman and Michael Foot. It argued many things domestic, but most importantly, on foreign policy, talked of 'a Third Force' dominated by Britain and France 'to hold the balance of world power, to halt the division into a Western and an Eastern bloc and so make the United Nations a reality'. Labour Britain 'must regain her independence' and escape Bevin's 'single and consistent note – a readiness to follow American strategic thinking'.

Over history of a longer span there would be something to be said for disagreeing with the Americans from time to time and civilly saying so. Arguments advanced 12 years later by Kennedy about going anywhere and fighting any battle are the bad rhetoric and worse policy which come from thinking the certainties of 1948 in 1960. A British government without an atom of illusion about any Communist regime might wisely have argued with its friend in the 1960s. But this was 1948 and the judgments of George Orwell and the policy direction of Ernest Bevin were, succinctly and without reservation, right. The Soviet Union's own tone and style could be summed up as Healey quotes it in his own memoir, with this broadcast comment on Britain, 'This little country went to war because it and its Fascist leaders love war and thrive on war. The attack on Hitlerite Germany was purely incidental.' Britain, rather than the US, had troops standing in unhelpful places like Greece, Iran and the Italian–Yugoslav border. Accordingly, Britain was the immediate objective of the juddering vilification machine of Soviet broadcasting.

Of the three authors of 'Keep Left', Crossman was a man to whom truth was as optional as it was plastic and for whom light-minded disloyalty, affably called mischief, was second nature. Mikardo enjoyed a long-term substantial income from East German business contacts only available to a friend of the Wall and shootings-to-kill regime. Michael Foot was a muddled, effusive, readily indignant literary man without malicious intent or disloyalty, and no judge at all of the world he lived in. Thirty-two years later he would be preferred to Denis Healey as leader of the Labour Party.

The butt of this group and their pamphlet, Ernest Bevin, as Foreign Secretary in a Government outstandingly radical, levelling and creative, spoke for the core of its leadership: Dalton, the Chancellor, Morrison, leader of the House, Gaitskell, the rising future leader, and supremely, that remarkable man, a cricketing revolutionary with military edge, Clement Attlee.

A single observation clarifies the Prime Minister's approach. There was to be much agonising during the creation of NATO as a defence against the Soviets as to who was morally fit to belong. Attlee brought a bracing coarseness to the argument. What about the questionable Turks? 'Fought against the Turk in 1915. Damn good soldier. Sooner have him on our side than theirs.' Healey, working enthusiastically for Bevin, was to a degree sharing the attitude of an older generation. Men born in the early 1880s, too grown-up, and in Bevin's case sensibly pre-occupied with union business, to be emotionally trapped by the mood of the thirties, did common-sense, realistic, unideological things. Such insensibility was shocking to many young enough to have in their adolescence seen the Soviet Union as a disinterested White Knight serving in the ranks of anti-Fascism.

There would be plenty more to share what was then called a right-wing view. But although the likes of Anthony Crosland and Roy Jenkins would accept the full pro-Western, anti-Soviet position, it was not their *raison d'être* and they would not come to it as foreign policy specialists tightly and busily involved with Socialist politicians of European countries who had had their own burnt or nearly burnt experience of the Communists. The exception was Hugh Gaitskell, whose Viennese year witnessing another (right-wing) *putsch* in 1934 had been such a mind-scorching experience. Right-wing totalitarianism actually experienced can be instructive about left-wing totalitarianism.

There would be refinements of view and temperamental dif-ference between these two and Healey was never a fully signed-up member of the set of single-purposed friends who met at 18 Frognal Gardens. But when it came to the general struggle and any particular fight, like the Scarborough Conference of 1960, Healey was in comprehensive accord with Gaitskell.

'What sort of people do you think we are? We are not the pacifists, neutralists and fellow travellers some people are. We will fight, fight and fight again to save the party we love', is very well and deservedly remembered from that febrile afternoon. But deserving of comparable billing was, 'We met Mr Khruschev and he told us that when he was a boy in the Donets Basin, he used to kill cats by swinging them by the tail and smashing their heads against rocks . . . Can I get it into your heads, comrades, that Mr Khruschev is not the George Lansbury type?' That is as perfectly Healey as the other is absolute Hugh Gaitskell, and it is the logical outcome of the years Healey spent fighting soft lines and Third Forcery, of which unilateral nuclear disarmament was a later expression.

But it is also perfect Ernest Bevin. Famously and to much genteel horror, Bevin had rounded on Lansbury and his pacifism in 1935, remarking that the old man had been dragging his conscience around from conference to conference and adding offstage that Lansbury also carried his martyr's faggots 'and I set fire to them'.

In the historic long term the George Lansbury type was far more important to the Labour Party's character than the fellow traveller. That model involves an honourable revulsion at war linked with an unwillingness to take steps inhibiting it. If honourable, it is also moralistic, dreary, and commonly delivered in high and piping tones. Such people could usually be reconciled to the broad direction of the party by the sort of blague and blur about unity and Socialist purpose which would come out of Harold Wilson on draught. But Healey was not the man ever to reconcile them. A good deal of his reputation for being a 'thug' derives from the post-war years and the putting of a plain case plainly.

This was what he was to do in response to 'Keep Left'. That pamphlet was historically important for gathering together the objections of the Left to the Labour Government. Of this the foreign affairs part, much of it written by Crossman, was the most urgent statement of how Socialist sensibilities had been offended by the brisk choices Bevin had made. This is what Healey set out to answer. With the war just over, a Greek Communist regime entirely thinkable, the French Communist Party commanding about a quarter of the vote and conducting lynch law against its enemies, loosely classified as collaborationists, sensibilities were the last object of Bevin's concern or that of his henchman. A henchman was something Denis Healey thoroughly enjoyed being and in his pamphlet 'Cards on the Table', 'Keep Left' was to be answered in henchmanly style.

Alan Bullock, in the last volume of his great life of Bevin, observes: 'For once Bevin had his case put for him by one of the ablest young men in the Labour Party, whose intellectual powers were fully equal to those of the Keep Left group ... The pamphlet is notable for a forthrightness of language which was a refreshing change in the Labour Party's discussion of foreign policy hitherto dominated by the Left.'

Bullock picks out the phrase 'a sustained and violent offensive against Britain by her Russian ally ... They thought they could see the British empire crumbling and that expansion to fill Britain's place in Europe and the Middle East would be easy.' The tone is as brisk as the Prime Minister's, Major Healey following Major Attlee to confront those questions of power, 'who whom' and 'who is to be master', equally implacably.

'The aim of an Anglo–American understanding is to prevent war by proving to Russia that an aggressive anti-British policy is doomed to frustration . . . Our hope is that sooner or later the Russians will realise that the policy they have pursued since 1945 is both impracticable and unnecessary.' As Bullock says, 'Cards on the Table' is 'in many ways, the best exposition of Bevin's views on the policy he had sought to pursue between 1945 and 1947'.

The events of the next two years, especially the Czech *putsch*, were to make it look, if anything, rather moderate. But it was a furiously controversial undertaking. It was attacked at Party Conference and not much defended at the National Executive meeting. But Healey had the satisfaction of having said exactly what he thought and having made an outstanding defence of a boss to whom he was devoted. Although he would later reach the conclusion that Soviet threats and the rhetoric of Stalin and his spokesman, Molotov, overstated any real threat, any mistakes which Bevin had made or for which Healey argued would be those of extreme alertness to danger. As pamphleteer, what he had really done had been to get history roughly right as it was happening. For the rest of his career, a tendency not anyway negligible to self-confidence and decisiveness had been mightily reinforced. That cheery arrogance which friends find amiable and opponents do not had been underwritten and, in the minds of an important minority, the cardinal sin of having been right on the wrong side had been committed.

The other aspect of Healey's Transport House apparatchik career was of going, seeing, learning and the making, over six years, of a vast acquaintance. In Italy for a second proper honeymoon with Edna supplementary to an earlier week in Wharfedale, he was to dine with the Italian Prime Minister, De Gasperi, and his Communist opponent, Palmiro Togliatti, a man different from the then basilisk norm of Communists. Healey would observe in passing that the British Ambassador, Sir Noel Charles, was drunk most of the time and his job effectively done by the Labour attaché. He met Alberto Moravia and Ignazio Silone, 'a sleek, morose man who spoke with flashes of humour', and took part in unsuccessful Socialist unity conversations with Pietro Nenni and Giuseppe Saragat, then about to go their long, forlorn, respective ways of association with the steadily more reasonable but no more electable Communists and a long miring in conventional Italian politics.

He made acquaintance with the French Socialists then

moving from the attractive leadership of Léon Blum – of Popular Front days and subject of the vicious observation on the French Right '*Mieux Hitler que Blum*' – alas to domination by the flavourless and intellectually anorexic bureaucrat Guy Mollet. The outstanding Lange in Norway, old Renner with his dodgy past in Austria and the furiously difficult Kurt Schumacher in West Germany, were all met and talked with. This was a time when Social Democratic parties with different experiences – rolled over by the Nazis, threatened immediately by Communists – were part of a world which insular Britain, for all its wartime exertions, knew little and in which it developed little interest. Labour, left to itself, can be atrociously narrow and unenquiring. But Healey was the courier and representative of Ernest Bevin who, despite the preoccupying limits of his union background, was furiously concerned with the world outside.

In the north, Healey struck up with the Norwegian Socialists who had learned about Stalin by once, long ago, belonging to the Comintern. He saw a little of Hungary and Czechoslovakia, which were in process of being taken over, also Poland, whose Communist regime never quite took on the Dracula quality of rule by, respectively, Rakosi and Gottwald in the former two countries. He was present in Brno at a conference of Czechoslovak Social Democrats when fusion with the Communists was rejected over the head of the leading collaborationist, Zdenek Fierlinger. It was only a glitch in a devouring, but it was instructive. Healey would later write, 'I shall never forget the wolfish snarl with which Fierlinger, white as a sheet, received the announcement of the votes.'

He would also commence through a series of contacts and friendship that private American lattice of influential acquaintance which he might sometimes overdo in conversation or debate – this is a man who drops the Dalai Lama into his narrative – but they were real enough and would give him every kind of access in Washington in later days of renewed office.

These were phenomenally interesting as well as frightening times. Developments since then have been very much the children of decisions made and crises faced then: the Marshall Plan, the Berlin blockade, the establishment of NATO, the Schuman Plan, which was to be the foundation trench of the European Union and, finally, the Korean War. Broadly, as America was roused and brought into Europe, Britain, with

Bevin running foreign affairs, was getting right a succession of hard decisions much as it had got such a series wrong in the thirties. Denis Healey had spent his best young years as a junior, but highly valued player in a group which could look back on what it did and say, 'We were right.'

CHAPTER THREE

If Healey were to become a Member of Parliament after so centrally involved and active a life out of sight of most Parliamentary concerns, it would not be as an ordinary MP.

He had not sought a seat in 1950, and the 1951 election, a product of exhaustion (and a vast error of historic timing), was hardly planned for. Healey had seriously considered a university chair at Aberystwyth, and might have taken up the foreign editorship of the *Daily Herald*, lineal (and unimaginable) ancestor of the *Sun*, except that, not being a member of the National Union of Journalists, he was barred from consideration.

Leeds South-East, the constituency where he would be chosen for a by-election, had become available largely through the determination of the Conservatives, squeakily elected in 1951, to control the chair of the Commons. Labour had accepted in 1945 the continuation as Speaker of Colonel Douglas Clifton-Brown, a Conservative who had succeeded to the place in 1943. They had expected his Labour deputy, James Milner, to follow. The Conservatives were not having anything as fair and reasonable as that and, despite the convention that the Commons not the Government fills the chair, saw to it that W. S. Morrison, an affable, popular Tory known as 'Shakes' from his fondness for quoting Shakespeare, was railroaded in. The affronted Milner took the hereditary peerage available and went at once, and if Healey's own rather high-flown account of his diffidence may be accepted, had he not walked away, the political career of Denis Healey might not have happened.

Leeds South-East was working class and heavily Irish; Leeds itself was a generally cosmopolitan city with a large Jewish population, mostly in the north, and an Indian–Pakistani population starting to arrive. The most devoted and driving personality in Leeds Labour politics for many years would be Ashok Bannerjee, who had come not only from India but via the university, where he lectured in electrical engineering. Leeds is the home of the most esteemed piano contest in the world, the creation of a local music teacher, Fanny Waterman, and the then Countess of Harewood. The Harewoods are library squires of distinction seriously interested in the city. The university is a real one and a future Vice-Chancellor would be the admired, liberal and scholarly former Tory Minister Edward Boyle. MPs included national figures, not just Healey but Alice Bacon, the handy Charlie Pannel, at a later date Merlyn Rees, the fine and anxious mind of Keith Joseph and of course Hugh Gaitskell. The single most important business was probably Montague Burton, the wholesale tailor; and the then head of the Burton family was in a quiet way a Labour supporter.

Diversity meant that there was some jealous looking out for undue influence by any one group. As noted, the Catholic Bishop, John Carmel Heenan, later Cardinal of Westminster, informed Denis of the date of John William Healey's apostasy, a card-index knowledgeability which reminded the candidate too much of the Soviet Union. Catholic influence and interest in many Labour seats was a factor, and the strongest candidate, John Rafferty, may have commanded clerical goodwill. Certainly Rafferty expected to win and, in a four-candidate contest, finished 20–10 ahead of Healey, who had been nominated by Poale Zion, the affiliated Jewish body. But Rafferty did not have an absolute majority.

Transport House, which had been running its own candidate and wasn't pleased with Healey, ordered a new poll to break the deadlock and Healey emerged as the clear winner. The contest was meant to be a replica of the first with identical membership. The swing is probably best seen in terms of Rafferty polling his absolute maximum but having spread around the other candidates a vote which was succinctly anti-Rafferty. Whether or not this was also a case of a Catholic candidacy against the other options is not clear. Whatever the components, Healey collected. For some time afterwards, Rafferty, a councillor with good newspaper connections, was resentful and threatened recriminations. But, according to Douglas Gabb, secretary–agent at this

time and a long-term ally and friend of Healey, Rafferty ultimately accepted that his opponent was popular and doing good
work and made his peace.

Gabb, an astute man who knows to paste the odd poster
upside down to attract attention, also knows more about Leeds
than most people, having been born there in 1920 and worked
as an engineer there, latterly at the university laboratories. The
son of a soldier and a theatre usherette, he has been poor,
paraded before his class by a teacher as the beneficiary of a
charity, 'Boots for the Bairns'. He has memories of terrible
housing and rotten poverty and remembers the courts on York
Street where sanitation amounted to throwing effluent into a
yard and hoping for rain.

Gabb's view of Healey is deeply sympathetic, but it had to be
won. He held, understandably enough, very left-wing views in
the early fifties. But there was never a social barrier. He speaks
with admiration of the way Healey handled his public. 'In the
working men's clubs,' he says, 'I used to introduce him to
somebody and then pull back.' The clubs were not party places;
one could not count on support. 'But,' says Douglas, 'he just
talked naturally and easily with anyone, readily getting into
fierce arguments where Hugh Gaitskell usually had a ring of
Labour Party people around him.'

He recalls the regular monthly surgeries, the availability and
the way Edna did what Leeds expected, turned up at key times
and was very nice, but concentrated on bringing up three
children. (Denis is also adept to the present day at the well-
judged friendly plug: 'Frank Child, the tailor,' says the local
paper, 'is retiring.' Frank was the former apprentice of Leslie
Rosen, another former pillar of the local party: 'Always bought
my suits there,' says Denis to the reporter.) But in those early
days of shortages and regulation, local demands through agent
or MP included those for licences to make ice-cream and buy
extra sugar and flour and, in Douglas's recollection, the four-
year-old National Health Service had not fully bitten and many
people needed to be told of their entitlements.

The constituency would also change, in the early sixties
becoming Leeds East, taking in the great Seacroft Estate while
giving up Hunslet in the south. Whatever its shape, and despite
the cultural strands and the university in another part of the city,
it constituted a world away from the circuit of ministers and
general secretaries and defence experts, symposia and cosmic
discussion. It was a hard, poor place which would by steady but

not obvious degrees get less poor, less hard, a very good constituency for a high-ranking minister to return to. In all the travails of left-wing lurches, the rise of Bennery and militant unionism, Healey's position, won in January 1952 and confirmed at the by-election in February, would not be disputed. He did not make the ardent ritual of Leeds East that Butler did of Saffron Walden, but he knew it, looked after it, had plenty of friends there and shifted about only as the Boundary Commission required him to.

The Labour politics he was entering nationally in 1952 were exceptionally unpleasant but not boring. Aneurin Bevan had resigned from the Cabinet in the previous year. Bevanism constituted a party within a party, but quite what Bevanism was, was something else. The quarrel had come ostensibly about small charges on Health Service goods, but more credibly out of the defence requirements which had indirectly precipitated them and, most convincingly of all, from the jealousies of ministers. Gaitskell had earlier succeeded to the Exchequer, now Morrison took on the Foreign Office from the dying Ernest Bevin (who would sooner have had anyone else, including Nye Bevan, in the job). This omission, along with Gaitskell's perhaps calculated quarrel over prescription charges, contributed to Bevan's 1951 resignation. The Third Force people (of whom Bevan was not one), much worked on by Soviet-friendly people, declared a dividend on Bevan's personal affront and acquired for a short time an incontestably first-rate champion.

Later in that same year, 1952, a left-wing group would sweep aside the established leadership, Morrison, Dalton and Gaitskell, in the constituency section for the national executive. The Party Conference at Morecambe at which this vote was announced was outstandingly unpleasant, the worst conference of the previous 25 years 'for hatred and bad temper', Hugh Dalton thought it. En route back from Morecambe, Hugh Gaitskell had paused at Stalybridge to make a speech, brave as always and contemptuous of tact as often. He had come from the unpleasantness of Bevan's supporters in their exultancy and he was very fed up with the sniffing malice of Kingsley Martin, Editor of the *New Statesman*. This explains phrases like 'end mob rule by a group of frustrated journalists' and 'a stream of grossly misleading propaganda with poisonous innuendos and malicious attacks on Attlee, Morrison and the rest of us', and above all a reference to 'the Communist element within the constituency parties'. This 'element' had been put at a sixth:

'That figure may well be too high. But if it should be one tenth or even one twentieth, it is a most shocking state of affairs . . .' It sounds like another age, but then, it was another age.

Dalton wrote of there being 'more hatred and love of hatred in our party than I can ever remember. Nye's defects of character are growing on him. Arrogance, conceit and personal animosities . . . now Mikardo and Co. are trying to undermine non-Bevanite MPs in their constituencies.'

The similarities with the Conservatives at present, a similar time of exhaustion, recrimination and open conspiracy, are obvious. The cliché about one's enemies being on this side and opponents opposite is usually glib and inaccurate. But in these two cases 'enemy' is the only word to describe the way two groups of party members saw one another. Healey rather enjoyed this sort of thing. At Morecambe he described Bevan's anti-Americanism as 'jingoism with an inferiority complex'. But he quotes a piece he wrote at the time for his Norwegian outlet, *Arbeiderbladet*, which stresses that further nationalisation had few friends, that 'further soaking the rich will no longer benefit the poor to any extent', and interestingly, 'Even among Labour economists there is a growing revolt against physical controls in favour of the price mechanism. A policy based on the class war cannot have a wide appeal when the difference between classes is so small as Labour has made it.' That has an oddly modern ring to it, though without, thankfully, the prose style of 'New Labour'.

In six years of government, Labour had done magnificent things. It had lost office partly through the physical exhaustion or death of its leaders – both Cripps and Bevin were gone – and partly through the fluke of an election which gave them a plurality of votes and a minority of seats. They needed consolidation, John Biffen's enraging word to Mrs Thatcher, and adjustment to the plateau onto which society was coming, largely through their efforts. They needed to say, 'Look what we have achieved. Let's now accommodate ourselves to it over a slow quiet period of settling down.' Instead, a quarrel about defence and personalities had turned Labour in on itself. Dalton's splendid phrase 'hatred and love of hatred' took over.

Labour were in opposition because they did not know how to shift from the high-energy mode in which they enacted ideas largely put together in their last long era in the wilderness. They never settled to bedding down comfortably. They missed the chance of becoming a natural party of government because they were not there to take the credit for those fortuitous returns upon steady government which would have fallen to a pro-longed Gaitskell chancellorship as they did fall during Butler's stewardship. They did not hang around for the terms of trade to turn because the patriotic devotion of Attlee, Bevin, Gaitskell and the rest demanded sacrifices for defence expenditure, that 11 per cent of GDP cited in the first section of this book. The stresses of the quarrel hit a physically tired party, exacerbated personality conflicts and abraided ambitions.

The party Healey was entering, ironically as chief defence and foreign affairs technician, had crippled its long-term useful future by giving up to party what was meant for government. It was a meaningless sacrifice. Bevan did not favour leaving NATO, quarrelling in any serious way with the United States or imposing any distinguishably more Socialist or levelling regime on the country. And in a moving Indian summer of conciliation the real Bevan, pragmatic, graceful and bewitching in argument, came together with a Gaitskell shedding much of his prickly righteousness. We had a short demonstration in the years after Suez and before Bevan's death of what had been lost before.

But in an interim long enough to brand deep enmities, the naïve Left, who derided an office of which they had no prospect, and the essentially vicious, in-mourning-for-Stalin Left both flourished and were given consequence outside the normal business of governing and choosing. (Pierre Mendes-France's favourite quotation, given currency at about this time, said that 'to govern is to choose'.) Labour, by retreating almost happily from the one, had no compelling need to do the other and debouched into a sandpit of faction.

All that a practical and useful person like Healey could do was to continue his education and, as he modestly sees it, extend the education of others. 'Gaitskell took my views on foreign policy seriously. I think I helped to form his position on Suez, the Common Market, Russia and the atomic bomb.' If that is a touch breathtaking, one might cite Gaitskell's first biographer. Philip Williams describes Healey and Alfred Robens working with Crossman and Kenneth Younger on his foreign policy ideas. He spoke with Healey separately from another group which included the young Tony Benn. That group he found 'much too pro-Nasser and equivocal about Israel', in Williams' phrase. (Gaitskell was also staggered by what he saw as the depths of Benn's naïvety and poor judgment.) The outcome was a statement which may reflect Healey distinguishing between legal action against a clearly offside Nasser and force, which 'could not be used and should not be used unless there was real justification for it ... that [control] should be through the United Nations and that Russia should be asked to the conference'.

As Williams points out, Healey also made from the backbenches the first speech flatly against the 'hypocritical and disingenuous ultimatum', as Randolph Churchill called it, of 29 October 1956. (Ironically, at that time Bevan, who described Nasser as 'a thug', was in terms of sympathies nearest to a moderate Conservative view that Eden had miscalculated in a good cause.) But Gaitskell and Healey were both truly shocked by Eden's conduct in colluding with the French and Israelis, and angered far beyond the call of Opposition disapproval. Healey asked the Speaker if he 'could please tell me what is the Parliamentary expression which comes closest to expressing the meaning of the word "liar" '.

As long as the operative word in that startling statement about forming Gaitskell's opinion is 'helped', it is fair enough. Healey was 35 when he entered Parliament. He did not come in as a routine backbencher, but as the Party's highly experienced officer on foreign affairs. By the time he was helping Gaitskell over the EEC, where his coolness fitted well with Gaitskell's own romantic post-imperial affections for the Commonwealth, he was a member of the Shadow Cabinet. He had made his first frontbench speech in 1954, two years after entering Parliament, and would be elected to the Shadow Cabinet in 1959. For all that, having once been an adviser feeding in information and making glosses upon it, he went on being and doing just that, indispensable, ready when called upon, a sort of stroppy West Riding Jeeves.

Healey writes with fervour about the year 1956, time of the Hungarian rising as well as Suez. He speaks of pulling his car into a lay-by near York when his radio caught the broadcast for help coming out of Budapest as the Soviet tanks entered the city, too emotionally affected to trust himself on the road. Suez ended his time as a stiff, dull speaker, a bureaucrat with words. Passion and aggression entered his speeches and the capacity to give offence, witness the lexicographical inquiry, came into its own.

It is said truly enough that Healey drops names but that he drops them having taken the trouble to know the people whose names they are. There was not too much interest in the fifties, less in the sixties, for the victims of Stalin's system, many of whom are such

Healey names. The consciousness of a monstrous empire, of crimes against unspecified numbers of people in countries as far away as Czechoslovakia was to Chamberlain very slight.

Every now and again some grim act would occur, the murder of Masaryk in the first Czech *putsch*, the tanks in Budapest, the events of 1968 in Prague, but most opinion, very much including Conservative opinion, was apathetic or ignorant or cynical or all three. A combination of Robert Conquest's book *The Great Terror*, the early books of Solzhenitsyn compounded by his exile and finally the treatment of Academician Sakharov would cause the Soviet Union, very late – from about 1977 onwards – to get a bad press, very much at the time that its own call on confidence and power began to run out.

At the time when Healey was logging hours in Eastern Europe and noting which Socialist international contacts had gone to jail, been tortured or died, the cream of liberal indignation went into opposing the admittedly odious Senator McCarthy. But Healey's attitudes failed to fit any preconceived pattern because, although he was more unequivocally anti-Communist and aroused on behalf of faraway countries and peoples, he was pragmatically talking to the sort of people in the East who could be talked to.

There was a period before Hungary and again after it, though never altogether the same glad confident morning again, when imaginably, a demi-liberalising of the Communist world might just have proceeded further. It was the time of Khruschev's secret speech denouncing the crimes of Stalin. The fashionable *Observer*ish word before Hungary was 'thaw'. The Gomulka Government, which came to office before the Budapest rising and survived it with Warsaw uninvaded, though it declined to a bad-tempered bloodless autocracy, aroused interest.

The Polish Foreign Minister, Adam Rapacki, wanted to fly a kite of his own, was not forbidden by the Soviets from doing so and it was thus suspected of being a Soviet promotion. It involved the military neutrality of Poland, Czechoslovakia, East Germany and West Germany. A response to this with Healey's fingerprints on it surfaced as the Gaitskell Plan. It launched a hundred thoughtful articles but came to nothing. There were to be no solutions except suppression and collapse, but Healey was a man of the thaw, an optimist who looked with interest at Khruschev, despite those savage things he remembered about him at the Scarborough conference.

He was to be an optimist again, memoiristically, about

Gorbachev whom, writing in 1988, he compares with
Khruschev. Gorbachev went to nothing because he had more
vanity than pride, attempted rather pathetically to please the
Americans, drove soft bargains abroad and was dismantled at
home. But Healey was perfectly right, in the teeth of much
looking under the carpet for wires and assumptions of Soviet
ploys, to think him entirely sincere – too sincere for his own and
arguably Russia's good. And Healey's optimistic assumptions
about Khruschev also seem right down the defile of 40 years.

Khruschev had lived through and co-operated in the
unhinged criminality of the *Stalinchina*, obliged in the Ukraine
to kill more than cats. But his efforts at accommodation look
like a liberal interlude, an attempt to make contact. And the
language of co-existence need not be seen, as twitchily it was by
intelligence people and professional cold warriors, as a ploy.
Living from hand to mouth, engaging in foolish adventures like
the missiles in Cuba, and choosing over Hungary between
repression and prospective collapse, Khruschev would finally be
ousted and replaced by a long period of prolonged reaction and
sterility after which Gorbachev would commence a total and
unintelligent embrace of America. Accepting the broad goodwill
of both men might be optimistic, but the judgment wasn't
actually wrong. And optimism, as we shall see, is a motif with
Denis Healey.

The period of CND, of renewed left-wing assault, which
followed defeat in 1959 and the death of Aneurin Bevan in
1960, kept all Healey's subjects in focus and would have made
him an adversarial politician even without his own genius for
calling spades bloody shovels. Labour would lose in 1959
largely because the Government had got over its headline
economic problems of 1957 and replaced them with a headline
lull. The crass modern notion of the 'feelgood factor' flourished
unnamed, while Gaitskell stumbled into a tax promise he
shouldn't have made. Conservatism, in the full sense of things
being all right and thus not needing to be changed, rode high at
a level it would never touch again. Labour's good behaviour was
noted, but not thought sufficient reason for electing it. Life was
better with the Conservatives without the Conservatives
knowing too much about it.

Clearly for Labour, with a deficit of 100 and five years further
exile, the time had come for another quarrel. CND, an odd
combination of anxiety, self-pity, that 'tinge of Christian feeling'
which Orwell had identified, and with all the Lefts tagging onto

it, became the fashionable, irresistible, wittering thing. Its effect upon local activists is best summed up in the action of Richard Marsh, an amusing politician who would later become a notably conservative Conservative in the Lords, wearing to his selection conference in Greenwich the ubiquitous semaphore lapel button of CND. As he observed, that stopped people asking him where he stood on CND, to which the answer was 'Foursquare against it.'

Two quick deaths atop the hierarchy of the Transport Workers' Union brought Frank Cousins to the command of a structure designed by Ernest Bevin to be marginally less democratic than the Vatican. Cousins was decent, pedestrian, honourable, not clever and in a moaning sort of way left-wing. His ascent also shifted above a million votes from support of the leadership. All that Gaitskell could do was argue back and then, when really pinned to the wall, make a magnificent statement of defiance. The campaign argued that nuclear weapons were wicked and that we, the British, shouldn't have them. By unacknowledged extension, it said that the Soviet Union was all right really and that the Americans, present in a military role, should as it was sweetly put, 'go home'.

This was the America not of Gingrich or Jesse Helms, but of Eisenhower shading into Kennedy. Now the Labour leadership – Gaitskell, Crosland, Jenkins, Healey and virtually all the university-educated element – were pro this America in ways entirely different from Mrs Thatcher's devotion to another US whose worst qualities so attracted her. The United States was very much a touchstone of Labour politics at this time and Healey, of all Labour politicians, had the widest network of US political friends – in Congress, in the State Department and the Department of Defense. (After Suez, when contacts at the Foreign Office and Conservative Party were severed for a while, even the CIA, again a more liberal body at that time, was briefly obliged to route its envoy, Kim Roosevelt, through Denis Healey, not yet in Labour's Shadow Cabinet.)

Accordingly, the CND battle was a peculiarly bitter affair. It went on to be won in the traditional ways of the Labour Party: a large union delegation which had voted undemocratically one way in 1960 was cajoled in corridors and at mandating meetings in 1961 into voting undemocratically the other way. But as Gaitskell had conducted himself with notable courage and flair, Labour emerged looking good and for once coherent.

We know it only in outline and as politics, while being hazy about the devil detail. As Healey himself points out, the recollection that Gaitskell at Scarborough was fighting, fighting and fighting again for an independent British nuclear deterrent is wrong. CND itself had begun in 1957 in the precise terms of its name: the Campaign for Nuclear Disarmament, which is to say general, international, consensual disarmament, what came to be known as multilateralism. In the usual exponential way of the British Left, this became unilateral British disarmament, then 'Britain out of NATO', then 'America out of Britain'.

There existed a perfectly intelligent and intelligible case for Britain divesting herself of the independent deterrent, its not being independent in any coherent sense being the crux. Again, Healey argued, serious Conservatives – Antony Head, Peter Thorneycroft, Nigel Birch and Aubrey Jones – had all been cool about the British private weapon on the grounds that cost and uncertain field of use made ownership different in kind from maintaining the independent lawnmower. The lawnmower has immediate local application, can generally be afforded and competently contains a threat readily recognised by the rest of the household; the consequences of a unilateral giving up of the lawnmower are not hypothetical.

The British weapons system cost money and bled other parts of the services, particularly conventional forces, and the tripwire aspect of war was one heightened by nuclear weapons exactly as the saving delay was diminished by the absence of soldiers and sailors. Healey at this time was pamphleteering again. His Fabian publication 'The Race against the H Bomb' was another good example of Healey optimism. He argues that the credibility of both sides should be taken as read, especially as understood by each other, and that their problem was to persuade the neighbours. Which since Russia had no one to persuade, was a polite way of saying that the US had to persuade doubting Europeans that her politicians would keep their nerve or maintain their interest. That pamphlet casts an interesting light on the CND debate within Labour politics.

CND took a purist position, a sort of *de facto* pacifist line since nuclear weapons were assumed to be the only ones with any contemporary meaning. It wished to be rid of the corrupting taint not just of own defence, but also of associated defence with the near neighbours and defence by the large, armed, distant neighbour.

Healey, and one may read Gaitskell as being in general agreement, was saying:

Having our own nuclear weapon is probably not useful, but since there are Soviet nuclear weapons, we in Europe wish to be defended against them by America's ownership of them and believable commitment to us. We don't doubt America's means. She doesn't need more weapons to impress the Russians, but we would like to be sure that when the next crisis comes, she will be sufficiently interested and clear-spoken about defending us to be understood by the Russians. To that end, we need to maintain close relations with the Americans in effect as lobbyists, and that makes NATO essential.

Considerations of influences at the UN and in America came into the calculations. In practice, Britain would find herself across the sixties keeping nuclear weapons, reasons of *amour propre* and vanity quite apart, precisely because they were part of her credibility with the Americans. They were perhaps totems, so many thermo-nuclear phylacteries. Healey quotes the committee set up by President Kennedy which recommended a substantial improvement in NATO's conventional capability sufficient to stop anything but a comprehensive Soviet invasion while calling for a phase-out by Britain and France of their independent nuclear weapons. This was joined with the judgment that the Skybolt stand-off missile, upon which Europe and its V-bombers had been relying, should be given up if it were not intended for defence of the US alone. The US Air Force did not want Skybolt, and Kennedy, without telling his allies, cancelled it.

It was at this point that Macmillan did his bit about being Greeks to the Romans – Greeks bearing requests – with a mixture of kitsch, tears and allusions to his American mother and to the 'special relationship'. Macmillan was the sort of Greek to beware of. Kennedy, soft-talked and flattered, let us have Polaris, to the annoyance of his own advisers, headed by Robert McNamara. Accordingly, in the teeth of a major policy-making decision and effectively by caprice, the British independent deterrent, not British, not independent and only incrementally a deterrent, found indefinite continuance. But it kept America involved with the people she had nearly overlooked.

Labour, in its democratic arguing-about-everything way, did not have an eye on the ball. As far as Healey and the consensus of soldiers and experts he could call up were concerned, Polaris was not the issue. What mattered was to replace the nuclear tripwire and strengthen conventional defence, not for resisting the all-out attack which wasn't expected and couldn't be stopped, but to police any crisis and make it a longer and thus safer crisis.

Healey would henceforth spend a lot more time learning – learning, he believes, largely what *not* to think – from American think tanks and crisis-management corporations, whose theoretical capacity for letting blood disturbed him, and coming to know senior British military like Sir John Slessor and Sir Ralph Cochrane, whom he found more congenial and better rooted on this planet. But what Macmillan had done would not be undone. Polaris had been ordered and Healey, after taking delivery, would have to live with it as Secretary of Defence.

CHAPTER FOUR

Before Healey could become Defence Secretary, Hugh Gaitskell would die. His replacement, Harold Wilson, never had been and did not become someone Healey liked, trusted or respected. His selection over George Brown – alcoholic, emotionally fraught, but brilliant and so often right in his policy judgments – looks to have been inevitable. But Wilson's conduct had long been noted and Healey knew roughly what to expect.

A latecoming joiner of the Labour Party (having been a nominal Liberal at Oxford), Wilson had moved from right-wing acts like the bonfire of controls at the Board of Trade, to left-wing ones like resignation with Bevan and Freeman over prescription charges to help pay rearmament bills. Then he had reverted to the right, taking Bevan's place on the NEC in 1954. In a final twist in 1960, he stood for the leadership against Gaitskell after the Scarborough fight. 'All rising to a great place,' said Francis Bacon, 'is by a winding stair.' Wilson's career was a ziggurat.

What was most held against him was that he had not been a unilateralist. Conviction simply didn't come into his 1960 candidacy. What, with deeper knowledge of the man, might have been a more damaging point was that he was not an assassin either. In the dismal world of putting down markers and watching one's rating, Wilson had been fearful that the threatened candidacy of Anthony Greenwood, as ephemeral and inconsiderable a politician as they come, might have damaged his standing. Royalty fretting over highnessdom and precedence could not cut a smaller figure.

Wilson's tragedy was that he brought to an outstanding intelligence – starred congratulatory first and very good economic judgment – a combination of lonely, untrusting ambition and a craving to please. He was a kindly and fearful person and there is a story which, if true, says everything about that apprehension. Allegedly, a young member, one of the 1966 intake whom Wilson had twitted at a parliamentary Labour Party meeting for his right-wing views, accosted him in the cloisters and said, 'Prime Minister, unless you apologise for your disgraceful attack on me, I shall never speak to you again.' The chutzpah attributed here to David Owen was matched by the nerveless passivity of Wilson in immediately finding him a post as a PPS, thus enabling him to commence an ascent to the point from which he would fling himself.

Neither villain nor hero, Wilson lacked the dimensions of his intelligence. He was born to be someone else's indispensable technician. Given his grasp of problems, and not obliged to make the moral decisions, he might, after two terms as Chancellor under a resolute leader, have been remembered with simple admiration and had us wondering what sort of prime minister he might have been.

Whatever Healey's criticisms of Gaitskell and lack of full Frognal Set status, there was warmth and regard between them. The advent of Wilson deepened Healey's own identity as a technician. Wilson would get the best possible practical advice. But the great adversarial politics, what Othello called 'the big wars', were over for now. Wilson had no intention of conceding anything that mattered to unilateralists or opponents of the military. On the contrary, he was going to be ardently patriotic in the usual Labour-in-office way. But there would be economies and it would be the Secretary for Defence's pleasure to find them. Healey would not get rid of Polaris in this mood of affirmation, but he could get on with the job of reorganising the administration of the forces which had been growing in the minds of defence specialists in both major parties. He would come in time to think that terminating Polaris for non-CND reasons might have been simple economy. He had benefited at the very start of his stewardship from a briefing at the hands of Peter Thorneycroft and started with non-partisan guidance on the problems that Conservative ministers had faced.

Defence has never been a popular job with Labour politicians, nor one thought good for the career, but between 1964 and 1970, it was actually a cool, rational, administratively minded sort of place, the peacetime equivalent of a good war. Oddly, the political sting had been drawn from the debate between parties. Conservative rhetoric against Labour, the unsound and semi-pacifist, was an empty ritual, though it is favoured to this day by the stupider backbenchers. The Tories had struggled with an involvement which had to be kept up by way of an independent deterrent which the sharpest of them saw to be superfluous and all Treasury ministers knew to be intolerably expensive. The Conservatives had got through nine secretaries of defence in 13 years and a melancholy litany of hardware: Blue Water, Sea Slug, Blue Streak, sad slogans with their tattered, bright, chatty names, all discontinued at fearful loss, 26 projects dropped at a cost of £300 million at the values of 30 years ago. (By 1967, after two and a half years of Healey, the figures were 32 cancellations at a cost of $500 million, but the pipeline had been long and full.) There was an unsolved problem about major aircraft and the pressing need to reorganise the entire ministerial structure so as to subordinate the expensively competing service interests.

Serious Conservative opinion which knew about detailed defence logistical problems was more interested in them and their solution than anything else. The left wing of the Labour Party disapproved of defence in principle and would have loved to cut *ad liberandum*. But the consensus was for cutting of an intelligent sort in pursuit of value for money, so to a degree the Minister was going with the grain of his party.

In fairness to predecessors, Healey was taking up administrative reforms Peter Thorneycroft had set in motion. Professor Michael Howard, in his RUSI pamphlet 'The Central Organisation of Defence', makes this point, but in ways most gratifying to Healey. 'Reforming ministers before Cardwell were not always given full credit either,' he says. As Edward Cardwell became a by-word for reform when he pulled the British Army out of a pageant of sacred 18th-century thinking suitable for the conflicts of 60 years before, the comparison from an outstanding military historian is a high honour.

It was broadly agreed within the Ministry of Defence, and had been from the late fifties onward, that the armed forces could not continue as Army, Navy and Air Force run by separate ministers – War, First Lord, Air Minister. The forces, co-operating semi-voluntarily, were duplicating orders, alternately squabbling with each other and operating a ring by which, for prearranged concessions, one optimistic, expensive idea would be nodded through in turn for another, worse idea from a conniving and bought-off brother service.

Defence had been hellishly expensive, made worse by Gaitskell's earnest commitment to Korea. But despite the Conservatives being less profligately 'sound' on defence, spending on it was still an inexcusable 6.6 per cent in 1964. For a country with mediocre growth rate this was an intolerable burden. Beyond that, complex weapons systems combined with an inflation in military materiel costs out of all proportion to the too-high general inflation. The £3 million aircraft-carrier which had gone up to £20 million, would by the mid-sixties be the smaller, less ambitious through-deck cruiser costing £60 million; transport planes costing £160,000 in 1950 would cost £3 million by the time Healey took over.

Ministers of defence, old style, were trapped between a justified Treasury determination to screw down appropriations and the mounting costs of what their services through the service ministries called for. Duncan Sandys, Macmillan's appointment to Defence (and Macmillan had been a very frustrated Defence Secretary himself), produced the White Paper of 1957. This chiefly involved giving a British nuclear deterrent first and second priority over everything, but understanding that deterrent was all it could be. Given nuclear war, we couldn't be defended and Sandys acknowledged as much. Whether the steps he took then quite made sense is more doubtful.

Sandys was a strange figure – driving, reforming, laboriously slow-minded and not desperately scrupulous, but different from the ministerial norm and with an instinct for the full picture. He fiddled figures, ignoring his own committee under General Hull, or rather mis-stating its report so as to justify a minimum safe lower total of men for a professional army. He had wanted to abolish conscription. The Hull Report gave a figure, 200,000, which was higher than he thought he could recruit, so he announced 165,000 as the minimum. Ballistic missiles would in due course replace the V-bomber squads which would have to do a stamp-edging act until then. The British, in coping with the financial military quandary, led the world in elastic stamp-edging.

With all his faults and mistakes, Sandys was a creative reforming Minister and he attempted next to change the departmental structure. But the Defence Board, which he had established to bring civil and military elements into consultation, came to nothing and he would be bundled on and out by Harold Macmillan who, like Harold Wilson, had an itchy shuffling finger, a distrust for colleagues getting overinfluential and an impulse to meddle. Not letting Wilson shift him despite two attempts was one of Healey's great achievements since it was the condition precedent to his reforms going through in the shape he planned.

As Professor Howard says, writing contemporaneously about Healey in 1970, 'He is an expert in his subject; he has been longer in his chair than any of his colleagues (and in Whitehall longevity confers a quasi-patriarchal authority); and he is impatient of formalities. If he wants a decision, he assembles his men and gets it.' The purpose of reform was, if not precisely to gain such facility, then its inevitable consequence if the transformation were to be fully accomplished.

Sandys had been taking sighting shots at reform and one of the unstated reasons for the abortion by Macmillan of the Defence Board was that, fully effective, it would have strengthened the hand, not just of Sandys and any successor but of the next Chief of Defence Staff, in this case the First Sea Lord. Earl Mountbatten was a man of talents which have been argued over, charm of a operetta-tenor sort, ambition to make a pharaoh catch breath, a vanity better confined to the catwalk and snake-in-the-grass tendencies. He had also fascinated and bewitched the dull-minded royal family upon whom he was eager to impose his family name. Any centralising of the structures which put more power into the hands of 'Dickie' was a centralising which quite reform-minded people felt they could happily delay. The Defence Board which Sandys told the Commons would 'have a most valuable and important part to play as a forum for the discussion of military policy and inter-service problems' didn't. And very specific express powers were laid down in respect of the CDS, leaving him as glorified minutes secretary to his Minister of the concerns of the chiefs of staff.

What Sandys left to Healey by way of his successors, the stand-pat Harold Watkinson and the cautiously reforming Peter Thorneycroft, was the ballistic-missile inheritance, warhead delivery systems whose costs got out of control often ahead of indications of their unsuitability. Polaris, of course, worked – almost too well, lasting long enough to let Britain in for Chevaline and Trident. He also bequeathed him Mountbatten. And in some ways Healey had the best of Mountbatten. The CDS had never stopped pushing for administrative reform, having in his time commanded men and equipment from all three services. He lobbied more successfully than he had run his ship, the *Kelly*, whose collision with another immediately after repairs followed the example of the aristocratic admiral in *Kind Hearts and Coronets*: 'Hard to port.' 'Surely, sir, you mean starboard?' 'Damn it, I said "port".'

Left to himself, Mountbatten would have had the Chief of the Defence Staff (Prop. L. Mountbatten) running that staff and its policy. The chiefs to whom he now reported would report to him and would cease to be professional heads of their services. That work would be done by three inspectors-general, a nice touch from a man inexpressibly grateful to be the great-nephew of the last Tsarina. It was the most extreme proposal for reform and created most grief and outrage among the service chiefs and their juniors while giving maximum purchase specifically to the Ministry of Defence itself, a sharing of stolen sweets which represented excellent policy for Mountbatten.

The beauty of such extreme proposals was that other people might subsequently temper and modify them and still outrun in radical change anything that had looked likely when the argument started. Accordingly, Generals Lord Ismay and Sir Ian Jacob began work, at Macmillan's request, in 1963 – 20 months before Healey took over – on a report completed in six weeks which indeed tempered Mountbatten, but moved sharply on. The abolition of the chiefs of staff was dropped and actual service departments would survive, though on a temporary basis, but the report did accept that the MoD would run the service ministries, with the Minister working directly through a small central staff, and that those service ministries which would be downgraded should be headed by junior ministers.

They also, going beyond Mountbatten (and Healey), wanted a single united service with common insignia and uniform. Whitehall-watchers might feel that such horror-comic material was put in expressly to be taken out when the reforms that mattered might be pushed through as a compromise. The detachable unit built into a controversial programme expressly for painless deletion as a prefabricated concession is well enough known. And in a force still, in 1997, arguing about cap badges, it cannot have been seriously intended.

In July 1963 Thorneycroft, having turned most of Ismay–Jacob into legislation, presented it to Parliament. There were to be only ministers of state running the individual services inside the Ministry of Defence and co-ordinating 'all questions of policy and administration which concern the fighting services as the instruments of an effective strategy'. In Whitehall the fighting services would fight no more. There would also be something called the Committee on Defence and Overseas Policy involving a body of senior officials and relevant Cabinet ministers which service ministers would attend only if asked. Like its predecessor, the Defence Board, it would come to little, though it survived a long time. But Healey did find himself in 1964 as part of a continuum and he inherited an official, Henry Hardman, strongly associated with the reforms.

His own first acts were to give general and vague powers to subordinate ministers. Christopher Mayhew at the Navy was given personnel and logistics. Lord Shackleton, Air Force, had research, development and production for all three forces and the defence budget as a whole. Unlucky Fred Mulley, Army, got 'matters of international policy relating to defence', as if Healey didn't intend to take charge of all that himself. Frank Cooper, later Permanent Under-Secretary at Defence and rising near the top at this time, observes uncensoriously, 'Denis liked the plums. Anything interesting, exotic, exciting, difficult – his hand would go out to grab it.'

He would, over his six years, have some able colleagues: Mulley, who was highly informed about NATO, Gerry Reynolds, a big amusing personality whose death at 42 surely stopped a Cabinet career, and an assertive young man, thought puppyish by the admirals, according to Cooper, named David Owen. None of them much interested the preoccupied Secretary of State, who might at this point have been developing a cadre of Healey liverymen but seems hardly to have noticed them. 'He didn't think much of junior ministers,' says Frank Cooper. 'Always wondered what they were for or what they were up to.' One can only mark and contrast the way Roy Jenkins brought on, fostered and was rewarded by Dick Taverne, Bill Rodgers and a set of long-term supporters.

The first draft of a ministerial pyramid wasn't the best of Healey's ideas. According to Howard, the designated responsibilities were 'spheres of concern' with no clear indication of who would take decisions. But in 1967, Healey took the decisive step of downgrading the service ministerial headship from Minister of State to Parliamentary Under-Secretary. The pride, pomp and circumstance of Secretary for War or First Lord of the Admiralty was reduced to oversight by a pushy junior. Actual responsibility went to two Ministers of State, one handling equipment, the other serving what was called 'administration' and covered troops and logistics. Both posts had trans-service responsibilities. And in the White Paper of 1970, even the shrunken PUSs were to be sacrificed.

Below the ministerial changes came a shift of responsibility within the civil service. The old notion of Whitehall military empires engaged upon permanent manoeuvres depended upon three civil service organisations. The Permanent Under-Secretary was, under Healey, to become very powerful indeed. The service departments had their 'second under-secretaries', as they were called but, even before they were scrapped in 1967, these were clearly subordinated to the Permanent Under-Secretary.

Responsibility for a service now stood with a Deputy Under-Secretary, which may not mean much to us, but in Whitehall spoke crêpe and funeral mutes. It didn't come with financial control and was no longer effective head of its own civil servants. In due course, the job would rate only an Assistant Under-Secretary – Vauxhall Conference status.

Finally, the civil servants coming into the department lost their old defence and services exclusivity. They were part of routine circulation of bodies. Para-regimentalism for civilians was being broken. By 1970, Healey had created five deputy under-secretaries, one for personnel and logistics (troops and transport), one for civilian management, one for finance, one for policy and programmes and one for equipment. A hostile critic might murmur things about the Habsburg Empire or the French Ministry of Education, such was the degree of centralisation. A Conservative keen to reduce civil service numbers might notice that the HQ staffs at the Ministry of Defence between 1963 and 1970 fell from 24,083 to 16,198, an increase of 5,000 at the central department having been massively overcompensated for by a fall of 13,000 in the service sections.

But control does not, or should not, exist for control's sake. Money is going to be spent by the Government, enormous amounts of it. It would be nice for Government to decide more about how much and on what. One vital development was the forward analysis of defence costs, something which might have saved us the travails of Blue Water. The idea being, as Michael Howard puts it, a simple one: to measure not simply what forces cost but what they do, so as to ask questions about cost-effectiveness.

Defence expenditure taken away from jealous service concerns would now be measured under 14 headings – nuclear, combat, European ground forces, research and development and training among them. Incidentally, the margin of error introduced into costing was called, with unintentional irony, 'Wedge'. Such analyses owed much to the American example; Healey was genuinely close to Robert McNamara, a relationship which Frank Cooper certifies as one of mutual and equal esteem. Listening to their conversation, he says, you would have to remind yourself that the American was talking about half a dozen divisions while we were referring to a battalion.

The attempt to reform procurement would be only one step in a process of attempted reform which would have a lively renaissance under Michael Heseltine 20 years later. Governments as custodians of armies and navies are great purchasers and, historically, since the time of that other reformer Pepys, have been regarded as very great mugs. They are stolen from by pursers and quartermasters and sold to by contractors; periodically, attempts are made to interfere with a climate of larceny seen as a natural state of affairs.

The reason why ministers had been struggling since Macmillan to grapple with defence was that £500 million at the values of the pre-general inflationary late fifties had been blown on Blue Water and its moral equivalents – missiles that were never launched, metaphysical notions of weapons which would never come into actual crass existence. The Labour Party would do its own bit for what is called 'expenditure overshoot', but it would be done on the civil side with Mr Benn's Concorde, the heroic cost of which would represent a very impressive margin of error. The Ministry of Aviation and its Labour successor, the Ministry of Technology, were created to hive off the procurement of the old Air Ministry, something mixed up with responsibility for state involvement in the civil aircraft industry, an involvement called Concorde.

In describing what actually happened at the Ministry of Defence, one can be caught up in vast trailing vines of bureaucracy. The structures created by Healey and his predecessors were awesome and piled up such things as the Defence Research Committee, the Operational Requirements Committee and the Weapons Development Committee (on which at various points the Treasury, chiefs of staff, Ministry of Technology and even the Foreign Office had representation). Progress through them involved a staff target, then a feasibility study (possibly taken in two stages), a staff requirement and a project study before final submission of anything for approval.

The system, as set out on paper, has been described as 'an

unwinnable game of snakes and ladders'. But, as Healey himself remarked to a Commons select committee, 'One of the problems about public investigation of organisations is that the organisation is compelled, by the nature of the inquiry, to make its activities appear infinitely more formalised than they are in real life.' In practice, as Michael Howard puts it, 'the committees were *in terrorem*'. They existed to make 'chaps down the line . . . consult and study complete problems and not each of them go off and study things on his own with his particular blinkers on'.

It was a good system for an active minister like Healey to jump into by phone and ad hoc meeting to get done what he wanted done. The personality of Healey lay behind the demise of that grand imperial divan the Defence Council. Writing in 1970 in the present tense, Howard observed:

> *He is impatient of formalities; if he wants a decision, he assembles the men concerned and gets it; and his choice of men concerned is not always what protocol would suggest. He will not wait for information to come up through the usual channels, but dives down into the machine himself. Policy is therefore made not by regular meetings of any formal body, but by ad hoc groups.*

It may be that procedures learned on Swindon and Halifax railway stations in 1941 had their impact here.

'He was always looking,' says Frank Cooper, 'for somebody who was rather good. Damn the hierarchy, find a major-general or a captain RN who was good and he'd talk to him. He was terribly good at dipping through the hierarchy to work with people who had something to contribute.'

In practice, to do the job, Healey had to carry with him three officers, the Permanent Under-Secretary, the Chief Adviser (Projects and Research) and the Chief of Defence Staff. Healey was a Secretary of State preoccupied with policy. For administration and equipment, he had, most of the time, a Minister of State and an Under-Secretary. Significantly, there was no such high-placed official or politician for policy. As Howard crisply expresses it, 'There is no point therefore in seeking a focus of policy decision-making anywhere in the Ministry as at present constituted, outside the office of the Secretary of State.'

There was a risk in such concentration and in such end-of-the-phone management, that it could become a system of hand-to-mouth and under-informed decision making. The usefulness of committees was partly educational and partly one of 'settling policies for the long term and keeping them before the eyes of the decision makers. If this function is not at present needed, it is again because of the personality of the Secretary of State who himself has such a long-term view which he allows no one to forget.'

That crisp comment is a phenomenal compliment to a minister from a cool, astringent source. From being a skirmishing ground anxiously surveyed by a succession of ministers struggling to escape from the role of a presiding and interested spectator, the department had become a command structure with the Secretary of State in command. Behind the trellises of anagrams with their tasteful placement of appositional brackets, Healey had made himself a moderately benevolent despot, a highly mobile and flexible general of the kind giving orders from a helicopter. He was functioning at his strongest as a cerebral Ernest Bevin. But he could do so much only by being an expert in his own right. And as Frank Cooper says, 'He had an intellect that nobody else in that job had had ... He was the best Minister we'd had.'

The watchword was 'Technician shall speak unto technician.' No ordinarily conniving mover of pieces in the bureaucracy could gain that sort of mastery. When the Defence Select Committee Chairman spoke of the whole system as an impossible garden, Healey jovially replied that it was quite an easy garden to move about in once you were familiar with it. Frank Cooper reports meeting Edna Healey on Whitehall years later when they had not spoken for some time.

And how was Denis enjoying the Treasury? 'Oh Frank, you know Denis. It takes him a full two years to know more than everybody else in the Treasury about the economy.' He would also complain about Treasury forecasts compared with those of Defence, saying that they did for economic intelligence what the Boston Strangler did for door-to-door salesmen.

But no one is altogether a despot within the shifting factions of defence. A very typical Healey creation of which his memoirs speak lovingly and Professor Howard regretfully was PEG, the Programmes Evaluation Group. It involved briefing the Minister independently of formal service staff reporting and equipping him against the special pleading, united fronts and general bamboozling of the chiefs wanting something. The group was tight: a one-star officer from each service, a scientist and a civil servant chaired by the deputy to the Chief Adviser (Studies). It didn't work overall for the good old military reason that the chiefs of staff didn't like it. They didn't like it because they had no control over it. As Healey himself tells it, the one-star from the RAF, Neil Cameron, for whom he had vast esteem, would later be punished by the Air staff for his treasonable independence in serving PEG with a series of below-calibre appointments which pushed him to the point of resignation until rescued by Healey's personal intervention.

Cameron's offence had been to confirm that the RAF didn't actually need a long-range strike aircraft. The group was very much PEG o' my heart for the Minister. But in Howard's view, for it to have flourished and be established would have involved greater ruthlessness and readiness to antagonise the chiefs of staff than even Healey cared for. But he got a great deal from its short life: independent studies of the services communications network, the application of flexible response in Europe, the Navy's anti-submarine programme and the 15-year combat requirements of the RAF, all covered independently of the official service briefings.

PEG went because of the pressure and was replaced by a policy staff and an operations staff supposedly less alien to the chiefs, but not as much under their thumb as the former joint planning staffs. Howard's evaluation of these two groups, though very useful, didn't provide a dispassionate check on his professional advisers. They were part of the machine and so acceptable to it. As long as Healey, with his knowledge, his demand for more knowledge and his willingness to go out and extract what he wanted, was there, and as long as service heads had a working relationship with him, they would work. Also the chiefs were sufficiently scared of getting PEG back that they were reasonably co-operative over the policy staff. But, says Howard, 'An indifferent Secretary of State, a conservative Chiefs of Staff Committee, a second-rate ACDS (Policy) and the policy staff's usefulness could wither'.

Even with the centralised powers that he had obtained, Healey was more circumspect and cautious than legend has it. Cooper, an ardent admirer, nevertheless thinks that he was less decisive than he might have been and that the unhappiness of the military – the resignation of Admiral Caspar John and the self-abnegating refusal of field-marshal's rank by General Richard Hull, convinced that too much had been surrendered – was communicated to him. 'All secretaries of state,' he says, 'become aware that they have to keep the chiefs on side and Healey also became aware.'

His way of working is revealing. Unlike Butler he did not cut through swathes of work at speed. His style was a mixture of deep investigation and minor sloppiness. Cooper comments: 'If he thought something was important, he liked to take his time . . . he'd ask six questions and then read a paper through quickly and say, "I'm not happy about this." Then he'd want six more things answered smartly . . . He was very much a lateral thinker. He genuinely wanted to feel that he was right, that it had been done properly.' On the other hand, he 'would use, or even abuse, arguments to prove that he was right, but always on the basis that he had actually made up his mind that it *was* right'. 'He could,' says this civil servant, 'misquote statistics accidentally and deliberately. He had this quaint belief in his memory. Sometimes you would say, "He's got it wrong." Sometimes he just didn't understand figures as much as he thought he did. Then we all had to rally round and patch it up, somehow getting the correct answer parroted somewhere. It wasn't done with malice aforethought. It was just Denis being Denis, really.'

But such glitches didn't get in the way of decisive and right judgments. Together with Roy Jenkins at Aviation, Healey could pride himself on an early and comparatively straightforward decision. Lacking a replacement transport plane, something which had vexed Conservative ministers for a long time without getting a decision out of them, Healey and Jenkins decided to buy one, the Hercules. It was a third of the price of the British alternative, came into service four years earlier and would have a notably long service life. Healey, not too heavily involved at this time in Cabinet politics, complains that he might have done as much over the Phantom but for the patriotic impulse, always a risk with a Labour Cabinet, which made him run it with British engines and finance the contingent redesign, all of which wasted the savings made. Politically instructive is the later matter of the F1–11 which, in the dispute of 1968, Healey wanted to keep and Jenkins, as Chancellor, wanted to scrap. The Cabinet, as sometimes happened under Wilson, took a vote. It went narrowly against Healey, but so narrowly that he asked for and got time for further discussion. Having spotted the hesitation of Lord Longford, Healey went to work on him and brought him round. At the second Cabinet, however, the vote moved to a clear majority against the plane, for Jenkins, better at this sort of thing, had spent the interval shifting several ministers the other way.

It was always Healey's belief that things could be done by

reason, a perilous assumption perhaps brought about by reading too much Kant when young. Frank Cooper recalls a conversation before leaving the office one night with Healey and Laurence Wilson, a senior civil servant now dead. It was the time of the earlier TSR2 dispute which was snagging horribly on Cabinet anxieties. Wilson said, 'You know, you really must get one or two Cabinet members on your side.' Healey responded with some emphasis, 'The day I can't persuade my colleagues that the case is intellectually sound, I shall leave.' So, says Cooper, 'I said "Shall I go and get your bag?"'

The Harrier aircraft is a good illustration of the way Healey's mind worked. He had a general, indeed a specific brief to cut expenditure. The Harrier, then called the P1127 and nicknamed the 'Flying Bedstead', incurred his dubiety, and his instinct was to scrap it. He was backed by Solly Zuckerman on the grounds that after that impressive vertical take-off, it could only fly a very short distance. But Healey came round to thinking that although the facts and numbers of here and now indicated cancellation, the plane was so original, so different that it deserved special treatment. 'And then', says Cooper, 'he did play a bit of politics because Harold rather took to it. Meanwhile, Solly was persuaded because the RAF showed how it could be supported with spares and ammunition.' The point is that the case was argued at a high level in terms of research and development and potential. It was done in the teeth of all expedient, cost-cutting instincts.

Cooper's judgment is: 'Denis loved politics, loved meeting people, having arguments, but I don't think he was a politician's politician at all. He loved mastering something intellectually.' What the Harrier episode shows is the difference which an intellectually interested minister makes.

Cooper also feels that the urge to be prime minister and do the ingratiating necessary for it was never all that strong. He enjoyed, says Cooper, 'the part of politics that he was interested in and didn't want to do the part that he wasn't'. He lacked the instincts of a real politician to glad-hand. Cooper recollects directing his minister during a short stop at a military airfield in Borneo to a group of young soldiers from Yorkshire. Healey, having been nudged, went, but without enthusiasm where 'most Labour politicians I know would have hared off to make themselves known'.

But the politics standing behind his job were secure. Wilson might have been a compulsive mover, a man who did reshuffles therapeutically, the modern equivalent of taking the waters in the 18th century. His unpleasant intelligencer, George Wigg, had certainly intruded into Defence in the early days. But Healey's operation was saving the Government money as bidden which, as the sixties progressed, mattered more and more. 'The money at that time,' says Cooper crossing his hands, 'was going that way, and all the costs were going *that* way, the exactly opposite direction.'

Wilson's paranoia (or justified distrust) of Callaghan vanished where Healey was concerned. He was the first-rate man doing a job and came to enjoy prime ministerial warmth. The only seriously contemplated move was one to Housing. Healey had lunch with the Permanent Under-Secretary, Sir Matthew Stevenson, came back and remarked to Cooper that Housing was a very good job for the Permanent Under-Secretary. In fact, he has since said that he regrets not making a move for the last year and Cooper recalls him being bored with speeches that he had made and jokes he had told several times already.

Looking back on everything in his career, Denis Healey said in interview that the two best times of his life were as International Officer of the Labour Party, when he had so much influence and enjoyed such political encounters when very young, and as Defence Secretary, 'when I was in effect, Foreign Secretary in certain fields'. East of Suez, perhaps fortuitously, this would not be an overstatement.

There is much irony stored in that phrase. 'East of Suez' is Kipling's term and was coined at a time of pride and dignity that Britain did so much, upheld a civilisation, governed and took responsibility. There would be a facile left-wing rejection of it and heavy unease among the traditional Labour leadership at its decline. 'Harold Wilson, George Brown et al,' says Frank Cooper,

didn't really want to leave East of Suez at all. They liked the world role. All the good old trade union people are conservative Britain. You might have Tony Wedgwood Benn saying, 'Let's get out', but he didn't really carry any weight. But at the Ministry of Defence, we realised that there was no way we could afford to provide such a police force. Politicians don't think very much, but money thinks for them which is how the decisions get made.

Healey had his own rather different prejudices – not the

residual imperialism of such conservative Labour men, but a
strong liking and affection for the East Asian leaders he knew.
'He loved people East of Suez. He thought they were charming,
intelligent . . . and *laughing*. He spoke all these European
languages – terribly badly – but he didn't come as *naturally* to
the people. They didn't laugh in the same way. So it took him a
long time to realise that the world was changing and he couldn't
follow his inclinations to stay.' There was a link between the
East of Suez argument and the inter-service dispute. The Navy
wanted a world role and the overseas stations Malta, Aden, the
Gulf, Singapore and Borneo. The RAF looked for something
else. So there would be the comic interlude of Aldabra, where
the great Tam Dalyell, using Parliament against the executive
and working with the biologist Sir Ashley Miles, routed the
intention of ministry and minister to use that Indian Ocean
island as a base at peril to its giant turtles.

Ultimately though, it was the Navy that Healey came down
against, the Navy which would be denied its aircraft-carrier,
the CVA–01, precipitating the resignation of one of those
unregarded junior ministers, Christopher Mayhew. But a three-
carrier force would with refits have meant one carrier East of
Suez: 12 fighters only being carried if the carrier was Hermes, all
at a cost of £170 million a year at the values of the late sixties.

'We would never have got out of Suez ideologically,' according to Cooper, and it was essential, he fervently believes, that we
should. 'But we did it because we had run out of the lolly – full
stop.' Cooper remembers Healey speaking regretfully on a
Comet somewhere over the middle of the Indian Ocean. 'We can
do all this better than anyone else can. And I love the people,'
and then saying, 'but I think we are going to have to concentrate
on Europe whether we like it or we don't like it. I don't think
we've got any real choice.' He simply recognised the economics
of the situation.

In his memoir Healey quotes Philip Larkin:

Next year we are to bring the soldiers home
For lack of money, and it is all right.
Places they guarded, or kept orderly,
Must guard themselves, and keep themselves orderly.
We want the money for ourselves at home
Instead of working. And this is all right.

In fact, Britain was cutting the house-building programme by
165,000 a year at this time, deferring the raising of the school-

leaving age and reducing the road programme. But then Larkin was not perfectly objective. He also wrote:

I want to see them starving
The so-called working class

Having acknowledged the feeling regarding withdrawal from the Gulf, Healey considers that the growth of nationalism made it impossible to stay, which was not what Lee Kuan Yew had been saying. The lolly Britain had run out of was more pertinent. He himself had clung to commitment and was on record with his Canberra speech as saying, 'We intend to remain, and shall remain, fully capable of carrying out the commitments we have at the present time, including those in the Far East, the Middle East and in Africa and other parts of the world. We do intend to remain in the military sense a world power.' Words, in the Spanish proverb, are feathers.

According to Frank Cooper, Healey got lucky when the Sarawak confrontation with Indonesia suddenly ended. It wasn't expected to end. It couldn't with any sort of face be backed out of or down on. It just stopped anyway for reasons good in Indonesia. It had been talked of as Britain's mini-Vietnam yet by serendipity she had more or less won. But the withdrawal from East of Suez is one instance where Healey is to be seen led by events and making himself come to terms with them against his instincts.

Recurring financial pressure existed at home, to a degree, though the yapping of left-wingers against all British presence anywhere ever should not be overestimated. There was also, as Healey himself wryly concedes, the attitude of the chiefs who, if they were not to get money and military goods, decided that they must cut back on undertakings. It was a case of Churchill inverted: 'You won't give us the tools, we can't do the job.' Finally, in the White Paper of 1968, Healey announced a cutting of troop commitments in Singapore and Malaysia by half in 1970–1. Six months later, withdrawal from the Gulf was scheduled officially for December 1971. All this was done in the teeth of American pressure, America being up to the gunwales in the Vietnam War and wanting no demoralising withdrawal of Britain's thin but emblematic forces.

Even so, this was not done without a last spasm of imperial anguish in Cabinet. Richard Crossman describes the events of 15 January 1968:

After that, there was a tremendous effort to get Cabinet to
reverse the decision on East of Suez withdrawal we had
taken with such a large majority only ten days ago. It was
clear that the weaker brethren of the Cabinet were
swinging back ... LBJ had certainly stepped up his threats
to George, particularly in the economic sphere ... They
were all swinging towards the position of the old junta and
when the score was 8–10, I knew the PM would have to act
... What he conceded was nine months further occupation
and instead of withdrawing by March 1971, we were now to
withdraw by December 1971. That was something for Harry
Lee to take back with him to his Cabinet and that was
something to satisfy my anxious colleagues.

Nine months is clearly a very long time in politics.

On Vietnam, the burning moral issue of the day, Healey was against any intervention even of a token sort and was in agreement here with Harold Wilson, though he did not play any very forward role in argument about it. His views perhaps paralleled his concern over Northern Ireland. Again according to Cooper, these were crisp, amounting to well-founded anxiety about when, having gone in, we would get out.

The East of Suez decision had been the right one and the events of the last 25 years have entirely justified it, but it had been a forced decision. New domestic necessities and the smaller Navy's limitations compelled a choice between European involvement and the beguiling ghost of a military role which turned out to have been pretty well accomplished. Healey had to recommend on the new facts and he did so very much in terms of that mid-Indian Ocean conversation on the Comet.

Overall, Healey had run his department and drastically transformed it. He was the creator of a smaller, better managed, more centralised, numerate and accountancy-wise military machine. He had done what Conservative ministers since Harold Macmillan's brief tenure of the office had wanted to do. The prejudices of the Labour Party made the operation possible as it would not have been for a Conservative minister. But only someone from the Labour Right and perhaps only a former officer mentioned in despatches could have given the entrenched military such a bad time without provoking a crisis of competitive resignation. And only a genuine student of the subject could have gone through and won.

Healey didn't exactly enjoy a love feast with his senior

military men. It was more a matter of grim respect, plenty of rough words and a gradual doing of what had to be done. It was an exercise in diminution, of thinking smaller and aspiring to less, of which the East of Suez retreat was the unacknowledged logical corollary. But not diminishing with diminished means, not retreating where there are neither means nor needs is delusive nonsense. Blue Water had turned into Blue Champagne and the point of Healey was to get us out of delusion. He assembled the facts, argued, dived down the line to bright younger officers, faced up to realities and made decisions. If Mendes-France's remark, '*Gouverner, c'est choisir,*' is accepted as a guide, then in his ministerial sphere, Denis Healey governed.

CHAPTER FIVE

In the fashion of hard-faced men and the First World War, Healey might be described in 1970 as a man who had done well out of the Labour Government.

Not that having Harold Wilson for Prime Minister is to be compared with the Battle of the Somme. Rather this had been a Government of disappointment. Its litany was discouraging: devaluation strenuously resisted, expensively fought and bought against in the markets before being surrendered to in a fashion rightly seen as humiliating; no breakthrough in growth and the economy admirably brought back to order in a thoroughly orthodox fashion by Roy Jenkins. There had also been a string of right-thinking liberal Sunday paper reforms – legalisation of homosexuality, and of abortion as well as abolition of the death penalty.

But this modest bundle was accompanied by failure to tackle trades-union powers generally thought excessive, something lost humiliatingly in Cabinet, much talk about technology (white heat of) accompanied by its manifestation in Concorde, a white elephant flying backwards. Education would be quietly remodelled against talent and performance, the grammar schools which would only ever be got rid of over Harold Wilson's dead body were got rid of if it was the last thing Tony Crosland did.

And the economy? Well, an economy that was much what it had been under the stumbling later Conservatives – solvent indeed, but hardly regenerated, in Mr Benn's poignant 1964 phrase. As for Britain's international influence, Harold Wilson liked to think that our frontiers ran to the Himalayas, while Lyndon Johnson liked to think 'I have his pecker in my pocket.'

Britain was a diminished, slow-growing, inflation-prone country with leaders who talked too much. In the midst of such imperfect achievements, a major financial saving and overhaul of the armed forces which could be put on a par with the reforms of Cardwell 100 years before looked terribly good.

In personality terms, most figures were devalued. Brown was out and finished; Stewart had fought with gallant flair in a doomed, mistaken cause, Vietnam. Crosland, who knew most about the economy, had been kept away from it; Callaghan might well be dead politically and though he had convalesced from failure as Home Secretary, notably in his handling of Northern Ireland, he looked seedy, back-numbered and over-lookable. Few better things can happen to a politician when he still has the means of advance. But the ability of Jim Callaghan to be the universal Goschen whom everyone forgot and, in ways endearing to the party and injurious to the economy, to make a brilliant comeback, was not yet appreciated.

There were two distinct winners from 1964–70 – Roy Jenkins and Denis Healey. There is no point in making comparisons of merit and the present author has no intention of taking sides. Both performed brilliantly in government and had a grasp and understanding which raised them above hack politics, raised them also perhaps above the arts by which a hack politician would become prime minister. The differences, however, are fascinating. Although it is always said rightly by Jenkins' friends that he had a party, a personal and dedicated following, and Healey did not, this was a dubious advantage.

The Friends of Roy Jenkins, or FORJ, as they were rather preciously called in newspaper articles of the time, were a limiting factor. This was a self-limiting club rather than a growth stock or the makings of a stampede. The Jenkinsites were too educated, too European, too middle class, too combative and too much of an elect to do Roy Jenkins any good. In everything except Europe, they looked back to Hugh Gaitskell, though he had been rather to the left of them. The driving instinct of the Jenkins group which would become the core of the SDP was resistance.

Even when Jenkins had gone to Europe they had quite enough cohesion. They looked back to Gaitskell for his courage and bloody-minded disposition towards dying in ditches. They were, to a degree, a Scarborough faction. The willingness was

there to make a sharp division from the creeping power of the
Left. The words 'fight, fight and fight again' were a perpetual
reproach to them across the Wilson years and Wilson himself an
object of scorn. He stayed in the middle way, dimpled and
ducked this way and that. He was a leader who toadied to
followers. On becoming leader, he drank a toast 'to Nye', but
left to himself, he was something of a Tory – devoted to the
House of Windsor and the ghosts of Empire. He talked plain
and blunt and acted baroque and furtive. In the words of
Gaitskell's and Healey's rough County Durham friend, the
former miners' leader Sam Watson, 'He couldn't lie straight in
bed.'

It was reasonable to think like that, though any leader of the
Labour Party would be buffeted by its natural factions and
would spend time damping the fires he was caught between, but
as a state of mind, it conjured very bad tactics. The weak middle
drifted, the educated liberal right fretted and grew isolated,
neglecting the party where Wilson was overconcerned with it.
This attitude led to disengagement and divorce and it minimised
the strength of the moderate interest which, in normal circumstances, should have the greatest public appeal. It did not equip
Jenkins for the long building operation through the party and
beyond his friends. Healey, though he had calculated nothing,
stood advantaged by *not* having a faction.

Even at this time, Labour was splitting. Disappointment with
the Wilson Government was part of it. The dropping of sensible
prohibitions against marauders – the Prescribed List and the
barbed-wire birch rod of Sara Barker, the authoritarian old
National Agent – made up another. Harm was done by the
sixties mentality, the outbreak of rather puerile liberties by
which undergraduates had come to cheek dons, demonstrate
and take seriously half-witted notions like Maoism and unhelpful ones like existentialism. (Labour would spend the nightmare
years of 1979–81 being an existentialist party.) Unintelligent
defiance of all authority, however moderately exercised, was
fashion, liberation, part of the chic of the times. Everyone did it
– so shirt-fronted a member of Mr Blair's chorus line as Jack
Straw was, at this time, briefly a student activist, almost a
troublemaker.

All this was given some purpose by the Vietnam demon-
strations, but the student rebel phase would come to a rather
pathetic immediate climax with the Garden House Hotel riots in
Cambridge in 1971, an infantile assault on the guests of an

unpleasant foreign Government (Greece) which ended in stiff jail sentences imposed by a judge of the old school who didn't know that this was the seventies and that you couldn't do that sort of thing.

Across the seventies Labour would have a terrible time from student unrest three or five years older which had spilt into the sleepy hollows of constituency parties on behalf of a general stirring up of radicalism. Only part of this would subscribe to the loopy off-Trotskyism of the Militant Tendency, but it would accept the targeting and tactics of fringe theoreticians better kept in their polytechnics. Such unrest could only blossom because Labour was unhappy anyway and because the traditional Left in unions and constituency parties felt emboldened to resume the war left off, more or less, in 1961.

This mood made itself felt very early in the life of that perplexing interim, that distraction from Labour's self-preoccupation, the Heath Government. In much the way that the right-wingery of Margaret Thatcher has since drawn Labour politicians into parallel imitation of an abject sort, Heath's approach of behaving from 1971 onwards like a Labour government pushed Labour leftwards. The leaders who had entertained 'In Place of Strife' imposed a three-line whip against the modest and tentative Tory union legislation. On the streets they heard the crowds chanting, 'Kill the bill. Kill the bill.' They were their leaders and they must follow them.

Labour would also stumble heavily into a primitive anti-European mood which Wilson, characteristically, would buy off with a referendum undertaken in order that it should be defeated. The contempt of Jenkins for a state of affairs in which the leadership contradicted what it had been about in government and lightly brushed aside problems which had earnestly exercised it a couple of years before was very just. But it would be the European issue which would push Jenkins out to the edge of Labour politics. This was what he believed in and had committed himself to.

Wilson's essential flippancy in reneging to the point where Europe could be used to feed the zoo pushed the former Chancellor into resignation from the deputy leadership and rendered him at heart semi-detached from the Labour Party. When Heath, in his one achievement as Prime Minister, got us past the French into Europe, Labour opposed the necessary legislation, a fairly contemptible thing in a party which a couple of years earlier had sought conditions not worth distinguishing from these. Jenkins resigned from the Shadow Cabinet and went with 69 rebels into the Aye lobby. The whole thing stemmed ominously from a decision of Party Conference. And Party Conference was beginning to take on the dimensions of that house guest on the backs of whose hands hair begins to grow.

Although Labour stands today as a thoroughly European party, the whirligig of time having brought in no end of revenges, that severance effectively set Jenkins on his way out of Labour and Westminster politics and on to Brussels and Hillhead. Healey could claim a fair conscience on Europe, though, as he concedes in his memoirs, he took a thoroughly pragmatic view of the whole issue. 'The overriding duty of a party leader in opposition is to keep his party together.'

Healey could fairly argue that, during the fight and fight again time, he had done his bit – Mr Khruschev and the cats – and that anyway he wasn't a passionate European, as the phrase had it, but a cool maker of reservations. Although he knew more about European civilisation from Machiavelli's Florence to Kant's Königsberg than most enthusiasts, he was always institutionally dubious. So he could support the party's latest lurch with a good conscience. And his acceptance of the Wilson line had nothing of manipulative or cynical politics about it. Wilson was doing a stamp-edging job as Attlee had done. He ought to be supported despite the intestinal contradictions wrapped round his neck. The heavy-conscience brigade were making a great moral to-do; sensible men would make dirty-handed compromises and keep the show on the road. That about sums up the Healey view.

It is respectable and rough and readily consistent, but it begs questions. The profound issue was not what Labour said but why it said it. The Left, kept hungry and disappointed by the 1964 Government, was a noisy expanding force. In the constituencies very much so; to a degree in the unions, though this was a more contrived strength, and most evidently at Party Conference, getting nastier every minute. Alan Ayckbourn wrote a play, *Upstream*, about a family in a narrowboat who take on board a stranger who, by degrees, asserts himself until he commands the boat, demands to be called 'skipper' and inflicts entire humiliation on the original occupants. Only by a fight to the death and a sharp blow on the back of the neck with a baked-bean tin is he prised out of the spoils of intrusion. For intrusion read entryism, the taking over of power points in the structure across the decade, and you are describing the Labour

Party – though Ayckbourn was probably talking about Britain as a whole.

It is fair criticism of Healey that he underreacted to the left-wing threat. Despising it, he couldn't take it seriously. Being the good party man which he would be, unrewarded and dis-interestedly in the eighties, he put party considerations like that metaphysical condition, unity, too high. Being an optimist, he thought things would come right which didn't come right. This cast of mind is the flip side of his accomplishing practical virtue and it may be a reason why Labour was not rallied, not called to be valiant for sense in time. Gaitskell may have slightly over-done conflict with his readiness to fight and fight again, but he wasn't actually wrong.

Europe was only an issue of contention, a handle. The left-wing pressure and the sheer spitting unpleasantness intensified generally. In 1972 Dick Taverne, very close to Jenkins (formerly Minister of State to him at the Home Office), was deselected by his ardently pure party in Lincoln. Taverne is very bright, brave, inclined to elevate intellectual consistency above tact, rather good in a fight and entirely capable of life after politics. He is arguably *plus Jenkins que Jenkins lui-même*. He reacted succinctly, applying for the Manor of Northstead, fighting at the consequent by-election, obliging the institutional Labour Party to jump through a hoop of its own making and to send down every Westminster MP, excepting a few recalcitrants, to cam-paign for the hack leftist replacement – and winning. Labour had, at that time, much of the quality of a dying elephant. The lines of the 1980–1 crisis were already being drawn inside a deeply unhappy party.

The ability of Edward Heath to lose to this demoralised, split, intellectually distressed band of non-brothers remains one of the great negative achievements of British politics. But somehow – by taking on the miners and a potential round of public service wage hikes and then weaseling out of the contest; by delaying an election which he would have won on 7 February until 28 February, then between those dates climbing down on its central issue – he did it. Healey's description of him in the Commons as 'a great marble statue being trundled towards the precipice' says it all. In the process he brought a bored, zestless, objectiveless and incredulous Harold Wilson to Downing Street and Denis Healey, who was none of these things, to the Treasury.

Healey, who had done some journalism in the interim, reminds us that an article in which he had contemplated the possibility that the oil-producing countries might agree to force up their prices by limiting production had been spiked by *The Sunday Times* in June 1973 as absurd fantasy. Despite such insights, he was starting very nearly from scratch in the economic job. He was a classics graduate who had spent the first part of his life on international relations and the next section on defence and military matters. He came to economics as Shadow Chancellor in 1972 after two years as Shadow Foreign Secretary armed only with a Latin quotation from the 12th-century Bishop of London who had doubled as Treasurer: that in the latter job, calculations are less important than judgments. He might also have recalled the words of Derby to Disraeli on his becoming Chancellor with no more experience of money than impressive debts: 'Oh, they give you the figures.'

It is the boring way of politicians to talk about the mess left by their predecessors and their role in clearing it up. But anyone following Heath and his unhappy Chancellor, Anthony Barber, has some excuse. Heath had dumped onto the system something called threshold payments which were effectively triggers. That dismal point was reached roughly in the following way. The Treasury Christmas party in 1973, so Leo Pliatzky, a senior civil servant to both Barber and Healey, tells us, was held by candlelight. Too-large tax cuts had combined with too-large public spending. There had been a last great burst of Keynesian faith, actually a sort of Andaman Islands Christianity followed to the letter without understanding. It was a spree undertaken in panic-stricken response to unemployment, the Joseph spending at the NHS and the Walker spending in local government.

This was the time of metropolitan county councils, new town halls (followed by Fraud Squad enquiries), the time of a sort of fiscal *fasching*, all of which would be joined by a float of the pound to disguise devaluation and then followed by a crude six-month freeze and statutory prices and incomes control. Rumours about William Armstrong, the senior civil servant most involved in policy, having a nervous breakdown and being found on his knees quoting from the Book of Revelations seem very apt.

Naturally enough inflationary measures were followed by counter-inflationary measures, but since price and wage freezes fall upon workers and unions take badly to the consequences, Heath and Barber were keen to show goodwill. All incomes policies, as Healey would have demonstrated to him later, do well in the early days and run into trouble later on. In the case of Heath they did so with what was called Stage Three. To make this last extension of restriction acceptable, threshold payments were undertaken – automatic wage increases for every point by which the retail price index rose above a certain level. They were meant to be psychological, a promise of succour in adversity and given in the earnest belief that such adversity wouldn't arise.

Healey's absurd little trope about the oil producers forming a cartel and ambushing the industrial world with it was the next interesting item of news. The consequence, as Pliatzky says, was that Stage Three of the prices and incomes policy fuelled inflation instead of containing it. The oil crisis strengthened the hand of Arthur Scargill, not yet President of the miners' union, but able to exploit rising wages and prices which accompanied a wage and price control regime. The miners were placed to break whatever the law sustaining that policy asserted. And the price of oil being what it temporarily was, they were only obeying rules agreeable to Adam Smith. Industrial action in the form of an overtime ban precipitated the energy crisis, cuts in electricity supplies, the three-day week, a hapless minister asking that we should follow him in cleaning his teeth in the dark, candles at the Treasury and the election which, along with everything else, Heath contrived to lose.

Politically, this was saddening. Heath had been the last party leader rooted in liberal Conservatism, the sort which accepted that there was such a thing as society, and desperately wanted good relations with reasonable trade unions. The parodic little figure of Arthur Scargill would dance on the grave of such accord and Margaret Thatcher with her devotion to the class war would inherit the Conservative Party.

The Labour leadership, still bruised by its own time in office, surprised and not altogether happy to be back in power, had inevitably played down the significance of the miners' action and the implied rates of wage inflation. But it cannot have come as any surprise to Healey to be told by Len Murray, General Secretary of the Trades Union Congress, that the going rate for public-sector wages would now be 30 per cent. The going rate for inflation would be adjusted as well. These were evils in the pipeline when Healey assembled his team of ministers, Joel Barnett, Edmund Dell and Robert Sheldon, with the amiable and ingenious Harold Lever floating nearby. They were advised by Sir Douglas Wass, Permanent Under-Secretary and practising Keynesian; Derek Mitchell, one-time object in Number Ten of the rage of Marcia Williams and, not for this reason, an ardent cutter of public spending; and Leo Pliatzky, an outsider from a poor background, brought long before from a warehouse in Manchester to Oxford University by the semi-divine intervention of Harold Laski. It was Pliatzky who would save the Treasury from the incipient hysteria of economic chatter by pointing out that its statistics were wrong by reason of double counting.

They were not always going to agree. They and their Chancellor would be caught between world markets immensely strong and largely capricious, and a Cabinet itself frightened by the social and political consequences of hard, necessary steps. Boots were on other feet at that time. The unions were demonstrably exceptionally strong. Somewhat to their own surprise, they had just breakfasted on the Heath Government. Power attracts power worship, and the satisfying of the unions played as great a part in the minds of ministers of all parties as the buying off of Norsemen did to the later Saxon kings. Healey, characteristically going to a book to make a point, quotes Joseph Schumpeter observing uncannily in 1946: 'The real problem is labour ... unless socialisation is to spell economic breakdown, a socialising government cannot possibly tolerate present trade union practice ... As things actually are, labour is of all things the most difficult to socialise ...'

One problem Healey did not have was the Prime Minister. Poor Harold Wilson, who would become such a tragic figure after his unnecessarily chattered-about sudden retirement, had at this time simply run out of animus towards and fear of colleagues. His trust and confidence in Healey, affirmed in the late sixties, was just as strong. With the old meddling and anxiety exhausted, he gave his Chancellor straightforward support. It was as well, because with heavy party duties as a member of the National Executive Council and facing an open-plan Hell in which crisis was laid like linoleum, Healey was about to be worked to the limits of even his bearlike resources. 'I went to bed dog-tired,' he recurringly wrote in his diary.

The first part of his time at the Treasury might be described as one in which things were worse than they looked. Later, things would look much worse than they were and much of what the Treasury did would be for ostentation rather than utility.

There was a large deficit. The PSBR, a minus figure after Roy Jenkins had gone to work, had stood at £4 billion in 1973, and in 1975 was at £10 billion. But the figures with which the Treasury worked were massively too low – £4 billion too low, 5.4 per cent of the year's gross domestic product. The time would come when the PSBR figure would be too high. But that was a pleasure in store. Wrong figures prowl beside the mystique of government, a sort of anti-convoy waiting to attack. Healey was trying in his first budget to follow the judgment of the Organisation for Economic Co-operation and Development, that the first risk to be avoided was a recession induced by book-balancing stringency. Unfortunately, given an underestimated deficit, the budget was reflationary. It was also harsh to business, with increased corporate taxes which won cheap applause in party circles and overestimated businessmen's ability to pay. But this last mistake would be put right through hastily introduced tax relief on stock appreciation. After that hiccup, the Healey regime would be overtly helpful to business and win early good figures by way of investment. Not for nothing was it Healey who later coined the cryptic observation, 'If you are in a hole, stop digging.'

As there are accelerando conductors and rallentando conductors, so there are economic chancellors and expansive chancellors. All Healey's personality and instincts put him in the second category, but debt and later the panic of markets would set him treading the heated wheel of enforced frugality. He was, in the early days, also festooned with Labour Party promises, manifesto commitments and other detritus of unreason. Money had to be found for beautiful, useless Concorde; British Leyland had to be saved all over again; Chrysler had also to be rescued and, by way of bonus, the social wage of increased pension and benefits had somehow to be fitted in.

Politics cohabited uneasily with the problem-solving function of the Treasury or at any rate a perfect Treasury. For all sorts of sophisticated reasons to do with not feeding a recession, meeting a wage bill put in the pipeline by the miners' round, and through working on grotesquely wrong PSBR figures, Healey was let in for an increase in public expenditure of 12.2 per cent in his first year. The last year of Heath–Barber had been 8.5 per cent. The increase in the share of expenditure per GDP went up from 38.7 to 45.5 per cent.[1] Inflation was going up and, against the supposed rules, unemployment was rising with it, reaching in the third quarter of 1975 the million figure below which it has never since fallen. Such nightmare arithmetic would win the battle over rhetoric.

The 1976 White Paper acknowledged that 'a married man on average earnings is paying about a quarter of his earnings in income tax compared with a tenth in 1960–1'. Healey had been plain with his party already at conference before the election, that increased spending, like public-sector wage increases, would have to be paid for. Broadly, all governments start upbeat and grow melancholy and punitive in their second year before organising themselves a little more optimism ahead of the next election. So it would be; so, with inflation now spilling into the high twenties by way of the 30 per cent wage norm of which Len Murray had adverted him, it had to be.

But rigour would, first of all, take the form of another incomes policy, voluntary but with reserve statutory powers. Healey had gone on with the Heath legacy and the manifesto promises on pensions and benefits as he should not have done. No government keeping its promises is altogether to be trusted. With PSBR at its revised, horrible, true level, Leo Pliatzky's point about expenditure was made. It is, he says, anti-Sisyphean. Government tries to push the rock downhill only for it to keep rolling up again.

In the summer of 1975, Healey had to push the Cabinet into acceptance, meeting resistance from James Callaghan and Michael Foot – they would be the party's next two leaders, which may signify something – but with Harold Wilson's late support. The most intelligent objection was that governmental authority, which had taken a terrible beating in the winter of 1973–4, was at stake if such a policy were again tried and again walked through by the defiance of Arthur Scargill or his moral equivalent.

This part of the job would be a success. It represented Healey getting policy back into realistic mode and making dark assumptions, but it was also a triumph of reasonableness on all or, at any rate, most hands. The trades union leadership at this time called itself left-wing, had fought in Spain and on the heavy radical circuit had seen it and done it. But neither Jack Jones nor Hugh Scanlon, the Marxist golfer, wanted the economy smashed and neither was the moral equivalent of Arthur Scargill. Both had sniffed something of a future which definitely didn't work; both set about being generally helpful, Jones actually getting Foot to live with the legal sanctions in the plan. And they were joined in this by Len Murray of the TUC.

The complex, tendril-trailing deal worked out in conjunction with Michael Foot, the Secretary for Employment, involved a flat rate of £6 a week for anyone earning less than £8,500 in return for a Government clamp on wage increases, limiting them to 10 per cent. Such were the neo-Argentinian circumstances of inflation that in reality this translated as an average cut in living standards of 2.5 per cent. The £6 meant doing something for the unskilled worker at the expense of the skilled people who could best face that sort of cut. The whole thing would then be copper-bottomed by the introduction of 'cash limits' on public spending. It was deflationary and it was enough. In the teeth of the boring Conservative charge of Labour being a tax-and-spend party, Healey was making this a tax-and-cut Government – something necessary made more necessary by wrong figures supplied and his own native euphoria at the start, not to mention a foolish manifesto. But if a government does do what is necessary, it will deserve well of us – not that it can count on getting such deserts.

There also existed an industrial strategy. It would be mocked today, not least by free-market Labour, but its working parties conveying information between unions, employers and ministers deserved testing in better circumstances. At the very least, they tended against ignorance. Government also had to attempt control of prices, and Shirley Williams, Prices Minister, described herself as 'under constant pressure to limit profits more'.

Healey had started off by doing the wrong thing and avoiding heavy outside pressure. He was now doing the right thing and that right thing would be until the start of 1979 a very remarkable success: rapidly falling inflation was down from 26.9 to 12.9 per cent between August 1975 and July 1976. These were Healey's July measures: they represented a triumph of sense and co-operation. In real economic terms, things would quickly start to look up. And at this point, Healey got into real trouble.

Or rather he was got into it by the Bank of England which, according to one theory, attempted a creaming-off operation. In March 1976, it sold sterling at a time when some pressure on the pound existed and the next day lowered rates which should have been raised. The pound fell ten cents in ten days. All the frugal things were being done, all the punishments of profligacy rained down. A controlled devaluation went out of control.

The Government, with Healey making all the key decisions, dragging a Cabinet screaming behind him, would now have to struggle with irrational forces. The market was as ignorant of what was going right as it had been dozy about what had been going wrong. But it had entered 'sell' mode and, despite falling inflation and a falling deficit, was disposed to sell. This created a problem to which the solution would be an ostentatious severity for the sake of being seen to be severe. The currency and the Government's general credit had been sustained through 1974 and 1975 on the prospects of North Sea oil. Britain was going to receive a great income and even if she was silly enough to go through a form of nationalisation (analogous to 'form of marriage' as understood by a bigamist) before a penny had come over the counter, the wealth would still be mightily discounted in our favour.

Now, with panic up, the spurious message went round that all the oil had been mortgaged. But those who want to sell will believe any bad news – that is what it is for. Government and Treasury got through the spring and, facing new selling, attempted to borrow new money. Standby credits from the major industrial countries and the Bank of International Settlements put noisily on display failed to do the trick. Confidence, that Holy Ghost of the markets, could only be manifested if cuts – a second round of fiscal repression on top of the July measures of wage control – plus cash limits were imposed. Otherwise the pound would fall and fall. Healey, looking over his career in 1996 and recalling International Officer and Defence Secretary with pleasure, observed, 'You couldn't enjoy the Treasury – except as an exercise in intellectual masochism.'

Masochism, pain for the sheer joy of it, is the word. And right-wing criticism, much of it rooted at the Philip Larkin level of wanting 'to see them starving, the so-called working class', would pour savagely onto the Chancellor while left-wing and ordinary Labour politicianly resentment fell as hard. The Conservative press, still quoting that untrue 'spending at 60 per cent of GDP', made injurious and harassing propaganda and, at this of all points, a Treasury forecast gaily projected the PSBR at a figure £2 billion above its later, ascertained true level. The misfortune of Job barely competed.

Interim cuts extracted from a moaning Cabinet yielded a billion, and another billion was raised through an increase in employers' National Insurance contributions; this plus £500 million for the Government BP holding saw off the high summer and let the Healeys enjoy a holiday in Scotland. Just as well it did, writes Healey with a wince. After further falls and further increases in interest rates, the pound fell and then fell again.

It was then that he did the thing everyone remembers. He had been due to fly to Hong Kong and Manila for two financial conferences, Commonwealth and IMF. He is sceptical about the utility of such conferences, but they would have kept him happily away from Labour Party Conference, a good idea at that time – a good idea at most times. But contemplating 17 hours incommunicado when the markets could sell Eldorado twice in an afternoon, he stopped at Heathrow and came back.

What followed – the application to the International Monetary Fund, the cuts which were first fought over between Healey and the IMF, then by the IMF proper and the US Treasury, insistent and uncomprehending, and, most of all, fought over between Healey and the Cabinet – represent a bitter and ironical chapter of British political history. Essentially the IMF proper, through its permanent official, was trying to be helpful. The US Treasury, under William Simon and Edwin Yeo, was anxious to give masochism its due by providing the sadism. At the same time there were differences within the Treasury, where Derek Mitchell was an ardent cutter and Douglas Wass, the Keynesian, on the sceptical side of agnostic. That was nothing to the division in the Cabinet with only Edmund Dell, Reg Prentice and the departing Roy Jenkins accepting any sort of cuts and with the new Prime Minister, James Callaghan, staunchly on the sidelines.

The debate here was between Healey, who did not think cuts intrinsically necessary for the real economy, a group of people headed by Anthony Crosland who agreed and wanted no action, and Tony Benn, who advocated protection. What Healey understood was that without the public display, the ceremonial scourging, a recurring free fall of the pound, would so weaken the currency as to do serious harm. The market was a hothouse which must not be allowed to generate a hurricane. The point about markets is not that they are right, but that their strength makes being right irrelevant.

He must also have been aware, though it is not a point he stresses, that his own elected policy of wage control would be psychologically strengthened by the crisis he hadn't wanted. It was also necessary to expose the eccentric desire of Tony Benn and Peter Shore to run a siege economy at greater cost in spending cuts and with all the attendant Cuban joys.

Before all this could come to a head, everyone had first to trudge through Party Conference. Healey, missing Manila, went instead to Blackpool to be subjected to the imbecilities of standing orders and a restriction to five minutes of his account of an economy facing heroic tribulation. The petty rules combined with the hatred which was beginning to bubble up in such gatherings and a great deal of applause and admiration from the saving core of Labour people.

Because of the conference experience, Callaghan's general support had to be fought for; having given it, the Prime Minister behaved with astute solid sense, holding back his own commitment and letting the argument run and run till democracy was satisfied. Anthony Crosland could then say that he didn't agree with the Chancellor, but he wasn't going to make this a resignation issue.

In practice, the IMF loan was the symbolic thing it looked. The final package was not the figure Simon and Yeo had wanted. Only half of it was actually drawn and, after a brief excursion to the midnight figure of a 15 per cent interest rate *à la* Norman Lamont in 1992, the nightmare began to recede at an accelerating rate, the mania of the market sated. Interest rates stood at 5 per cent in October 1977, the pound fully recovered and Labour Party Conference in 1977 gave Healey a standing ovation. What had happened is best explained in a complicated way. He had done what he had to do, which involved doing what didn't intrinsically have to be done. But as the will of the market made this necessary extrinsically, he had to do it. Ed Yeo, using language natural to Denis himself, spoke of the Chancellor's 'iron balls'.

Ironically, in the midst of all the immediate concerns, there was one thing which Healey, following Callaghan, had *not* done which over a longer term would have been both splendid economy and welcome politics. An intelligent reproach to Labour is that it spent too much on defence. As the arguments against nuclear weapons systems came from moralists and persons overtolerant of the Soviet Union, Labour never did fully address what might be called the accountancy aspect of the nuclear question. It had loomed for both parties in the late sixties after the failures of Blue Streak and other home-made ballistic cookies, but, because Harold Macmillan had engineered a cheap, sensible deal over Polaris, immediate cost-questioning of the whole independent-deterrent undertaking receded.

The costs that would come with the replacement of Polaris never got the attention they deserved. Healey spoke of his hindsight on this to Peter Hennessy's outstanding *Analysis* programme in startling terms. 'I think the case of the Left was nonsense. They believed that if we gave up our nuclear weapons, other countries would give up theirs. On the other hand, I think with hindsight that if I had known then what I know now, I would have cancelled the programme.' But that regret, a marginal judgment, was as nothing compared to his thoughts on Chevaline, the successor to Polaris. Chevaline had been secretly tee-ed up by a small discreet group of ministers in the Heath Government in 1973 when they were busy with the industrial crisis which would destroy that administration. The Labour Government which would operate on this matter in secrecy untroubled by party clamour was perfectly placed to make a purely financial judgment. Such low motives, never mind the charm of avoiding political conflict later, letting Polaris run out its maximum time without new costs and conflicts, might have saved Britain many billions of pounds. No such low self-interest occurred. James Callaghan, decent son of Portsmouth, behaved in a patriotic, responsible and ruinous fashion.

He told Hennessy,

> Our predecessors, the Conservative Government, had taken the decision on Chevaline, and I think in the press of government business that day, it came forward. I don't know that there was a great discussion about it. I don't remember a great discussion. When I came to office as Prime Minister, I could then have said, 'Well, all right, we'd better cancel it.' But it's awfully difficult, unless you have the virtue of hindsight when something is going on, has been going on for three years, and you're told, 'Oh, it's going to be pretty soon now, can we have another £100 million, or £50 million?' to say, 'No, put it all on one side,' to be so certain that it's not going to succeed. In fact it did succeed; but it cost a lot more than anybody expected. And every time they called for a new tranche, I used to write 'agree' on the minute, or whatever it was, because one always thought it was just round the corner.

Chevaline had been costed in 1972 at £175 million with inflation discounted. Callaghan, coming in as Prime Minister in 1976, faced a bill of £388 million. By the time Chevaline's mere existence was disclosed in 1980, the constant price was £530 million (a billion on paper), three times the original estimate. But beyond that, if Chevaline had not been bought, the question of its successor, Trident, ardently elected and cherished by Mrs Thatcher, would never have arisen. A single knife stroke and we should have been out of the *amour propre* of the independent deterrent, in which Healey had long since ceased to believe. The costs of Trident by the time HMS *Vanguard* put to sea would be £12 billion. Chevaline was never discussed in full Cabinet. If domestic ministers had done so, says Shirley Williams darkly, things might have been different. Policy from any computation of housekeeping was insanely wrong. Yet Denis Healey had seen Polaris, a genuinely economic buy, as a marginal preference for continuity in 1964.

His comment to Hennessy is bleak: 'Actually, I regard myself as having failed in my duty as Chancellor, especially with the knowledge I'd gained as Defence Secretary, in not subjecting the whole Chevaline programme to severe scrutiny right from the word go.'

Healey is less self-serving than most politicians precisely because he can think analytically and see his own error, but the defence he offers is one that anyone should understand.

'People forget we won the election in March. I decided I had to produce a budget within three weeks, and the physical effort of getting that done, I think, wiped pretty well everything else out of my mind.' A better insight into how decisions are taken and mistakes made in government could not be found. The Prime Minister is lax, uncritical, conformist, trundling along in the best Micawberish manner. Lacking expert knowledge, he does not seek it. The Minister with the knowledge and the analytical grasp is so burdened by work and the rush to keep an early timetable that he simply can't focus on an issue which doesn't loom big, can pass for routine, but whose ultimate consequences are an absurd expenditure which the public finances must dumbly endure. Anyone reading Section D of the Scott Report, which showed how sales of arms to Iraq happened without coherent and settled intent, will recognise the process.

Healey reproaches himself as Callaghan does not. It would make more sense to reproach a system which so weighs down ministers as to make it impossible for the most perceptive of them to take a proper view and see straight.

But, whatever he says against himself, by any reasonable standards, Healey had been a successful Chancellor; he had also been an heroic one. 'For 12 hours,' he says of the day he resolved upon the IMF loan, 'I was close to demoralisation.' All special pleading apart, it ought to be recognised that nobody else could have done it. Healey has physical and intellectual stamina. He loves struggle and furious argument. He is brave and he has intellectual grasp. He is also, which is just as well, someone who learns. The mistakes came at the beginning; the tough, correct, coherent answers came afterwards. He stopped digging and got out of the hole.

The last mistake came at the end and if it was essentially Callaghan's, made for understandable reasons, Healey went along with it. The years of creative restraint, the sort of restraint from which stability and growth are created, had put heavy pressure on the union leadership which had actually behaved with the sort of wisdom we credit to German unions. Jack Jones had been booed at his own conference and he was now giving way to the vision-free and dull-minded Moss Evans. There was a new stage of incomes policy, the loosest and most vulnerable yet, and it required a line that would accept some increases. The Government was not placed to impose the preferred low norm. Callaghan inexplicably said 5 per cent, an unenforceable figure which would set union discontent crackling.

In October, when Callaghan decided that he would not hold the election generally expected, Labour had a lead of 7 per cent and he was far ahead of Thatcher on the personal poll. Demand at Ford for 15 per cent, twice the inflation rate, a couple of haulage strikes and the nightmare of the council workers' demand for 40 per cent and the subsequent Winter of Discontent would destroy everything politically.

The breakdown of rational consent came most prominently and injuriously from workers in the public-services union, NUPE, people who with the flat-rate cash had done better from Healey than any group. But in the way of all incomes policies, what had been held down insisted upon standing up. In the circumstances of high employment and the expectation of its continuing, comparisons with other earnings and determination to make up for lost purchasing power follow naturally. Talk of guidelines had to be political, the least injurious that could be got away with. Five per cent, a number Callaghan let fall almost casually, was explosive.

It is speculative to estimate the effect of a larger figure and Healey himself deals with the whole matter philosophically, but the problem of gently relaxing a wages policy in the absence of endemic unemployment remained unsolved.

The events of the winter 1978–9, strikes which left black plastic bags piled up in the streets under the cameras and the eye of the *Daily Mail*, was far more damaging politically than economically. It made up the public mind in broad terms against the unions and against Labour. The unions were their own worst enemies until Mrs Thatcher claimed the role.

Economic policy had been damaged, though far from shattered, but events simply demoralised the Government. Callaghan, who had postponed an October election in the belief that the success created would breed a more secure backing for Labour, declined to hang on to the very end. Events had brought an exhausted party to the election they would lose. What lay ahead was two vicious years of political civil war and systemic decline into a decade and a half of opposition. Winter was only a bit of it. The party's suppurating political dispute, also suppressed, would explode, producing eight seasons, two years, of the blackest discontent.

The problems of third stages of incomes policy had turned up as they always do, but the economy Healey had managed was a healthy one. Mrs Thatcher would lighten the burden of wage inflation by the dazzling inadvertence of creating 3.5 million unemployed and finding that the south of England, the middle classes and workers in work could live with it as no one in the previous 40 years had thought they could.

Healey had tried to run an economy, real wage cuts, taxes, IMF terms and all, without such aids. The unions which did not understand what Jones and Scanlon had understood would inherit Mrs Thatcher and her inadvertence. They did not understand then, but within a short time, they would be told as the God of Jean Calvin told the Scot in Hell, 'Ye ken the noo.' The 'problem of labour', as Schumpeter had defined it, would be solved, accidentally and ferociously, at huge cost in benefit spending and at a social price not yet worked out. But there was nothing in Mrs Thatcher's calamitous success and Healey's last-fence failure to diminish his major achievement under different, harder and more humane rules. No one, Mrs Thatcher included, knew how to run an economy without major unemployment at the low point of the cycle. If it should prove to be impossible we would be profoundly unjust to blame the last man who tried.

---

[1]Before Pliatzky detected the double-counting element, it was briefly supposed, with some hysteria, that public spending took up some 60 per cent of GDP.

CHAPTER SIX

The facts can be swiftly assembled.

Labour was defeated at the general election of May 1979. There was at that time a solid left-wing majority on the National Executive. In that same year Party Conference voted to adapt a report *compelling* all constituency parties to consider the fitness of their sitting MPs. This became known as mandatory reselection. The same conference also voted to give the NEC control of the next election manifesto. But it rejected the idea of an electoral college to choose the next leader of the party. However, a committee of enquiry, biased heavily to the Left, had been created just before the conference to look into constitutional changes.

In mid-June 1980 that committee, meeting at the Bishop's Stortford country HQ of the General and Municipal Workers' Union, recommended an electoral college made up of 50 per cent MPs, 25 per cent trade-unionists, 20 per cent constituency party and 5 per cent other groups. This college would elect the party leader. This proposal, which was seen, when combined with mandatory reselection, as creating left-wing extra-parliamentary control over MPs, provoked the first meetings to discuss the possibility of a group defecting from Labour and forming a new Social Democratic Party. Party Conference in 1980, by the defection of a single delegate vote, accepted the Bishop's Stortford proposal but rejected the mechanisms proposed to enact it.

A special conference was then set up to meet in January 1981 to decide on how to implement the college. David Basnett, leader of the General and Municipal Workers, publicly asked James Callaghan specifically not to resign before a successor could be chosen under the new rules. Callaghan declined and on 15 October he did resign. The candidates for succession were Denis Healey, Michael Foot, John Silkin and Peter Shore.

In February at the special conference held at Wembley, the formula for the electoral college was amended, the engineers abstaining in well-meant error. Voting power would now split: 40 per cent for the unions, 30 per cent each for constituency party and MPs. On 26 March 1981, the Social Democratic Party held a press conference at the Connaught Rooms to announce its foundation. The Labour Party's essential work for the period immediately following electoral defeat was complete.

The point at which Labour emerged from office, the electoral defeat of 1979, was a miserable one. The 5 per cent norm which had proved so rebarbative to unionised workers had triggered the 'dirty jobs' strike and left the Conservatives with an image they would be reusing with full impact eight years and two further elections later. It was also a conflict between a Labour Government and 'its people'.

Labour in power had actually done what was necessary; the economic numbers they could quote, in spite of those politically damaging troubles at the end, were extremely good numbers. They had governed responsibly and with creditable results. The affinities with the Conservatives in 1996–7 are substantial and the Conservative Party today shows equal appreciation of its responsible Chancellor, Kenneth Clarke.

But responsible government on a small majority damages the fabric of that lesser, necessary thing, a political party. There had been a steady guerrilla campaign against the party leadership in Parliament and a series of defections on important votes. Parallel with these there had been menacing outside pressure, what soon became known as 'entryism'. Labour constituency numbers were commonly small and thus vulnerable – though Healey's friends in Leeds never let this take place there – small, vulnerable and elderly.

In the forties and fifties, when a rather different Left attempted to utilise the constituencies for their own royal road, Transport House, through the briskly intolerant Sara Barker, the party had maintained a power of veto on moves to reselect and on the choice of candidate. It was widely deplored by enlightened opinion and got rid of with Harold Wilson's consent in a move at once lackadaisical and ingratiating. Just how necessary

Miss Barker's short way had been would soon be demonstrated. (Ironically, one of the achievements of Tony Blair has been to impose a centralised control on local parties which makes her look like a latitudinarian.) But, for the time being, the party leadership was paralysed and inert.

A few determined, aggressive youngsters could hector their way forward, take up unwanted chores, stage late-sitting and frankly intolerable meetings to induce a widespread quiet death, a steady falling away of traditional loyalists and a taking up of reins by themselves. Such control would be followed by two things, a drafting of conference resolutions directed at changing the party constitution by way of weakening the say of the parliamentary party, and a menacing surveillance of the sitting member. The magic word was 'reselection'. A member might be dropped by the resolve of his local party. Alternatively, the mere threat of deselection would induce fearful and compliant conduct.

At the same time, trades-union developments had accentuated the drift to the left. Jack Jones and Hugh Scanlon had long been part of the picture – respectively, a hardish if realistic leftist replacing a soft one (Frank Cousins), and someone well disposed to the Communist Party – not at this time and place an extreme position – who had replaced the trusty Catholic Right. (In fact the Catholic Right had begun to come back in 1978 in the person of Terry Duffy, a man of exceptional niceness and decency, but late into politics and naïve about it; also, as we shall see, a rotten tactician.)

The worst thing that happened to mainstream Labour occurred when the General and Municipal Workers (a generic name to cover the 101 names the same union has taken after mergers and spring-cleans) had fallen in 1973 to the leadership of David Basnett. Basnett, who would emerge as something close to a personal enemy of Healey, was a man of towering demerit. The *Dictionary of National Biography*, seeking to be kind, says of Basnett, who died in 1989: 'In his 1978 address to Congress, Basnett outlined his strong commitment to the view that union leaders had a right and a duty to participate with government in developing policies.' It was a right and duty in respect of matters concerning which he had very modest understanding.

This overreaching mentality, an autonomous operation of the Peter Principle of promotion one point above competence, was given a mirror image after the 1979 election. Basnett, self-

important and weak, set out to meddle in Labour's power structure as he had aspired to meddle in government. From being a
redoubt of support for the leadership, the G and M turned into a
fussing, unreliable neutral which insisted upon building bridges
between people who didn't want to cross them and arranging
dialogues between people who didn't want to speak.

He was supposed to be part of the Right, and his creation
'Trade Unionists for a Labour Victory' was meant to comple-
ment a right-wing politicians' group, Campaign for a Labour
Victory. But Basnett's vanity was exceeded only by his limpness.
He was a low-grade Harold Wilson without the intelligence or
the occasional illuminating shaft of despair. As for the vanity, it
equipped him to distribute danegeld like maundy money. The
G and M was, and would become again, the ultimate garrison of
the Labour Establishment, but having Basnett in charge there
was like passing cannabis round the Household Cavalry.

One other personality counted and that was Tony Benn. We
have seen Hugh Gaitskell nearly 25 years before conferring with
the youthful Benn, one of a young group lobbying him with a
view on Suez. Gaitskell had minuted, 'Tony Benn . . . talented in
many ways, a good speaker and a man of ideas, has extraordinarily poor judgment. He is the last person in the world I
would go to for advice about policy.' Philip Williams, Gaitskell's
biographer, must have written in that quotation in 1978 with a
happy feeling of perfect aptness. In his memoirs Healey
compares Benn with Stafford Cripps, 'a political ninny of the
most superior quality'.

Benn, who had once called in effect for liftmen to prevent
publication of hostile newspaper articles, who talked of the
transfer of the means of production to working people and their
families, was seen late in the Conservative era which he helped
create, as unreal. His blissful notion of generally contented
Socialists sounds like the talk of dream children. If it suggests
any other notion of government, it recalls Eamon de Valera with
his Celtic vision of wholesome youths and pious maidens
dancing at crossroads. But although Benn and Bennism have
since been, like Bunbury, exploded, for about three years the
ideas were sketchily credible and the man a national preoccupation.

He was the leader the Left had never had since Bevan had
grown bored with them. And for Bevan's decelerated and drink-
tempered inertia in rebellion, he substituted most of the qualities
– as to words, effort, intensity, sobriety, intolerance and daily

travel – of John Wesley. Not only did he regard the whole Labour world as his parish, but he was bent upon doing 'all the good you can in all the ways you can, in all the time you can, to all the people as long as ever you can'. It would make him, this endearing fellow, for a time, the most hated man in Britain. But his purposes towards a Labour Party whose rules put power in the hands of constituencies and the still oligarchic but now erratic unions were serious business. With responsibility for government sensibly got out of the way, the Labour Party could now settle down to the important matter of nervous breakdown.

The parliamentary party was in the position of people defended by a carapace, the obligation – which is also a shield – of being a government. Once this had been removed they found that enemies made during the period of immunity now stood poised for what huntsmen call 'the death'. Unlike Butler, Healey would face his great prospect of election in exile and under fire. Butler was menaced by a single, well-placed sniper. Healey, Chancellor through those hard times, imposer of freezes, cutter of public spending, all-round iron housekeeper, faced a ring of rifles. Butler at least lost the prime ministership (and lost it twice). Healey was about to lose the leadership of the Opposition and the reversion of a premiership which the man defeating him would then put out of reach for a decade and a half.

The situation in 1980 was of a leadership election at a time which made it almost a distraction from the party's main business – and the party's main business in 1980 was despair. The Left were in the saddle, reselection was in prospect of becoming mandatory reselection, the envisioned collegiate process was thought certain to impose a left-wing leadership. Callaghan threw in his hand as leader a little earlier than he might have done, precisely in order that this last choice should be made by the parliamentary party in the old way: choice by a moderate group, choice also by an electorate which knew the candidates properly. The argument from competence had never been properly deployed in the preceding debate; presumably it was thought too élitist.

At the same time, the possibility was growing that Labour would not stay as a single party to be put back on conventional tracks by a new effective leader. The right wing contained people willing, as they would say (again and again) to break the mould, certainly to break something. For the moment they were simply fighting back without too much mutual co-ordination on the constitutional issues where the Left, accommodated by Basnett, hoped to draw up the constitution of a party institutionally ultra.

The sharpest of those who would later join the SDP were pitching at this early point for 'one man, one vote'. Having lost a comfortable small constituency, they aspired to the largest possible one, trying at all costs to avoid being mired in the middle way of union and constituency delegates. All sorts of theoretical/theological arguments could be used to make that case, but if you were a quick-minded threatened MP, you had a shrewd idea that the broad Labour-voting public was with you, as the parliamentary party was, and that the people who had won too much equity in the constituencies and the unions were not. It is a wise child who knows its own electorate.

So David Owen was making speeches about 'widening the franchise on a basis of genuinely greater democracy' at the same time as Bill Rodgers was speaking about the time having come to 'assert the rights, duties and role of the parliamentary party without equivocation'. Owen, despite sometimes having the judgment of Benn, was right about this. The events of the next few years – polls, by-elections, the temporary success of the SDP and the discreet charm of Blairism – would make his point with overwhelming numbers. The ineluctable Left of 1980–1 would shrivel into dust and prove, after all, eluctable.

But this was in the future. In 1980, the Left were the bosses and the chic. Denis Healey had an election to fight. He was the choice of his predecessor, he might expect to win the contest in normal circumstances and so the PLP was the desired arena. Though on the right, he was not in that group whose revulsion at recent developments had made them increasingly ready to leave the Labour Party. He existed to make the best of the party. When the special one-day conference took place at Wembley in May 1980[1] he went to the tribune to speak accompanied by a chant of 'Out, Out, Out.' It was a folk echo of the catcalls of 1976.

There was a lot of that sort of thing about. The same conference abounded in talk of 'weak-hearted traitors and cowards', and Tony Benn made a fool of James Callaghan by contradicting him in everything he said. A floor delegate called on the leader to 'retire to his farm and make room for someone who will do a better job'. (They were about to get Michael Foot.) But angry as he might be, Healey, the candidate, could not and did not offer himself as a vehement partisan candidate of the Right against the Left. There were good reasons why he should not do so. The marginal votes among the unity-at-all-costs people, the natural responders to Harold Wilson's appeasing instinct. The nearest thing to a fully shaped right-wing bloc was centred upon devotion to Europe, about which Healey was less than sacramental, and upon Roy Jenkins, who wasn't Denis Healey.

That group's complaint against institutional Labour went back to 1971–2 and Wilson's decision to hold a referendum on Europe. To use a phrase later coined in another party, they were semi-detached. But they were ready for a fight and many of them felt that Healey was not.

Crewe and King, in their excellent account of the SDP, quote the bitterness against Healey into which one of this group slipped: 'Healey as you know, likes to bluster and shout and bully people, but he's really just Ferdinand the Bull. He gets up and bellows once in a while, but most of the time he just sits there, sniffs flowers and drinks gin and tonic and listens to his records. He'll fight for himself if he's attacked, but fight for a cause or a principle? Never.'[2]

This is massively unfair. The principles dearest to this group were, after all, not Healey's. The nonsenses which would be loaded upon Labour at conferences after the election of Michael Foot – unilateralism, promiscuous nationalisation, actual withdrawal from Europe – would provide causes for him to fight against.

Tactically, Healey could argue that he had votes to lose from the nervous centre to balance any he might gain on an exasperated and disappointed Right. The language we use about politics at this time is inadequate, too much an affair of hard and fast 'blocs' (Labour has always liked transforming the French word into 'block' as in 'block vote', suggesting something you could be hit with, which, on reflection, is fair enough). But the word oversimplifies. There were no monolithic blocs. There were at least two rights, both frayed: the roughly identifiable Jenkins group and another, looser body, linked to traditional Labour and continuity, a sort of heritage group, much concerned about the state of the roof, but anxious now over the loaded shotguns in the conservatory. If one wants to be genealogical, the first group descended from Gaitskell, through Jenkins, refined as to purpose (and reduced in number). The other, more traditional set – municipal or trade-union based, lowbrow, wrong knives and forks, and rooted –

was made up of Herbert Morrison's sort of people.

Both elements detested what Benn was doing. None of their members had watched the rise of Arthur Scargill with any satisfaction. But all the affinities were negative. Less clear-minded than the lady in the art gallery, they knew only what they *didn't* like. But then again, the second group was divided from the first by different things. Some people didn't much care for Europe, some people felt split off socially. Many Jenkinsites, including their now absent leader, were extraordinarily ill at ease with working-class or non-university-educated MPs, including those whose support they naturally expected. It was a very Butlerian failing.

I have seen it with my own eyes: an uncomfortable shuffling politeness on both sides, the man with the vocabulary and the points of reference not seriously differing in belief from the man who left a coal-seam at 40 or had come into Parliament from a borough council, but both hovering near that town-and-gown, young-master-and-decent-yeoman relationship which the British do so well. There are terms, like 'staunch', to which Mrs Thatcher was devoted in her cloth-eared way, and 'salt of the earth', which are used by the aboves about the belows and form a nexus between man and man too fragrant and sur-refined to be pressed further. But the notions that surround them – the two-way communication of clumsy goodwill becoming patronage and acceptance becoming resentment – had played their part in the heavy rejection of Jenkins in the 1976 leadership contest.

Healey was, on the whole, good and clear of this sort of embarrassment. He was a man from Keighley with a first-class Oxford degree. If he went on a bit about Yeats and Mahler and was at home with foreigners, he didn't give offence by it. He had no supersensible tastes in food and drink as long as there was plenty of it. Unlike Rab Butler, he was not aloof, still less shy – he must be the most clubbable lone wolf in zoological history. The accent helped; it was all over the place with the occasional Balliol vowel, but it was far more Yorkshire than anything else. Then again, he had a sort of civil servant's standing. He had done two jobs – pretty acceptable in all but doctrinaire left-wing or extreme Tory opinion – but only two, and over long terms. So he was remembered in them which, after Harold Wilson's way of playing chess with a Parkinson's disease shudder, could not be said of many former Cabinet ministers.

Healey had all the strengths of non-membership of a group. Of course he was on the Right, but what was the point of spelling it out? In a period of febrile excitement begun with defeat, marked by strategic assault, accompanied by bubbling hatred and to end in schism and exodus, the case for *not* raising the temperature was obvious. He was also, for all the lone-wolf chatter, part of the Establishment, things as they were and should be, continuity! He was Denis-after-Jim-after-Harold, only not so feebly devious as Harold and a crisper executive than Jim. There would be, among the people advising him, much talk of applecarts and the not upsetting of them.

Talk of bullying and blustering and Ferdinand the Bull hardly applied to Healey the beachmaster or Healey facing the British economy. Even the argument, used for instance of William Whitelaw, that a man may be brave, even heroic in soldierly conflict, but nervous in civilian disputes, has little application here. Healey was the Minister who had turned that economy round by doing things which left-wing Labour hated and middling Labour was scared rigid of doing. He had come back to Labour Conference, reared up into all the feral malignity of which it is capable; come back to the ridiculous five minutes which its bureaucracy afforded a Chancellor not on the executive. He came back rationally and with an argument, but chiefly with defiant courage.

His principle now of treading softly because Labour in the griefs of the early eighties should be handled as something fragile was perfectly sound. But omitting the scorn and the charge of pusillanimity, it is possible to argue that nevertheless he made a mistake. Called upon to speak to the Manifesto Group, a right-wing tent inside the parliamentary party, he was wilfully unforthcoming, brushing off his questioners. John Cartwright, it is thought, was the MP who said flatly, 'Your answers have been very unsatisfactory. There are an awful lot of us. Why should we vote for you?' And Healey answered bluntly, 'You have nowhere else to go.' As the history of the SDP would demonstrate, that was strictly correct, though Liberal Democracy has made a decent billet. But correctness, like patriotism, is not always enough. The final election for leader would fail him by a handful of votes, and some gesture of empathy and warmth towards the manifesto people might well have reconciled to him the handful he would lack. Against this, until we know the names of every one of the five (or was it seven?) right-wing MPs credited by conflicting sources with having voted for Michael Foot, we can't say so with certainty. Some people are more reconcilable than others.

One of the five (or seven) is on record, anonymously (and pusillanimously) as saying: 'It was dirty politics. I admit it. I – and quite a few others – thought that Foot had to be elected in order to convince the waverers that the game was up and that we had no choice but to move. I was particularly concerned about Shirley. If Healey had won, I still think she wouldn't have come over.' This speaks the preoccupation of suicide, someone fretting that the gun is decently oiled and the noose properly adjusted. It is not clear how Healey could have won over such a committed martyr.

But since the actual vote would be horribly close – first ballot: Healey 112, Foot 83, Silkin 38, Shore 32; second ballot: Foot 139, Healey 129 – every vote would count. If the five future SDP votes, the acknowledged minimum, had gone from Foot to Healey, then the first-round lead, with Healey on 117, and Foot on 78, would have been 39.   Identical redistribution in the second round would have produced a score of Healey 134, Foot 132. But with the wider first-poll gap, there would not have *been* identical redistribution. A larger lead creates its own precipitation, the camp of victory beckons, especially to scared rank-and-file politicians. So every increment weighed heavily. The perfect silliness of Neville Sandelson, who excitedly told everyone of his Herostratan ballot, and the decision of so unlikely a person as Tam Dalyell, who informed the author that he had voted for Foot, made major contributions to the deciding tilt of probability.

Tam Dalyell's complaint was that Healey had, on one particular occasion as a minister, been dismissive of his own serious purpose, a visit to Borneo. It may sound frivolous, but nobody is less frivolous than Tam. Nobody is less interested in free trips. He had nurtured a painstaking interest in the territory where we had just fought a war and, having entitlement for his excellent voting record, made approaches through the Chief Whip, Ted Short. Healey had been explosively dismissive and made it clear, in Dalyell's words, that he had 'no time for people who fuck him about'. Healey's own remark had been, 'The defence budget East of Suez hasn't got helicopters to take you bloody around.' That sounds terribly authentic.

Now, Tam Dalyell is not a petty-minded man any more than he is a tripper. But he takes his own seriousness seriously. He quotes Crossman's remark to him that Healey had a typical ex-Communist Party cast of mind, intolerant of other people's opinions. Dalyell, with typical honesty, couples all this with two sad points. His wife, Kathleen, had 'never been so angry with me as she was for not voting for Healey. She said I must be off my rocker.' Then, he said, after quoting the Crossman remark, 'In spite of all that, I might have been wrong. He might have made a very good prime minister indeed.'

This case history, honourably placed on the record by its subject, has its own minor tragic quality. Dalyell is the exemplary backbencher – free spirit, maker of justified trouble, goer-on – rightly about the Belgrano and (at Healey) about the island of Aldabra. Healey, in the way of Butler, is the exemplary executive minister, like his friend Helmut Schmidt, a *Macher*, or doer. You would expect them to collide and bounce off one another, but they shouldn't fall out. And Dalyell's other comments resonate beyond his own case. He felt that 'Healey would split the Party'. So much for Ferdinand the Bull sniffing the flowers and going back to his records. Also he complains that Healey could communicate only with the great, not colleagues.

But Peter Hardy is not a great man, though an excellent and devoted member. His recollection is of Healey coming down to the constituency dinner in Rother Valley to back him when Arthur Scargill, in his role as king of south Yorkshire, had plans for changing the rules and the MP, and of Denis standing up to speak. 'Peter Hardy isn't perfect.' Silence, intake of breath – odd thing to say. '*Denis Healey* isn't perfect.' Rising expectation. 'And Arthur Scargill isn't perfect, either.' Explosion of delight.

Hardy also recollects his elderly father being drawn cheerfully into a long conversation with Healey many years before on the seafront at Scarborough. The thesis of Healey being only at home among the great doesn't fit a thoroughly democratic if affably homicidal person. But it is true that Healey can be very rude indeed – often therapeutically. Frank Allaun, not a man who would vote for him in a million years, was harassing him in a backbench meeting in the late sixties after the main cuts, and demanding more, in the way Allaun did, through piping and interminable Commons questions and letters to the *Guardian* over 30 years.

Healey snorted. 'You lot think we're in London Zoo. You're the pelicans and I'm the keeper. Well, there ain't going to be no more.' That sort of truculent joshing was essential Healey and one is thankful for it, but said a degree more sharply and to a marginal backbencher with a thin skin, it could alienate. And when the vote came, it did not need many to have been alienated. Incidentally, among those who were was a member of his Treasury team.

Those few prospective SDP people who stabbed at Healey on their way to the door voted on the principle that things must get worse before they got better. And there were others on the Right who, despite voting for Healey, and like David Owen, displaying their ballots to friends as proof of it, nevertheless regarded his defeat as that hopeful worse because they did not expect him to take on the Left. And King and Crewe endorse them. Putting the hypothetical, but fascinating question, what would have happened to the SDP if he had won, they run the options of his making a stand and winning, making a stand and losing and 'turning out to be not a Gaitskell, but a Callaghan, doing deals with trades-union leaders, prepared endlessly to compromise with the Left in the interests of party unity' and relate them to their own concern whether or not the SDP would then have been precipitated.

A Healey victory against Foot would have postponed the break, but, say King and Crewe, 'One's judgment in the end depends on what one thinks of Denis Healey and one's assessment of the balance of forces inside the Labour Party'. 'Our judgment is,' they continue, 'that he would not have fought and that if he had, he would have lost. The Labour Party in the early and mid-1980s could only be led successfully from somewhere on the left.'

Respectfully, the Labour Party at that time could perhaps only *grant* its leadership to someone on the left, a very different proposition. Labour in its collective parliamentary shape was scared and willing to tell itself tall stories of things coming right in the end. Healey would underpoll at least in part through the faint-heartedness of other people. But this does not mean that Labour could only be led successfully from somewhere on the left. Neil Kinnock would be elected with left-wing credentials crudely sweetened and toned down, only to amaze the Left by his ingratitude. The term 'Soft Left' was one of the most elegant, if improvised, pieces of political camouflage ever devised. It covered the common-sense disillusion of a good-faith, if lightly moored, former leftist with better sense than anyone in 1980 envisaged.

Kinnock's election led onto a betrayal, that therapeutic, necessary betrayal essential if the Labour Party was to be saved for politics. The tactics followed by a succeeding Healey would have been different, the sugar on the pill thinner and less convincing, but he would have been trying to assert the same common sense. What King and Crewe are really saying is that you had to start on the Left to be able to leave it and that, on turning right, people would follow you.

Healey, when questioned, sees all of this in a different perspective. Exhaustion, he says, 'plays a bigger part in politics than anyone thinks, and we were exhausted'. He makes a comparison with 1951, when Labour didn't even complain at being represented with fewer seats when it had a majority of votes and when a slightly later election would have enabled a Labour chancellor to bring in Butler's second gratifying budget. 'We could,' he says, 'have been in power like the Social Democrats were in Sweden.' The Swedish Social Democrats have been either in absolute power or the dominant members of a coalition, less about six years, since 1932.

Exhaustion in 1979 meant that subjection to the left-wing assault and the campaign for constitutional changes particularly hit the tired ex-members of a five-year Government. Healey reckons that Callaghan's lingering in office even the little time that he did made his own chances of election weaker. If Callaghan had gone in 1979 before the threats of constitutional reform 'and the conference that was forced on us by Basnett's stupidity' got going, the election would have been a normal one. As it was, Parliamentarians making their last independent choice were crowded by constituency activists, had people looking over their shoulders and were picking a leader who would have to live with a new regime. The charm of not giving offence to what were supposed to be the new masters played a part not owned up to by the confused number who fell for it.

If the PLP had voted in the autumn of 1979, the leader would have been chosen without such looming threats and the charges of illegitimacy. Logically, Healey would have won. As it was, he says, he had to push Callaghan to go as early as he did and, in the worsening atmosphere, he then lost. Healey, not surprisingly, does not share Crewe and King's opinion of what he would have done if elected. A programme of 'compromise with the Left in the interests of Party unity' is not what he had in mind. Nor is eternal deference to the unions. He distinguishes between lefts. 'I should have had to take on the *far* Left,' he says. And expands,

The weird thing that happened in those disastrous years, the early eighties, was the Trots, who weren't even the far Left of the Labour Party – they were doctrinal entryists. They were a section of the Communist movement which

thought they could create a revolution by destroying the
Labour Party. I would have had to take that lot on and draw
a distinction between them and what we now call the old
Left. And I would have had to take them on because I
couldn't have done anything without.

The unions, properly handled, would have been allies against the assault. Healey would in particular have engaged himself to work with Terry Duffy. Duffy needed to be dissuaded from the odd belief that he shouldn't use union votes against an expansion of union electoral power which was being proposed for the electoral college. Healey also speaks of the SDP people as 27 allies in the parliamentary party who would still have been there *because* he had won. Healey can show a purpose to those who believe that he would have submitted, compromised and accommodated the Left.

He is accused of not being solicitous enough of the possible ship-jumpers and of being a mere noisy continuation of the old weak Wilsonian line. But his experience as Chancellor had made him increasingly unhappy with the union mentality. 'They were not democratic organisations. They cast their bloc votes without consulting the membership ... the pressure by Thatcher to make union decisions more democratic was absolutely right and long overdue ...' The unions began to realise, he adds, speaking of a rather later period, 'that they were the obstacle to the election of a Labour Government'. He was pleased to find Hugh Scanlon, the old hard man of the engineers, for whom he had always had respect, conceding that his union had done most to wreck the British motor industry.

But that is hypothesis and hypothesis in the past conditional tense. Healey was defeated, through defections, offence given, exhaustion and an uncertain campaign. On 10 November 1980 Michael Foot was chosen by 10 votes on the second ballot to lead the Labour Party, a hard blow to Healey and a calamitous one to Foot. Foot's candidacy had been a composite: some wifely enthusiasm, an element of affection for an old trouper with a disjunctive charm, a hoping, quite rightly, that he might not be excessively left-wing after all. There was a belief on the calculating Left that he was an instrument weak enough to be serviceable. And an aggrandising sort of trade-unionist like Clive Jenkins trusted that his deference to unions would make him their creature.

Quite simply, Foot's leadership was a crucifixion. And though his poll figures didn't plummet until the summer, crucifixions have no honeymoon. He was the object of cruel, derisive contempt *ab initio*. The jibe 'Worzel Gummidge' celebrated a scarecrow with a funny walk and a strange voice who was altogether kind and lovable, but not quite the leader of Her Majesty's Opposition. The fact that he was left wing in a platonic, democratic, romantic sort of way did not stop him from being left-wing, and the Conservative tabloid press knew exactly what to do about that.

The age may be censured for its enchantment with what are called 'boyish good looks' – witness David Owen and Tony Blair. It may be excessive for Peter Mandelson to worry about a Shadow Cabinet member having too round a face for TV, but Mr Mandelson, like Mrs Thatcher's hairdresser doing a set every day, is the legatee of Michael Foot. Appearances may be deceptive; good looks, in Miss Prism's phrase, may be a snare; John Kennedy wasn't actually a very remarkable President. But the snare and the deception are preconditional to any imaginable merit of a candidate having the least chance of use in office.

Public relations may be a shoddy thing, but to have no public relations is to go to the Cenotaph in a donkey jacket; the fact of it being a new, best donkey jacket and worn in as great a reverence for the war dead as any suit over a stuffed shirt are good points that will never be taken.

It was open to Healey at this stage to decelerate, to go through motions and look for a pleasant alternative life outside Parliament. In fact he would stay as deputy to Foot, continuing to conduct foreign affairs as Shadow until after the defeat of Labour and resignation of Foot in 1983. One shouldn't make too much of merit in a politician and I am not accusing Healey of solitary virtue. Labour would stay in the lead for some time yet. The first three years of Mrs Thatcher's Government were marked by spectacular unpopularity, the riots of 1981 and unemployment figures about which we are now blasé and in 1980–1 thought apocalyptic. Again Healey, as one keeps saying, is an optimist, excessively so. The possibility of being Foreign Secretary must have seemed real. But the jobs on offer in and about this time were luscious affairs. The secretary-generalship of NATO would come up (twice), also the equivalent post in the IMF, and to the taker of spoils, irresistibly, the chairmanship of GEC. Healey didn't 'want to be an international civil servant carrying out other people's policies' and specifically didn't want the managing directorship of the IMF because he reckons 'from bitter experience' that nothing can be done in that organisation against the wishes of the US Treasury.

In recent years we have seen a raft of Conservative ministers take up chairmanships and directorships in companies created by privatisation which they have conducted through Commons legislation. It isn't illegal, but it isn't fastidious either. The instinct of Sir Norman Fowler's generation had been to follow the advice of Guizot, '*Enrichissez-vous*'. Healey's reaction to the GEC offer from Sir Arnold Weinstock, a highly cultivated tycoon with whom he had good relations, was, 'It's not me, and it took me about 25 seconds to say no to that. I refused on the spot, which Arnold still finds difficult to understand. But apart from not wanting to do that sort of thing, thinking it over later, I couldn't *possibly* represent as an ex-Defence Secretary a firm which made most of its money out of selling defence equipment to the Government.'

Not too many politicians of either party with options like that would stay after a humiliation at the hands of a much lesser man in return for the wobbly option of possibly becoming Foreign Secretary in three and a half years' time. But there is a profound streak of institutional loyalty in Denis Healey. He is a good party man indeed but also a good Parliament man.

Healey himself, when asked about this, goes back reflectively. There was more coherence as to ideas in his time but there was something more important.

> The thing that was branded on the inner core of everybody in the Labour Party was the need for loyalty. The memory went back to what was perceived as the desertion of MacDonald and Snowden which had destroyed the Party and kept us out. So whatever happened, we had to keep the thing together. We did feel we were part of a movement. It had got us where we were and it was our duty to go on working with it.

He also cites wartime military service. 'It made everyone, whether Tory, Liberal or Labour, realise that there is such a thing as society and that we all depend on one another . . . and that was a dominant feeling in my generation on all sides – Ted and Willie Whitelaw; Peter Carrington was just the same. And that's completely gone now.' Without moralising heavily, he observes with sorrow that the social purpose which followed the war has completely disintegrated in favour of looking after oneself and adds that insecurity of employment has heavily contributed to this.

The best side of a puritanism now generally abandoned had governed him. Disinterested motives outweighed the optimism and the entirely honourable ambition to serve in the post of Foreign Secretary for which he had equipped himself over a lifetime. He stayed on and gave himself the unspeakable pleasure of being challenged in the deputyship he disliked, a conflict which would determine long-term whether the Labour Party would survive as a serious force. Considered as personal conduct, that course of action represents what Conservative moralists like to call old-fashioned values.

[1]Not to be confused with the constitutional conference also held at Wembley, which took place in January 1981.
[2]Quoted anonymously in Crewe and King, p. 76.

CHAPTER SEVEN

By staying as number two after defeat for the leadership, Healey took on many burdens, the first of which would be defending the challenge of Tony Benn for the emblematic bauble of the deputy leadership. A contemporary speaks of Healey's 'hatred for Tony Benn'. But if one reads Benn's own account, Michael Foot seems hardly more sympathetic to the challenger. Healey is not a hater; he may be rough, brusque, rude, liable to knock one over in getting more quickly to the point, but he is also genial and inclined to forget the affront received almost as readily as the one assuredly given. That is part of a general optimism and incapacity to brood, an interesting and emphatic contrast with his friend and close parallel, Helmut Schmidt, a man of similar gifts and outlook who did make the highest office but who has always laboured under intermittent crushing depression.

But Benn for a couple of years would dominate everyone's calculations. What might have been Labour's time for recovery and rebound became its great tearing apart, with the innocent champion of the Left weirdly standing calm at the centre of unacknowledged calamity. Accordingly, such spare bad psychology as Healey has, plus vast contempt, would be directed point-blank at the member for Bristol South. Benn might be sincere, but he was bidden on by a meddlesome destiny and the least touch of vanity to a conflict which would irreconcilably divide a party which had just lost an election, would drive a tenth of its MPs into a new one and leave Labour, 15 years later, still in opposition.

It was a bitter time generally. Healey reckons that he was as busy between 1980 and 1983 as he had been at the Treasury. He was stuck with a Foot leadership, honourable enough in its discombobulated way, but injuriously left wing in rhetoric and assumptions, no good at administration and a presentational catastrophe. Healey was obliged to assent to a unilateralism-and-nationalisation-happy programme with which he had no sympathy. He had to defend the indefensible until it could be got rid of and hear the duller sort of Tory call him a twister for his pains. He sat on the NEC ex-officio and the NEC–TUC liaison committee as well as functioning as Shadow Foreign Secretary. It was a career structure deficient in halfpence and vivid with kicks.

A flavour of the brief, bitter Foot era comes in the exchange reported by Benn himself during a meeting of something called the Policy Co-ordinating Committee in February 1981. Norman Atkinson, Party Treasurer, a man of inordinate dullness of the sullen, stolid, resenting sort, had rounded on Roy Hattersley.

> 'Look, we are trying to get a fundamental reconstruction. Is Hattersley really trying to run a social democratic ticket? You' – turning to Hattersley – 'can't deliver 3 million jobs without a fundamental transformation of the economy. And there is no hope if the Treasury is in charge. We have got to think it through.'
>
> Denis Healey said, 'I agree with Norman Atkinson that we must think it through, and we shall all watch with interest while he attempts that task himself.'
>
> Atkinson replied very angrily, 'We shall watch your demise too.'
>
> Hattersley asked, 'What the hell does that mean?'
>
> 'Well, what the hell did Denis mean when he said he would watch me thinking?'

The Left had gained apparent great advantage with the Wembley conference decision. Forty per cent of the leadership franchise was a vast gain in power. In *The Benn Diaries* – which in their charmingly candid way, have odd little cameos of people like Joe Ashton coming up to Tony Benn and mentioning that the unions were moving to the right and of Benn receiving that important information with perfect blank non-reflection – Benn talks at one point about history not being understood by his opponents. History would fairly soon roll oceanically over Tony Benn, but in 1981 it didn't seem like that.

His decision that year to challenge Healey for the deputy leadership was pressed for by some of his circle as a necessary striking while iron was hot, though it is interesting to find one supporter, Reg Race, observing that the Wembley vote was 'flukey' and advising caution.

But the people who most disliked the candidacy were those with power in, and responsibility for the party, including a furious Foot – who could barely bring himself beyond minimum civility towards Benn – and the likes of Clive Jenkins who, having helped block Healey's leadership and enjoying his piece of brokerage won at Wembley, clearly favoured consolidation and a period of quiet. But the oil of Jenkins, who presented the challenger with a handsome, gold-rimmed loving cup with the slogans 'Elections can be poisoned chalices, Tony' and 'Don't do it, Tony', made no more impression than Foot's phuttering anger.

In June came the sharpest of all rebukes from the leadership. Michael Foot, in a statement which Benn airily attributes to Healey, Peter Shore and others – the Establishment – invited him to stand in a different contest. 'In view of what he has said and done over recent weeks . . . I have told Tony Benn that, in my judgment, his only course now is to stand against me . . .'

Benn is widely and rightly liked as a man. But part of his nature is to be innocently impervious, almost autistic. Quietly convinced of the perfect rightness of what he was doing, he strolled on, a little miffed to be rebuked, but putting it down to the machinations of people clearly getting at Foot. Individual colleagues made no more impression on him. Leo Abse came and said very angrily, 'You are destroying the party,' only to be told, 'Look, Leo. You are in a minority. I support the Labour Party. Anyway, I don't know whether *you* are going to stay or go.' Abse replied, 'Nothing will get me out of the Labour Party except death or expulsion.'

'His voice,' says Benn, 'was raised so loud that everybody crowded round: the clerks in the Lobby heard every word of it, and I came home feeling slightly distressed about the bitterness in the parliamentary party.' With such insouciant good manners, such coolness under fire, Benn might in another age have been a great, disastrous naval commander.

The contest itself would be a paradox. In one sense, it was a stunning achievement for Benn that he came within less than a percentage point of victory, and Healey might feel that, even under the new rules, he ought to have crushed Benn. On the other hand, the whole episode was a public airing of the struggle inside the Labour Party expressed in precisely those personality terms which Tony Benn has memorably denounced. He favours 'issues', and issues lack front-page flavour, while a Manichean struggle between eyebrows and pipe registers, resonates and makes for the taking of sides. That struggle also demonstrated, only months after it had been exalted to even greater strength, the grotesque elephantiasis of union influence inside the party.

How far Denis Healey benefited from the campaign waged for him by the *Sun* and *Daily Express* – for which at this time he wrote a column – and others is dubious. The shrill, fatuous Cummings cartoon showing Tony Benn of all people in full Nazi regalia with the caption '*Ein Volk, Ein Reich, Ein Fuehrer*' is the sort of thing which makes all Benn's points for him. On the other hand, the Left likes to talk of 'raising public consciousness'. Tony Benn did that all right, though hardly to his own advantage when the Left had done so well lately by stealth. The contest would show the British press, 'the most prostituted in the world', according to Aneurin Bevan at a time when it was altogether more fastidious, conducting a wholesale and hysterical assassination of Benn.

On the other hand, the devices by which he hoped to rise had nothing in common with the democracy in which Benn sincerely and earnestly believes. It would all hang upon meetings of constituency parties whose collapse in numbers and extensive subjection to shell operations had long since been reported by the National Organiser, Reg Underhill, and that report shelved. Even more would depend upon meetings of union executives or delegate conferences which undertook to cast the votes of members who resembled nothing so much as the Dead Souls of Gogol.

The Transport and General, the biggest player in the contest, would carry out a poll among its regional organisations – and find a big majority for Healey. The executive decided that, membership be damned, they couldn't possibly support him so they would seek another candidate. They found one in the affable former Chief Whip John Silkin, who would be knocked out in the first round. Alec Kitson, for the union, then announced a planned abstention on the second ballot only to have a last-minute executive huddle resolve that no, they would vote for Benn after all. This, as Healey phlegmatically notes, made the difference between his getting in by a whisker and having a thumping majority.

The word 'democracy' was rarely off anybody's lips at this

time and the question of the people who broadly supported a party actually making a central decision about it never arose. But if it had, then as that T and G poll had shown to the union executive's averted eyes, Healey would have won. For that matter, with such a real electorate he would have won the leadership itself. This was demonstrated again, and very sharply, within the public-services union, NUPE, which, in contrast to the T and G's hugger-mugger off-floor meeting to dispose of a million votes, behaved with great rectitude. The NUPE executive was left-wing, containing people who had been involved in the Winter of Discontent strikes. But it held a consultation of its members on the deputy leadership, received the answer 'Healey' and voted for Healey. If every union had behaved in the same way on major issues, the bloc-vote system might have begun to be defensible.

Tony Benn's diaries ring with hypothetical totals appearing on his son Joshua's computer supposing that Arthur Scargill could swing a roomful of Nottinghamshire miners. The contrast with what Labour-supporting public opinion demonstrably wanted was too vivid. But Joshua's computer reflected power as it stood disposed, the admired exertions of members of executives. The union bloc vote had always been undemocratic, never more so than when Arthur Deakin, Ernest Bevin's nominated successor, used it to keep down the Bevanites whose support was confined to the constituency parties. But Deakin and Bevin were despots cutting with the grain of public opinion. It is very doubtful that they ever contradicted general feeling among Labour voters. Benn's words to Leo Abse, 'Leo, you are in a minority. I support the Labour Party,' were true only in the most etiolated form, in a Pickwickian sense. But Labour at this moment, was a Pickwickian party.

The Gogol analogy is irresistible. The opinion of a minority was inflated by committees touched with megalomania into the 'voice of the people'. It was no such thing, and the millions of non-voters cited were an exact echo of that roll-call of deceased serfs. Brilliant organisation and stupid mistakes had worked with the inertia of the union system to give activists the rewards of activism, a constitution geared even further towards union power at a fleeting moment when the unions were left-wing. In fact, the whole thing was a chimera since the unions, already moving right, would soon revert to their traditional stance. The longer-term implications ten years and more on would lead away from union influence and towards a form of one man, one vote which, under Tony Blair, would itself have acclamatory and authoritarian qualities.

But it didn't seem like that at the time. The election for the petty post was emblematic of the entire quarrel within the Labour Party. It had to be fought and Healey had to fight it. He travelled the country, published a pamphlet, 'Socialism With a Human Face', and generally became more the public politician than ministerial burdens and inclinations had permitted before. These were, according to Healey, 'the most disagreeable six months of my life' and involved two or three broadcasts a day and three or four meetings a week. All this, as he says, for a job which he didn't enjoy and which wasn't worth having. Life became Ixionic with the hero, bound to his wheel of fire, under an additional requirement to smile at the cameras.

But Healey is not altogether good at elections. His campaign in the leadership contest had been underpowered and had failed to reach out to the dubious. In this one he would make a wild charge that booing and heckling at a particular meeting had been organised by Jon Lansman, Benn's highly effective young assistant. It hadn't been and there was no reason why Healey should have thought it had. Sheer anger at the unpleasantness never far away in the doings of the Left, including the travelling claque which dogged him, led to a momentary blurring of his judgment and a consequent lashing out.

But the memory of that time, a memory over several years, is of so much bullying public rage, of crowds used as weapons of intimidation. And intimidation, though Benn would never consciously and deliberately employ it, was part of the battle. A resolute minority – not a tiny one, as the cliché puts it, but a minority for all that – which goes Millwall supporter from the floor is an horrific thing. Anyone who followed Labour Party conferences at this time, never mind more particular meetings, remembers a feral hostility vented on Parliamentarians or anyone daring to speak plainly for a non left-wing line. But it didn't start in 1980; it had been a factor at big meetings and notably Party Conference for some time and it was an acknowledged factor in the coming split.

One of those who would leave for the SDP described his reaction to the atmosphere on an earlier conference occasion on which Denis Healey had tried to do his job:

In my case it goes back to the '76 conference. There were a lot of very unpleasant people there who just didn't give a

damn about trying to save this country's currency. Healey
was on his way to an IMF meeting and was brought back to
the conference from the airport. And he was booed all the
way to the rostrum. I was horrified, I hated it: that bloody
mob, those clenched fists, those pointing fingers.

Ultimately, it didn't matter that Jon Lansman specifically was
innocent, though the charge had been a silly thing to raise.
Healey had long endured a full share of the destructive and
malignant crowd rage, upon which, in its innocence, the
campaign of Tony Benn floated.

For a long time now Benn had been in a state of exultation.
Back at the Wembley special conference when, through Terry
Duffy's tactical naïvety and David Basnett's strategic folly, the
unions had emerged with 40 per cent of the vote and MPs with
30 per cent, Benn commented to his diary. 'It was an important
day. It will never be reversed and nothing will ever be the
same again.' Nor would it. On 26 January 1981, Roy Jenkins,
Shirley Williams, David Owen and Bill Rodgers had issued
their Limehouse Declaration, the preludial salvo to the creation
of the SDP.

Healey had thus been given another task. As he put it himself,
'I would spend months as unpaid social-psychiatric counsellor
to people contemplating defection to the SDP.' The long crumble
of central authority and morale in the party which had
accelerated through the election of Foot, the revision of the
constitution and now the Benn candidacy, had persuaded two
groups of people, Roy Jenkins' circle and a looser group of
moderates, that the party was irrecoverable, probably
unelectable and anyway not one that they wanted elected.
Benn's earlier phrase about an 'irreversible transfer of power'
might or might not do anything for the 'working people and
their families' he had designated for this undertaking. But as
sure as could be, it was transferring power (and self-respect)
away from Labour Members of Parliament. Coupled with the
sheer nastiness injected into conference and crowds, the feeling
picked up by anyone attending, as I did, was that Members of
Parliament sitting as a group were objects of contempt and
hatred, rather like the First Estate of the French assembly, the
nobility, in about 1791. It all made for an unprecedented and
widespread inclination to have done with a party in such a state.

We are not concerned here with the ultimate failure of the
Social Democratic Party. It lost momentum, small mistakes

turned big and personality incompatibility problems familiar to the divorce courts occurred. But it was still a momentous thing just to have happened at all and it stood a very tolerable chance of destroying the Labour Party as a useful force. Shirley Williams would win Crosby for the SDP, Roy Jenkins came very close at supposedly impregnable Warrington. By Christmas 1981 the combined SDP and Liberal support as measured by Gallup was 50.5 per cent. Prophecies were intimated which would flower on May Day 1997.

Healey was perfectly certain and unequivocal at all times that in no circumstances would he contemplate joining the exodus. As a close follower of the domestic politics of foreign countries, he was familiar with the Italian experience where another Social Democratic Party had broken from the Italian Socialists (PSI) over links its leader, Pietro Nenni, had with the Italian Communists. That had split itself and dwindled after an early efflorescence. He foresaw Jenkins as another Giuseppe Sarragat and was fundamentally right to do so. But whether he was personally right to be quite so much of a loyalist and to slog on in harness with Foot is something else.

The SDP, merely by existing, caused a Labour defeat in 1983 to become a humiliation. The latter part of Denis Healey's career, as leadership, never mind premiership, receded, is one of considerable disinterested service to his party. Labour did indeed enjoy a lead in the period when Mrs Thatcher's monetarist policies were creating 3.5 million unemployed, when riots broke out in London and other cities. But the combination of the Falklands War (about which, ironically, Michael Foot was hot and Denis Healey cool) and the Labour split would make a Conservative victory inevitable after spring 1982. The Falklands War caused a jump in Conservative support to nearly 50 per cent. And Foot's leadership, his vulnerability to a sustained hail of cruel but credible derision in the press, had sealed things.

The effect of the Falklands War was to defeat not Labour, but the 'Alliance' of SDP and Liberals which had at one stage established that absolute percentage majority in the polls. Labour had been electorally doomed from the moment in early 1981 when the SDP was established. From then on, Healey was not realistically looking forward to renewed Cabinet office, still less the leadership or the prime ministership. Without being too pious, he was, from that date onwards, the responsible member of a leadership group in a time of travail. He might spin himself occasional yarns about heroic sequences of contingent events but, in practice, he fought that miserable campaign to stay as deputy leader in the knowledge that his defeat would make Labour an unredeemably extremist and unelectable party. Even with that disaster seen off, Labour almost hit third place in 1983. He was bound to his wheel, felt that he must endure and did so. What followed was an epilogue to a career, one which took full part in vigorous opposition, showing the general public the full fire-spitting genial profile of a man so long confined to the desk and ministerial preoccupation. Possibly the public enjoyed it more than he did.

There are no automatic rewards for virtue and there would be no question of his inheriting the leadership four years ahead of the next election at the age of 66, but he could have slipped away there and then to a distinguished and splendidly remunerated business appointment.

As we have noted, Healey rejected two major international posts and the chairmanship of a great company. Passing the deputyship to Roy Hattersley, he went back to the front bench until 1987 and stayed in Parliament until 1992. At the urgent invitation of the new leader, Neil Kinnock, Healey ran in 1983 for the Shadow Cabinet, came top and served on as Shadow Foreign Secretary in a party with 209 seats in Parliament. It was immensely helpful to Kinnock, who needed the old guard as friends and colleagues rather desperately. And when Healey did finally go, the Conservatives would have an enviable time comparing and contrasting their foreign affairs man, Douglas Hurd, with Gerald Kaufman.

George Robertson, who in 1997 would himself become Defence Secretary, had as a young MP seen a good deal of Healey, having been a junior spokesman first on defence, then foreign affairs, when Healey was shadowing them. He reports something close to a shift in personality. Having observed Healey's brisk, impatient, too-busy manner he then, when working to the man, found him quantifiably sweetened – solicitous, kind and interested in the younger man's future. Healey's new mood showed in a self-mocking humour which could surface even in grim circumstances. Don Anderson, who was his deputy handling foreign affairs in opposition after 1983, tells of attending the funeral of Yuri Andropov at the Kremlin. The old men of Soviet decline were grouped about – stooping, white-haired, octogenerian generals and politicians headed by the interim leader, Konstantin Chernenko, already the visible victim of the emphysema that would soon kill him. 'Denis looked around at these ancients and their decrepit leader and murmured, "There's hope for me yet!" '

There was nothing for Healey in the political life he was now resuming, only chores and a good number of debating triumphs and a letting loose of a wit which the years of departmental toil had rather muffled. The greatest of these was a speech I chanced to hear in debate on the GCHQ affair.

Mrs Thatcher, in the teeth of Cabinet opinion, had resolved that the inoffensive non-closed-shop representation of a civil service union which existed at the information and intelligence station GCHQ in Cheltenham should be closed down. It was Mrs Thatcher at her paranoid, John Birch Society worst. She had alienated moderate trade-unionists and prevented Sir Robert Armstrong, head of the civil service, from putting through a compromise. Healey playfully, as he would describe it, 'beat up' the Minister handling things, Geoffrey Howe, the effect of one of whose speeches on another occasion he had immortally likened to 'being savaged by a dead sheep'. This time he observed that some of Howe's colleagues 'must be a bit tired by now of his hobbling around from one of their doorsteps to another, with a bleeding hole in his foot and a smoking gun in his hand, telling them that he did not know it was loaded'.

He then launched into one of those bursts of sulphur and magnesium which make politics memorable.

The Foreign Secretary is not the villain in this case; he is the fall guy . . . Who is the Mephistopheles behind this shabby Faust? The handling of this decision by – I quote her own backbenchers – the Great She-Elephant, She Who Must Be Obeyed, the Catherine the Great of Finchley, the Prime Minister herself . . .'

The Prime Minister, for whom I have great personal affection, has formidable qualities – a powerful intelligence and great courage – but these qualities can turn into horrendous vices unless they are moderated by colleagues who have more experience, understanding and sensitivity . . . I put it to the Government front bench that to allow the Right Honourable lady to commit Britain to another four years of capricious autocracy would be to do fearful damage not just to the Conservative Party but to the state.

It went beyond rapier play into prophecy, for we now know that poor Geoffrey Howe had been fearfully abused – 'screamed at', in the report of a Cabinet colleague – for advocating compromise. The words of John Biffen, leader of the House, in the aftermath of the GCHQ Cabinet dispute, when he talked about the need for 'consolidation', led to his being publicly abused by Bernard Ingham and subsequently dropped from Government. We also know that in 1990, for the first time ever, this political party removed its leader from power. It did so not from any disinterested objection to capricious autocracy (though the Tories were not enjoying it), but because the exercise of such caprice had landed them with the poll tax and electoral haemorrhage.

The intervention was characteristic Healey, witty, literate, aggressive, at once giving offence and making people fall about laughing. At the same time it went to the core of Thatcher, her strengths and that awful element which would assert will against reason, see treachery in dissent and crow from a midden. Incidentally, the slashing comment he made during the 1983 election about 'this Prime Minister who glories in slaughter', which he had to take back, stands in the context of the sinking of the non-combatant *General Belgrano* – not perhaps glory in slaughter, but a plain failure of imagination and conscience.

The Commons fights were splendid, but with them came the chores, and one of these was to speak for Tony Benn who, defeated in Bristol in 1983, had found a new seat at Chesterfield. Eric Varley, a former minister, had chosen to accept the business option. Healey was able to speak of his friendship with Varley and turning to the candidate and unable to pretend affection, he said, 'As for Tony, well he and I have been inseparable for years – like Torvill and Dean.' This reference to the ice skaters was accompanied by the slow collapse to the ground of the red banner on the wall at the back of the platform. It was rather like the lightning which struck York Minster a year or so later during the enthronement as Bishop of Durham of the heterodox (and admirable) Dr Jenkins.

In these years, there properly developed something we assume always to have been there, the popular public figure of Healey. As a minister, he had not been the memorable speaker he became during the years of winding down and doing duty by the party. The harsh wit had been there: we have seen him asking comrades in 1960 to get it into their heads that Mr Khruschev was not the George Lansbury type. But he had been burdened with huge duties and anxieties. Five years of Defence, not a jolly subject, and six of the Treasury, including management of one of the great financial crises of the century, do not make for badinage. Busy as he still was, he could now spread his stylish, deeply read understanding into general public politics. He could also lark about rather, going on the *Morecambe and Wise* programme and showing himself to the non-political public. But the Healey high style with its easy access to a great culture is something we may not see again.

Healey, out of all races, became ever more popular both in the trade and beyond. One can't quantify such things, but to have heard as I have, committed left-wingers saying, 'What fools we were not to choose Denis,' is its own measure. The customary journalistic cliché for him was 'the old bruiser' but it was affectionate, if massively simplified, and there is little doubt that the Labour Party and the country both at last regretted not having seen him at the top.

They were right to do so. He did not become Prime Minister or leader of his party, but he had more grasp and decisiveness than Wilson, a better mind than Callaghan or Kinnock, better executive talents than any contender. He was manifestly up to any job including the top one. His not getting it has affinities with Butler's failure. Both men were governmentalists, doers of heavy work rather than fingertip politicians. Both qualify as Marthas in the company of Marys and Magdalenes. Butler and Healey were alike in giving up to party what was denied to themselves. Both stayed on and served; both had clearly defined strands of addiction and duty. So both the Labour and Conservative parties had better service than they quite deserved.

But there are great temperamental differences. Rab Butler was a timid man with no taste for a fight. Macmillan could affect to see him as a Jesuit in a soutane up to some conspiratorial purpose. In practice, Butler flinched from the low politics of building up backbench support as well as the hard politics of saying, 'I mean to have that and will resign with colleagues if I don't.' The rhetoric was different. There are no dead sheep or Catherine the Greats of Finchley, still less gloryings in slaughter in Rab's repertoire. 'Part mad baronet, part beautiful woman' is wonderful stiletto play, but in the way of Rab's more biting remarks, it was said privately. Indiscretion was Butler's form of assault. Healey was full-frontal, something which reflected a directness and an ingratiation deficit welcome in a politician. And it created that late public popularity which came when he stepped out of the shades of grinding office.

But Healey, like Butler, lacked the art of accumulating friends against the great day. He had lots of people who liked or admired him, but no Healey Party, no group flattered by being cultivated by him. And some, like Tam Dalyell, he affronted into voting the other way. It was a terrible waste. And like Butler he made enemies, creditable ones – Clive Jenkins and David Basnett being the two most injurious. But although relations with Wilson and Callaghan had their collisions – Wilson's innate suspiciousness, Callaghan's anxiety about the hard Treasury line – basically, the central political ties to leaders were good despite the lack of any attempt by Healey to nurture them. The good Minister getting on with the job came to be appreciated by all his bosses.

He was pursued by no 20-year-long animus of the kind which dogged Butler. There was no manic Randolph Churchill keeping up a steady rage in print. The Left were against him, he was against them and, compared to the underground drainage of Conservative enmities, it was good clean factionalism. But the rejection in favour of Foot in 1980 occurred in the absence of a factional majority. Healey's rash, rough, noisy style clearly frightened some people who were already frightened enough of the Left. One has only to watch current Conservative back-benchers edging further right and more anti-European than they would freely choose in anticipatory terror of right-wing assault.

Among ordinary MPs, there were two reactions to the Left ascendancy, a wish to say '*Il faut en finir*' which had been in certain minds since Dick Taverne's explosive by-election in Lincoln in 1972, and a desire to avoid giving offence, to accept expanded left-wing influence, to worry about the ill-effect on the voters later. Either you bristled or you were cowed. As nobody at that time was actually in a position to crush the Left, something which only electoral defeat and a crisis in Labour's national standing would make possible, Healey couldn't offer a trumpet call to Labour's moderate traditions. He was compelled to trim.

Indeed, though neither of them would applaud the comparison and their styles are oceans apart, there is some affinity between Healey just short of the leadership and John Major exercising it. Major is an accomplished ex-Whip accustomed to conciliation, Healey a man widely accused of percussive aggression, a charge reduced by some enemies to one of blustering. In fact, both had to face parties split between inert sense and militant hysteria, and both had to compromise. Major was lucky to start as leader before the assault, something brought about by the absence of a true right-wing candidate.

And he did his necessary compromising as leader, managing a historically rather good Government for nearly seven years. But because of that compromise, he took dreadful punishment in terms of press hatred and Parliamentary disloyalty.

Healey got most but not quite all the votes of the right wing of the Labour Party. A small, irreconcilable band of splittists rejected him as an obstacle to crisis and he missed more votes among people frightened of a heightened conflict. It is much better to be damned by both sides *after* getting power. Facing in 1980 a Commons electorate fearfully ready for swamping, he looked to the weaker brethren likely to provoke the people menacing them. Kenneth Clarke would have the same problem in a far more acute form. And Kenneth Clarke, successful Chancellor, consistent upholder of his party's moderate tradition, non-sufferer of fools, enjoyer of a non-political hinterland, has a great deal in common with Denis Healey. His having been obviously the best man to succeed merely caps the affinities.

If Healey had been outspoken from the Labour right, would he have reconciled rather fraught people like Neville Sandelson and Tom Ellis who are thought to have voted for Foot to bring on the fever? One doubts it. Would he have scared off a larger number than that group of about five by heightening the panic of those already running scared? On balance, Healey had more to lose from the mice than the rats.

Kenneth Clarke has been heroically plain-spoken and was rejected for an infant phenomenon. But then, he serves a party in which loyalty is a weapon so secret as to have been lost. The best judgment is that Healey was the right man at a dreadful and thus wrong time, that he had done the necessary hard business of cuts and squeezes which had weakened his political position, that he had bruised a few people and failed to soften others.

As to the question of what sort of prime minister Healey would have been, the ifs of 1980 are hardly helpful. The best he could have hoped for in the light of the Falklands War and Labour's continuing division would have been a more respectable defeat in 1983. Even if the SDP had not happened – and Healey's presence at the helm would have stopped it – one cannot imagine a better result than perhaps 270 seats instead of 209. The 'if' which provokes argument is one which supposes Callaghan had gone to the country in October 1978 and won. Office, as the Conservatives have discovered, is the great container of division. Labour still governing the country would have been far less likely to go through the travails of Wembley one-day conferences and the options on Joshua Benn's computer. Power may be an aphrodisiac; it also keeps marriages together.

The shift in economic thinking characterised as Thatcherism is actually something which was taking place at the Treasury and in the mind of James Callaghan, especially as advised by Peter Jay and the writings of Samuel Britten. Callaghan's Ruskin speech was an historic turning point, the idea of an eternal champagne party, eternally publicly funded and direct-tax-fired, was going down – and politics under any party must have become, shall we say, more arithmetical. Healey's own exhausting struggle at the Treasury underlines that three times.

But a Callaghan-to-Healey succession would have meant not pursuing the monetarist delusion until the pound stood, on oil and interest rates, at an employment-annihilating level. It is doubtful if a former Defence Secretary would have made the petty cuts or fed out the abandonment steers which left the Falklands undefended, thus facilitating both slaughter and glory. There would have been no GCHQ episode under any Labour Government, no abolition of the GLC or weakening of local government generally. Despite a Winter of Discontent which would have marred the early months of the second Callaghan Government, an attempt to make incomes policy work would have been tried again. And who is to say it would have failed?

The major union leaders, men like Jack Jones and Hugh Scanlon, old leftists both, had worked for it as dedicatedly as the best German union leaders in the fifties. Their problem was uncertain control at plant level and the difficulties of the lower paid and unskilled. So much of the policy of 1976–9 was right and successful that, given what had been learned, and given a moderately tight monetary policy, its second version might well have worked. Callaghan–Healey would have listened to Sam Britten, but would have shared none of Margaret Thatcher's blind nationalistic insistence on overvaluation. Less would have been got back from Europe by way of rebates, but the mania against Europe would not have taken off despite the best efforts of the far Left. These exertions, ironically, might well have left the Tories in opposition much stronger Europeans.

There would still have been Arthur Scargill, who indeed would not have been smashed, but then neither would the miners have been, which would have been nice. But does one see as much being demanded or pursued into a year-long strike against a Labour government? There would have been little or no privatisation, but it is doubtful if the taker of a Treasury hard line in the late seventies would have favoured open-ended subsidy to nationalised industries unchanging in structure and obligation. 'Cuts or break even' would have become the formula at some stage.

Finally, the Denis Healey who blamed himself for letting Chevaline through because he was too bogged down at the Treasury would never have continued with Trident. A saving of unquantifiable billions would have been achieved through cancellation of that heart-warming undertaking which was such second nature to Mrs Thatcher. Britain would not have opposed German reunification: the head of Government's actual knowledge of foreign affairs and defence, coupled with sensible rationality about Europe would have given Britain more influence there and unimaginably less distress and bad feeling without her being in any way rolled over. Healey was sceptical in the true sense – sympathetic, but highly conscious of difficulties.

Although there would have been no poll tax and no poll tax-induced political crisis, Healey would have had, sooner or later, a furious row with Labour councils of the extremist or high-spending sort and one wouldn't put it past him to have instituted something like rate-capping.

With luck Britain should have practised more arithmetic and had a better regard for gravity than was apparent in the Labour Party before 1976, but without an atom of the class-war-cum-personal-hang-ups which marked true Thatcherism. The party led by Denis Healey in government, though confined by office to some restraint, would have still possessed a Utopian-coercive wing which would have made trouble we can only guess at. And Healey would naturally have been damned for his right-wing stand over a course of conduct systematically leftward of Tony Blair's residual Labour Party to which these radicals now submit.

But being blamed is something Healey is good at. He tells the tale of meetings in his Communist Party days which discussed the question: 'Under Socialism, who will do the dirty jobs?' The answer he says, then and subsequently, 'seems to be Denis Healey'. It is a matter of deep regret that he has never been given the dirty job of governing us.

PART
THREE

IAIN
NORMAN
MACLEOD

CHAPTER ONE

We didn't have a telephone by the bedside in those days. So when it rang in the middle of the night, I didn't hear it. But it did wake me later at about quarter to seven. I went down and took the call. After about five minutes, my wife came in wondering what was holding me and found me in floods of tears.

When I went to the Commons I came across Nigel Birch and he said, 'It's a very sad day, especially for the Treasury,' and it was all I could do to make it to my room to dissolve into tears again in private, and I found myself doing that all day.

When it came to the funeral, I went up by train to Yorkshire with Terence Higgins. We were spoken to by this large, grand man, Sir Frank Figgures, who said very severely, 'You are never to travel by public transport with red boxes. Your department will supply you with special brown boxes for the occasion.' We were two very new junior ministers being crushed by a Permanent Secretary.

But when we got to the cemetery, we just stood there, near the grave, Terence and I, these two juniors who had worked with him for three and a half years and admired him for much longer . . . and we just felt like a couple of orphans.

Those are the words of Patrick Jenkin, Economic Secretary to the Treasury in 1970; the man who had died was Iain Macleod, who had been Chancellor of the Exchequer for just a month.

That reaction of intense personal grief beyond ordinary sadness over the loss of a senior colleague echoes the feeling expressed so often by those who knew him for Hugh Gaitskell. A few politicians do exert the claims of paternity. They stand for a set of ideas or attitudes; they have personalities which, however quirkish or irksome to others, induce something like love in friends. They have been in some notable fights and have their loyal lieutenants and footsoldiers. Yet given a different course of fortune or, as he might have said, a different turn of the cards, Macleod might have lived out his life in obscure disgrace.

His biographer, Robert Shepherd, relates an evening during the war when, very drunk and bristling, Macleod returned to military quarters at Wye in Kent from a frantic evening and spoke to his friend Alan Dawtry, future Town Clerk of Westminster and acting Deputy Adjutant. 'Alan,' said Macleod, 'I want to play stud poker.' It was late, he was drunk and Captain Dawtry declined and, after refusing several times more, went to bed. The next thing he heard were the words, 'I'm going to shoot you.' He took evasive action, trying not to be in the immediate line of fire. Several shots were fired into the door before Macleod emptied his pistol; he then declared that he would find ammunition, failed to do so, smashed the door down with a piece of furniture and collapsed into a drunken stupor.

If Dawtry had been unlucky, if a shot had passed through the door and killed him, then although Macleod, as a young serving officer of good character and someone temporarily unhinged by drink, would almost certainly not have faced the death penalty, he would have gone to prison. The likely outcome might have been five years for manslaughter, dishonourable discharge and a subsequent full-time career in the more louche bridge clubs quickly making at the tables money as quickly got rid of. One would expect ever heavier drinking, but with death coming rather later, there having been no war wound for the officer cashiered too soon for action, though in shabbier surroundings than 11 Downing Street. It would have been a life which would never have crossed that of Patrick Jenkin or, for that matter, Winston Churchill who, 11 years after the shooting incident, made Macleod Minister of Health.

This is all part of the slight weirdness of Iain Macleod. He doesn't fit a pattern and he is, as the Marxists used to say, full of internal contradictions. By comparison, Healey and Butler are easy. Heavy psychiatric musings are not called for. Both were academically outstanding, both cultivated, Healey with a wider, hungrier reach. Butler inherited pro-consular and headmasterly traditions of service with minimum partisan content. Healey's more aggressive mind was energised by thirties leftism. He was, quite usefully, a short-term member of the Communist Party which taught him any intolerance he didn't have already and excised all tendency to slop. Both found in politics a rail for their wheels, wheels intended to go round and round rather quickly. For both Healey and Butler, being a minister was what they were for. The alternative occupation would have been as dons of the more intimidating type.

In Macleod we meet a near-philistine, mediocre at school, never excited by sixth-form discovery of art or science, an equally mediocre undergraduate, attending Cambridge as a privilege which went with his minor public school; a sports enthusiast, the kind of man to be found cheering at rugby matches, a cricket buff – a hearty for Heaven's sake, the sort of person from whom R. A. Butler would have flinched and about whom Denis Healey would have said something cutting.

On top of which, he was a card-player. Now card-playing is difficult to dismiss. It involves memory and some strategic thinking. If it doesn't have the intellectual cachet of chess, it isn't exactly a stupid activity. But the social and political overtones of bridge are less encouraging even than those of rugby. Philip Toynbee's remark about Fascism being set back 20 years by a bomb in the west stand at Twickenham and the extreme enthusiasm of most top-class rugby players to carry on happily playing South Africa in the days when Nelson Mandela was settled on Robben Island are matched by Belloc's crack 'women and champagne and bridge' to describe Edwardian moneyed politics. Then again, bridge is a bitter game full of recriminations, grudges and ill-will, witness the virulent attacks made on Terence Reese and Boris Shapiro by opponents. And Macleod was not just a bridge-player, but a professional who for years made his living playing cards for money.

Yet the dull schoolboy and duller student turned out to have the brain of a dominant minister who, to conserve his strength when half unknown to himself he was dying, would clear the Chancellor's workload on a ten-to-five, no-red-boxes schedule. The rugby and bridge man showed himself as fervently liberal a Conservative as ever graced that party (and the people who knew him best, like Patrick Jenkin, would endorse the word 'grace'). The rugger fan organised the decolonisation of British Africa and in a speech touching on greatness proclaimed: 'I believe quite simply in the brotherhood of man.' He would protect the Health Service from any suggestion dear to pressure groups in his party that it be watered down, diminished or creamed off. The minor public schoolboy took a fierce concerned view on poverty of a kind that his fellow old Fettesian the contemporary Labour Prime Minister seems not to share.

You could have predicted Butler and Healey for public life near the top at 20. Macleod one would have got completely wrong. The potential within him hadn't been touched. The talent was directed in early years to a seemingly trivial, if mind-sharpening occupation. He was never in business and he had no academic affinities whatever. The likeliest guess about Macleod at 20 would have been that he would continue rackety and raffish, drinking rather too much, getting through a quota of women and, if he had a political thought in his head, then, in the way of such people, it would be a distinctly right-wing one. This surely was the sort of person to be seen in tweeds and a flat cap at Twickenham pulling on a hip flask and wishing fortune to good old Smithy in his fight against the reds. He might even have married an ambitious woman politician. It wasn't so. Lord, it wasn't so.

Macleod was the fortuitous politician. Perfectly equipped to do the job well and lit by a good light, he turned to it late, stumbling upon perfect mentors in David Clarke, the head of Conservative Party Research Department, and indeed in R. A. Butler. As a new MP he made his famous attack on Aneurin Bevan under Churchill's nose and found himself taken up by the ministering angels. Gray's flower 'born to blush unseen' would not be Macleod. He blushed frantically to an admiring assembly of helpful people.

He was fortuitous also in his political colouration. In no sense was the Macleod radicalism opportunistic. He took great risks, ran ahead of the field and found that large numbers of slightly surprised people were following, and he made undying enemies in a right wing admittedly different from the powerful Tory Right of today, and not so influential. But being defined, hated and loved was natural to him. Straightforwardly, he detested the death penalty, flogging and racial distinctions. The opinions were natural opinions, swiftly taken on, furiously held. He was remarkably clear-cut, a sporting instinct perhaps that this was his team, his group, and that would be who and what he would be fighting for. This in turn accounts for the rather startling partisanship with which he attacked the Labour Party when his views were different by very measurable distances, when indeed, as over the colonies, he could be to the left of them.

He came in as a talent at a time when the Conservative Party, knocked sideways by the 1945 election, was rebuilding and recolouring through Butler's charters and never more unsure of itself. The Tories have always recruited capable men of no standing, Disraeli being the cliché example. But a glance round reveals the mature Joe Chamberlain, the rich but plebeian W. H. Smith; the provincial cad with the Romany look, F. E. Smith, for that matter, the dull, but dedicated Addington at the start of the 19th century and Frederick Robinson, Lord Liverpool's Chancellor of the Exchequer, or the poor law student from Newcastle, John Scott, later Lord Eldon and for 26 years an outstandingly immobile Lord Chancellor.

But a new man who was also a radical and who, given other friendships and encouragements, might have arrived in the Labour Party, was something else. Unlike almost all the others except Joe Chamberlain, Macleod rose among the Tories on his own terms. To be slightly cynical and borrow a trope from Marxism, the period after the war was one in which the collective self-interest of the Conservative Party and the interests behind it – land, the City, the inheriting class – felt sufficiently afraid of losing their place to be willing to make very pliant terms with reform.

A young, able and ambitious entrant who said, 'Leave the Health Service alone, show that we are not interested in taking from working and poor people what Labour has given them,' would be seen by the shrewdest of the rich as a sensible man. Self-interest has its own enlightenment from time to time.

Another aspect of Macleod's political life was its shortness. He was in Parliament for 19 years compared with the 35 of Butler and the 40 of Healey, though his 11 years of ministerial life[1] is set against the 18 of Butler and the 11 of Healey. Death at 56, the same age as Hugh Gaitskell, in Parliament for only 17 years, explains much, but not the rocket-propulsion of that brief life.

Macleod was a phenomenon, known almost as soon as he appeared at the centre of business and controversy, an instantly recognised, sharply defined public face. Unlike most politicians, he was saved the burden and diminution of seeking out patronage. It must be a vast liberation never to be a parliamentary private secretary. This was something he had in common with Denis Healey. Each avoided the vale of subordination through the recognition of a great man, respectively Ernest Bevin and Winston Churchill, who would clap hands and enable. Butler, by contrast, overwhelmingly the most prudent and anxious of the three, though blessed by a succession of patrons, ascended by elaborate degrees, not indeed ever a toady, but what neither Macleod nor Healey ever was, a mandarin.

Macleod had another distinction rare in politics, he was a wit and an outstanding debater. 'Verbal skills' is the educationalists' lip-curling term for poetry, eloquence, the art of words. 'Communication' is the educationalists' other term for the English language which they tend to dislike. And communicating is the thing which children brought up with that scorn of verbal skill in their ears commonly lack. If I said a moment ago that Macleod was a near-philistine, that should be rapidly amended. He had no eye for art and no ear at all for music, but he read, loved and could quote at length, the great poets of the English language. Shockingly, he had learnt a great deal of poetry by heart, something which would grieve the educationalist even further. He was one of those like Patrick Leigh Fermor who recalls in *A Time of Gifts* that he could walk down a road in the middle of Bavaria quoting hundreds of lines from the works of dead white males.

The memory of Macleod's debating skill lingers in discerning minds. Robin Cook, in his speech on the general European debate in December 1997, was interrupted by the fixed eyes and upraised index finger of the egregious Bill Cash. 'Oh yes, I suppose so,' sighed Cook. 'After all, if I don't give way, it will be Hamlet without the first gravedigger.' Congratulated by a Liberal Democratic colleague, he murmured under his breath, 'Iain Macleod!' The compliment comes from a proper source.

We have a way of saying, 'There are no great debaters left. Things aren't what they were.' That one can positively rebut that overstatement with the example of Mr Cook, or stretching a point, Tony Benn or, in his dry way, John Biffen, and that there were catalepsy-inducing dullards flourishing around Gladstone and Bright, F. E. Smith and Lloyd George, doesn't alter the fact that the ability to move the heart or achieve wit is valued less. Detail and simplification, respectively the third schedule to the act as amended and the spoonful of babyfood called a 'soundbite', twist at opposite ends of the rope.

No one today would become a minister overnight because of a single Parliamentary sally which, though well informed, was most effective for its verbal felicity – 'I want to deal closely and with relish with the vulgar, crude and intemperate speech to which the House of Commons has just listened' – and the grave-digger remark, directed with startling nerve at Aneurin Bevan, another of those giants of eloquence and wit we don't have any more. Then, of course, being eloquent in front of Churchill was much more useful than being eloquent in front of Attlee or Chamberlain. Even so, being witty and using memorable phrases would get one noticed in any assembly. The ear for poetry saved Macleod from the cliché and jargon in which so many strong intellects lose their identity as if paddling in sheep-dip.

But the rise by means of that single assault on the biggest public personality on the other side signified something else. Macleod, the young gunslinger, went for the old gunslinger because he was brave, direct, theatrical and bold. What he would do in Africa, what he would do taking on the London busmen, what he planned to do with a major reform of the tax system and of course what he did in his resignation from the Cabinet in 1963 were all the actions of a natural attacker. Obvious analogies suggest themselves with the bridge which he played outstandingly well and wrote a textbook about. It might be more apt to say that the temperament attracted by intelli-gent gambling – playing on odds shortened by skill – was one to be equally attracted by the planned, calculated, but risky political stroke.

For that matter, there are affinities with someone who did become Prime Minister, Margaret Thatcher. Macleod would speak highly of the young Mrs Thatcher, seek her for his team and say ritual words about her future. But too much shouldn't be made of that. Thatcher rose as a capable, hard-working tech-nician with a little noticed and as little advertised philosophy. She kept boldness in reserve until under impossible pressure, as over the Falklands, and was anyway at least as vindictive as she was bold. Above all, Margaret Thatcher was the militant middle class, a class warrior with a measure of downward-directed fear and loathing, nothing imaginably like Macleod. She developed oppressive personal fears and enmities which would be worked out in a Cabinet regularly scanned for disloyalty. Macleod, for all the physical pain he endured, and despite a quickly flaring-up temper, had no grudges and expressed dislike by dismissing the individual from comment. He was immeasurably more balanced and, boldness notwithstanding, nothing like her. His research assistant at that time also recalls him saying of the lady, 'We made a mistake there.'

But notoriously, for all his brilliant rise, he did not feel himself quite to belong. His quarrel with the appointment of Douglas-Home, the essential cheating of Butler which of course cheated him too, the whole business which he denounced in his *Spectator* article as the 'Magic Circle', was an expression of rage at over-smooth, official Conservative enemies. An opponent might have used the term 'paranoia', though with only debating effect. He was for a start, right. The solidly Etonian group immediately surrounding Macmillan, which included numerous members of his family, were either people speaking openly only to each other or sherpas of this elect. Patronised by Macmillan, while praised and flattered, half backed by the Prime Minister where he was owed full support, Macleod had been angered and set at a distance by the Macmillan group.

But in the 1963 succession crisis, Macleod, not a little naïvely, had taken the public-school code literally. It was ridiculous, he told friends, to think that Alec Douglas-Home might run; Alec had given his word that he wasn't running. That was the bright-eyed reaction of the Fettesian ignorant of the Beelzebub potential of an Etonian eyeing the main chance. It was the minor public schoolboy's mistake and one which the bridge-player, if on duty that day, would never have made. The gentry cheated and Macleod, very attractively, exploded with indignation. It wasn't very good politics or, one guesses, cards, but it runs along the seam of what is so admirable about Macleod.

His biographer Robert Shepherd has a quotation from Peregrine Worsthorne in the *Sunday Telegraph*: 'What is boring and irrelevant is the suggestion of an upper-class conspiracy, particularly coming from a man who has sedulously and successfully modelled himself on that class, and whose complaints against the magic circle only began when he failed to square it in his own interests.' This is Sir Peregrine being silly. The reality was that Macleod had choked on the dishonest conduct of Macmillan and his immediate clique, especially in the context of the high tone and old-fashioned honourability upon which Macmillan traded. And having such feelings, he walked away in contempt.

Macmillan would voice and Robert Shepherd surprisingly gives some attention to theories about highlanders and islanders and their romantic emotional nature. Macleod was proud, occasionally tedious about his roots, but they have nothing to do with the case. Macmillan, by indulging such airy waffle, was attempting to mystify a clear case. Macleod, although he knew how to calculate advantage and act in terms of rational self-interest, had an interest in Butler's succession as Butler's natural heir. But that was an open matter played straight. If Macleod had said that he would not be standing, he would not have stood.

One of the wonders of British politics has been the surviving reputation of Lord Home as a grand old nobleman, a gentleman of the old school, an example (*pace* Paul Johnson) of quiet Christian duty. In fact, Home remains a man who, whether from weakness, vanity or self-serving incoherence, lied his way into Downing Street. The fact that he could do a Lord Emsworth act, and charm the class-silly element as a decent old cove getting the very best thing by endearing oversight, does not alter that essential fact. If he had not said he would not contest the position, he would not have got it.

A thought crosses the mind. Hectares of indignation were invested in denouncing John Profumo 'because he lied to the House of Commons'. That, rather than sexual intercourse with a pretty girl, was always given as the reason for his Lucifer-like disgrace. But Profumo's lie, extracted at the urgent need of jittery colleagues at a time of great distress and personal pressure, makes an interesting contrast with the untruthful statement made by Home to his Cabinet colleagues under the pressure only of a Prime Minister anxious to have Home succeed him.

The highlander rubbish disguises two central truths: that when it mattered, Macleod was straight and Home crooked. It underlines a key fact about Macleod: that never mind the worldly side – membership of White's, the champagne, the bridge, and occasionally the women – Macleod was enough of a puritan, whether by way of Fettes or Calvin, to have a salutary sense of wrong. Go back to Africa or poverty or anything that drove him in politics and, for all his happy hedonistic flurry of enjoyment and superficial cynicism, it is at the heart of him.

[1]The odd status of Health as a full ministry outside the Cabinet means Macleod was a Cabinet minister for nine years.

CHAPTER TWO

The start Macleod had in life was to be born the son of a hard-working professional man, Dr Norman Macleod, more amiable than Monty Butler and less clumsy than Will Healey. He was also on his mother's side the grandson of a doctor, Rhoderick Ross, something of a hero on the Isle of Lewis for his devotion.

Dr Macleod came from a family of tacksmen, or tenant farmers, rooted on Lewis since around 1500. The Macmillans, though more mobile, had similar connections in Argyllshire then Arran, before a move to the Irvine in Ayrshire which John Galt chronicled. Daniel Macmillan, Harold's great-grandfather, would leave Scotland for London in 1833. Norman Macleod went via Glasgow University on scholarships to Skipton in north-west Yorkshire in 1907. 'It takes three generations to make a gentleman,' said Robert Peel, Etonian son of a rich industrialist and grandson of a smallholder–weaver.

Iain Macleod's father sent him to prep school (St Ninian's in Dumfriesshire) and as a fee-payer to Fettes, the Edinburgh public school, then to Gonville and Caius College, Cambridge. Macmillan went to Eton and Balliol. The distinctions are subtle but vital: very English and very Anglo–Scottish distinctions between older money (and more of it) and new, between the established and the tentative, between those for whom Scotland was a rhetorical memory and those still linked with it.

Scottish nationalism has, in the years since Macleod's birth, become a more furious and impactive force. Anglo–Scots are less comfortably placed than in Macleod's childhood, when a sort of free trade in talent allowed Scots to rise within the British system, to be based in England while proclaiming a general Scottishness, an approach which has spawned so many Burns' Nights in Guildford. Something of that remains, but for all the men with Home Counties accents calling themselves 'Jock' and beginning sentences with 'We Scots', anglicisation is the reality for second and third generations. What is being lost is the enjoyable and fruitful business of being both at once. Macleod, beyond the call of the politician's identity ploy, was genuinely proud of both Scottishness and Yorkshireness. With separatism the goal of about a fifth of the Scottish population and London more remote and resented than at any time since the Porteous riots, he would not easily have done that today.

The education through which he was put was English in Scotland. He played cricket and was beaten by a clergyman and prepared for Fettes, a school self-consciously developed on the English public-school model. It was a long way from the world of his grandfather, a fish-curer and general merchant. So, for that matter, was his parents' attendance at the Anglican parish church in Skipton.

But none of this should be flung in a reproachful, puritanical way at the Macleods. People do make their way, do get on, do conform upwards. A doctor in 1920s provincial England had a social status despite his usefulness, and the idea of the doctor's children going to the local school would have been thought slightly odd and not quite nice. Dr Macleod, on all evidence a devoted physician with a significant poor-law practice, was behaving naturally, not being a hard-eyed careerist. Norman Macleod seems to have had a good deal in common with his son. As well as the conventional Scottish doctor's golf, he too played bridge, as well as poker with a coterie of Bradford wool traders, and was also a regular follower of and putter of money on horses.

It was all within prudential limits and co-existed with Liberal politics and poor-law medicine. Dr Macleod also shrewdly bought back into his native Lewis, obtaining for £1,000 a house, Scaliscro Lodge, and 8,600 acres of moorland and waters. Shooting and fishing were among the doctor's other interests and, given the massively depressed land market in remote parts of Scotland, he was able to expand the pleasant middle-class life of a general practitioner in the twenties through ownership and recreational use of the beautiful but declining island he came from. It was a sensible thing to do and injured no one on the island, but it underlines in a melancholy way the doom of rural northern Scotland. What had been a decent, small economy of fish, agriculture and textiles could not support its talents. And those talents flourishing in England, while bringing a minuscule injection of cash, could use Lewis only for fishing, grouse-shooting and the enjoyment of its good air. If of course Scotland had been an independent sovereign state, Lewis would have been quite as poor and Norman Macleod would never have had access to England to achieve his prosperity.

The effect of this house purchase was to give Iain Macleod a lot of healthy arduous activity and the friendship of Alasdair Alpin Macgregor, chronicler and traveller of the islands. With Macgregor he walked the moors and there is no reason to doubt the strong affections for this place which he would later express in indifferent poetry, but the experience made him no more than a recreational and rhetorical Scotsman. His visits as an adult were few (unlike those of R. A. Butler, who fled to Mull on every reasonable occasion). Butler's connection was only a mother from Aberdeenshire and he never went on about Scotland, but he went back.

Macleod's real home after leaving Cambridge – perhaps even before he left a university which did not engage him – was Mayfair. From being a keen bridge-player he became an habitual and preoccupied bridge-player and in due short course a professional bridge-player. At Cambridge he had teamed up with a Magdalene undergraduate, Colin Harding, to establish the first ever Oxford and Cambridge bridge match, and if blues had been awarded for remembering diamonds in an intense atmosphere, Macleod would swiftly have had one. His degree (in Modern History) was mediocre, a 2:2. However, the fact that Cambridge didn't get Iain Macleod interested in history may be something for Cambridge to reflect upon.

Instead he became a familiar at Crockford's, Lederer's and other West End places where serious money was wagered. The very job which he occupied in the daytime after going down – with De La Rue, the printers, at their offices in Old Street – was the result of meeting the Chairman, Bernard Westall, over the bridge table. Relations with a martinet-like immediate superior at the office were not happy, and business, like school and university, never caught Macleod's imagination or interest. However, Shepherd describes a popular colleague willing to work very hard during a rush of business, and someone, as he would always be, open-handed and generous without reserve. But he was also someone for whom the dullness of routine on a wage of £150 a year could only be an underattended-to filler of space between evenings of intense serious play.

He would eventually be fired, but fired in the happiest of circumstances, to get on with earning far more than his business salary doing what he liked. He would make, despite occasional losses which prompted an urgent appeal to his father, an average profit on the year of about £2,500. That is a phenomenal sum of money at a time when people talked admiringly of the '£1,000-a-year man'. If it was only half of what the majestically rich Courtaulds settled on their protégé, Butler, it was 17 times what Macleod earned in the office at De La Rue. And it was two and a half times the price of Scaliscro Lodge and 8,600 acres of moorland, loch and river on the Isle of Lewis.

Macleod lived like this for four years until the outbreak of war. He would be employed by Crockford's as a host, something rather more skilled and busy than a greeter at Caesar's Palace. He was employed on the Nash principles of 18th-century Bath – to avoid fraud, see off sharpers and be on hand to take a place at play. His skills, now very high, at or near international level, allowed him to earn his living pleasantly and he was, by all accounts, very well liked, having got rid of a certain under-graduate rough and untidy appearance. But it was employment not very different, except in money terms, from that of the professional dance partner.

Quite how the contemporary *Daily Mail* or all those Conservative politicians who talk tediously of 'family values' would have responded is not hard to guess. Fully known in a spelt-out, detailed way, Macleod's prewar life could have killed his political career after it. In practice, the Conservative and Unionist Party is a wonderful coalition between grandees and the suburbs, infinitely tolerant at the top of debt, serial fornica-tion, sexual virtuosity and experiment and no more than prudentially alerted to business irregularity. Compared with Disraeli – about whom we know enough to send him down post-humously for five years – Iain Macleod was a playful kitten. Even the charges, encountered only through police gossip, that he was warned off a couple of clubs for playing for money below his league, a bad sin in the card-playing world, would, if true, be lemonade in the catalogue of Disraeli's debts, Lyndhurst's expansive adultery, F. E. Smith's suicidal drinking, Lord Randolph's syphilis or the pecadillos of a dozen more careers in the Conservative Party alone.

As John Profumo would discover, being found out is a capital offence. But before Profumo, finding out was discouraged. The craven press of the forties was a better dog than the prurient press of today. An editor hating a decolonising Colonial Secretary and enjoying the kill and torture licence of the Murdoch era, by telling all and alerting responses from Banstead to Enfield, could have published and would have damned. Lord Beaverbrook's newspapers did detest what Macleod did, but they organised no public stoning.

As it was, by way of the gambling milieu, Macleod was mixing with the grandee element, no doubt taking a little of their money as he did so. The mutterings of Peregrine Worsthorne 30 years later that he had 'sedulously and successfully modelled himself on that class' implies toadyism and aspiration and is wildly wrong. If anything, Macleod seems to have learned not to like the upper class very much, certainly not to feel fully at ease with them. But he enjoyed their pastimes. Membership of White's Club gave him great pleasure. It was White's (founded by an Italian waiter called Bianco), of which Alan Brien once wrote in the *Spectator*: 'When revolution comes and Buckingham Palace is a People's Hall and Westminster Abbey a Ministry of Cults, White's will remain a bunker of the huddled and defiant old class.' Ironically, by living as a playboy, if a diligent, well-remunerated one, Macleod was mixing not just with Jack Marx, Rixi Markus and other stars of bridge, he was encountering more Etonians than is the usual lot of a Fettesian.

But he was not intentionally mixing with Conservatives. Astonishingly, for someone who would become not just a minister – that function has been performed in a fit of absence of mind before now – but a fascinated, preoccupied, and for that matter principled, politician, Macleod seems at this time to have had no politics. He had opposed the death penalty in debate at school, an opinion he would hold with fervour all his life; he had spoken once and effectively in the Cambridge Union against the Imperial Protectionist Ottawa accords, and, also at Fettes, he had offered himself as candidate in a mock election for Mosley's New Party. This was the same respectable thing it was for Harold Macmillan already in Parliament. The New Party at that date (1931) was a Keynesian, public-spending, work-creating force against which the knuckles of Fascism had not yet brushed.

But these are just three opinions in ten years between the ages of 17 and 27. The contrast with the sedulous involvement of

Butler in the Cambridge Union and the learned Marxist of Keighley working his way through and out of the CP is dumb-founding. Macleod had also enjoyed none of their intellectual stimulation. Butler was getting on top of idiomatic French and German and the authors of those languages, then on his honey-moon, repairing the limitations of Marlborough by reading the Greek classics in translation. Healey was criss-crossing Germany on a bicycle, seeing off Kant and his antinomies of pure reason. Both were getting very serious about art. Macleod was playing cards for a lot of money.

Even the Macleod gift for learning poems by heart, something he could do in a burst of intense concentration, was a facility akin to his recall of spades discarded, though no one doubted that he truly loved poetry in an eclectic way which embraced T. S. Eliot and Richard Church. Essentially at this time Macleod was an apolitical bridge ace, keen on horses, on ladies whom he cheerfully pursued, frequently a fairly heavy drinker[1] and an ardent follower of rugby and cricket. But he was going to be one of the half-dozen dominant politicians of mid-century, a role-model and hero to gifted and far more earnest men. He simply hadn't started yet.

Macleod gained from war what he had signally missed at Cambridge: a gauge of his abilities and a direction in which to point them. But, like so many urgently joined-up soldiers of 1939, he spent a great many of his early military days hanging about. And being Macleod, he spent it breaking stupid rules about curfews and lights out and in going back to the Mayfair bridge clubs to augment his income. He was also, as at Cambridge, a minimalist of study, seeking only to pass his officer-training course, having all the ability and using a fraction of it to coast through something he couldn't take seriously.

His first encounter with soldiering involved retreat and a serious wound. The regiment to which he had been transferred as second lieutenant after early training, the Duke of Wellington's, was sent to France in the melancholy spring of 1940. Within a fortnight the Germans invaded Holland and Belgium and the Dukes were among troops sent with the doomed objective of heading off that terrifying roll into France. They faced enemy fire and their train stopped just short of Abbeville – the Abbeville where Butler, 20 years before, had spent hours in the railway signal box to feel in touch with a world beyond the small town where he was perfecting his French.

The Dukes, under air bombardment, mapless and candidly
lost, made in several groups for Dieppe or Neufchatel. Macleod
was in the Neufchatel-bound set, getting there on 22–23 May.
At this point he was involved in the setting up of a road block of
logs of wood. Like most things the British did in the first year of
the war, it was hastily prepared, not finished and not much use.
A German armoured car drove contemptuously through it and a
flying log struck Macleod, badly fracturing his thigh. He would
be patched up and in due course evacuated via St Nazaire and
sent to hospital in Exeter. This accident was not related to
the spinal condition, ankylosing spondylitis, which would
near-crucify him for the last 20 years of his life and indirectly
accelerate his death. It contented itself with leaving him quite
independently lame and limping.

The first experience of war over, Macleod, duly promoted to
captain, perfectly cheerfully waited for something to happen
and waited in his usual way, playing cards and breaking tiresome regulations as well as doing administrative work with
admired despatch. It was in this long lull that the shooting
incident at Wye which might have killed the Deputy Adjutant of
his regiment took place. The drunken shooting at a senior officer
who had denied his demand to play poker is the sort of thing
from which Socialist morality, no less than Christian, tends to
draw conclusions. Gambling, drunkenness, irresponsibility,
homicidal rage: Macleod got uncomfortably close to providing
the text for a Hogarth illustration.

It is the rage that lingers in consideration of the whole life.
Notoriously, Macleod would have a short fuse during his public
career. It would be accentuated by the grievous pain of his spinal
illness and it would be a rage without petty vengeance or
grudge-bearing. It sat beside the compassion, the personal
generosity, the untrumpeted charitable work and a general blaze
of good humour and affection. There is no point in moralising
about it, but though never again lethal, it was there.

Before the shooting at Dawtry, Macleod had done something
more sensible: he had married Eve Mason. The widow of a
sailor drowned off Ireland on convoy duty, Eve came from a
discreetly aristocratic background – seven centuries of land-
ownership on one side, the Blois family; granddaughter of a peer
on the other, the Pakingtons – and had been presented at court.
She had into the bargain talents in tennis and lacrosse to conjure
an image of Miss Joan Hunter Dunn. She would prove a fierce
defender of Macleod's left-wing Toryism. Like the Healeys, the

Macleods honeymooned at a country pub in Wharfedale, the Devonshire Arms near Bolton Abbey. (The Healeys went to the Buck at Buckden.) Macleod would have a happy marriage with two children, but his illness would be grimly paralleled by that of his wife who, in 1952, would be stricken first by meningitis then by polio. Everything necessary to reinforce a natural toughness would be heaped onto the couple.

But important as Eve would be in Macleod's life, the greatest impact upon it was not marriage, but the last burst of higher education which at the age of 30 was thrust upon him with secondment in 1943 to the Army Staff College at Camberley. It would do for Macleod what prep school, public school and Cambridge had never done – arouse his abilities, alert him to his own depth of talent and animate him to ambition.

The Camberley course, telescoped from two years to four months, put him up against first-rate minds in an intense atmosphere. And there may lie the trick of it. It was an intense atmosphere which brought out the brilliance concentrated on bridge. Macleod, who had no aesthetic sense outside poetry, was ill equipped to stand and stare and could not bear to spend any part of a holiday looking at a landscape, however beautiful. His was a functional mind able to do things outstandingly well, not fitted to linger, absorb, slowly enjoy and accumulate.

Apart from which, this hedonist was furiously but selectively competitive. Against the selected minds of an Army which was itself truly valuing cleverness for the first time since Cromwell, he chose to run and excel. As he told his brother, Torquil, of his reaction to the brilliant competition, 'It was there that I found to my genuine surprise not only that I could keep up, but that I could beat them.' It was Macleod's own clear conviction that the bridge club and race meeting man became the deadly serious, driving political animal during that short course. Not that he gave up cards and horses – they brought, after all, an income as well as pleasure – but cards and horses, like Macleod himself, now had something to compete against.

In terms of military action, Major Macleod (promoted once more) again paralleled Major Healey. The beachmaster of Anzio was shadowed by the landing officer directed to take troops on shore in Normandy at what the Army delighted in calling 'H plus 40' – 40 minutes after initial landing. He was now on the staff of the 50th (Northumbrian) Division, a distinguished one with two years in North Africa behind them.

With characteristic disregard for propriety and correct

discipline, Macleod knew, because he had looked at papers he was not supposed to look at, where the D-Day landings would take place. A map sheet relating to Overlord, the invasion plan, corresponded to an exercise he had done at staff college and indicated that they would be staged in Normandy, not the Pas de Calais, which all informed opinion had supposed.

Having gone ashore, he had commandeered a police motor-bike to make contact with forward brigades and observed British troops moving into Bayeux and command over St Leger. 'On the 50 Division front,' he said echoing and answering Shakespeare, 'the day had gone well.'

The story he told himself in a *Spectator* article 20 years later about finding that his batman had put boiled sweets into his ammunition pouch shows the same old soldier's wisdom as Bluntschli, the ironical Swiss mercenary in George Bernard Shaw's *Arms and the Man*. It was a happy conclusion to every-thing Macleod ever had to do with revolvers. And as he said in that *Spectator* piece, he had survived that battle and now believed he would see his second child, due to be born later in the year. Fatalism had tipped to the light in his own mind. Even the cleverest, most arithmetical gambler believes in fortune.

What mattered now was not so much involvement in D-Day, which gave admirable cachet to a future candidate's credentials, as that Macleod was a man transformed. He now networked among senior officers with Conservative Party connections, cheerfully telling one of them, William Urton, at the bottom of the slit trench in which they had taken sensible refuge from enemy fire, that he aimed at the prime ministership.

He had distinguished himself at staff college, been given serious responsibility, played a full and honourable part in the D-Day landings which were to become part of the national legend, one not less fabulous for being true. In November 1944 the valiant Northumbrian Division, having done its job, was withdrawn and Macleod was able to return to Britain to his father's home, where the two of them proceeded to do some-thing very cheeky and very shrewd indeed.

Norman Macleod had made two moves in recent years away from Skipton, first to the Scottish spa of Strathpeffer (where Rab had been taken by his mother after Cambridge finals), then back to England and Blackpool. But he had maintained his Lewis connections and Scaliscro, something which would now be put to use.

Conservatism lacked appeal in the Western Isles, lacked it so much that no organisation of any sort existed for that party in the constituency. Dr Macleod, a Liberal all his life, but giving regard for Churchill as an excuse, set one up. It was an association whose selection conference was attended by two people, Norman and Iain Macleod, and at which Iain Macleod was selected as Conservative candidate. For the doctor who so enjoyed his poker school and outings to Wetherby Races, this last punt – he would die early in 1947 – must have been a source of slightly glinting satisfaction.

Conservative Central Office, never quick-minded and doubtless glad of a candidate, made no trouble. Churchill's message of endorsement came out like rations into a salient and Major Macleod commenced his campaign having issued a rather preposterous address which accused the Socialists of actions leading to Fascism, which he spelt wrong. He also proclaimed island credentials in violent excess of his father's full-time residence there 40 years before, ownership of Scaliscro and summer holidays a decade earlier. 'I am a man of the isles,' he thundered untruthfully. He also warned in the best Pickwickian fat-boy tradition of the Conservative and Unionist Party, that 'the croft or loom or boat' of the islanders was at risk from Mr Attlee. 'Under the Socialist threat of nationalisation, these things will go.' Not that any of this nonsense has to be taken at face value. It was, as Shepherd records, the sort of election where, when the car carrying the Labour hecklers broke down, the Conservative candidate gave them a lift to his own meeting. The benign ghost of *Whisky Galore* seems to have presided over that election. And while Malcolm Macmillan, the Labour candidate, took the seat and held a majority of the 13,000-strong necessarily overrepresented electorate until the seventies, Macleod, in third place with 2,756, had done extremely well in a dreadful year for the Conservatives.

The important, if less amusing aspect of his campaign was its natural unConservatism. This would be a time when the Tory Party would go to considerable lengths, many of them sincere, to assert a social and protective role towards the citizen. The Hobbesian dog would be sent to kennel. But that sort of thing was more in evidence at the top *after* the Labour victory. Macleod went out and endorsed without reservation the Beveridge Report for the purchase of copies of which queues had formed. He demanded Social Security in capital letters. Over that election, with its legion of candidate officers with thirties memories and the politicisation of the war, hung the mocking rubric of 'the land fit for heroes' proclaimed in 1918 by Lloyd George. Macleod, undistracted by his champagne metropolitanism, became without effort or simulation a representative Conservative type firmly in the liberal mainstream. This would be unremarkable except that he had, so far as we know, entertained serious political notions only since his staff college experience. He was always quick when he moved, but clearly there was something else.

Norman Macleod might masquerade as a Conservative, but he was an old Liberal and he had seen enough poverty in rural north Yorkshire. The world which Dougie Gabb, Denis Healey's Chairman, knew, the world of 'Boots for the Bairns', had been at a tangent to Dr Macleod's path. Beveridge in his Bunyanlike imagery had spoken of the 'Giant Want'; Dr Macleod understood. Accordingly, when Iain did turn to politics, he would have received more from his father than a crafty constituency ploy. He was 31 years old, a wartime major with a creditable record. His abilities were the high ones they had always been, but were now directed to a single preoccupying end on behalf of clear-cut political convictions which would not vary for the rest of his life. Like Major Healey, Major Macleod would now become a rather elevated and superior sort of apparatchik. He would go to work for R. A. Butler as Healey went to work for Ernest Bevin, a parallel not only in career pattern, but in rival apostolic succession.

---

[1]He was an 'American drinker', says the political commentator Alan Watkins. He would have a couple of large martinis before lunch then drink water with his meal.

CHAPTER THREE

Defeat, involving an absolute majority for Labour of 146 seats, did for the Conservative Party all the things that Dr Johnson attributed to the prospect of being hanged in a fortnight.

As we have seen, of the Tory leadership only Butler had expected defeat. Churchill's wartime prestige was supposed, in the 1945 election, to perform a major act of intercession for the Conservatives. Endemic unemployment in the thirties; the memory of vapid, rhetorical promises to returning heroes lying unfulfilled after 1918; the great raising of political conscious-ness in the armed forces (to use the language of the leftish current-affairs tutors who raised it); Beveridge and Labour coming sweetly together as a programme and its advocate – none of these registered with the Conservative leadership. Accordingly, they were found during that contest giving vague assent to the Beveridge mood, but lacking all credibility as a social party willing to make it happen. Defeat made them pull themselves together and they responded to annihilation in a positive manner.

'We have had,' said Kipling about the South African War, 'no end of a lesson. It will do us no end of good.' It was in that spirit that Churchill entrusted a major revision and redefinition of policy to Butler. What Butler would do in the preparation of his charters, subsequently accepted by the Tory leadership and endorsed by its conference as a new direction, was to accept most of Labour's postwar social settlement but subject it to a critique on cost and efficiency. The Conservatives fervently rejected the idea of themselves as a party of hard times and economic gravity.

Friedrich Hayek's *The Road to Serfdom*, published at the end of the war, would be a Conservative watchword in the eighties. But publication of a book has never been less happily timed. A Conservative Party arguing then for Manchester School economics, resistant to welfare, bent on aborting the National Health Service, and accepting substantial unemployment as 'a price worth paying' would have remained in fixed and institutional opposition. Labour in 1979–80, committing itself to unequivocal Socialism and unilateral disarmament and electing Michael Foot leader in token of all this, produced a mirror image, an experiment which concluded in the election of 1983, Mrs Thatcher's Roman triumph. Like Heaven, Hayek could wait. The price of that unemployment, though demanded late, was paid by the Conservatives in 1997.

Butler's instrument in refashioning Tory thinking to the age in which it found itself was the Conservative Research Department, housed in Old Queen Street, an address amusing in those innocent days only to the very knowing. Beyond the research department, there was a new body, the Parliamentary Secretariat, in which Macleod would find a post. Butler's lieutenant in the work to be done was David Clarke, a social and enlightened Tory before the letter and one who astounded Macleod with his entire want of parliamentary ambition.

Macleod himself owed employment at this admirable establishment to the goodwill of a friend of his sister Rhodabel, who knew Ralph Assheton. Assheton, old squirearchy but sharp-minded and realistic, was Chairman of the Tory Party and had used his influence to create the secretariat. Macleod was an extra to David Clarke's original allocations and money had to be found to pay for him. Despite flippant comment, much of it deriving from Macleod's own dismissive way of talking, about anyone being able to get such a post at that low point in the market, the quality of the intake was breathtaking. Its principal other recruits were Reginald Maudling and Enoch Powell. David Clarke at 85 recalls with a chuckle sitting Macleod and Powell down next to each other at small desks like schoolboys.

Both Maudling and Powell were intellectually outstanding, but Maudling's good nature lacked the last necessary element of fastidiousness, and Powell's prophesying mind wanted a sense of proportion and occasionally sense. Maudling would be Chancellor of the Exchequer and Home Secretary and still fail;

Powell would later preach market economics which would come about, and bloody communal war involving immigrants which would not. His notion of failure was expressed when he told a radio interviewer of his regret at not having died in the war.

According to Nigel Fisher, Macleod's first biographer, Clarke ranked Maudling as the most mature mind, Powell as the strongest intellectual force and put Macleod third. Ten years later he would describe Macleod as the best politician of the three. Butler was to make the judgment of Macleod that 'he was so quick . . . he seemed able to write a minute or produce a brief in record time and he was extremely clear'. As became someone who could learn a poem after a concentrated reading and remember a bridge hand weeks later, Macleod worked by mental composition which he would then dictate whole to a secretary.

Macleod, as a Scot, was given Scotland as a subject, and onto his desk were also piled the Home Office, Local Government, National Assistance and, appropriately as it turned out, Health and Labour. He showed himself able to work extremely fast and efficiently, but, as Fisher says, not for long hours. Being quick and lacking Powell's perfectionism with its dash of masochism, Macleod and Maudling favoured hard, effective bursts of work and long lunches. Macleod also acquired a taste for political history and biography, reading books which Enoch Powell had perhaps read at 16, but which were now suddenly part of his new interest and purpose, his late life-focus of politics.

In 1948, the secretariat and the research department were merged, also taking on the Library and Information Department of Central Office. Separation of the sharpest sort from Central Office was an article of faith to Clarke, for broadly, the reputation of Tory thinking as against the operations of its office has always stood higher. In the enlarged body Macleod would also play a part in drafting the election documents, 'The Right Road for Britain' (1949) and 'This is the Road', an abridgement which became the manifesto for the 1950 election. He was concerned that the Tories, though learning to be moderate and supportive of social policies, were not getting themselves the credit for it. His essential message to his superiors was to be something which Labour and Tory politicians would both employ across the decades. 'The schemes are right, but we must have growth to pay for them.'

He was blessed in Clarke and Butler – though not in grand, dull Henry Hopkinson, who succeeded Clarke – with the sort of intelligent heads who knew what they wanted and how to get best use out of a talent. But at the same time as Macleod was earning every penny of the £1,250 a year to which his salary would rise (not bad money for the day), he was also equipping himself as a technician of government. He would go into Parliament knowing a great volume of detail on half a dozen departmental subjects. The absorbent, fast mind and the lucid, often elegant fluency were coming together.

At no time did Macleod think he was in the secretariat or the research department except as a step before entry into Parliament and ministerial office, though he would maintain close associations with the department long after his ascent. Having put behind him in the Western Isles the customary ritual of fighting and losing an unwinnable seat, he could get down to business. The bridge which had got him a job with De La Rue now got him onto the shortlist at Enfield.

He had in the card-playing world a reputation separate from the one in politics at whose foundations he was now at work. Dr Fraser Allen was an Enfield medical practitioner with no reason to seek out an obscure Tory aspirant still looking for a job. But he was very keen to ruff and finesse with Macleod, the star bidder when the chance occurred at a tournament in Harrogate. Then, fortuitously, the telegram from Clarke offering Macleod the job in the secretariat arrived, triggering an invitation to lodge temporarily with Dr Allen while he looked for a house. Macleod's clear determination to be a candidate produced the phone number of the local party Chairman, Douglas Waite, an Allen patient. Within the day, a call to Waite and the cheery observation that his long list of 47 could bear a 48th led to Macleod's inclusion for selection. By June of the same year, Macleod, not without controversy, was the Conservative candidate for the Enfield constituency. So much good fortune rarely comes so neatly packed.

The contrast with Butler who also landed on his feet through acknowledged merit is not great. But very different was the experience of Healey, who was not driven by the parliamentary demon, though much later it would charm him. Denis Healey perhaps had to have Leeds South happen when it did if he was to continue along that line. Macleod actually needed politics, meaning Parliament and the pursuit of office. They were the substitute in his competitive nature for the struggle which was card play. The decision to take up politics had been abrupt, conscious and arbitrary – 'This is what I shall do' – and it was now a compulsion.

Healey was entering the Commons after the apogee of Labour power. He was naturally more fascinated by the great milieu of world affairs in which he had walked for six years – sympathetic American and Scandinavian examples and the tenebrous hangman regimes of Eastern Europe – than Macleod could ever be by sensible documents on social amelioration. For Healey Parliament was an anti-climactic option to be thought of once he was no longer working directly for Government. Macleod would always be a delightful and delighted parliamentary performer. Healey would stumble into wit, rhetoric and assassination *after* his governing experience and do so almost as a consolation prize. Macleod had far more in common with the first man at whom he was going to aim a passing kick, Aneurin Bevan.

The Enfield selection did have its controversy. Douglas Waite had overlooked the need to announce the rule that any lead of under ten votes did not constitute outright victory, and Macleod, well below his best form, had trailed the strenuously unremarkable Wing-Commander Bullus by fewer than eight votes. But once that was smoothed over (Bullus duly won a seat in Wembley) and grumbling subsided, Macleod was fighting a winnable seat. And in the general election of 1950, thanks to the inane virtue of Sir Stafford Cripps, when the Conservatives enjoyed a gratifying near miss, Macleod was elected to Parliament.

The point is made elsewhere that with a little restraint in dispute, some sense of timing and a modest measure of guile, Labour might have returned to office in the spring of 1950 with the sort of majority which would have carried over into favourable terms of trade, abolition of rationing and general public gratification, before calling a further and opportune general election. But Cripps's tedious insistence that Labour must not risk charges of using a budget for electoral advantage led to a February election – wrong weather, devaluation still recent news and no happy upturns. It produced a Government majority of six, less than on any calculation they deserved.

There followed an unhappy and unedifying period of 18 months, time for the Korean War to be signed up to, expenditure to leap and the bleak postponement of all the cakes and ale of good politics. For the now avid Opposition this was a time of 'harrying' the Government, ambushes, a multiplying of votes, loud and overstated verbal assault and the occasional accelerated and piously regretted death of a Government backbencher, a sort of parliamentary natural selection. Stafford Cripps died at this time (to be replaced in office by Hugh Gaitskell and in his Bristol seat by Anthony Wedgwood Benn), as did Ernest Bevin. Attlee was not well himself, the Government was older on average than the Opposition and the means to pay for the war led to a quarrel, *the* quarrel of mid-century politics, Bevan against Gaitskell.

Labour could and should have sat things out; governments almost always should. So much can go right if they wait for it. But exhaustion and exasperation played their part; Attlee went to the country and in October 1951, the Conservatives, loudly flourishing the Union Jack and making oppressive display of their now spasmodic great leader, Winston Churchill, were re-elected though with fewer votes than a Labour almost too weary and distracted to complain

Macleod had done well enough in the interim. He took, two years before it was offered, one of the two pieces of advice given by Attlee to Roy Mason when he entered the House in 1953, 'Specialise and keep out of the bar.' The specialism would be health. He knew a good deal from his father's work and he had handled health as one of half a dozen subjects devilling for Clarke and Butler. He became deputy then full chairman of the backbench Health Committee. He made a sensible, unsensational maiden speech, part of it dealing with dentistry (in a state of undermanned crisis at the time), much of it given over to a modest reflection on selectivity in social provision. It was expert and crisp, not crudely partisan but not the waffling generality and fey charm half expected in maiden speakers.

He might conceivably have hoped for minor office when his party took power 18 months after his own entry into Parliament. Luckily, he didn't get it. Instead. from a seat below the gangway at a bound, Jack would become a full-dress minister, seizing his share of power by a *coup de théâtre*. If Macleod's reputation was to be made by his famous assault on Aneurin Bevan, and it certainly was, we should perhaps understand that attack best by looking at it from Bevan's point of view.

Bevan in 1952 was in the middle of the Gaitskell–Bevan rift. As seems to occur every 25 years or so in one party or the other, the real division in politics was internal. When this happens, politics *between* the parties goes onto auto-pilot until the real hatreds are sorted out. If there was one thing that Bevan was not thinking about in March 1952 it was the Conservatives.

The whole business of the secretariat, the Butler-inspired trend to acceptance of most of Labour's social purpose, including the National Health Service, had not communicated itself to Bevan. He was 55, tired from a great creative exertion, too much the prisoner of the left-wing group which adored and exalted him. His mind was focused on how Hugh Gaitskell with his prescription charges had eased the way for what must inevitably follow, the Tory onslaught on the NHS. He was at this point thinking in legendary and mythic terms. Undermining the Health Service was what Conservatives did. They must therefore be eloquently denounced. His speech that afternoon was sub-standard stuff.

As Bevan's scrupulous biographer, John Campbell, puts it, Bevan's attack on the minor increases proposed by the Health Minister, Harry Crookshank, was 'a ludicrous reversion to his apocalyptic predictions of the thirties'. He also talked windily about the Treasury. 'Once more the little men are adding up their silly sums.' Crookshank's minor adjustments were proclaimed by Bevan to be 'the beginnings of the end of British parliamentary government'. With an enemy like that, Macleod hardly needed friends; he had an inadvertent one in the Speaker who, accommodating a maiden speaker, pushed Macleod down the list, thus introducing him after Bevan's contribution, which came from the backbenches to which the former Health Minister had banished himself.

It is worth marking the context to understand the famous opening: 'I want to deal closely and with relish with the vulgar, crude and intemperate speech to which the House of Commons has just listened.' This was not an exaggeration. Bevan at this time was talking hysterically and thinking not at all. Macleod's comments were fair enough. As Campbell observes, 'With detailed figures and skilfully quoting him against himself, Macleod took Bevan's wilder allegations apart.'

Not often do politicians establish themselves in a single early speech. The defiance with which Disraeli ended his disastrous maiden made an impact. F. E. Smith, another raffish wit from the clubs, impressed at once. Bevan himself made a speech in February 1930 which registered his quality in many minds: 'We have a right to say that if it means slightly dearer coal, it is better to have slightly dearer coal than cheaper colliers . . . you cannot get from the already dry veins of the miners new blood to revivify the industry.' And that speech was directed at Lloyd George as Macleod's was at him. But all these four were orators, and for most parliamentarians, oratory is a dangerous optional extra, best left alone.

Generally, the path of political assent, outside the cringe simple, is one of demonstrating intelligence and grasp where the whips can see it while showing suitable devotion to the party's correct line of that moment. A good modern instance would be Michael Howard's defence of council-house-sale asset-freezing in 1984, not a dazzling speech but a sturdy one among a chorus of Conservative reservations. Whips insist that there are two words which count in the notebook which covers every colleague's speech: 'effective' and 'supportive'. Have that written about you reliably often and advancement follows. The whips filter through their chief to the Prime Minister the names recommended for junior office. A Cabinet minister may successfully press for an individual, but the whips determine the great mass of political starts.

But then Macleod had been both effective and supportive, and in concentrated, high-quality form, at a dramatic moment, upon the head of one of the two great speakers of the time and in the presence of the other, who, being Winston Churchill, didn't need whips to tell him anything.

James Stuart, the Chief Whip, murmured something about Macleod being very young, which with Churchill, who had entered the Cabinet 45 years earlier at the age of 33, carried no weight at all. Churchill had also been harried, effectively and healthily, by Bevan, whom he had called 'a squalid nuisance' in a wartime campaign of guerrilla democracy against the cult of the great leader. Here was the squalid nuisance being knocked about by someone whose name Churchill had to ask. He had, like all prime ministers, autocratic powers of selection and was minded to exercise them.

Churchill in October 1951 had largely formed his Government from old shoes and from *vin ordinaire* like Crookshank, and he was saddled with 'dear Anthony'. But Macleod had declined to make Oliver Lyttelton, the conventional favourite, Chancellor of the Exchequer on the grounds of his being too City of London, too brashly the rich businessman. For all the reasons to which Bevan was blind – determination not even to look like the General Strike Churchill or Tonypandy Churchill, recognition that Conservatism must be conciliatory and social – he had appointed Butler, as he had sent good-humoured Walter Monckton to the Ministry of Labour.

Macleod's appointment was not an intentional part of such a sweetening scheme. Churchill, now more than ever, was very broad-brush about colleagues. He had simply seen a big talent, recognised it and liked it, though it is worth mentioning that James Stuart, despite the mutter about youth, was a Butler man. At any rate, splendidly, it happened. The attack on Bevan took place at the end of March 1952; in mid-May following a minor reshuffle, Macleod became Minister of Health. It was not of course the great department involving housing and local government over which Bevan had ruled. It was Health *tout court* and didn't command a seat in the Cabinet, but it would do very nicely. Macleod, for all his assurance, had gone to Downing Street half wondering if he was going to be told off for annoying the whips by refusing a second year on the Council of Europe and, on emerging slightly dazed, asked his wife to take him to a telephone kiosk. He needed to look up the address of the Ministry in the Yellow Pages!

The appointment broke all the rules of precedence: the requirement of a sedulous climb from junior office to higher. Butler was reckoned a lucky fellow with a brilliant start in government, but he put in nine years as a junior before making Cabinet office. There were still in 1952 far fewer posts in government. Macmillan, Wilson and Heath would double the numbers, devalue the word 'minister', which today means any underling in the department, multiply secretaryships of state, create little courts of parliamentary under-secretaries and practise origami with the PPS. The big department over which Bevan had presided had been redistributed (by Attlee), but Macleod was head of a department on call to Cabinet when its business came up. And the appointment, a hunch, was a stroke of genius. It was also something overwhelmingly unlikely to be done in our own time.

Sensibly, once he found his office, Macleod showed a measure of humility, staying quiet and waiting to learn from civil servants before he plunged into major initiatives. He was to be, in fact, a thoroughly conservative minister in the sense that he would defend what Bevan had created, find extra money for it and resist the call going up from many Tory throats for inundations. He was confronted from the start with a campaign inside the Conservative Party to make cuts or charges. In part this derived from a certain social malice against an instrument created by Labour for 'their people', one, moreover, which was much too good for them. There was also a good-faith belief that too much money was being spent and that economies of little pain were possible.

Naturally, the Treasury facing the startling bills created by the service inclined to the second line of thinking. Macleod's own instincts, reinforced by his involvement in the 'One Nation' group of which he was an early stalwart, pointed him in the opposite direction and he had an ally in the Prime Minister who had appointed him. But a weaker minister would have temporised and made concessions. Crookshank, Churchill's first Health Minister, socially remote, suspicious of Labour creations, busy with a second job, leadership of the House, and anyway not much good as a minister, had been disposed to do just that. And Macleod's 'One Nation' friends had been active backbench critics of Crookshank. The possibility of a stormy split existed. It would never in that party at that date have been so bitter or destructive as Labour's, but the difference between accepters of the welfare state and those who disliked it were real. With clumsy or weak handling, the question could have disoriented the Government.

Macleod, coolly, without raising his voice or starting an intra-party war, would see off all the economisers politely. Very early on he devised a ruse which governments would employ heavily for a dozen issues far beyond Health across the next 25 years: the Royal Commission established as a reason for not doing anything just yet. But Macleod owed a major debt to the Chancellor. Butler, with the deft and refined skills which were his hallmark, composed a question for the commission which simply asked how the 'rising charge' on the Exchequer might be avoided. An aggressive direction to an inquisition into assumed waste was blocked by the Chancellor warning colleagues not to fulfil Labour expectations of an attack on welfare.

The instrument would be not the talkative former Tory Minister Ernest Brown as first proposed, but the Cambridge economist Claude Guillebaud, a man rather of the Left than otherwise, but a thoroughly professional technician. He would examine the costs of the NHS and adjudicate on the claims, made by Gaitskellites as well as Tories, that great economies might be made in a supposedly inefficient, overspending service.

Macleod was thus taking over the precise issue on which the Labour Party had split – costs and charges for the NHS. To put things very plainly (and familiarly), the Health Service was a brilliant success, but the demand for its services was very high and it was costing much more than its creators had expected. This had led to the belief that the cost should be trimmed by charges.

Possibly Gaitskell, as his new biographer Brian Brivati thinks, may have been scheming politically with his 1951 imposition of the shilling on prescriptions. But Gaitskell also seriously believed in charges and thought that the NHS must be brought under financial control. This ought to have been the basis for a reasoned argument about management but, given the personality clash, Bevan's intense dislike of Gaitskell and resentment of his appointment to the Treasury, the issue turned into a highly unstable explosive.

The Conservatives ran fewer risks and by the time the commission reported found themselves, little as they realised the fact, following the left-wing option, the views of Aneurin Bevan. To quote Campbell again: 'Gaitskell, backed by Morrison and others, thought that he had an irrefutable case that spending on the National Health Service was too high and continually rising and needed to be checked, not only in the interest of rearmament, but of the other social services.' Stafford Cripps, the previous Chancellor, had held the same view. The function of Guillebaud would be to tell the Conservative Government in 1955 that this was wrong.

He 'authoritatively acquitted the service in this period of the sort of extravagance of which it was widely accused', says Campbell. The big increase in costs at the inception of the NHS came from an underestimate of the effect of a sudden surge of demand for a free service. The core area of cost was the hospital service where, in fact, early financial control had been weak, and that was under control now. Charging would have only marginal effect.

Macleod could know none of this for certain from his single-handed studies of health along with half a dozen other subjects in the secretariat. But it chimed in with his instincts. What Guillebaud would proclaim 30 months on, Macleod would be happy to hear. In setting up the commission, he was saving himself and the Tory Government from the political consequences of a series of unpopular imposts which would have given credibility to the stereotype of the uncaring, NHS-undermining Tory Party. He might annoy activists and right-wingers, but he was exactly following Churchill's own instinct to frighten none of the domestic horses.

In the short term, merely by appointing his old Cambridge economics tutor to make a leisurely study of the problem, he was procrastinating, wasting time, avoiding the issue, dithering – absolutely and in every way the right thing to do. The appointment of Guillebaud should be seen as an example of the benignity of shrewd politics. A rancorous argument was stilled in the short term through pious talk of not prejudicing the Royal Commission's solemn deliberations; money which might have been slashingly cut back by a politician trying to demonstrate his decisiveness went on being allocated and a politically charged issue was taken away to the laboratory for a long cool look. Any mere politician adjudicating performance would have marked up Macleod at once for good sense under pressure. He was living up to his own judgment that the NHS needed 'a period of tranquillity in which the resources available, however limited, are being used to the best advantage'.

He was also able to contribute to such tranquillity with his success in persuading the Cabinet to accept the high pay award recommended by the arbitration of Mr Justice Danckwerts. It put £40 million of the real money of 1952 onto costs but, like Bevan's decision to keep the consultants in line, it helped entrench the service. As the American poet Edgar Lee Masters put it:

A moral truth is a hollow tooth
And must be stopped with gold.

Speaking of which, Macleod, who had discussed the dental-service crisis in his maiden speech, was unable for some time to act as he wished. A Dentists' Bill had been introduced by Crookshank and then dropped. But the pressure created by vast new demand and strict closed-shop restrictions on performance of a dentist's less skilled duties was startling. Eventually, after setting up an enquiry to tell him what he knew, a necessary ploy, Macleod brought in his only piece of actual legislation, the Dentists' Bill of 1955, just before he left the department. It conferred responsibilities upon assistants and made it easier for dentists qualified outside the UK to practise.

Crookshank had deferred to the pressure of the lobby. Not deferring to lobbies was to be one of Macleod's great charms as a minister. A good example concerned family planning. In the mid-fifties, when sexual intercourse was still considered not nice and the views of celibate clergymen about its exclusive purpose were treated with unwarranted respect, contraception was a shocking, if narrowly legal thing. You could do it but shouldn't talk about it. The Roman Catholic Church, then in the triumphalist afterglow of the Marian year of 1950, with Pius XII in the Vatican and the Second Council not thought of, inspired real fear on the subject. Contraception was immoral, a nonsense half-conceded by official conduct. Setting up a family-planning clinic was a hushed, word-of-mouth undertaking, a doing good by furtive means. Macleod, tentatively invited to a clinic to see that they were not really so bad, at once brushed aside the minute discretion he had been assured and made a public event of his visit, proclaiming the common sense of women not getting pregnant if they didn't want to. In the process, he simply brushed the mystique of the Catholic lobby aside. Neither humbug about sex, nor cringes to supposed big battalions were his style; he was a worldly man and a brave one.

This non-moralising approach came in the stuffy mid-fifties, but it would have been welcome from the Conservative Party during its 'Back to Basics' phase in the nineties. And Macleod got away with his actions. The Catholic hierarchy was bluffing even with its own congregations. David Lodge's elegant novel *How Far Can You Go?* records a subtle change just beginning then for Catholics. As for the country generally, we were nearer to 1963 in 1955 than anyone quite realised. Accordingly the Family Planning Association dared to speak its name and get on with its work.

For a minister outside the Cabinet and not superficially well placed for leverage, Macleod did notably well over his three and a half years at Health in his dealings with the Treasury. Not only was he able to postpone and finally resist altogether the clamour for charges, he did quite well eventually over capital expenditure on hospitals as well. In his early days Macmillan's housing plans had hogged a great piece of the public spending equity – and launched the Macmillan rocket towards the premiership. Schools were also getting cash, but the stripped-down Ministry of Health was kept short of capital for building. And the money that Macleod did get from Butler in spring 1954, a £1.5 million increase as against the £6 million he sought, was lost in Lord Swinton's economy exercise that summer. As Macleod pointed out, investment in hospital-building was desperately low. Across the five years since 1948, a two-party period, it had averaged £7 million annually contrasted with the £35 million spent in 1938–9 under a Prime Minister, Neville Chamberlain, who had been Minister of Health. (Macleod would raise eyebrows in 1961 by writing a short biography of Chamberlain.) But elections are useful things for spending ministers, and Macleod used the prospective contest of 1955 to get £3 million extra for 1955–6 and £8 million extra for 1956–7. And the plans survived the post-election aggravation which produced the pots and pans autumn budget. Butler, ill advised, might have cut too much tax, but the temptation to renege on hospital proposals was successfully resisted. Shepherd quotes Macleod's speech in the finance debate (31 October 1955), 'That programme stands, every hospital, every ward, every bed in it. I am deeply grateful to the Chancellor that he has been able to keep the green light fixed on that particular programme.'

It was the sort of victory which has implications for the victor's future. Macleod was generally seen by Conservative and non-Conservative commentators alike as a successful minister. He had seen off an assault on his charge; he had got money for expansion. He had done other sensible things like putting stress on preventative medicine and mental health in response to people who knew about the whole subject. It wouldn't do to say so, but he had done very roughly what an outstanding Labour Minister of Health operating in a more sympathetic environment might have hoped to do. However, a Labour minister would have walked very softly over family planning with all those Catholic voters on Merseyside and Manchester, the sweetening of whom with 100 per cent grants to denominational schools would be Harold Wilson's first cringe of government. Since the Conservative Party was doing very nicely electorally from a discreet stewardship of Labour's concerns, such a minister would be commended and advanced.

CHAPTER FOUR

In fact, the job to which Anthony Eden, the new Prime Minister, directed Macleod in 1955 involved a sideways move. Labour and National Service had, for five years, been run in an even more conciliatory style by Sir Walter Monckton. Churchill's instinct, which Eden, insofar as he took in domestic affairs, shared, that the Tories must not be brutalists, was met in the workplace. The fact that Britain did not succeed, as the Germans did in a similar enlightened atmosphere, in creating a systematic climate of *Mitbestimmung* with unions alerted to the importance of productivity and competitiveness, is too large and melancholy a truth to be gone heavily into here.

Industrial relations postwar were marked by managements eating, living and thinking apart from a workforce about which they complained on the golf course while workers gradually warmed to the implications of full employment and, the boot being on the other foot, found themselves kicking.

The two sides never did manage to be civilised and rational at the same time, but engaged in a kind of two-way Hobbesian conflict. Monckton's instinct was to use the Ministry to make peace and, where pressed, to make it on the unions' terms. Beer and sandwiches were coming onto the menu and a number of settlements were reached which were fundamentally injurious to the economy as a whole, but Monckton's brief from Churchill – peace with the unions – was met. The consequential slowly developing inflation was a great threat, underestimated because it contradicted a political consensus, decently intended but unarithmetical. At this time Britain was sovereign, not properly assailed by the bond markets, and thus able to take the weak options and gather the penalties later.

Matters were made worse by a change of guard in the union leadership. Arthur Deakin, Ernest Bevin's old T and G henchman, might be a despot, *was* a despot, both in Labour Party politics and in running the union. But he was a despot on the side of sense. He shared Bevin's dislike of Communists, Trotskyists and anyone stirring up trouble in his union, and he was no friend of unrealistic settlements. But when in 1955 Deakin died, the T and G succession, though fixed by predecessor for successor, took time to become operational. Deakin's own successor, Albert 'Jock' Tiffin, was in the apostolic line of bunch-fisted moderation, but within months Tiffin died and the general-secretaryship passed to Frank Cousins.

Cousins would be a good argument for despotism. A model of old-fashioned working-class and Socialist virtues, he was a sentimental, warm-hearted member of what would later be called the soft Left, but very tolerant of a harder Left. He was readily pushed from below by the sort of people whom Bevin and Deakin had knocked on the head. The union was hopelessly uncohesive without autocracy, a sort of Portuguese empire of islands, coastal regions and land-locked territories. Ernest Bevin had fought a bitter internal battle in 1937 with the Communist leader of the London busmen, Bert Papworth.[1] His ruthlessness in doing down the busmen was widely deplored at the time – no class solidarity there, rather 'Who is to be master?'

The heirs of Bert Papworth were now about to win serious power and Bevin's point would be made with bitter clarity. Bevin was an autocrat in time of depression, Cousins a complacent liberal in an era of full employment. The argument of Schumpeter's argument picked up by Denis Healey about union power under Democratic Socialism would also be confirmed. Cousins had another contribution to make in his heavy naïve way. By shifting his bloc vote in 1960 to the CND lobby, where it would stay, he would do great things for the Conservative Party.

Back on the shop floor, it would become increasingly easy for local shop stewards to practise autonomy, increasingly usual for the national leadership to be dragged along by the chariot wheels of such local commanders and indeed to develop a protective remoteness. Arthur Cockfield (later a Tory Cabinet Minister in the Lords), wearing his business hat, recalls meeting Cousins socially during a strike and Cousins saying, 'I think we've reached the stage where you and I will have to get involved.'

'As an employer,' he says, 'I had been involved all the time.'

Cousins, demonised by the Tory press, seen as arrogant by colleagues jealous of his high profile, became a target. Macleod would in due course enjoy a victory over him which looked at the time like a turning point, but proved historically to be no such thing. The conflict would concern the bus drivers.

The early months of 1956 were economically bleak. Wage increases achieved in those months equalled the total for the whole of 1955 – £250 million added to costs. A hard line by Standard Motors imposing redundancy to follow automation had produced an unofficial strike, something which did not stop BMC sacking 6,000 men without consultation on a week's wage severence. Whatever the faults of the unions, peremptory thick-headedness in key boardrooms did everything it could in a union-strong market to immoderate the entire workforce.

Ironically, BMC, so swaggering and masterful at this time, would when reconstituted as British Leyland enjoy the attentions of Tony Benn and a species of trade unionism which might have been devised as punishment by Gilbert's humane Mikado. Monckton's approach from Government is unfashionable today. The field is strewn with the scorn of men talking hard after the event. His attitude may have involved too much intervention, but if managements at that time could have achieved half of his good manners, respect for the workers' side and inclination to consult, the story of industrial relations would have been very different and much happier. If it is argued that workers and spectator unions now endure much more adverse decisions, they do so at a time when unemployment has become part of the landscape.

Macleod reacted to the BMC decision with what newspaper headlines call 'fury' and it was anger enough for the message to be picked up by Jack Jones, the new Midland organiser of the T and G and Cousins' ultimate successor, who was startled to find a Conservative so critical of 'the bosses'. What followed fitted the pattern of recent events: a short but official strike, followed by ministerial intervention ending in company agreement to pay limited compensation and to engage in proper consultation next time. At the price of a lot of slow-burning ill-will, the company had had the best of the dispute. But the longer-term pattern would be for interventions which cloaked union victories. Macleod was left telling Conservative Conference that automation ought to be 'handled by way of consultation from the very beginning at all stages and all levels'. The disputes, or rather the peremptory leg-breaking style of motor manufacturers who lacked the real strength to sustain such swagger, would be reflected in new language from the top of the unions.

At Brighton that autumn, Frank Cousins made the famous pithy remark that if there was to be a free-for-all, the unions wanted to be part of the 'all'. A not desperately bright, emotionally charged but also fundamentally decent union leader with a line to the genuine anger of people put casually out of work was talking a new old language.

Bevin, Deakin, Walter Monckton and the brighter managements had, at some cost in wage drift, managed a social contract. Macleod had the ill luck to come in when that contract was starting to flake. The job was living up to the title which a future occupant, Ray Gunter, was to give it, 'the bed of nails'. Yet, in a low career sense, the ill luck was good luck. Two years later, under the prime ministership of Harold Macmillan, circumstances and the new mood would oblige Macleod to fight and win a battle with the unions which translated into crude *Daily Express* terms as very good internal Tory politics.

The dispute was a complex affair involving London busmen, the heirs of Bert Papworth's lads. It was wished upon Macleod by the uncharacteristic hawkishness of the Minister of Transport, Harold Watkinson. A demand in the autumn of 1957 by the T and G on behalf of busworkers for 25 shillings a week, one which was to have been almost automatically granted a court of enquiry, was stopped dead in its tracks in the office of the Chief Industrial Commissioner, Sir William Neden, by the fiat of Watkinson that nothing should be done to let the busmen think they were going to get any money. Macleod was not consulted. At this stage he would not have been anything like so categoric – indeed, he recommended as Minister of Labour that there should be a committee of enquiry, since 'to refuse the request would be a very marked departure from normal practice and would be construed as a definite Government move to have a show-down with the unions'. A showdown with the unions, or at any rate with Frank Cousins, which was almost the same thing, was what Macleod got and it did him no end of political good.

But oddly enough, neither he nor Cousins was looking for the fight they both got into. The enquiry Macleod proposed to his Cabinet colleagues was gently rejected – by R. A. Butler. Macmillan being on his Commonwealth progress, this was one of the 13 or so occasions when Butler functioned as acting Prime Minister. It was an instructive one. Butler, supposedly weak and indecisive, suggested with an edge of velvet in his voice that an enquiry 'would be interpreted by public opinion as the beginning of a surrender to the unions'.

As Shepherd reasonably comments, had Macmillan been present, anxious as ever not to have any strike that might spread to the railways or the docks, Macleod would have got his enquiry. And Frank Cousins, who wasn't spoiling for a fight, would have got something he could sell to his members. Macleod was being pushed into the arena against the supposed wild beasts of the unions at the graceful request of the acting Caesar. Butler coolly stopped him from resigning, his first reaction, by holding Cabinet back from any decision until it could approve a letter to the T and G drafted by Macleod. He was being manipulated but not allowed to lose face.

In fact, due to the tendency of the leader of the Opposition to make furious attacks too soon, Macleod gained an unscheduled Parliamentary triumph as pure bonus. Gaitskell, despite owing no favours to Cousins, tabled a motion of censure on the Government at a moment when shrewd, insincere expressions of goodwill and a sitting back to enjoy things would have been in order. Alf Robens, former and Shadow Minister of Labour, opened with a speech of great detailed command in moderate language criticising not Macleod but general Government policy.

Macleod wasted no time answering that, but made instead the sort of bitter, concentrated, contemptuous attack which he reserved for major occasions (to the great satisfaction of Robens). For a moderate and essentially good-humoured man, his physical pain notwithstanding, Macleod knew how to be savagely partisan and knew that it worked. His ferocity towards Labour on key occasions rather recalls an explanation of the contrast between the impenetrable accent of southern Scotland against the pure English of Inverness. John Laurie, the actor, said that Dumfriesshire people like himself had to speak like that since being so near to the English, they could never risk being confused with them.

Macleod was not about to be confused with Gaitskell. 'I am bound to say that I cannot conceal my scorn and contempt for the part that the leader of the Opposition has played in this,' he said. Politicians in group formation are not a sophisticated audience, but they know what they like, and the sinking of teeth into the throat of an opponent is what they like best. The Tory backbenchers were in excelsis. With irritation elevated into a burst of politic fury, Macleod was getting himself talked about as a future leader.

But the actual dispute continued. Cousins took an ostentatiously moderate and consultative line, getting the busmen to agree to the principle of arbitration by the Industrial Court. The award, not a high one – 8/6 a week confined to central London crews which Cousins wanted to spread across to the outer London crews at an average of 6/6 – had a rough reception. Watkinson insisted that the whole award must come from London Transport's own cash. In a similar spirit of compromise, the busmen themselves rejected the offer and demanded 10/6 for all crews. Authority in that section of the union ran from the garages to the delegates to the General Secretary in something close to descending order.

The risk now was of a strike involving other transport workers. So, for 3 per cent quickly conceded in a huddle, the National Union of Railwaymen and the Underground workers were accommodated. Macleod would later claim to Geoffrey Goodman, the *Mirror*'s astute trades-union specialist, that he had been advised by major figures in the TUC to keep the fight going and win. Cousins unfairly inspired the sort of peer dislike which Arthur Scargill would deserve, and other trades-union chiefs may have decided to roll themselves a little *schadenfreude* by encouraging the Minister. Much more creditably, such union leaders could see that if the Government gave in to Cousins, who was in turn harried by a militant autonomous faction, they, who had militant autonomous factions of their own, would have a bad time later on, as in the seventies they assuredly did.

Macleod was now standing by a hard figure only to find London Transport offering more to the country busmen and a review to others outside the award. Meanwhile, garages rebelled against Cousins and the delegates who wanted to resume negotiations. The conflict dragged on but Macleod understood what hung upon the next round of negotiations with provincial bus-drivers and his own standing as winner or loser. He had more stomach for the fight than the busmen and, with the country drivers on 5 shillings and the London men on 8/6, he emerged with what would count as a victory. In terms of long-term mastery of the unions that would not be true and relations with Harold Macmillan, never happy with a clear-cut stance, had not improved, but the political credit was very large. The Tories had trailed in the polls, and had lost a by-election, something that didn't happen in those days. The polls would shortly turn up and Macleod would be seen by people well to the right of him as providing 'the smack of firm government', the phrase of Donald Maclachlan's in the *Daily Telegraph* which had writhed under the thin, afflicted skin of Anthony Eden.

Fighting the London bus drivers was very much better business than fighting the Egyptians and Macleod like Butler had endured the events of August–November 1956 in the disquieted dark, told little and not liking what he was told. Macleod had supported the principle of using force in honest circumstances. He had done what he could to fix trades-union contacts to pre-empt a resolution against it at the TUC Conference. But he was in the dark about the Sèvres deal, the famous collusion agreement for Israel to make a back for France and Britain by her own act of war. This was dishonest force and the act which invalidated the Suez operation to what might be called the scrupulous hawks. Macleod was noted by Norman Brook, the Cabinet Secretary, as one of those 'who will want to postpone the use of force until all else has been tried, or until Nasser provides us with a good occasion, whichever happens earlier'. Though excluded from Sèvres Macleod had, as Minister of Labour, been first alerted then restrained in the business of seeing what resistance there might be to industrial war production. By the end of October refinements of attitude were swamped by the common-sense fact that everybody else – Commonwealth, UN and the United States – was against military action. World opinion can be brushed aside as rhetoric but if the world includes the United States, defiance will be ill advised. Perhaps also a good gambler recognises a bad gamble, in this case one which involved kicking over the card table.

There are conflicting reports about whether or not Macleod contemplated resignation. Candidly resigning or not was a dividing line between the pure and the very pure, the proper politicians and men less or more than politicians. Macleod was less of an idealist than either Edward Boyle or Anthony Nutting, who did resign. Nutting's career was over; Boyle's would revive, though he had no passion for it.

Macleod, as he would demonstrate six and a half years later, had a resignation in him, had indeed a hot sense of honour. But he was realist enough to stay and would have opened to him after the travails of fighting Frank Cousins an opportunity to do something in Africa which was at violent odds with the underlying imperial assumptions of Suez. Suez, not just in Eden's excitable hands but in those of Harold Macmillan, its most violent advocate, was counter-devolutionary, a resiling from the first retreat out of Empire, abandonment in 1954 of the canal zone. The policy of accelerated decolonisation which would form the high plateau of Iain Macleod's career, a thing natural to him, was not natural to Macmillan for all his progressive credentials, nor to the ten members of the Eden Cabinet recorded by Norman Brook as 'pretty steady' for force. The awful view of the Egyptians as 'wogs', as people who didn't quite count and could be peremptorily and ill used, hardly fitted with the idea of people far south and much darker-skinned than the Egyptians being given self-government. The Cabinet which Macmillan had shrilly urged to war would respond to the humiliation of war by acts which defeat had made possible, indeed almost necessary and which Macleod was the man to execute. He had been very wise not to resign.

[1]See Alan Bullock, *Ernest Bevin* Vol. 1.

CHAPTER FIVE

The first thing which it is necessary that we should realise is this: that what we are face to face with is essentially a crisis of confidence . . . I know that Rhodesia was the most British, in the fullest sense of that word, of any of the realms and territories of the British Crown. Now, within the space of a few months, those feelings have given way to others of a very different kind: of suspicion, of contempt, almost of hatred of the home Government. How has this terrible thing come about in so short a time? . . . the main responsibility must rest on the present Colonial Secretary . . . I believe he has adopted, especially in his relationship to the white communities of Africa, a most unhappy and an entirely wrong approach. He has been too clever by half . . . I believe that the Colonial Secretary is a very fine bridge-player . . . It is not considered immoral or even bad form to outwit one's opponents at bridge. On the contrary, the more you outwit them within the rules of the game, the better player you are. It almost seems to me as if the Colonial Secretary, when he abandoned the sphere of bridge for the sphere of politics, brought his bridge technique with him. At any rate it has become, as your Lordships know, the convinced view of the white people of Eastern and Central Africa that it has been his object to outwit them, and that he has done it most successfully . . . The Europeans found themselves completely outwitted [of the Kenya settlement], and they were driven, if I may revert for the last time to the bridge metaphor, to think that it was

the nationalist African leaders whom the Colonial Secretary
regarded as his partners, and the white community and the
loyal Africans that he regarded as his opponents in the
game he was playing.

Lord Salisbury continues, including a remark about the population of African Northern Rhodesia being 'primitive'. The phrase 'too clever by half' is the one that stuck (and which did Macleod real harm). But it was the reference to bringing his bridge technique to politics after describing bridge as a game directed at outwitting opponents which was the most savage.

The hostility, not far from hatred, expressed here speaks eloquently of the conflicts into which Macleod had entered in his time at the Colonial Office. A couple of years on, 200 Tory MPs would attend a meeting at the Commons addressed by Sir Roy Welensky, Prime Minister of the Federation of Rhodesia, and Macleod's adversary in a relationship which suffered its own immiseration. Martin Redmayne, Macmillan's Chief Whip, would report that between two thirds and three quarters of that number supported Welensky.

The relationship between any decolonising colonial secretary and the imperial right was never going to be happy. *A fortiori*, the colonists were going to like such a reformer even less. Macleod made nothing easier for himself by conducting matters not only with (very necessary) negotiating skill and reserve, but a steady zeal. The end was a cause for him. He also had a clear dislike of white settlerdom. About that Salisbury was right. He *did* regard the settlers as his opponents. He would do what he could for them. As engineers or farmers, they were useful people. They should stay and would, he was certain, prosper. His brother Rhoderick was such a settler in Kenya. But if they thought that being Europeans entitled them to primacy as a boss minority, they would be fighting him. (However would he have handled Northern Ireland?)

At the end of his time in the Colonial Office, he would be physically exhausted and would have accumulated enemies in British Conservative politics by whom he would be defined. He would also stand in a different relationship to the man who had put him into the job. It was Macmillan who had started the entire operation when, after the near landslide victory of 1959, he offered Macleod the office, assessing it as a major task and thereby bringing him forward as an identified young runner in the leadership race. Macmillan's fearful and melodramatic nature, always on the alert for a new catastrophe, had something worth being scared of in the French Algerian crisis.

To the five syllables of 'Algérie Française' played on car horns, French civil government had been brought down in May 1958. 'Algérie Française' meant total identification of France with the settlers, many of them (off-French), with Fascist-minded generals ready and able to mount a paratroop-led *putsch* if denied their shrill wishes. The subsequent delicate and long drawn-out betrayal of the settlers by General de Gaulle, beneficiary of that remarkable thing, a drawn coup, was in 1959 laboriously underway. The General had flown to Algiers and immortally remarked '*Je vous ai compris.*' Indeed he had, and a comprehensive welshing on commitments made under duress to colonists threatening the state would be accomplished as Macleod's problems in Central Africa moved into top gear.

How sympathetic Macmillan actually was towards black people and their hopes is debatable. He disliked mannerless and triumphant ex-military rightists, though he was always a little afraid of them. But dealing with Macmillan alone Roy Welensky would have obtained more by way of concession than he would ever get from his Colonial Secretary, and the Prime Minister's diaries teem with the amateur race psychology – 'a highlander, so highly strung', for instance – to which Macmillan was given. (When Lord Devlin had delivered his damning report on the Hola Camp massacre in Kenya, Macmillan would confide, 'I have discovered that he is (a) *Irish* – no doubt with that Fenian blood that makes Irishmen anti-government on principle; (b) a lapsed Roman Catholic.')

For all this witter, Macmillan scared was Macmillan urgent for action. And his fears in the light of French colonial experience, though probably overdone, were of the kind which lead to a search for the way out. The great streak of melancholic, rather whimpering defeatism which ran through Macmillan – 'weighed down with grief and foreboding . . . almost a sense of despair' – had its uses here. Macleod's brief in his new job was to meet Macmillan's apprehensions by moving events and institutions on in Kenya, Tanganyika and Uganda, and in Nyasaland and Northern Rhodesia, the two other territories of the Central African Federation in existence since 1953. The task was a curate's egg – parts of it were manageable.

Tanganyika, with a negligible settler presence – this was the old pre-1914 German territory (Mr Nyerere is not called Julius for nothing) – and with an African Chief Minister already established under colonial rules – was almost easy. Kenya with its horrific experience of Mau Mau, its small and not over-illusioned white population under a leader, Michael Blundell, who meant what he said by the word 'partnership', still had serious problems, but might be brought off.

Nyasaland would be very difficult indeed. It was a near all-black territory (7,000 settlers in all) and not at all valuable, having neither oil nor metals, industrial or precious. No crusade for a new world order will ever be fought over its thin bones. But it mattered to the whites of Southern Rhodesia as a pawn sacrifice that would signify retreat. They didn't need, or intrinsically want, Nyasaland, but giving it up implied that the federation of three territories was mutable, even that black people not very far from Salisbury, might, by governing them-selves, give ideas to uppity natives not currently allowed into Meikles Hotel.

Over Northern Rhodesia the issue was even simpler. It was rich in copper, cobalt and other industrial metals. It had a few more whites than Nyasaland, though not enough to make for a great fight. But it was treasured by Southern Rhodesia, eyed by South Africa and the Soviet Union and marched neatly with a province of what was still the Belgian Congo, Katanga. And Katanga was a place where most of the European dark scenarios would soon be played out in ways which would make those fears look a touch optimistic. It would be the scene of a vicious tribal war, cost the life of the one truly independent Secretary-General of the United Nations, Dag Hammarskjold, and call up American anxieties to match Macmillan's.

In respect of all the Rhodesian-attached territories, Macleod was on his way into an uncomplicated *realpolitik* which would spin off skeins of constitutional options, plans, voting rolls, consultations, and flights by Welensky to London to address discontented Conservative MPs.

But Kenya, Macleod's first heavy preoccupation, was the other reason, and one more specific than the French malaise, why he had been appointed. Kenya had seen the Mau Mau rising in the early fifties. Its murders of settlers, and its leaders calling themselves 'General Russia' and 'General China', fitted the nightmare of all ascendancies rather as the Phoenix Park assassinations had confirmed for Englishmen the bog-atrocity image of Ireland in 1882.

It had been possible to crush Mau Mau and hang violent African leaders like Dedan Kimathi much as Joe Brady and the

Invincibles had been dealt with. The remarkable thing was that thereafter the Irish pattern, with British minds closed and unable to make deals, was *not* followed. Jomo Kenyatta, 'a leader to darkness and death', had been acquitted of capital offences and convicted of lesser ones. Was there an element of the Albert Speer case here, involving someone obviously very intelligent and interesting, a pupil of Malinovsky, whom it would be bad form to execute? And like Nelson Mandela, Kenyatta was an African aristocrat, though that would not have inhibited the junior minister I have heard regret the failure to hang Mandela.

The innocence of Kenyatta is almost irrelevant set against the wisdom of not making a martyr of a negotiating partner. Macleod inherited this volume of good sense, but he also inherited a state of emergency which had run for seven years since October 1952. Under that emergency there had occurred in March 1959, only six months before Macleod took over, the episode at Hola Camp. There had been a riot among detainees and in their respone to it, guards had left 13 prisoners dead. This Kenyan event harmonised with events in Nyasaland, where Robert Armitage, the Governor, had responded to riots by proclaiming his own state of emergency, arrested Hastings Banda, the local African leader, and alleged that a massacre of Europeans had been planned.

This crisis would produce the comment from Gaitskell, 'Will they never learn?', his criticism reflexively pigeonholed by Macmillan as party politics, and the commissioning of that report with its Fenian overtones from Mr Justice Devlin. The Hola massacre inspired a speech of blinding authority from Enoch Powell. Macmillan, not entirely indifferent to party politics and working rapidly with Armitage at Chequers, had knocked together in two days a second, short report offsetting Devlin's account of the Nyasaland conspiracy massacre, soothing the anxious Tory Party and getting himself out of what he characterised as 'a jam'.

Macmillan also found the press 'excellent' in swallowing the operation. Hola, as his biographer Horne interestingly puts it, was 'put into perspective'. Anyway, that 'was an accident'. However, Alan Lennox-Boyd, the Colonial Secretary, fairly conservative but a man of some conscience, wanted to resign both because he had family business to take up and because he was shaken by Hola in ways different from Macmillan. Macleod was thus the heir in Kenya to a major act of wrongdoing and in Nyasaland to a governor's blunder which had produced a piece of prime ministerial misrepresentation to make John Profumo look like George Washington. Things would now be handled very differently.

One of Macleod's first acts was to get past Cabinet a suspension of the Kenya Emergency and to release 2,500 prisoners held under its provisions. He would much later release Jomo Kenyatta, parole 120 convicted offenders and establish a constitutional conference. But his immediate objective was to find Europeans able to accept that Kenya would be governed sooner rather than later by Africans. Whites of the die-hard stamp with whom he would have to talk in the Rhodesias, he simply brushed aside. In Kenya Group-Captain Briggs, leader of a right-wing faction, sympathiser with apartheid and general blowhard, made Roy Welensky sound like Metternich.

Macleod had, luckily, a natural ally in Michael Blundell and the New Kenya Party. (In particular, he would strike up a good working relationship with Wilfrid Havelock, Blundell's deputy and a man with a helpful grasp of detail.) There were minority tribes federated under the moderate leadership of Ronald Ngala into the Kenya African Democratic Union (KADU), and he had the Asians. All these could co-operate and behave very reasonably. But without the Kikuyu, the great dominant tribe of Kenya, all such reasonableness would be nugatory. And it was the Kikuyu who were led by Kenyatta, the Kikuyu who had enrolled in Mau Mau.

It was as if the Chinese of Malaya, from whom the terrorists had been recruited in that emergency, had been the majority population. If real business was to be done, it would be done with the Kenya African National Union (KANU), the party of the Kikuyu. Macleod would be working for some of the time with Tom Mboya, a Luo, a significant cadet connection of the Kikuyu. It was Mboya who had coined the phrase 'scram out of Africa'. But, in his noisy way, he was a man one could do business with, especially as the business, at least as far as old-style colonial command went, was scramming out of Africa.

Allied with Mboya, and in opposition to him, was Oginga Odinga, a sort of horror-film leftist and maker of imprecatory speeches which frighten horses and Conservative MPs and who, with Mboya, made up a sort of Spenlow and Jorkins partnership: 'I don't want to be difficult, but Jorkins wouldn't hear of any easier terms.'

The mechanism for progress was a conference at Lancaster House marked by a thicket of wrangles about accreditation and the date of Kenyatta's release. There were walk-outs and boycotts. Macleod knew better than to get indignant. For a man who could snap and grow short with friends, he was unaffrontable so long as a conference, even one taking place in separate venues to accommodate those not speaking to other people, actually took place. At the outset, the Colonial Secretary said the words which mattered: that the time had come to recognise that majority rule would come in Kenya and that the Africans were the majority race.

In fact, as Michael Blundell was finding out, Macleod's chief concern was to push towards a version of the common electoral roll which Mboya and his delegation wanted. All colonial institutions worked on fancy franchises and separate rolls, given tribal division and a clear wish to hold the hand of any majority likely to assert itself. Lennox-Boyd had left behind a notably baroque set of rules and rolls. Macleod now offered a smaller legislative council, 65 members instead of 91, of whom 53 would be elected by a common roll; 33 seats would be open with their franchise qualification – literacy, office-holding or £75 a year – quite low, while 20 seats would be set aside for Europeans and Asians. (And much good *that* would do them a few years later.) This deal wasn't everything the Africans wanted, but it was an essential advance and, when Macleod threatened a commission and a year's delay, he won immediate African assent.

He then faced uncovenanted resistance from the Europeans. The New Kenya Party, Blundell's people, were unhappy about things moving further and faster than they wished and were conscious of losing settler opinion behind them while the unspeakable Group-Captain Briggs, whom Macleod had barred from seeing Macmillan, gained momentum. They made an issue of certain questions about European rights over land. Macmillan was called up for the sort of honey-and-butter oration – change inevitable in human affairs, often less disagreeable than it seemed, setting a pattern for the whole of Africa – which he did so well. Macleod put up money (development costs and resettlement, £6.5 million in all), but did not give the legal safeguards on ownership which had been demanded. The Europeans, already men bowing to the inevitable and putting their money on the African partnership working, wearily agreed.

As for the British Cabinet, it was stressed to them that advance in Kenya was slower than in Tanganyika or Uganda, which it was bound to be. The Cabinet accepted; Macleod was through. And historically, though Kenya is a highly imperfect state, notably in its treatment of Asians, the outcome 35 years on makes his strenuous efforts here look well. Blundell went home to have 30 pieces of silver thrown at him, but Africans and Europeans did and do rub along in independent Kenya in the ways Macleod and Blundell had hoped for.

In fact, no narration of these years can convey the anxiety and the hustle of what was done. The several parts of the imperial problem were not dealt with seriatim, in neat sequential order; several baubles were spinning in the air at the same time and Macleod was effectively commuting between conferences. The final conference session which put sealing wax on the knots of the Kenya package occurred on 21 February 1960, at the same time as a very bitter phase of the Nyasaland crisis over which he nearly resigned.

Nyasaland, part of the Central African Federation, brought Macleod (and a twitching Macmillan) into dispute with what was then Southern Rhodesia. Southern Rhodesia meant Roy Welensky, half-Jewish, half-Afrikaner, not stupid, not blindly reactionary, but not subtle either and gifted in making serious and noisy trouble. It was a common, rather snobbish observation that after the war, officers went to Kenya and NCOs to Rhodesia. Arguably, there was a gentlemanliness about Blundell and his friends which was manageable. Welensky had been a trade unionist and was untouched by fears of giving offence or making a scene. He made some of the best scenes of his generation.

Macleod was working smoothly and well with Butler, acting Prime Minister again. He was encouraged by Macleod to exercise discretion in what he told the Cabinet. An enquiry from Macmillan, returning on the Castle Line from his 'Wind of Change' speech, about the effect of developments on Southern Rhodesia brought the flat reply, 'I am afraid there is naught for their comfort wherever Rhodesians look in Africa today,' lines to be echoed later in a book title by Bishop Trevor Huddleston.

What Macleod would say about African rule in Kenya would make hardly any impact; his opinions about Rhodesia were private. But his position was unambiguously for the end of both Empire and its settler extension. The procedural arguments were secondary and the elaborate dispute over electoral rolls related to the terms of retreat. Retreat itself – recognition of numbers, the impossibility of holding a position, the need for liquidation – was the order of the day.

But the immediate question in Nyasaland was the release of

Dr Banda. According to old received colonial opinion, Hastings Banda, the first African from the territory to qualify as a medical practitioner, something achieved after trekking via the Cape to Edinburgh to a practice in Kilburn, was the focus of violence, surrounded by men who would start a riot at the drop of a hat. The Governor, Armitage, had put his name and reputation to a state of emergency and a wave of arrests. By old practice people like Armitage were the men in the field to be given implicit backing at Westminster whatever the contrary judgments. Devlin had poured water, fairly hot water, all over Armitage's assumptions, and had talked about 'temporary states of totalitarianism', something so injurious to right-thinking assumptions and morale that the second report had been faked up to muffle the sinister Irishman. Meanwhile, Walter Monckton, as certain a liberal as any member of the Government, had been delegated to report on the future of the entire federation.

Flux was the only word for it. If you didn't like Devlin you weren't going to like Monckton, and how much of this confusion could be attributed to Macmillan's own havering state betwixt pushing reform and running back to the status quo, how much to ordinary, unstructured muddle, is a nice question. What was clear was that, as Lord Beaverbrook liked to say, the trumpet gave an uncertain sound. Macleod began trying to shift the landscape by dropping hints in routine speeches like the one at Leeds saying that 'the time must come when the question of constitutional advance in Nyasaland must be tackled again'.

If constitutional advance meant releasing Banda, Armitage as Governor wanted a lot more troops to prevent the riots which, consistently if inaccurately, he ardently expected. Armitage's professional credibility rather turned upon such riots, and with neighbouring Katanga about to be plunged into civil war, and Evelyn Hone, Governor of Northern Rhodesia, backing him, there was nothing implausible about such anxiety. But the judgment was wrong and Macleod's private estimate that Banda, for all his vanity, uncertain temper and touchiness, was *not* the sort of man to conjure up riots, was correct. (Living, it seemed, for ever, he would in due course become an unengaging old tyrant, but that is another question.)

Armitage wanted to extend his emergency by at least another six months, and, backed by Welensky as Federal Prime Minister, put pressure on Macmillan, hoping to have Banda exiled while Monckton, now on the road, carried out his investigation into the federation.

But Macmillan at this stage was still backing his Colonial Secretary and seems to have formed the view that panic and overreaction were the Nyasaland administration's only instincts. If Armitage wanted to get rid of Banda, Macleod set to work to get rid of Armitage, choosing as his instrument Glyn Jones, north Wales-born, grammar-school boy, a reform-minded member of the Northern Rhodesian colonial administration as Chief Minister of Nyasaland. Measures are conditional upon men and Jones would later work closely with Butler, who greatly admired him, when the time came to wind down the federation. The Southern Rhodesians were drawing febrile conclusions and making the first hints that, denied federation and with dangerous black men released, they would start thinking of independence for themselves, an independence to be reached by unilateral declaration.

While this crisis was simmering, the Kenya conference was coming to successful conclusion and Macmillan was completing the Commonwealth tour which would include his famous 'Wind of Change' speech. The Prime Minister was also, on these travels, having his ear violently bent by European farmer opinion and being assailed by Welensky and the Southern Rhodesian premier Edgar Whitehead, a man physically frail but virulently willed. The possibility that Banda's release in Nyasaland would trigger new elections held on the issue of Southern Rhodesian flight from federation and Commonwealth existed prominently among the scares and fright scenarios of the day. Lord Home, Commonwealth Secretary, who on the whole had worked well enough with Macleod in their double-yoked task, conveyed the flavour of his own meetings with Welensky and Whitehead. They would favour Banda's release only if it came after the Monckton Commission had done its work in Nyasaland.

So the leader of the blacks in a territory 98 per cent black must stay in jail until the British team adjudicating the future of his and neighbouring countries had gone on its way. The natural reaction of any Cabinet caught between fires was delay. The natural reaction of Macleod to next-door settlers limiting his authority to do what he judged right in a colonial territory was to resign. Such a decision 'would greatly increase his difficulties in the discharge of his duties as Colonial Secretary . . . he would have to consider the implications of such a decision on the colonial policy in Africa'.

This was not the point at which Macleod and Macmillan

fatally fell out – Kenya was going fine, after all – but it was a dress rehearsal, and it offered a clear indication that where the Colonial Secretary had a clear, driving purpose, the Prime Minister could be deflected if bullied and cajoled enough. Macmillan would accuse Butler of lacking steel, but his own nature contained a long streak of what often resembled liquorice. For the moment, the difficulties were got over. A compromise date for Banda's release was mooted by Home as Commonwealth Secretary three weeks later than Macleod had wanted, but just within Monckton's timetable for still being present in Nyasaland. A free Banda would talk to the Monckton Commission. Macleod had won an essential principle, but he had been obliged at the height of his prestige over the Kenyan settlement to use last-resort artillery.

It had been worth it. Macleod had gone himself to meet Banda and, without being naïve about him, had been willing to plunge deep on Banda *not* creating riots in Nyasaland and indeed having the reverse effect. Quite simply he banked on Banda, conscious of his general support and of things going the right way, being the greatest force for quiet and order in the territory. Actually, he underestimated Banda, expecting his power and appeal to wane with exposure 'unless he proves himself an effective leader'. In fact, 'the little doctor' (also an elder of the Church of Scotland), would assume power and hold it with a tenacity and narrow preoccupation which the die-hard whites of 1960 could never match. Despite many failings, he proved an effective leader.

Macleod had endured the intense pressure of the Government in Salisbury, the flesh-creeping warnings of Robert Armitage and the warning of another Nyasaland eminence, Sir Malcolm Barrow, to expect 10,000 dead. When Banda did come out of detention in Gwelo, his first act, together with a meeting with Macleod, was to make a broadcast saying that he was back and calling for non-violence. The non-violent response was complete, leaving Macleod exultant. As he said, 'Nothing whatever happened,' a terrible let-down for Welensky's people locally, members of the United Federal Party, who responded by complaining that Banda's call for peace should not have been broadcast.

In a message to Macmillan, Macleod remarked with every reason, 'There is really no measuring the bottomless stupidity of their members here and in all three territories.' That was true enough and Macleod was enjoying a triumph after displaying bloodyminded will and courage against a mountain of white African prejudice, British Government compliance with it, and generalised fear of atrocity at a time when real atrocity was lively recollection. He had been right. There *were* no disturbances in Nyasaland. Welensky's people *were* stupid. The great breakthrough was happening and a constitutional conference at which Banda displayed great good sense would subsequently prepare the way for the creation of Malawi, a sovereign state within the Commonwealth. Given the opposition and the fluttering trepidation, it was an extraordinary achievement. But back in the domestic world, the observations of Reggie Bennett, Macleod's long-term PPS, about losing the support of natural Conservatives and slipping from party hero to leader of a group was also true. 'Too clever by half', the Marquess of Salisbury's epithet, was simply the angry and frustrated man's name-calling of someone cleverer than either himself or sound people generally. Macleod was being both brave and intelligent, but not career-adroit. He would get perfunctory nods for courage, while loathing for his cleverness would gather like poison gas.

Salisbury would speak with writhing animus about Macleod's skills as a card-player. Macleod had indeed followed the instincts of an experienced gambler, particularly on the question of Banda's non-violence. He had been proved absolutely and intolerably right, had swept the table and would, by implication, be called a cardsharp.

Part of the problem was that in those late imperial days Britain had two departments, the Colonial Office and the Commonwealth Office, dealing respectively with the subordinate and independent parts of the old Empire. This was complicated further by the Commonwealth states having opinions and communicating them, sometimes, as in the case of Canada, very liberal opinions, on the future of Africa which would feed into the complex trellis of political vines. Here and now, self-interested, pessimistic and perhaps understandably hysterical views were fed in by Southern Rhodesia, nominally a colony, but treated in every way but legal form like a dominion. There had to be exceptional trust and agreement between Colonial and Commonwealth Secretaries for this push-me-pull-you animal to go in one direction at an agreed speed.

With Home, a considerate colleague, things had gone well despite this difference of opinion and Home had come up with a sensible compromise (producing heartfelt gratitude in the Colonial Secretary). Nevertheless, the place of Home's heart might be judged from a story printed in the *Spectator* just before Macleod became its editor. In the summer of 1959, Home spoke at the Oxford Union and was heavily defeated on a motion supporting the (Southern Rhodesian-dominated) Central African Federation. Home was shocked – 'Oxford usen't to be like this' – but remarked he had heard that 'the right people were probably on the river'.

Macleod's pitch would soon be queered by Home's advance to the Foreign Office and his replacement by Duncan Sandys, prejudiced in different directions to Macleod and temperamently as unlike him as could be, a slow, deliberate, painstaking worker who in today's euphemistic vocabulary might have been called 'challenged'. Rab Butler, as mentioned elsewhere, had said that dealing with Sandys made you want to drink whisky in the morning.

It was with Sandys that Macleod would have to work in respect of Northern Rhodesia. This, like Nyasaland, was a colony and Macleod's business. Southern Rhodesia was a concern of both, being a nominal colony but internally autonomous. And Southern Rhodesia, federated with its neighbour and with its sought-after and desirable mineral resources, would make trouble. Southern Rhodesia had three resources only: tobacco, a quarter of a million whites and a line to the Conservative and Unionist Party. Perhaps a fourth was the clear possibility, as communicated to Home in 1960, that it might declare for independence. Everything that looked right for Northern Rhodesia in Macleod's eyes, and for that matter in isolation, was bad for Southern Rhodesia, with which Sandys was dealing. And as long as Southern Rhodesia was linked into federation, it wasn't isolated. It might paraphrase John Donne and say of its neighbours, 'Every man's independence diminisheth me.'

For any Labour Government the issues were clear-cut and Hugh Gaitskell had equally clear-cut plans to put troops into the northern territories aimed at pre-empting anything the Salisbury Government might do. Macmillan instantly flinched from any such thought, the Right proving pacific and the Left bellicose as sometimes enjoyably happens. 'We cannot send British troops to fight British settlers. There will be no battle of Bunker's Hill . . .'

A great moral stand of the Left on Africa generally, and South Africa in particular, was coming into being. An important minority of Conservatives would identify themselves with that stand. A much larger minority would have a distinct tendresse for a polite and pragmatic form of European ascendancy – not indeed doctrinaire *baaskap* apartheid, a piece of Afrikaner literalism – but a farmers' and engineers' prejudice that white men did things better than black men and would go on doing them better for the foreseeable future. The Rhodesians were people like us, usually related to us with sisters and cousins in Conservative associations from Plymouth to Wick. They might be a touch rough-handed, but they should certainly be supported.

Against this came in September 1960 the report of Monckton that there should be early and advertised constitutional advance with secession contemplated if necessary. Macleod seized the recommendation and used it to push Macmillan towards the African solution he believed to be the only right one. Monckton and the Tory backbenchers existed side by side as pressures on Macmillan, for whom the whole question became more and more a concern of domestic politics.

Like Europe today, Rhodesia was almost certainly a less weighty consideration among voters than activists. The electorate is a wonderfully unidealistic body. Macmillan's diaries contain electoral and national anxieties of an upmarket sort about which Mr Robert Worcester and sophisticated polling would have put him right. For a cynic, Macmillan did a lot of unnecessary worrying. But when he spoke of the issue poisoning his second premiership he was not exaggerating. The comic side to the poison lay in the farcical relationship with Welensky who, back in the federation, had bugged Banda in his cell while Macmillan, through Butler as Home Secretary, was bugging the visiting Welensky in his Claridge's suite. On the other hand, Welensky, as Alistair Horne points out, was throwing Macmillan off balance in conversation by knowing things – about British military concentrations in Kenya, for example – which he was learning from British sources.

Oppressed as he felt himself, Macmillan's view of Macleod was changing. Macleod had 'undoubtedly leant over too far towards the African view', yet interestingly the Prime Minister believed that if Macleod had resigned, the Government would have fallen. It wouldn't. Macleod didn't have that much clout. But the overestimation of difficulties is a recurring Macmillan trait, as we have seen. He was afraid in an emotional, distressed way about the Rhodesians turning to 'open rebellion' putting the Government 'in a ludicrous as well as an impossible position'. He imagined 'strife and conflict on a terrible scale, white versus white, black versus black, all against all'.

In this mood, Macmillan gravitated towards Sandys, 'as cool as a cucumber, methodical; very strong in character, has gradually mastered the art of parliamentary speaking, tremendously hard-working; not easily shaken from his course – ambitious and rather cruel . . .' Sandys protected him from Welensky, 'rude, blackmailing, coarse, silly', as the Prime Minister recorded him. Ultimately, Sandys wished to give Welensky enough of what he wanted to suit his own instincts and give Macmillan a quiet life.

What Welensky wanted was a weighting of the two-roll franchise in Northern Rhodesia in ways which strengthened the upper, white-dominated roll. Macleod was clear in his mind that if he did any such thing and the whites effectively ruled Northern Rhodesia on comfortable terms with the federal authorities in Salisbury, not only would Kenneth Kaunda, the Northern Rhodesian black leader, not wear it, but violence of a concerted kind would occur, starting with disobedience but likely – planned or otherwise – to get worse.

Whereas in Nyasaland the established white authorities – Robert Armitage, Malcolm Barrow, with the whole Salisbury set behind them – talked massacre and thousands dead which didn't happen, in Northern Rhodesia it was Macleod who genuinely feared a breakdown of peace, while the white leadership was relaxed – relaxed, of course, in the knowledge that such violence would suit their book. In January 1961, a conference had kicked around the constituency numbers with Macleod advancing in a White Paper the idea of an assembly resting on a 15:15:15 ratio, the races enjoying parity and sharing legislative authority with a balancing bloc. Such an arrangement would in time edge towards African objectives, if in a slightly Augustinian way. But, following the institutionalised stymie of British two-minister involvement, Sandys kept Welensky sweet by treating his colleague's proposal as negotiable.

The conference in stalemate, Macleod talked privately of resignation, groups of Tory right-wingers in Parliament made calls for the old 1958 constitution (written before blacks got above themselves), the Tory press rumbled – the *Express* calling Macleod calamitous – and made space for Welensky, though *The Times* backed Macleod. Kenneth Kaunda walked away and spoke of the violence there might be.

The quarrel, which describes it as well as anything, dragged deep into 1961. On 7 March, Lord Salisbury made *that* speech:

'Miasma of mistrust'. Meanwhile, Welensky spoke to *that* Commons meeting, the one at which a great majority of 200 assembled Tory MPs impressed the Chief Whip as sympathetic. Macleod had to live with the active hostility of a great tranche of the party he belonged to. And he had to stop Macmillan and cucumber-cool Sandys from buying the options which Welensky now offered with clumsy guile. To Welensky's people he wrote: 'A multi-racial approach means working with the Africans they choose; to us it is co-operating with those whom the Africans choose.'

In late May, compromises would seem to have been reached, of one of which Welsensky, with his usual gracelessness even when winning, said, 'Like all such solutions [it] would probably please nobody.' Certainly it didn't please Macleod and was very much Sandys' doing. It allowed for consideration of a scheme in which the upper roll had a 60:40 ratio of electoral power. For Macmillan, it was 'a miracle' by which 'we have achieved a solution of the immediate crisis'. Macmillan was more interested in escape than in a solution, which it was not, nor miracle, either. The African population rioted as Macleod had said they would, while Evelyn Hone, Governor of Northern Rhodesia, imposed internment.

Sandys, very stupidly, had disregarded Macleod's detailed and often repeated warning and accorded the Europeans a run for the sort of minority primacy which accorded with white rule of the copper belt from Salisbury, postponed black hopes in Southern Rhodesia indefinitely and gave the south resources and economic muscle for comfortable survival under South Africa's wing. It meant, and could only ever have meant, a nice balance of white rule and black riots. Macleod was working for black rule, one evolving generally as equity and as necessity. The two sides which mattered summed him up accordingly. Welensky described him in a letter to the Marquess of Salisbury as 'the most sinister influence in the British Cabinet'. Kenneth Kaunda had said earlier in the year, 'Mr Macleod as a person . . . remains the only hope in the British Government . . . Mr Macleod left to himself, could have done the right thing, but he suffers because of his collective responsibility to the Cabinet.'

The Sandys deal would collapse in violence and African rejection, proving Macleod right in his fear of it in Northern Rhodesia as he had been in his expectations of peace in Nyasaland. The Cabinet agreed that 60:40 was not a runner. Macleod had a last go at amending his own White Paper plans with a requirement that the third group of electors would have to have the support of one eighth of voters from both African and European rolls, the equivalent of what was then needed to save a deposit in Britain. In June, with this modification, a deal of sorts become possible. The support of Sir Evelyn Hone, himself wearied by Welensky's bluster, helped. Kaunda, far from overjoyed at a settlement which made everyone wonder who had won, but rightly trusting Macleod, who talked to him seriously in his own flat – the sort of domestic diplomacy he used for all his African work – agreed to try to make it succeed.

So he did, but he ran into heavy opposition from his party, not least because the Welensky people made great public play of being pleased with the deal. Nothing could recommend it less to Africans, and violence and the usual arrests followed. Macleod wanted essentially something to be conceded which would allow Kaunda to make claims to his followers on the streets to get them off them. Since this involved revision of what had been agreed in June, he was in difficulties, especially with Macmillan, who wanted none of it and Sandys, with whom he was now on terms of jarring contradiction. Macleod proposed a firm line and private words to Kaunda about order coupled with an open letter to Sir John Moffat, a Northern Rhodesian white liberal, designed to keep the agreement open to amendment after order was restored. Even in the modified form of a statement, this idea was clogged at every point by the resistance of Sandys whose dull mind understood that something had been agreed and should not be disturbed even though it was seen by Africans as a white victory. Like Salisbury he thought Macleod tricky and deceitful. But then, Sandys would also confide later to Welensky, 'We British have lost the will to govern.'

Here and now the balance was order then amendment, but did Macleod really mean to insist on order first? He did, but, as he stressed in a note to Macmillan, there had been 25 deaths and 2,000 arrests and powers of internment without trial. Effectively the June deal hadn't worked, had conceded too much to Welensky. Ironically, this judgment would be sustained, and in February 1962, the sorts of changes Macleod favoured would be instituted. But that work would be done by a new Colonial Secretary, Reginald Maudling, who proved, ironically, slightly more pro-African than the man he replaced. Maudling, as Horne puts it, 'prepared the way for an African majority'.

But before Maudling could carry out Macleod's policy, which Macmillan was resisting, Macleod would have to be moved. The change, as the Prime Minister cryptically called it in notes to his Secretary, Bligh, involved shifting him from the Colonial Office to the party chairmanship. It wasn't publicly seen as demotion and, with his wit and fluency, he was certain to be a chairman in high focus. But it was a rejection nonetheless, a loss of trust and an easing of Macmillan's troubles. Stamina and energy came into it. Macleod might have been faulted for pushing through developments in Uganda as quickly as he did. But Uganda, like Tanganyika, having few settlers, made very little trouble in Parliament. Lord Salisbury had no kith and kin to speak of on whose behalf he could thunder. Horne heads his chapter 'The Continuing Burdens of Africa' and it is the burden upon Macmillan to which he seems to refer. The business of getting things disinterestedly right with an eye to the future might have been missed by Macleod in his zeal, but in such territories where the Prime Minister was little troubled, no reproach was made.

In 1962 Macmillan would read a lecture to the still complaining Roy Welensky warning him against force.

> *The French have a million men under arms and they have suffered a humiliating defeat. It is too simple a reading of history to think that you can exercise control simply by the use of power. Indeed, I cannot guarantee that British troops would undertake the kind of duties that would be necessary.*

But this accurate judgment had been his at the outset. It was because he thought this that he had hired Macleod to pre-empt an Algerian situation anywhere. As Macleod himself remarked, the object was to be quicker than Algeria and slower than the Congo.

When doing this proved burdensome and fires were lit on the other side by Welensky and the Tory backbenchers, Macmillan tired, decelerated and withheld his support. In respect of Africa, he wanted to go, but didn't quite have the nerve to get up. Nor did he have the nerve to stay. He abandoned Macleod in the job he was doing, then, carelessly rather than guilefully, appointed Maudling. Given such unfixity of purpose, he thoroughly deserved to find Maudling '*plus noir que les nègres*' more difficult and intransigent than his predecessor. He threatens resignation.' Then Monckton's report on the federation, indicating the implausibility of its continuing, came back into play. Butler, of all people, Macmillan's *bête noire*, would be called in to do a private (and brilliant) job in finessing the end of that impossible arrangement. Of all ironies touching Butler and Macmillan, the supreme one came from Roy Welensky, who had the last word, describing Butler as 'very flexible in negotiation, but when he has reached his decision he does not change it . . . The best Prime Minister I had to deal with . . .'

Macmillan, having judged shrewdly, even wisely, on macro-policy, began something; it was accomplished more or less in his time (independent Rhodesia was something else, Harold Wilson's pigeon, and finally brought to an end by civil war and a bemused Margaret Thatcher). Yet, in doing what he had understood must be done, Macmillan found himself flinching, evading, pulling back, denying support to one Colonial Secretary and being startled to find his successor insisting on an identical course of events. Africa was a vast, calamitous territory which would reduce Macmillan to a state of immobile agnosticism.

He wasn't necessarily wrong to be afraid. He might perfectly respectably have set out on a different course, a more conservative one of sharply defined limits. But that would have meant starting from somewhere else and employing someone other than Macleod who, right or wrong, had throughout a clear-headed, illusionless idea of what should be done. He represented 'the smack of firm government' and Macmillan did not. Macleod stayed coherent at great political cost to himself and in the face of a chief not quite resolved upon irresolution.

An intelligent case could be constructed against Macleod's conduct of affairs. Liquidation was precipitate; it anticipated the development of a large enough class of competent Africans and a governmental tradition. Alan Lennox-Boyd, not a crude reactionary, had also looked to Africanisation and independence, but had dates scheduled 10 and 12 years on. Uganda, after Tanganyika the easiest of the transfers, was to be ruled twice by the atrocious Milton Obote on either side of the nightmare of Idi Amin, a psychotic sergeant made into a general by independence. Tanzania, as it became with the accession of Zanzibar, the jewel in the crown, became a depressing despotism. A more paternalistic approach, one worried more about the readiness of the hands into which power went, rather than the essential rightness of their being black hands, might, with a few years' delay, have given Africa later, better government, better black government.

What has gone wrong in independent Africa – village despoliation in Tanzania, open-ended atrocity in Uganda – can blandly be described as their problem, part of the business of being free to get things wrong. Except that what is got wrong is done on the heads of innocent people who are there while Britain and the British Government are not. Africa, like Czechoslovakia, is a faraway country.

The fear in 1959 was of Britain being subjected to an Algerian experience: local war with troops committed, furious reaction in Britain, mounting costs, runs on the pound; also the pressure of the Americans, self-righteous on such matters even while practising their own form of apartheid and great believers in snap decisions with damned consequences. Macleod was the instrument of such imperatives, but an instrument with his own true-believing convictions. It is also in the nature of change that if essential decisions are made, those making them seldom or never attempt the moulding of gradual reform. If doors have to be knocked down first, what follows is a charge. In a better world, we would have shared Macleod's inclinations earlier, spent money, made preparation, built schools, opened scholarships and perhaps adhered to something rather nearer Lennox-Boyd's timetable. We would have been neither complacent nor precipitate instead of being both in scrambled succession.

But Macleod had both his brief and his own instincts. The object was *Il faut en finir*. The instincts were genuinely elevated and idealistic. The speech he made to Party Conference at the very end of his term at the Colonial Office quoting Burns, 'That man to man the whole world o'er, shall brothers be,' and saying, 'I believe quite simply in the brotherhood of man' was not rhetoric. Macleod finessed, dummied and bodyswerved as a negotiator, but in his central purpose he drove a straight line. And, politically, he paid a very high price.

Macmillan, whose far from foolish apprehensions had set him to work, would withdraw favour, doing so because other pressures, those of the Southern Rhodesians and their allies in the Tory Party, weighed upon him. The Southern Rhodesians did have something for their comfort, a body of Tory opinion. This had been anaesthetised in the early days when Uganda, Tanganyika and Kenya were moving to independence for the very good reason that paternal care for what might happen to tribal people too soon exposed to tribal conflict through independence was the least of their concerns. These Tories were British, accustomed to Britain commanding an Empire, but more importantly, white people roused to action on behalf of other white people – kith and kin.

Reggie Bennett describes going into the lobby at night with Macleod and, having so often seen Macmillan arm in arm with or making keen salutation of his colleague, 'I just saw his eyes swivel about and avoid Iain's. He had used Iain and now he wasn't useful to him any more.' Bennett has no doubt that Macleod's involvement in the entire colonial operation killed him for that succession which had earlier looked wholly feasible. Everything, he says, that Iain had done at Health and Labour made him naturally popular. He was phenomenally effective, he dominated the House, he was liked, he was funny. (If he had denied the Right their assault on the NHS, that didn't matter. He had done it subtly and, anyway, it kept the Tory Party popular.)

Bennett adds, 'All that opinion which one can call naturally Conservative was against him on Africa, and they sent in motions to prove it. I should know. My association [in Gosport] passed a motion condemning what he was doing and passed it over my head, knowing that I was his PPS.'

All this, he says, went beyond activists in the country. Macleod was losing support among backbenchers, people who should have understood that this was the only rational policy given Britain's resources, the ending of National Service and the strain of the Cyprus Emergency. They should have understood that it made sense, but day-to-day pressure in the associations counted for more and 'Iain, from being a leader of the whole party, became identified with a particular faction'.

There is a parallel here with the change in perception of Healey when he was at the Treasury from strong, capable minister to specifically right-wing cutter and squeezer, so that the soft, quiet-life, middle of the party on which he ought to have been able to count flinched away from him. Both Macleod and Healey did the brave thing, the act by which a whole Government is remembered. And both lost support for the key periods of time when they might have succeeded to the leadership. It would seem to be a precept that courage and the accomplishment of painful necessary policies can be fatal obstacles to anyone serious about leading a political party.

But Macleod's time at the Colonial Office had been momentous. No other word describes it.

CHAPTER SIX

'Can you imagine Iain using one of those bloody awful screens to make a speech or getting his speech cleared with the left-luggage people at Number Ten?' Nicholas Scott's question about the politician he admired and loved, demands and gets the answer 'no'.

The period following Macleod's two years of controversy and creative energy at the Colonial Office embraces the crusading (or huckstering) work of a party chairman for which, as a wit, lover of good words and truculent political fighter, he was very much designed. It also takes in an earth tremor of a scandal, the Profumo affair, and a row over the succession between Macleod and the new Conservative leadership only a little less sensational, which ended in refusal of office and damaged him savagely with sound men, team players and observers of good form. The whole interlude – only three years – concludes with him taking up the editorship of a political journal and flings up the question, can one imagine Home or Heath or any Tory leader, except Arthur Balfour, editing the *Spectator*?

Nicholas Scott has another story. As Chairman of the Young Conservatives in 1962, he was severely told off by the official who looked after the tiresome youth faction for having proposed to raise funds to buy a tractor for a group of Indian peasant farmers, a project connected with a charitable campaign against world hunger. That wasn't what money from wine-and-cheese parties was for. Young Conservatives raised money for the Conservative Party: was that understood?

'I just hauled off down the corridor to the Chairman's office.

Iain listened and then said, "You want permission, you've got it." ' As Nick Scott readily says himself, the whole undertaking wasn't naïve. It had indeed a sincere, helpful purpose, but it was also intended to spell out the fact that Tories, breaking out of their stereotype, could do such things. They had become more sympathetic people, they should publicise the fact. Macleod understood both aspects and approved of both. He wanted the Tories to think generously and he wanted them to get the credit. (One hears this story with considerable nostalgia.)

This was 1962, change hadn't quite happened, public relations and preoccupation with style were a little way off; preoccupation with youth was tremblingly close, but had not quite arrived. Youth having been around now for three decades, and with the surviving Beatles pushing 60, it is possible to deride that sort of ardour. Sciatic chic now scorns the whole thing and yearns for stuffy, responsible men in striped trousers talking unintelligibly across this television thing.

But during Macleod's party chairmanship we were about to undergo one of those rare identifiable generational changes. We were also, had we known it, about to go downmarket. In January 1963, Hugh Gaitskell would die, to be replaced by Harold Wilson. A man born in 1906 was being succeeded by one born in 1916; an earnest, fervent man was giving way to a high intelligence without fixed purpose, obstinate passion to short-winded facility. The first hint of the soundbite would be heard.

Macmillan, meanwhile, had been born in the previous century and the entire tone of his Government, despite his own good jokes, was that of people inheriting authority and expecting to be shown respect. The remote and elevated notion of the statesman (a word which, instructively, we no longer use) benevolently telling a public as much as he thought it wise for them to know – telling it, moreover, through newspapers still respectful – and being rewarded with grave approval or dissent, still held true. Look at any party political broadcast until the mid-sixties, notably the one that William Deedes has offered for his own and our derision, of Mr Deedes the junior minister gravely urging the Conservative case in the mid-fifties.

All that was to change shatteringly. Satire arrived, politicians might be mocked, should be mocked, were good for little else. Government became hell. The Opposition had an easier time of it by reason of being an opposition, and also because here they were led by Harold Wilson who, his best gifts being analytical, rapidly understood that something had changed and adapted himself to pleasing in the new necessary way. For 18 months before the tragedy of being elected, Wilson rode the wave of derision by the simple device of himself deriding. Being cheeky protected him – for a very limited time – from being cheeked. His own cruel humiliations would come, but for the moment he could handle the climacteric and Macmillan could not.

From now on, politicians could not rely upon the natural protection of their status. Acceptance by the critical, mocking, disrespectful people who set the tone had to be earned, not necessarily by merit, but by a shrewd avoidance of being dull, heavy, pompous or stuffy. Butler, despite his old-fashioned ways, had a light time of it and Macmillan himself, until the final blunders, seemed to be staying afloat. Both were too humorous and too obviously clever for easy scorn. But you could not afford even to *look* like a fool. The serial martyrdom across the early sixties of Butler's successor at the Home Office, Henry Brooke, with his pronouncing manner and inflexible adherence to a bleak brief, is a case in point.

Of all Conservative politicians, Iain Macleod should have been the one to cope with the incipient new mood. He had Wilson's quickness. He was funny, and for a young audience which was essentially, if shallowly, radical, the abomination of Lord Salisbury and 'the white people of Rhodesia' left him very well placed. And Macleod genuinely liked and was at home with the young. Nothing in the package of death-penalty abolition, easing of divorce and homosexual law reform which back-benchers would bring in with the Labour Government's happy assent would trouble him. There was a lot of unfocused idealism about and Macleod, for all his practical grasp, was an idealist by temperament. The trope he delicately turned against Wilson – that J. F. Kennedy had 'in a brilliant phrase' described himself 'an idealist without illusions' while Wilson was 'an illusionist without ideals' – puts the case well. The Macleod of Nick Scott's anecdote, who wanted the Young Conservatives to raise money for a peasants' tractor and knew that it was good politics to do so, makes him an idealist with a sense of theatre. Kennedy was the substitution of image for content.

Macleod was something else, something which could shine through the new climate, a genuinely inspirational speaker. The 'Brotherhood of Man' speech leapt across party and generation and did so without contrivance. It was Macleod's best self, best projected. That the wit who could down (an admiring) Harold

Wilson at the top of his reputation, the man who could find heroic words for a political avowal right in the gut of all young, ardent, disinterested faith, should then feel compelled to walk away from a Conservative Government, become the target of rumbling old men (and old men in preparation) for letting the side down and general outsiderishness, defines in action the superabundant folly of the Conservative Party of that calamitous day.

It should be said that, at the very start of his new job, Macleod showed his pragmatic side less than attractively. He had been offered the chairmanship, something relinquished very happily by Butler much as Martha might give up one of her shawls. However, Butler had no wish to surrender the leadership of the House, a role in whose ambiguities, winks and touches of charm he excelled in ways later approached only by John Biffen. But Macleod understood the importance to himself of underscored authority and pressed for the job. Macmillan needed little persuasion and, to Butler's annoyance and minor hurt, the office was taken, though the Home Secretary squatted tight in his office just behind the Speaker's chair – typical Butler in all manoeuvrings, giving way on the key thing while fussing about the small comforts. Yet, within two years, the seizer of this main chance would abjure office because Butler had been bilked of the premiership. Politics are not sentimental but in judging the second great event we ought to recollect the early minor one.

The early part of Macleod's chairmanship was marked by sharp-edged difficulties. The Government, in the way of governments, wasn't doing very well. It lost or nearly lost by-elections. The Chancellor, Selwyn Lloyd, showed some courage but very little imagination. Journalists with nothing better to do reached for the word 'malaise'.

The by-election shift was part of the general worm-turning of the times. The voters had discovered the frivolous pleasure of doing down the high-ups at single contests instead of earnestly voting at all times with their general election convictions. As much as *Beyond the Fringe*, a swing to the Liberals at Oswestry in November 1961, followed by a very poor Tory result in Blackpool North and third place behind a Liberal in Middlesbrough East, represented public disrespect. It showed a combination of independent-mindedness and frivolity in the electorate, neither of them qualities which commended themselves to politicians. It was rebellion of sorts, but then again, though this wasn't realised, it didn't really matter. Votes were going the way the pound would soon go, electoral inflation reflected in the size of swing.

It would all come back to normal in the general election of 1964, if one can treat as normal the turning of a 100-seat majority into a deficit of four. But politicians were used to stability across parliamentary terms and associated rare big votes against a ministry with great statements of will – witness the Fulham by-election which Baldwin cited to argue against vigorous rearmament. As a consequence, urgency among ministers in the early sixties could easily turn into panic. At Orpington in March 1962, the Conservatives, putting up Peter Goldman, a candidate of genuine distinction, if not a cheery one, saw a majority of 15,000 in a middle, middle-class south London constituency on the Charing Cross to Hastings line turn into a Liberal majority of 8,000. The sky, if it had not fallen in, was distinctly seen to sag.

Macleod would respond by showing his ruthless side again in lobbying for the removal of Selwyn Lloyd, the put-upon, faintly resentful career Lepidus[1] who had been endlessly subordinable in very high places. It was a reasonable mistake, but a mistake for all that. Macleod was irked with Lloyd for not doing anything to excite the voters. Lloyd thought that by resisting inflation through a rigorous pay pause on public-sector incomes, he was doing the right thing, with excitement a low priority. At that time, Macleod, who hadn't yet done serious thinking on the economy, almost certainly shared Macmillan's upbeat instincts for promiscuous post-Keynesian reflation, a point of view heard these days mostly from bishops. Macmillan's little comments to Heathcoat Amory, Lloyd's predecessor, would make Treasury blood run cold. 'He was terrified of one thing, a slump . . . he did ring me up occasionally. "Don't you think there might be a slump in a month? . . . What is wrong with inflation, Derry?" I'd reply, "You're thinking of your constituency in the 1930s." "Yes, I am thinking of the under-use of resources – let's over-use them!" He believed in import controls, but the Treasury wouldn't let him.'

The Prime Minister was meddling and he was wrong. At that time, the removal of Lloyd in a modest, businesslike reshuffle involving a couple of other Cabinet changes would have been reasonable politics bringing no plaster onto the Cabinet table. Such a move required Lloyd himself to be gracefully handled, ideally offered exactly that Commons leadership to be given him in October 1963 by Home when Macleod had no use for either the job or Home. But it would be handled as badly as it could be.

After Lloyd's budget had denied excitement, Macmillan began to talk to the Cabinet about 'risk-taking', hoping that 'the Chancellor of the Exchequer will not think me too ambitous', and argued as Macleod had already argued 'for expansionist measures now'. Macleod had a serious part in all this. Broadly, the Conservatives appoint two sorts of chairman: one after an election to pick up pieces, replace money just spent and superintend the general ticking over, and another at the start of the pre-election run-up, to be barker, publicist and general firework. This was Macleod's job. If he was thinking about the economy, he was thinking through an electoral filter. He was concerned about Selwyn Lloyd's hard line on nurses' pay. It had 'done us an immense amount of harm. It is really very difficult to project the image that Conservatives care after this.'

Lloyd was not a remarkable chancellor, but his pay pause made more sense than what Macmillan himself wanted: expansion modified by a voluntary incomes policy, itself supposedly made effective by publicity exhorting the unions openly. Sacking Lloyd made very little sense, yet not just Macleod but Butler, Home and the Chief Whip were for it. The dismissal, as we shall see, led to the Night of the Long Knives, an acknowledged disaster, but the dismissal of Lloyd itself was a mistake, however clamoured for. Inflation was enormously important even if grander men thought not. Macleod was preoccupied with a caring image, Macmillan wanted to know what was wrong with it and even Hugh Gaitskell was being insouciant about over-anxiety and instead urging greater productivity. At least Lloyd had his priorities right.

As for the politics, Edmund Dell puts it very well:

Politically, Lloyd carried the cross of having introduced the pay pause; but if the Government, having designed an effective incomes policy, intended to introduce it, it would have to accept the attendant unpopularity and persuade the electorate at the polls that it had been right in what it had done. Lloyd was the wrong man to persuade an electorate with words, but it could perhaps be persuaded by steadfastness. It was less likely to be persuaded by the ritual slaughter of the author of the pay pause.

The errors of this time which fortuitously boiled over as the Night of the Long Knives would achieve critical mass. Dell describes it:

> *Macmillan was given to panic, as Suez clearly illustrated. He knew he was unpopular and his mind had become permeated with suspicions of conspiracy against him. Panic is in any case encouraged by the British electoral system under which quite a small swing in votes can lead to the overthrow of a government, and by June 1962, Labour in a national poll had a lead of 11 per cent. On 13 July, Macmillan sacked not merely his Chancellor, but a third of his Cabinet.*

Macmillan did not err alone. Not only had a bunch of ministers, including Macleod, urged the dismissal, but Butler's one-man freedom-of-information unit had led to the story leaking. A small fire was then doused with petrol – a strong, decisive act. Macmillan's diaries are full of self-justification, putting the slaughter of a third of the Cabinet down to inadvertence. He had planned two things, an autumn reshuffle advancing younger talents and the sacking of his Chancellor. Butler chatted; Macmillan, fearing the resignation in protest of Lloyd's pay-pause associate and personal friend, the Minister of Labour John Hare, panicked again.

So in the high summer of 1962, the two ideas, like iceberg and *Titanic*, came together. The quality of disaster was deepened when David Eccles, a minister with first-rate qualities who had hoped for the Treasury, resigned (from Education) after being passed over. Inadvertence runs through bad government like 'Blackpool' through rock.

The reaction was calamitous. Macmillan and Macleod had both wanted to please the voters, but the July massacre earned their contempt. The figures on Macmillan's personal rating (Gallup) for 11 July (pre-cull) were Satisfied: 47 per cent; Dissatisfied: 39 per cent; Don't know: 12 per cent. Those for 20 July, after the events, were respectively 35 per cent, 52 per cent and again 12 per cent. Jeremy Thorpe would make his gloss on the New Testament: 'Greater love hath no man that he lay down his friends for his life.' Nigel Birch, veteran of the little local difficulty of 1958, would write to *The Times*:

Sir,

For the second time the Prime Minister has got rid of a Chancellor of the Exchequer who tried to get expenditure under control.
   Once is more than enough.

Butler told Macmillan's Press Secretary, Harold Evans, 'I feel my neck all the time to see if it is still there. I do understand the Prime Minister's motives and I am behind him. I know why he got rid of Selwyn after six years. But it wasn't done properly.'

Gaitskell, during a motion of no confidence, made a comparison with Stalin and the Old Bolsheviks, observing that of Macmillan's 19 Cabinet colleagues of 1957, there remained only six. Macmillan's Government, he said, 'would be remembered not for the leadership they gave the nation, but as a conspiracy to retain power'. All governments are that, but it was remarkable professional incompetence to make it look so obvious. From Macleod's own point of view, the vast blow to the Government's credibility sustained while trying to restore it made his immediate task more difficult, though personally he was almost a beneficiary.

Tory Chairmen expect to be blamed for defeats, but *this* Chairman would not expect to be blamed, even though his pre-occupation with the caring image had contributed its portion to the crash. In simple horse-jostling terms, Macleod stood after the reshuffle where he was; the chancellorship which he certainly fancied went to the technically trained and accomplished Maudling. What perhaps really mattered to any ambitious member of the Cabinet was the serious prospect now arising that Macmillan would be replaced himself. Macmillan, not for the first time, had wielded the knife, but the knife had slipped.

'When sorrows come, they come not single spies, but in battalions.' The cry of King Claudius needs the amendment that one sorrow weakens the constitution for resistance to the next. From violence, the Conservative Government moved on to sex. Adultery in politics gives some pleasure to participants but more surely to those speculative onlookers, the electorate. There is probably little more sexual adventure in a Parliament of 650 MPs than in a convention of 650 dentists. (Though dentists, lacking star quality, may be shaded on the final tally.) But sex involving politicians arouses outside interest. Lord Chesterfield's remark about the position being ridiculous is important, especially when politics is supposed to be dignified. The slipping of togas provokes guffaws.

What Mr Profumo and Miss Keeler did together was not illegal, nor was it uncommon. Macleod himself enjoyed a vigorous extramarital life, notably with a constituent and a colleague's wife; Gaitskell had the Fleming affair. The adulterers of whom Lord Hailsham would soon complain were well distributed on both sides and on all gradations of benches. Even among the double-barrelled right-wing backwoodsmen with Southern Rhodesian sympathies who bristled about Macleod were those known to the Whips' Office, from their mid-afternoon departures to old-fashioned gallantries, as 'the four o'clock fuckers'. Tolerant, worldly and unshocked, politicians in Britain have usually ordered things almost as well as they have in France. At the height of mid-Victorian propriety, the whole political world knew and liked Lord Hartington, put-upon lieutenant to Gladstone and, from his longstanding affair with what was gracefully called a courtesan, knew him as 'Harty Tarty'.

But there had always been a law of discretion. Ian Harvey, caught out in a homosexual episode a year before, was a dead man, resigned and gone from politics at once. (Nick Scott recalls half-strangled public remarks of sympathy with Harvey from Macleod which rather died away.) But no assumptions about the Tory Party being rotten to the core had been drawn from the episode. The conviction and four-year term of imprisonment given to Sir Ian Horrabin for homosexual offences with under-age partners was somehow managed as one of those bad events without political implications. Why a minister's sleeping with the sort of pretty girl most men would like to sleep with should light the sky with a blaze of crazed pronouncements can only be explained by circumstance.

The standard Tory apologia – that of course they are as tolerant of sex as the next man or political party, but that it was the lie that did it – won't wash. The lie was uttered after a panic summoning of Profumo and his examination by a panel of four ministers in the middle of the night.[2] Clearly the sex mattered to *them*.

So many things come back to Macmillan and panic. Getting not just a denial from Profumo, but a formal, unchallenged personal statement to the House, might look like clearing the air.

It also gave the matter heightened prominence. Macleod, as Chairman, found himself not just in the middle of all this but asking the germane question, 'Did you fuck her, Jack?' What sort of state had the Conservative Party got itself into when one non-monogomous, worldly politician has to ask that of another? One, surely, in which the answer 'Yes' would have been furiously distressing.

There had been the earlier, non-exploding cases and there had been Thomas Galbraith, a junior Scottish Office Minister actually, if not quite credibly, exculpated of homosexual entanglement with the spy Vassall. But of course the stories partitioning Miss Keeler with Captain Ivanov of the Soviet Embassy made a great difference. Even so, at the end of all the investigation that captivated the nation that year culminating in Lord Denning's bestselling command paper, there *was* no security dimension, just sex and baroque speculation.

The story proper arose through press knowledge that Christine Keeler had failed to sell her account of the Profumo affair to the papers and might have used her position as a wit-ness at the trial of a West Indian heavy called Edgecombe to speak out – exactly what Norman Scott would do in the Thorpe affair. She didn't turn up and a group of Labour MPs used parliamentary privilege to suggest that Profumo might have been involved in a cover-up. The sex mattered to them, as to Profumo's inquisitors, but it didn't do to say so.

As already observed, Butler got the whole situation right. He thought Profumo should have been given more time, should have stepped down from office pre-emptively and not been forced into a rushed Commons statement, while an enquiry should have been made in Parliamentary form. Profumo, who would lie under interrogation and tell the truth at leisure, would surely then have conceded an unwise and mistaken association with no security implications; there would have been a short gratified buzz and the summer of 1963 would not have celebrated the sexual equivalent of the Popish Plot. Butler's words, on being asked to accompany Macmillan for the emergency statement, deserve immortality for their comfortable good sense: 'Not on a Friday morning, surely!'

But Butler wasn't leading the House; Macleod, at his own urgent insistence, was. And 'Did you fuck her, Jack?' wasn't a very sensible question to ask. A good lawyer would have known what had to be denied and what was superfluous. The actual charges raised by the Opposition related to 'perversions of justice' and implied that Profumo was 'connected with or responsible for Keeler's absence from the trial at the Old Bailey'. Since there wasn't a cover-up and Profumo had nothing to do with Keeler's absence from court, a limited but unchallengeable statement – unchallengeable because true – could have been made. The Opposition, and for that matter the press, would have been confined embarrassingly to the narrow issue of a sexual affair. It would have looked like a prurient witch hunt and they had been burned over Galbraith. The press of then not being the press of now, would have had good reasons for desisting. Profumo would have been under no anxious pressure to face that question in the solemn circumstances of the Commons. He could have told the truth later or lied off-oath. Politically, nothing would have mattered very much.

As it was, on that Friday morning, Profumo, with Macmillan on one side of him and Macleod on the other, said, 'There was no impropriety whatever in my acquaintanceship [sic] with Miss Keeler.' As Robert Shepherd comments, it was the only lie in his statement. It was enough. Macmillan's anxiety had been joined by Macleod's partisan instinct to get a denial in terms, one which would flatten the Opposition. It was very odd that those two non-monogamous worldly men could not, privately, away from the Chief Whip and the Solicitor-General, have agreed that you might fuck her, didn't have to say so, but could confine yourself to denying the false charges. But of course sex *did* matter, so much so that Profumo denied it privately and ministers insisted on him denying it publicly.

What would follow when Profumo, still pursued, could not sustain the act and in June came clean, would be blackly funny and then horrible. It was also the closest thing government can get to collective nervous breakdown. Open day was called on sexual allegations. So contrary to Philip Larkin's assertion, sexual intercourse, far from beginning in 1963, had apparently been going on (in secret) for a long time.

There were the eight high-court judges involved in an orgy. 'Eight seems a bit much,' said Macmillan with a flash of the old charm. Duncan Sandys actually arrived at Cabinet with a written resignation having been linked with the Argyll divorce case, that year's alternative scandal. There was the Man in the Mask, there was royalty and there was Lord Hailsham blazing away on TV on behalf of beleaguered and rather unattractive virtue. It is incidentally a startling irony that at much the same time as Britain's little show, the admired President Kennedy, who had told Macmillan that not having sex gave him a headache, was sharing a girlfriend with a leading member of the American Mafia.

The Cliveden establishment from which all this had sprung appears to have been a serial wild party at which sexual intercourse did indeed sometimes occur – very shocking but neither without precedent nor the end of civilisation as we know it. Captain Ivanov, the excuse for the great dirty-minded public wallow, appears to have been more sinning than sinned against and not seriously spying at all.

The real orgy was a public one and the far from transient pleasure was prurience. It is hard to know who appears more odious, George Wigg, Harold Wilson's evil little spy-truffler, or the prosecutors and judge in the case of Stephen Ward. Ward looks from any decent perspective like a naïve dabbler in influence for reasons of self-gratification and vanity, not profit, who, in the hysteria which marked the entire season, was turned upon as a scapegoat and whose suicide ahead of an assured vengeful sentence fell like ice upon the riot.

Macleod may have been uncharacteristically clumsy in the investigation. He was characteristically large-minded and generous on the personal side. Happening to be in the United States when confession and resignation broke, he said to American reporters, 'I was, and am, a friend of Jack and Valerie Profumo . . . I think it is a personal tragedy that this should have happened.' He had actually been the one lied to and could have been justifiably bitter, but Macleod genuinely lacked the instinct for grievance.

What the Profumo affair had done most of all was to destroy the self-confidence of Macmillan. The actual occasion for his stepping down – fearful overestimate (by doctor and patient) of a manageable prostate condition – would surely not have run away with events if the summer had been spent calmly continuing the policy programme interrupted by Profumo. Macmillan was a man who lived on anxieties and whose anxieties had come true. He truly thought he was dying, perhaps he almost wanted to be. Certainly, he wanted to escape.

His animus against Butler and determination to bar him from a premiership which Butler would never have brought to this near-shipwreck has been dealt with. What concerns this account is the course of dealing which would end with Iain Macleod's angry refusal to join the Government of Alec Douglas-Home. The Chief Whip, Martin Redmayne, would remark, 'It's too late; it's all been fixed.' It was an historic quarrel whose implication, though injurious to Macleod, would bring an end to such fixing.

---

[1]'This is a slight unmeritable man, meet to be sent on errands.' *Julius Caesar*, Act IV, Scene i. Lloyd was better than that.
[2]I once interviewed John Biffen in his office when he was leader of the House. 'You might like to know,' he said cheerily, 'that you are sitting where Mr Profumo sat when shamefully denying his guilt to Cabinet colleagues.'

CHAPTER SEVEN

Macleod's relationship with R. A. Butler was complicated. He had worked for him early, was a sincere admirer, thought of his own sort of Toryism as Rab's and had enjoyed his support in Africa. Indeed, over the Central African Federation, Butler would conclude the rejection of white settlerdom which Macleod had begun. But he had not been a Butler supporter for the leadership in 1957 nor above taking the leadership of the Commons out of Butler's unwilling and unhappy hands. It is conceivable that, along with mounting considerations of his long-term interest, some embarrassment at this snatch may later have helped edge him into stronger support for the older man.

But the self-interest was clear-cut enough. Among promoted younger men, Macleod had been the first off the mark with his 1952 Ministry. Macmillan had advanced Reginald Maudling, while Heath, a 1950 entrant who had very early become Chief Whip, was pushing obdurately forward. Considerations were in order worldly enough to be associated only with a papal conclave. An older pope would be better politics for any young cardinal than any other young cardinal.

On the other hand, if Macmillan went in 1963, an idea with force after the Night of the Long Knives and greater force after Profumo, Macleod would not be Pope. 'Too clever by half' had done its work. Creative policy had made its enemies, Macmillan among them. At a time when the leader had influence on the emergence of his own successor, Macleod needed a leader who liked him better. A general cooling of relations had taken place over the troubles of Africa, but also out of the capriciousness which kings show to favourites. Indeed, the Prime Minister contemplated dropping him as Chairman only to be warned off by Macleod's co-adjutor, Oliver Poole – no friend of either Butler or Macleod, but resistant to that febrile mood. Succinctly, Macleod could live with a continuing Macmillan and more time, better than with a Macmillan organising his succession now. So he was for Macmillan.

But if the Prime Minister did go, Macleod needed promotion to one of the great secretaryships in the service of another man born well before himself. Butler at 60 made very good sense. But there was nothing fundamentally improper about such calculations. They are part of normal politics in its non-angelic state. And a Butler succession winning the 1964 election to make way for Macleod ahead of the 1968 election was a desirable combination making much better sense for the Tories than anything they have now.

This Prime Minister's relations with his Cabinet colleagues had their affinities with those of Margaret Thatcher. Both enjoyed patronage, both busily practised discards. Both had enthusiasms which turned readily to disillusionment; people kept letting them down. Leaders of governments commonly suffer from both scorn and fear. Having got to the top, they despise climbers. Being generally able themselves, they cannot quite believe in the ability of others but, once they acknowledge it, frequently do so with intense dislike. They watch the manoeuvring of aspirants and go in fear that aspirants will become conspirators.

It was, for example, a hard thing in the late eighties to be John Moore, spoken about as a crown prince at one moment, then flung dismissively aside after an episode combining too much of a desire to please and a poor Commons performance when too ill for debate. But Thatcher, though she revelled in power and lacked sympathy for colleagues, was not sadistic; she did not toy with prey before despatching it. Macmillan, incomparably more graceful, better mannered and generally civilised in display, did have a streak of cruelty. He didn't turn violently or irrationally off people as she did, rather he would become irritated, as when Macleod's African policy gave him trouble. That might be understandable enough, but having originally demonstrated affection in the rather showy way he favoured, he would deliberately withdraw it. Reggie Bennett's account of the episode in the lobby is a perfect single shot of Macmillan's nature shown through his odd, unmasculine way of punishing by denial.

The likely outcome of a prime minister running through colleagues like snooker balls is that a lucky one will find himself out of reach in the wrong part of the table. With Thatcher that off-angled colour was John Major. With Macmillan, it once looked very like being Reginald Maudling, another later promotion. And, for all Maudling's faults, one might have done much worse. The *Financial Times* of 19 June 1963 reported, 'Increasingly as one canvasses backbench opinion, it becomes plain that if a straight vote were taken at this moment, Mr Reginald Maudling would succeed Mr Macmillan.' But events were to move so quickly and irrationally that when in October the new Chancellor failed a test – making a dull speech at conference – an absurd degree of significance would be attached to it by the frantic circumstances of the hour.

The last 18 months of Macmillan's leadership were the cruel counterpart to his brilliant opening in government. Where he had restored morale, he now broke it. His breezy cheerfulness which picked up party and nation between 1957 and 1959 was replaced by a self-directed *Weltschmerz* which imparted easy desperation. He had opened doors and pushed talents among successor candidates he was now denying and confounding with a round of 'she loves me, she loves me not' which would have done credit to a tiresome adolescent. Also, and depressingly, the consistent thread of this period is a certain quest for the inferior. Butler, Maudling and Macleod were all, in their different ways, first-rate men. Hailsham had charisma and high intelligence, though flecked with silliness. Events (and Macmillan) would conspire quite needlessly to advance the second-rate Home and beyond him the second-rate Heath.

The Prime Minister was, in fact, perfectly well placed to stay and fight himself. His diaries are packed with whinnying little bursts of introspection: 'I shall probably be humiliated if I stay and everyone will say that failure has been due to the old limpet.' Yet he was being told, by Macleod for one, but also by his son Maurice and brother-in-law James Stuart, that he could in fact win an election. James Stuart talked of 'pub-crawling' for him and reported on it: 'Your position is immensely stronger than it was in mid-July. Whether you want to go or not there is now no serious rival to you who is visible!'

The Conservative Party had plenty of talent and very little need to quarrel. In the absence of democratic procedures, it could still have reached intelligent consensus in Westminster away from press and conference hysteria. Butler was someone with whom all the younger candidates could have gone along. A short elderly papacy under a pope placed to win the election, with everyone else comfortably postponing intact hopes, was the easiest option. He had enemies on the executive of the 1922 Committee, but Tory MPs looking for a pre-election change to a respected leader would have been happy enough.

For that matter, if the parliamentary party had positively rejected Rab, it would have been able to find by an honest canvass who it *did* want. Honestly surveyed, the Westminster Tories would probably have rejected Hailsham, whose way of vitiating intellect by noise was well known. They would certainly have rejected Lord Home, for the good reason that they hardly knew him. (This would be the country's trouble in 1964.) Macmillan could have left his party in a good temper without quarrels and with reasonable expectations by the modest expedient of doing nothing very much.

The Prime Minister's longstanding hostility to Rab and its roots and pathology have been dealt with in another section, but the element of cruelty shone through this relationship which probably got worse as it fed upon itself. Divorced from day-to-day contact, Macmillan would, long after the event, confess that Home wasn't up to the job and that he should probably have left the leadership to Butler. Certainly what he would soon do to stop him would inflict nothing but damage – to Butler of course, to Macleod as he reacted against sharp practice, and chiefly to the Conservative Party.

The temporary alienation of Iain Macleod from the party establishment, the walking away of the most gifted warrior in that command, is the measure of the disaster, telling us more about Macmillan than it does about Macleod. The events are now roughly apparent. Macmillan, having promoted the younger men and having become readily and now restlessly discontented with them, began to contemplate other options. Fortuitously, he would be encouraged in this by Anthony Wedgwood Benn, as he then was, a peer trying to make lordship optional in order to pursue his own political life in the Commons. How much his Labour colleagues in the seventies and early eighties would yearn for a silken law of aristocracy, an immutable binding of the Viscount Stansgate into a heroic niche of nobility, was an irony which could never then have been guessed. For the moment, he was wrecking the Tories.

The Second Viscount had been campaigning through the courts and in pursuit of legislation since his father's death in

November 1960. And the charm of disregarded impediments was not lost upon ambitious or even activist Tory MPs afflicted that way. When, in 1962, a joint parliamentary committee narrowly approved extending a right to disclaim peerages, possibilities emerged. An amendment allowing immediate disclaimer ahead of the next election, one rejected under Macleod's Parliamentary leadership, was reasserted in the Lords and accepted by the Commons on 30 July. That decision made it possible to consider for the prime ministership two thoroughly unsuitable men.

There had been an early prime ministerial conversation with the Earl of Home which had come to nothing, but Home was being encouraged by Major Morrison, the chairman of the 1922 Committee. And Edward Heath, grasping what to do next in ways that would have surprised members of his Cabinet, sought the company of Major Morrison on his Scottish island and became a supporter of Home's candidacy. With his successor as Chief Whip, Redmayne, alerted to these possibilities, something close to a conspiracy of inferior men was afoot.

Home was to do for Heath what Butler would have done for Macleod. A competitive search for older men with limited political lifespans was underway. Meanwhile, Macmillan was looking for not-Butler and in the process, was making war on the young men by using someone who, however disguised by shape and mannerisms, was their contemporary, Hailsham. To Hailsham, whom he had treated roughly after the 1959 election and that pre-election bell-ringing and John Donne-quoting conference, Macmillan now returned. He did so first in casual conversation with other people, then in June telling Hailsham himself that he was the right man to succeed him if he retired before the election. Hailsham, as noted, was allocated a piece of the limelight, being sent to round off a diplomatic advance with the signing ceremonies in Moscow for the partial test-ban treaty.

But the goodwill faded again. Hailsham would have every reason for thinking that Macmillan had treated him shabbily. Given his popularity among activists and bounding public style, he would be reached for as a useful tool, pushed forward, found unsuitable and superseded.

Macmillan had dithered through the late summer. In August he had been demurring at staying on in office after Parliament resumed. 'I don't particularly want a tiresome eight weeks from November to Christmas, with the party in the House of Commons making trouble and then resigning at Christmas.'

Only a great international prize would detain him. 'So it is the choice between finishing my political life at the end of October, or going right through to and including the election.'

Having judged thus in a rational vein, Macmillan's too-present emotions kept him bouncing between the supportive Stuart ('Your position immensely stronger'), and the morose Poole who,

> *deeply moved and almost in tears, told me that he thought it was his duty as Chairman of the party, but even more as a personal friend with a great affection for me, to warn me against such a course [staying on to fight the election]. He thought we should lose the election anyhow ... a collapse which is likely anyhow, while bad for my successor, would be humiliating for me. Why should I endure it?*

Poole, on the strength of this, sounds more lachrymose and devious than Macmillan himself.

The Prime Minister, though, was giving to his diary a fair demonstration that while Stuart and the optimists were almost certainly right about his electoral prospects, the anxieties which he hugged to himself – about how he would look and whether he would be hurt – had begun to make him a liability at 10 Downing Street. Macmillan had always flirted with disaster and, though he would pull himself together in early October and make a clear resolve to carry on, he had left himself in no emotional state to face any sort of illness, still less another incompetent doctor reacting to a prostate problem as Oliver Poole responded to the election.

When, on 7 October 1963, only days ahead of Party Conference, Macmillan found himself unable to urinate and in considerable pain, his doctor, Sir John Richardson, happened to be away. The substitute, a Dr King-Lewis, after draining, con-sulted A. W. Badenoch, a surgeon. Having conducted Cabinet next morning in some pain (for which Butler very aptly offered him a tablet of Valium), Macmillan was told by the consultant that he was suffering from inflammation of the prostate gland by either benign or malignant tumour. It was the sort of bad news which Macmillan at this point was made for.

John Richardson, his own physician, rushed down from the Lake District and at once contradicted the official guidance that an operation would incapacitate Macmillan completely for three to four months. He also told Lady Dorothy and Maurice

Macmillan that 'he can go on if someone takes the strain for a few weeks'. Macmillan's words to his secretary, Tim Bligh, ahead of the press conference announcing the operation, determined his departure. Bligh said he would have to answer the question, 'Does it mean he will have to resign?' 'Of course, I am finished. Perhaps I shall die. You can say that it is quite clear that I shall be unable to fight the election.' He was ill, he had had a very bad political time for at least 15 months. But self-pity and defeatism had always been part of Macmillan and the words of his own self-dismissal encapsulate both. A little local difficulty became catastrophe, the unflappable flapped.

The upshot would be a succession resolved in the atmosphere of Party Conference – fraught, malignant and nasty. As Alistair Horne observes, 'It was clear that over the summer the younger contenders, Macleod, Maudling and Heath, had been relegated, leaving Hailsham and Butler the clear favourites.'

Macleod learned of immediate events at Blackpool by phone from Downing Street. His growing distance from Macmillan had not helped him to any priority information. Indeed, the Prime Minister had been doing his confiding to family members like Maurice, friends like Stuart and innately inferior figures like Poole, Redmayne, Major Morrison and the Lord Chancellor, Viscount Dilhorne. And in such company, a name like Home's had natural attraction.

As David Watt would write in the *Spectator* in October: 'The hard core of old-style Tories with the semi-aristocratic backgrounds (or connections) and membership of White's Club have been formed against Mr Butler since 1957.' This was not on account of any specific policy 'but because in a vague kind of way "he stands for the wrong thing if he has the guts to stand for anything", as one irreconcilable put it'.

The confederacy of dull men was at work. The Chairman of the party was kept in the dark and had also to contend with a threat of death more real than Macmillan's. Macleod's daughter, Diana – clever, vivacious, very dear to her father and with a touch of his quality – has always suffered wretched health. In the week of the Blackpool crisis doctors feared that her acute back condition would kill her. Macleod was naturally preoccupied with this. Diana survived, though she was recurringly very ill, and, seven years later, would have to be brought to her father's funeral by aircraft and ambulance.

Reggie Bennett, whom fastidious good sense normally kept away from Party Conference, undertook the social and reconnaissance work impossible for Macleod. And it was Bennett who would report back the Home candidacy, only to have his head bitten off. 'Don't be bloody ridiculous. Alec told us in Cabinet he wasn't a runner.' Dennis Walters and Ian Gilmour were giving similar warnings to Hailsham. Hailsham was just as certain. 'I simply don't believe it. Alec has told me that he is not a candidate, and we have agreed that we could not possibly leave the House of Lords simultaneously.'

Even the idea of Home as contender had not been part of general political conversation, a reflection on his obscurity despite service and surprise advancement to the Foreign Office. Notoriously, Macmillan liked a lord and, in imitation of Salisbury's Hotel Cecil, had advanced a number of them, including his nephew by marriage, the young Duke of Devonshire, into Government. This was thought larkish and Trollopian and may have once been intended so. Now it was becoming serious. But people as important in politics as the party Chairman simply did not know of Home's encouragement and own growing ambitions. Like John Major 25 years later, Home spent his late rise sensibly shutting up.

That would have been fine – perfectly legitimate politics. But Home did a little more than shut up. When Cabinet met on 8 October, Macmillan, bravely but not wholly convincingly, attempted to conceal his illness. The misdiagnosis was not actually revealed, and then privately, until 12.45, when Cabinet was over, and only Butler was given so much as a garbled indication of a serious condition. That Cabinet was backing Macmillan's continuation but eventualities were touched on after his departure. Dilhorne announced his willingness as a non-contender to conduct any consultation around the Cabinet about a successor.

The Earl of Home, whatever Major Morrison and Mr Heath might wish, told that gathering what Hailsham and Macleod would so soon repeat to friends who reported rumours of his candidacy, that in no circumstance would he be a candidate. He would be glad to help Dilhorne. Dilhorne would be helping him. The change of mind which Home underwent came just late enough to make him stand after telling his colleagues categorically that he would not. Among grammar-school boys, Jews, professional bridge-players and other people outside Macmillan's circle, that was called cheating. Home, of course, was none of these things.

Butler, in a private letter, would later express belief that

Home had got the resignation statement out of Macmillan. He would read the statement out to the conference of which he happened to be that year's Chairman. Without it, the conference might have buzzed with possibilities, but it would not have influenced selection. The announcement, which moved the Conservative Party to the sort of tearful excess to which it is prone (*The Times* detected one in Macleod's eye; he would have good reason soon enough), did Home no end of good, a messenger placed not to be shot but to run for office. He was in the limelight, he was conference Chairman and thus neutral and above conflict. He was speaking the laudatory forms for a suddenly departed leader. Alec Douglas-Home had few of Mark Antony's strengths and none of his interesting vices, but at this excitable funeral, Antony was the part he got.

Meanwhile, Hailsham was being urged on by Julian Amery and Maurice Macmillan, son-in-law and son of the Prime Minister. Their message 'was conveyed straight from Harold himself' and would be confirmed by Poole, Co-Chairman, Macmillan's man (and Butler's and Macleod's enemy). Hailsham should renounce his peerage and declare his candidacy. It might be overstating Macmillan's natural chicanery to think that this was intended as an invitation to sprinkle oneself with petrol and strike matches. Macmillan was interested in not-Butler, whoever that was.

Hailsham was to give a lecture in the atrocious Baronial Hall of the Winter Gardens. He was already embarrassed by the raucous, bright-eyed presence of Randolph Churchill (having access to Macmillan, friendly with Macleod, hating Butler) who was handing out American-style buttons marked 'Q'. Hailsham made his own sort of speech – boisterous, excited, romantic – culminating in the announcement that he would disclaim his peerage after much unedifying noise and cries of 'We want Hailsham!' and 'Declare yourself!'

It is Hailsham's nature, not unlike Michael Heseltine's, to combine respectable, indeed rather liberal views with a ranting manner (calculated in one man, second nature in the other) which conveys the South American balcony and arouses worst instincts. Some observers said 'Nuremburg'; the unengaging Major Morrison, labouring for Home, said 'Dull and dreary'. 'The Establishment,' wrote Harold Evans, the PM's Press Secretary, 'reacted with curled lips.' Consensus in an atmosphere where mood was king said 'Quintin? Impossible.' What Sheffield would do for Neil Kinnock, Blackpool would do for Hailsham.

He had gone to the conference armed with Macmillan's blessing for the succession, but, crucially, thinking it would arise perhaps at Christmas. He had been harassed into declaration. Having done it in the foreseeable rapturous way, he was immediately damned by Macmillan's people for bad taste and self-seeking. The chutzpah was magnificent but Hailsham was done for. Horne heads his subsection dealing with this episode 'Hailsham Pops'.

Butler, as we have seen elsewhere, would react to everything slowly and passively, encouraging the Macmillan camp to say 'Rab doesn't really want it.' Hailsham had responded *con forza* and the Macmillanites said, 'Quintin wants it too much.' Both men did themselves an injury. But they did so in a set of circumstances created, out of mixed neurosis and malice, by the Prime Minister and serviced by a clutch of infantry. Home's name would now be filtered to journalists through Central Office staff and sympathetic right-wing MPs like the pink and furious Sir Cyril Osborne, to whose campaign for flogging Macmillan had contemplated concessions frustrated by Butler. It was at lunch on Saturday at the end of conference that Home, at lunch with Butler and his wife Mollie, crystallised what the floor whispers had suggested. He was going for a medical check-up as a prelude to his candidacy.

Iain Macleod, Chairman of the party, senior Cabinet Minister and its finest speaker, was nowhere in all this. He was to write in a few months' time in an explosive *Spectator* article of 'the Magic Circle'. It was rather a circle of cronies, 'hard-core, old-style Tories with semi-aristocratic backgrounds'.

As the unbriefed onlooker seeing very little of the game and certainly not the fouls, Macleod was left with a statutory duty of oration. He made a well-received speech mocking Harold Wilson as Ethelred the Unready and describing the Tory Party, without intended irony, as 'dry tinder which a spark would set ablaze'. No intelligence is too severe and no conscience too chaste not to be diminished by a party conference. Macleod's random rhetorical dismissal of 'faint hearts' would very soon be flung back at him when he came to give his account of events in the *Spectator* early the next year.

In fact, Macleod, distracted as he was by Diana's condition, was playing a modest hand for Maudling. Macleod and Maudling – staff workers under David Clarke at the research department 15 years before, both very clever, both unreserved liberals, the one succeeding the other in the colonial task – went together naturally, the Bobchinsky and Dobchinsky of young liberal Tory talent. They couldn't both run for the same thing and, though not inseparably close friends, they were on good enough terms to co-operate, although less well placed to make a back for each other. Given that he had attracted positive enemies and needed time for his own best chance, Macleod found himself promoting Maudling, which would probably have meant his own succession to the Treasury.

Promoting included help with Maudling's speech to conference, advice about timing and on delivery. It did no good. Maudling, son of an actuary, had a logical mind which worked at very great speed. He solved problems, he was generally cultivated, but, no more than Nigel Lawson a generation later, could he make a big conference speech. Lawson would sound scornful and indifferent; Maudling simply lacked the arts of waiting, word-stress, audience-encouragement and pouncing. He sounded like plywood with the gift of speech. It was his misfortune to be tested in the shrill and meretricious moment of a fraught conference at the one thing he did badly. Macleod must now concentrate upon Butler who, from a self-interested point of view, had always been his own best option. A Butler–Macleod succession was a natural development.

As it happened, Butler also made a poor speech, which is to say quite a good speech, but not the inspirational, flame-throwing affair that the crazed circumstances demanded. The fact that he had just been sweetly told by Home about his plans to run did not help. Circumstances and Macmillan's premature vision of mortality had condemned aspirants to a sort of *Meistersingers* contest with press comment as its Beckmesser.

After conference had wrecked Maudling and injured Butler, the succession struggle moved from its provincial try-out to the West End. Again, Macmillan would use speed to confound his enemies, the idea being to sew up the Home succession before Parliament resumed on 24 October. Butler and Hailsham had both quite reasonably made assumptions about things being settled around Christmas. Home was still only a name put about at conference, though a group of modest talents like Selwyn Lloyd and Duncan Sandys was now gathering behind him. But the essential drive for his succession (or 'uniting the party', as it was chuffily to be described) lay with the people supposedly charged with the disinterested collation of opinion, Redmayne, the Chief Whip, and Viscount Dilhorne, the former Reginald Manningham-Buller (Bernard Levin's immortal Sir Reginald

Bullying-Manner). It was Dilhorne whom Alec Home had offered to help as a fellow non-contender. What followed was crass conspiracy. Even at Blackpool, Redmayne's questions had first tilted clearly to Hailsham and then veered. Witness this conversation with the young Jim Prior:

> *MR: Who do you favour?*
> *JP: Reggie Maudling as first choice, but if not, Rab, of course.*
> *MR: Not Quintin?*
> *JP: No, not Quintin.*
> *MR: Thank you very much. By the way, what about Alec if he decides to stand?*
> *JP: I don't really know him and in any case he's in the House of Lords.*
> *MR: So he's not a runner?*
> *JP: Well, we don't know yet, do we?*
> *MR: But if he does renounce?*
> *JP: I suppose he would be possible.*

Shepherd quotes Prior as having 'little doubt that even at that early stage, I was put down as an Alec supporter'. Humphry Berkeley describes being asked, 'If there is deadlock between Rab and Quintin would you accept Alec Home?' Reginald Bennett was asked, 'If Alec were nominated, would you vote against him?' William Whitelaw, then a junior minister, having opted for Butler with certain reservations, was asked, 'But if Alec Home were available, would you be prepared to support him?'

If the putting of questions with the Chief Whip's *nolle* to get the right answer, together with supplementaries so as to draw in second or third 'not actually objectings' as votes for, were not enough, the actual counting of more senior heads was suspect. Dilhorne claimed ten first preferences for Home in the Cabinet. Macleod would point out, when he came to refute the whole case in his *Spectator* article, that he was present at a sandwich lunch of ministers and of the five present, not including Boyle, Hailsham and Butler, no one favoured Home as first choice. Of five others, exactly two were known to him as pro-Home and three as not. Even if Home had all six of the remaining members, Dilhorne's numbers would be wrong. Of the 13 Macleod could account for, 11 were not for Home against two who were. Yet Redmayne would soon be saying to people, 'It's too late, it's all been settled'. Settled it had been, to the point almost of having been fixed. There is a name for this sort of thing. It is 'guided democracy'.

The actual dishonesty of what was being done in response to Macmillan's scheming would disgust Macleod. The words of Salisbury about it 'not being thought immoral to outwit one's opponents and the more you outwit them, the better player you are' acquire a bitter aptness here. Macmillan, identified as the bookish old burrower in his beloved Austen and Trollope, was playing cards himself – cards not in the deck. Macleod, too clever by half, certainly *thought* too clever for his own good, Macleod the professional gamester, had been snapping at Bennett and contradicting the political scientist David Butler with his perfect certainty that Home would not stand because he had said that he would not. Never were two men respectively more blessed and more ill served by their stereotypes. Macleod's conduct throughout Blackpool and until the Thursday following was, despite its mild dabbling for Maudling, correct, very close to being naïve and, perhaps because of his preoccupation with his daughter's health, almost sleepy.

As the prime ministerial plot proceeded, like all good plots, quickly, Macleod would move from a trusting and near-passive stance to intense activity. He had been excluded from information and had to learn it from intermediary friends like Lady Monckton and William Rees-Mogg of *The Sunday Times*. It would be decided that afternoon, said Lady Monckton (who had it from Dorothy Macmillan) on the morning of 17 October. The decision had been made and it was for Home, said Rees-Mogg on the afternoon of the same day.

Confirmed in this by conversations with lobby correspondents, Macleod consulted Enoch Powell, was contacted by Hailsham and finally, late that night, reached Home by phone. It was a message of polite refusal. He told him, as he recounted in the *Spectator* piece, 'We were now proposing to admit that after 12 years of Tory government no one among the 363 members of the party in the House of Commons was acceptable as Prime Minister.'

Next day there was a gathering at Powell's house, including Frederick Erroll, President of the Board of Trade, Lord Aldington and Maudling, as well as Macleod, and linked by phone to Hailsham. As Macleod would argue, if Maudling and Hailsham both opposed Home's succession and were happy to serve under Butler, that surely pointed the succession only one way. Butler rang Dilhorne to ask for a meeting of the three candidates other than Home authorised by Macmillan. He received no answer and Macmillan avoided further developments by formally making over his resignation to the Queen. In doing so, he also tendered advice as to the succession and this, as Macleod would write, 'purported to be not the advice of one man, but the collective view of a party'. Almost certainly at this point, if Butler had been the sort of grit-blasted, strong-minded politician willing to make trouble for what he wants, Home could have been stopped. Messages had been conveyed to the Palace. A raft of very senior politicians were saying, as Enoch Powell put it, 'to Mr Butler and one another, that they did not consider Lord Home should be Prime Minister, that they would serve under Mr Butler, and that they would not serve under Lord Home unless Mr Butler had previously agreed to do so'. Powell lists Macleod, Maudling, Hailsham, Boyd Carpenter, Erroll, Edward Boyle and himself as taking that stance.

Butler's line when talking to Home – that he would not serve 'unless it was the only way to unite the party' – was fatally weak. I have argued in the Butler essay that this does not vitiate Butler's fitness for the job. He was a Government man, a doer of business and blessedly without Macmillan's mania and panics. But, despite the ironies and the remarks behind the hand, he had never been a true intriguer and had no aptitude for the near-physical struggle for power. Like Maudling, called upon to make a rousing speech, he was being tested on the one thing he really did badly. Since Macleod did it so well, the thought of what kind of government they would have run together is a poignant one.

While Butler used this sort of good party language, Hailsham, under pressure from Home's people, very understandably weakened too, though Dennis Walters' picture of Hailsham, then offered a miserable odds-and-ends job, trying to be delighted with it, is a sad one. The resistance party needed Rab to break the habits of a lifetime and kick over the table with a refusal to serve. He could not, and lived to fulfil everything that Shakespeare has to say about the alternatives to tides taken at the flood. Butler, submitting to the old Tory humbug about party unity, was quickly followed by everyone on Powell's list – Hailsham first, then Maudling and Edward Boyle most reluctantly. But he was not followed by Powell nor by Iain Macleod.

Macleod was about to do the great, unspeakable thing. He would spurn party unity – indeed, would give it a couple of good healthy kicks – first by refusing to serve, then by publishing his

January article in the *Spectator*. He was about to become a bad hat, a cad, a nasty bit of work, a total outsider – by refusing to be accessory to a piece of fraud and by telling the truth.

Standing where we do at the end of the century, with election by parliamentary party looking a distinctly confined standard practice, the model of a chief whip's run-round of the chaps by intimidatory query with heavy hints of the reply desired, and all assessment and counting subject to honour and discretion among three or four elder confederates, looks grotesque.

It always was grotesque and it would have been a bad way to do business if Chief Whip and Prime Minister had behaved with immaculate dispassion. But Macmillan placed upon this frail structure of public-schoolboy honour the whole burden of his own shifty dealing. That system required mystique and suppression of the critical faculties as much as any tank of decaying tissue exhibited as art in the Serpentine Gallery. Macleod's function – and it was a historical function – was to play the little boy remarking that the Emperor had no clothes, and the sheep stank.

CHAPTER EIGHT

A *Spectator* summary of the previous week's events published on 25 October 1963 encapsulates immediate adjustments and the confusing mood of the day quite perfectly.

The publication of Fanny Hill, Woman of Pleasure *is to be contested at Bow St Magistrates Court. Mr Niall Macpherson is to become Lord Drumalbyn, Mr John Hare is to become Lord Blakenham. Lord Hailsham has been adopted as Conservative candidate for St Marylebone and the Duchess of Kent is to have another baby.*

The period following the leadership episode was to be a particularly bitter one for Conservatives. The true 1960s were upon them. Having achieved the leadership of Home (a commoner now new made, but by reason of his longstanding Order of the Thistle, Sir Alec Douglas-Home), the Conservatives could reflect on Harold Wilson's speech at Scarborough only the week before. It had been delivered with such verve and style that Home's journalist nephew, Charles Douglas-Home, had had to be restrained by a colleague from bursting into applause. It was a speech with a thousand disappointments coiled within it by way of later reproach when white heat proved tepid, but for the undemanding present, it did brilliantly. In terms of surface dazzle, Labour now had a Harold of their own.

But these were the sixties. Respect and deference, the old hermetic sealing of politicians away from the breath of familiarity, were done for. Parliamentary Question Time, which

Macmillan had developed and been good at, was perfectly designed for the undoing of a man sequestered in the House of Lords since the beginning of the reign. 'He will ... be a dud when it comes to exciting the electorate, and Wilson will make rings round him,' wrote another new commoner, Anthony Wedgwood Benn. As Benn also wrote, Wilson was 'amenable to suggestions and has none of Hugh Gaitskell's rigidity in sticking to dull economic phrases that could and should be simplified'. What possibilities lay waiting in *that* sentence.

Home did the only sensible thing in the circumstances. As he had every right to, he pushed the election to the full statutory distance. Maudling, his Chancellor, had wanted an earlier election, disliking the political uncertainty clouding economic management. This is the oddest of ironies, for Maudling's economic management is best understood as politics.

At a time when incomes policy was the standard, not very good, restraint on inflation, he had none. Unemployment was thought high but falling – at the figures, unimaginable today, of 2.4 per cent in May 1963 and 2.1 in June. Prospective inflation was a serious threat, and the way out of it, taxation, was politically unavailable. He had handled tax in a political way, giving reliefs worth a 2 per cent increase on wages, pleasing the TUC Economic Committee no end.

He was thus caught up in what Edmund Dell calls 'wild reflation', though it was less than Macmillan had urged upon him. On top of everything, he had a balance-of-payments problem about which Labour during the election would grate-fully go on and on. This was the famous dash for growth – much too fast and, as the song has it, too hot not to cool down. It was already underway when Douglas-Home succeeded and, though he made no attempt to discourage a politically advantageous wave, it was people with more plausible claims to economic competence, Maudling and the former Chancellor, Macmillan, who had put the word 'political' into political economy.

And politically, it nearly worked. Champagne is said to be the political drink. Maudling has produced a champagne budget in 1963 and followed it with champagne growth. The forecast large Labour victory did not materialise, but the small Labour victory that did sufficed. As Dell says, 'The policy behind the 1963 budget was a gamble fashioned by politics,' and it was a gamble lost. Harold Wilson's professional rhetoric, his modern manner, his vocabulary compounded of grit and oil – indeed, his actual great abilities, not yet vitiated by tests of courage or party quarrels – saw Labour through with an overall majority of four.

Home had been given power he was always likely to lose, always certain of being blamed for losing. Though he did not disgrace himself, we had arrived at the hour of the image. And Home's image was the grouse moor. He was recorded in November that year as shooting 199 pheasants and 19 partridges one Saturday. He was the man who called a social security increase a 'donation' and who managed to injure himself during an interview with the soft-edged Kenneth Harris with a joke about counting with matchsticks.

The extent of defeat is blurred in many minds which recall it. There is much talk among Tory politicians about 'Alec having done very well'. If losing by only four seats against worse expectations constitutes achievement, he had indeed done well. But to suffer a loss of 6 per cent of the vote and 1,748,434 votes was to fall farther than either party had done since 1945. The actual Tory vote was half a million below their modest total in 1950. And they saw Labour into government despite a 10,000-vote loss of their own. A dreadful result might be explained in terms of Conservative turmoil, the Profumo affair and the sheer absurdity of the succession struggle. But, though the economy was not academically in a creditable state, it had been run in the most voter-friendly way imaginable, through high employment, easy credit, every mistaken occasion for feeling good.

So, bribed but not bought, the boom-proof electorate was saying fearful things. In 1966, when Labour not unreasonably held up the Maudling deficit of £800 million (actually about £400 million, but who is counting?) as the key issue of their shrewdly judged renewal election in March 1966, the rejection was continued and deepened. The shift in Conservative support then brought them down to 253 seats against the 365 with which they had gone into the election in 1964. Until very recently, those were considered exceptionally bad results.

Almost as soon as the Tories went into opposition Maudling made a career mistake to compound his economic errors. He did not, in 1965, insist upon handling Labour's Finance Bill, that long, arcane but sexy annual deliberation where reputations are frequently made. He left the position open to Edward Heath. Heath was tortoise to almost everyone else's hare. He didn't think quickly; he didn't speak well; his charm is reported, if at all, mainly by musicians and sailors. He didn't, for that matter, have the grasp of the economy he imagined and in due late course he would panic on a scale to make Macmillan look cool. But he worked hard, read his briefings, was conspicuously busy and used the sort of non-specific language of modernity and efficiency which Wilson with so much more flair had turned to account.

As Douglas-Home wilted in the House of Commons, enemy territory into which he had been parachuted, Heath grew in reputation. Replacement always looked likely. Macmillan would write to his friend Lady Waverley, 'Alec did his best – with courage and dignity. But he could not impress himself on Parlt. or people enough for a PM . . . He was an Edward Grey, not an Asquith.' Such comparative historic felicities are rarely wise: an excitable journalist would one day compare Edward Heath with Peel! Anyway, the Conservative Party would not tolerate its Edward Grey figure much longer and Harold Wilson, with justified confidence, did not choose to play safe in timing his inevitable follow-on election to assure a contest against Home.

An announcement on 26 June 1965 by Home that there would be no leadership contest that year was flattened by an announcement by Wilson the same day that there would be no election either. Getting rid of Home was now as practicable as it was desirable. Various heavy persons pronounced in the bowel-like way of the institutional press. Rees-Mogg, with his usual command of cliché, applauded 'a captain's innings' and rumbled that the Conservatives 'will not win a general election while Sir Alec remains their leader'. In those days captains tended to be amateurs with an average of about 14.

They weren't going to win an election *without* him. But Home had his Charles I touch: 'nothing petty or mean' marked his departure on 20 July, less than a month after his rejection of a leadership contest that year. But reverting to his speciality of foreign affairs, he would, in opposition and in the Heath Government, prove quietly hintproof and unbudgeable, one member of the 1970–4 Government to emerge with something like credit.

Macleod's role in all this was, without intended irony, that of spectator. He had been installed by his friend, Ian Gilmour, in the editorship of the *Spectator*, in those days a liberal Tory weekly rather than the fashionable journal of shrill high-church reaction it would become. After October 1963, it seemed a refuge. Macleod, for all his card-playing long before, had never had money. A friend like Anthony Sumption of Lombard Bank might give him moneysworth, a large car and a driver which, as his health declined and his back bent, he dearly needed. But he was one of those Tory ministers, not as rare nowadays as they were then, who actually need their salary. At £5,000, the hike of a rich and generous man, he was back at ministerial level, something which says poignant things about the inflation which from the late fifties would define the British economy.

Not that Macleod was in any way wiser about economics than his colleagues. Like his Cambridge education, it never held his interest. His instincts would have been the same as Maudling's but very much less well informed. Even so, being Macleod – a learner, a student of detail and a very fast worker – he would do things to change this state of affairs. For the moment he was simply watching politics with no idea that he would necessarily be let back into the game.

The election of a new leader would be a hand he would not play. Nick Scott recalls a desultory meeting at Macleod's house and his own opinion that a candidacy was unrealistic. Eve Macleod said sadly that she had never expected him to speak so gloomily and Scott, very much the young enthusiast, personally attached to Macleod since his recent Young Conservative days, mournfully assented. It was the last thing he would have expected to say. But it recognised a reality made up of the support lost at the Colonial Office, the resignation over Macmillan's conduct and a certain article of 19 January 1964 in the *Spectator*.

Randolph Churchill, that strange, emotionally charged, brave, impulsive, drunken, generous and virulent man, had a thing against Butler, was a White's Club friend of Macleod, a noisy partisan of Hailsham and had easy access to Macmillan. Wanting service in a grand restaurant, he broke wine glasses against a marble table to attract the waiter's attention. Wanting to contribute to history, he published at speed a book, *The Fight for the Tory Leadership*, which owed most to his connections with Macmillan and described events triumphally in Macmillan's terms.[1] As Editor of the *Spectator*, Macleod wrote a review at double main-feature length (4,000 words), comprehensively rebutting this orthodoxy, setting out the depths of the real division and making clear how a high-placed faction had adjusted the truth.

On publication of the book, Macmillan had sent Churchill a 'Dear boy, too kind' note on old 10 Downing Street paper,

Dear Randolph,

What you write about me is too flattering. But I will not pretend that it has not given me much pleasure.

Yours ever
Harold

From Macmillan's point of view, it would have been better for him if Churchill had never written it. The publicity given to Macleod's account, coming from such a source and in contradiction of the line his friends had fostered, was explosive. It was headline news in daily and evening newspapers and it sent the broadsheets into magisterial mode. David Wood of *The Times*, with his own source in Maudling, would swiftly follow up with strong confirmation. Macmillan made no denial or dissociation until months later, and then feebly. The word 'Establishment' was just coming into satirical vogue to describe the limp but lethal conspiracy of highly placed persons and their connections. Macleod was the man defying the Establishment. His phrase 'the Magic Circle' became common currency. The article – far more important than the book – served as a further detonation of the very Establishment it described. Randolph Churchill, like Christine Keeler, simply did not know what he was starting.

Two things flowed from Macleod's extended review. It changed the perception of government, uncovering the sly, back alley arrangements of official persons. Demonstrating, as he was able to, that 'from the first day of his premiership to the last, Macmillan was determined that Butler, although incomparably the best qualified of the contenders, should not succeed him', Macleod made it impossible for any magic circle to do such things ever again. Secondly, he made Iain Macleod furiously and sensationally unpopular with the Conservative Party in all its manifestations. His status as cad, card-player and disloyalist was underscored three times. From some of the *Spectator*'s letter-writers – 'What a nasty little bit of work you are. First noticed your eyes at the Blackpool conference' – much of the underlining was in green ink.

As all this happened at a time (January 1964) when an election was in immediate prospect, the author of the piece was double-damned for an act injurious to the party's re-election. There is no higher crime. Macleod was not horsewhipped on the steps of White's, where one of his oldest associates was

Randolph Churchill. But he was cut in the Commons smoking-room, insulted by Nigel Birch, who also managed, more famously, to insult Macmillan by quoting Browning at him. He was censured by his own constituency, though in those days de-selection was a word waiting to be coined. And an attempt was made by three drab Birmingham right-wing MPs to bar him from a meeting in that city.

Macleod himself was wrongfooted and genuinely shocked by the hostility. But then, he was in an odd position. He had risen by merit alone. A GP's son attending a minor public school and a Cambridge college neither King's nor Trinity, enjoying a war-time rank establishing him as what was then called 'a temporary gentleman', he was an acceptable Conservative candidate and member. But without spectacular abilities (and Winston Churchill's short way with the career structure) he had no assured access to advancement. His biting *Spectator* headcount of Etonians in the Macmillan circle was considered bad form. As a blinding truth, it surely was. The ability of the English upper class to conspire without noticing it, in the manner of Monsieur Jourdain's talking prose for 40 years without realising, was something of which Macleod, the outsider, was jarringly aware.

But he was a Tory partly because the externalities – White's and the Carlton, the Army and state occasions – all charmed him. Emotionally he was a cavalier. Policy for policy, he was substantially a Liberal. The career open to the talents, hatred of cruelty in the penal system, wide sexual tolerance, support for civil liberties before the phrase had currency, contempt for racialism when the all-Christian golf club was a commonplace, all described him. He was divided from the Labour Party because, a libertarian before the letter, he lacked its puritanical and authoritarian streaks, not its broad compassion. Being a Tory at a time when that Party wanted to sweeten its nature made sense. With Butler as chief thinker and Churchill (a capital 'L' Liberal long before the vulgar bulldog stuff attached to him), the Tory Party he entered was in just such a mood.

But the upper-class garrison and its style which Macmillan, in Vincent Crummles mode, liked to accentuate, was also there. It didn't like Macleod, he didn't like it and the quarrel was something long waiting to happen. He was, after all, a hireling, a *Hofjude*, the clever little woman every dowager turns to for the running up of a dress. When he quarrelled, he broke the rules of a circle at whose periphery he stood. The scorn would be loud and it would be loudest from those whose own social coinage most invited enquiry, like Peregrine Worsthorne.

There was another factor behind what he had done. David Rogers who, hired in 1965, served Macleod as Research Assistant for the rest of his life, is convinced that Macleod's intensifying illness played a part. The spinal pain of ankylosing spondylitis was at times so savage that Rogers, like Scott, recalls hours of sheer inability to speak a word in this happy conversationalist. Arthur Cockfield, who would work with Macleod as a fiscal expert from 1966, had no doubt that he was going to die quite soon. 'I had seen it once before, in a senior partner at Peat's [Peat Marwick, the accountants], the look of having the Angel of Death in attendance.' Rogers believes that Macleod's whole course of action, which went against every calculation of self-interest, sprang from an intensified need to do the right thing in the short time available to him.

After revelation, rage and catharsis, the question for Macleod would be one of utility. Snubbing and back-turning in the smoking-room is one thing, but he was a frightfully clever little *Hofjude*. As Alec Douglas-Home stumbled after 20th-century vocabulary and made the best of an elected chamber, could the Tories manage without Macleod? Evelyn Waugh, another member of White's and much more of an outsider (Lancing and Hertford, father employed in publishing), but someone for whom the charade mattered with unhealthy intensity, devoted much of *Brideshead Revisited* to hatred of two characters – Rex Mottram (based on Churchill's confidant from nowhere, Brendan Bracken) and Hooper, social outsider accelerating through the Army. Both had Macleod's sort of provenance without his genius; both face running rage.

But art trailed behind life. The immediate and anxious needs of the Tory Party after the defeat of Home and the great electoral shift away from the Conservatives made Macleod indispensable; so too, perhaps, did changes in society which underlay under all that. So Home himself realised that the means by which he had come to office, descent by baroque stage machinery with too many wires, could not continue. A Macleod disciple, the eager and ingenious Humphry Berkeley, proposed an election system involving a secret ballot, second-ballot entry of new candidates and invocation of a ballot by a demanding quorum. (The Chief Whip was to be confined to his own vote.) It was accepted. So far it has both elected and rejected Edward Heath and Margaret Thatcher and elected and resecured John Major, as well as keeping the political world, press and parliamentary, in a happy state of recurring speculation. It is imperfect, especially with an electorate of 165. But until the Conservatives get a franchise in their party, it beats 'emergence'. William Hague is as yet unjudgable.

Macleod would run the *Spectator* with a good deal of pleasure. He employed Randolph Churchill to write a sporadic column about the press; he even published a batch of Hailsham's poems:

> Let others picnic off champagne
> And rich brown croutes of pink foie gras
> Or greedily fierce vodka drain
> Helped down by heaps of caviar
>
> Just give me beer and bread and cheese
> To feast on in the open air
>
> I shall have lived as well as they
> And live just half as long again

He printed a series, 'John Bull's First Job', which included this from the ever-terse Lord Attlee: 'My father was an eminent solicitor and it seemed natural that I should be a barrister.' Then, of his time working in an East End mission, 'After a year the cynical young Tory had become a fervent Socialist. Being a street-corner propagandist for the Independent Labour Party at least cured my shyness.'

Reflecting on the murder of President Kennedy, Macleod wrote in an editorial: 'It is very rare (and not always creditable) for politicians to have anything to say to people under thirty-five ... A political attitude is taken up early and soon ossifies into a statuesque attitude antipathetic to all those who have no use for attitudes at all. It is the pomposity of politics and politicians which threaten their influence.' At the end of that year he wrote, 'The best thing that can be said about 1963 is that it has finally come to an end.'

But for all the fun of journalism, there was never any doubt in his mind that active politics at the top was what he wanted. After the election defeat in October 1964 Douglas-Home offered him what looked dull, should have been crucial and turned out to be thoroughly unimportant, responsibility for opposing Labour's renationalisation of steel. If Harold Wilson had obliged by pushing that item and if the expected second election defeat had come after that argument had been made in full, Macleod's leadership chances might have become serious again. He would have been on show doing what no colleague could do, making war with bright words on an issue which united all Tories.

Wilson, lumbered with both a controversial policy and a couple of right-wing troublemakers, Donnelly and Wyatt, unwilling to vote for it, did something he was good at and which was often a good idea: he prevaricated. Macleod made one, below-form, speech, but steel as central business of government slipped away. 'No doubt,' wrote Macleod with a snarl in his *Spectator* diary of the prospect of the policy being temporarily dumped, 'Mr Wilson in his cold calculating way would be ready to do this.' He was, and very sensible of him! Equally inconsiderately, Wilson did not hurry an election because, at the top of his form, he felt equal to beating better men than Sir Alec. Neither Heath nor Maudling worried him while Macleod, whom Wilson very much admired professionally, would not get the job. The Tories, said the Prime Minister, didn't have the sense. Macleod was a boxer on a comeback denied his big fight.

Home was deprived of that immunity which a prospective election was supposed to give him. He had given Heath far too good a platform and, faced with a press campaign and itching fingers, lacked all of John Major's Darwinian instincts under internal threat. The new democratic arrangements were in place and proceeded. When Heath suitably celebrated Home's demise and his subsequent close defeat of Maudling by motoring down to Glyndebourne to hear Verdi's *Macbeth*, a third victim was Macleod. The timing had been all wrong. Democratic selection had been established and it was too late and too soon for Macleod the democrat to benefit.

But from Heath, sensibly confident enough after so much upheaval to appoint on merit, he received the shadow chancellorship, a lien on the second-best job in government. He would die within a month of inheriting the actual office, but his time from 1966 on would be given to intelligent preparation for it and in something he was good at, opposition. He would be in every way loyal to Heath, though there was no affection in the relationship. His judgment before Heath's election and appointment imposed their obligations had been succinct. 'God forbid that Ted should lead the party,' he had said to Reggie Bennett. 'He'll put us in the wilderness for a generation.' It wouldn't be for want of trying.

Macleod had already, in the 1965–6 steel phase, begun to

gather round him an exceptional group of attractive talents. Like Butler he was good at younger people, even if he never quite found another Iain Macleod. To Scott, who had been an ally from the Young Conservatives, and Rogers, who would be the very first Parliamentary Research Assistant to anyone, there would be added Patrick Jenkin, Terence Higgins, Barney Hayhoe, Humphry Berkeley, his future biographer, Nigel Fisher, and many more. A small or maybe not so small point: the Macleod people had careers shortened and diminished by the Thatcher succession, but one looks in vain through a list of his friends for anyone unattractive or unpleasant.

To his political circle Macleod now added an expert one. Heath to his credit was determined to use Opposition to plan. He had mistakenly produced for the 1966 election a manifesto of what seemed like 100 proposals. Turning such earnestness to sensible account, he set up the Economic Policy Group. Actually he created 36 policy groups which covered everything coverable before splitting them into subcommittees to cover more. But then, Ted Heath had a weakness for trees as a source for the wood he hoped to see later. As for Macleod, he was repeating in a highly Hegelian fashion the experiences of his very early career working for Butler and David Clarke at the research department.

But the core of the work which was to be done concerned tax. Heath, having done that stint on the 1965 Finance Bill, was preoccupied with the iniquity of its main tax provisions: Corporation Tax and Capital Gains Tax, not to mention SET (Selective Employment Tax), the notion of Wilson's adviser, Nicholas Kaldor. Tax reform, which had not attracted Conservative thought in the past, became a first concern and Macleod was set to work with experts to find a Tory answer. The preoccupation of the last four years of his life, paralleling the fun and fury of the frontbench, would be 'Sub-Group A'.

Sub-Group A concerned itself with tax reform or, more cynically, with replacing Labour's new taxes with new taxes of its own. But cynicism won't do. Taxation needed drastic reform and from the deliberations of these years, major changes would materialise though Macleod would not live to see them. Key members at meetings which went on across the second half of the sixties would be Edward Boyle and Keith Joseph, both inclining to an egalitarianism which, even for *that* Tory Party, would prove unrealistic, as well as younger men like Hayhoe, who would do useful work on child poverty, and Terence

Higgins. There would be input by way of a separate report from a CBI group, but the crucial support came from academics, the young Brian Reading, Ash Wheatcroft, who would do the specific work on a VAT system, and Arthur Cockfield.

Cockfield, later Sir Arthur, then Lord Cockfield, a somewhat wry member of Margaret Thatcher's Cabinet, was the Conservative Party's contract intelligence on taxation. A former civil servant and a precise, formal man with a disguised sense of humour, he had been working to ministers since the mid-forties. He had also watched Paul Chambers of ICI boss an earlier committee and get it to concentrate its mind. Cockfield, working very closely with Macleod, had a critical mind not readily charmed by politicians' style and blarney. His judgment of Macleod is a key test.

Through much of 1966 and 1967 the committee talked round issues and failed to coalesce on hard conclusions. In Cockfield's view it was a forum for senior shadow ministers to discuss immediate issues and the tasks of the moment to the detriment of the long-term work. Accordingly, with large input from Reading, Cockfield produced a draft report of his own. In a talk delivered in 1970 he described the reaction.

The effect so far as Iain Macleod was concerned was quite remarkable. In his early days as Shadow Chancellor, his main interest had been in the cut and thrust of debate in the chamber. But the moment he saw the report, he realised that here he had to hand the opportunity of radical reform. No longer was it a question of tinkering with the existing system . . . he had, if he chose to use it, the opportunity of remodelling the whole system on a simple, more coherent basis and in a way which would assist and promote growth and opportunity. He seized this chance, in just the way he seized the chance to make radical change at earlier stages in his career. Without reservation, he threw his formidable energies behind the programme . . . so far as the party was concerned, both inside and outside Parliament, the battle for tax reform was won long before the general election.

Sitting in Cockfield's study Macleod confided to him, 'My only remaining ambition now is to be a great reforming Chancellor.'

Cockfield was an interested party, of course. His ideas were on offer; Macleod took them up and promoted them. But the admiration is that of high technician for politician on account of the ability to see a point and to think big about it. Douglas Allen, Lord Croham, talking about Butler, remarked on how he (along with George Brown) had the gift of understanding your expert point before you had quite finished explaining it. Cockfield was persuading Macleod to think very big. In his unpublished monograph on the taxation work, he recalls himself saying early on:

> The income tax is a good tax, a very good tax indeed. But it has been strained beyond the limit in our endeavours to make it carry, as the cornerstone of fiscal policy, the vast weight of present-day government expenditure. It has been expanded to the point where all sorts of undesirable side effects have emerged . . . I am convinced that the inequities of the income tax cannot be solved with the tax at its present level. They can only be solved concurrently with a drastic reduction of the level of the tax. The income tax will always be an important tax, but if it is to be a fair tax, a less damaging tax, it must be a much smaller tax.

The central purpose, achievement and electoral charm across four elections of the Conservative Party is stated there.

In the early thinking of the group, Macleod and others, notably Boyle and Joseph and the young Nigel Lawson, had hoped to balance the abolition of SET with a wealth tax. It is a reflection on the way politics mutates that the present Conservative leadership has sought to denounce a narrow and specific windfall tax proposed by the Labour Government when a Conservative policy group itself gave very serious thought to a general wealth tax. The coarsening of Conservatism is a subject in itself. But no account of Iain Macleod should ignore the realistic, hard-nosed element which complemented his human sympathy. As Professor John Ramsden points out in his study of the research department, Macleod, even in those days, was given to adding little notes to earnest discussions about 'the E factor '. 'E' stood for election. He unhesitatingly settled against this attractive idea which offended against a vested interest best not taken on: money.

Cockfield had sensed that unease was in the air. Recording a meeting on 9 May to discuss investment incentives, he observes, 'The most important thing that happened did not appear in the minutes. I had become increasingly apprehensive about the proposals for a wealth tax . . . The almost enthusiastic welcome the proposals had received at Swinton [the Conservative college where a meeting had been held] I regarded as quite misleading.' It was 'a tribute by the pessimists of the party to what they thought, in the difficult situation following two general election defeats, their leaders wanted'.

Cockfield had sensed doubt in Heath's mind and felt that he himself might be being used as a stalking horse. 'Accordingly . . . I took the first opportunity of confronting Ted Heath . . . At the end of the meeting, I stayed in my seat directly opposite Ted. Iain Macleod sat on Ted's right. None of us moved until the room had cleared and the door was closed.' Cockfield then made his pitch, saying that a great deal of detailed work would have to be done to bring the wealth tax up to date. He had to know 'whether the wealth tax would form an integral part of the package'. He had his own doubts about its acceptability, but if it was to be retained he would be ready to do the work. However,

I was not prepared to spend a number of months reconstructing the package on the basis of including the wealth tax, only then to have it knocked out at the last minute, bringing the whole edifice down like a pack of cards. For what seemed to be a very long time nobody spoke. Then Ted said, 'It would not be acceptable to party opinion.' Iain looked up. 'I agree,' he said, 'it simply is not on.'

In the official minute of a confirmatory later meeting, Macleod's opinion is given in 130 words. But with those seven, as Cockfield succinctly put it, 'so ended the wealth tax'.

The move, which Edward Boyle and Keith Joseph both resisted, left the tax plans lopsided. The original idea had been to abolish SET and impose the wealth tax. If the latter had been deleted for political reasons, abolition of the former had very early, and for reasons no less political, been settled upon. The Conservatives had committed themselves to that almost from the moment James Callaghan as Chancellor had introduced it in 1966.

Macleod had been particularly culpable. In his occasional Rupert of the Rhine way of charging splendidly without quite working out what was in the next field, he had announced to Party Conference at Brighton in 1966: 'We have no proposals to amend the SET. We will abolish the SET.' But SET raised a lot of money: £300 million in the first year, twice as much by 1970–1. Promising to abolish it meant promising to raise £600 million by some other means which, like the South Sea Bubble prospectus, would be intimated at a time to be disclosed. There is more than one PhD to be written on the injurious effects of politicians speaking at party conferences.

Macleod and Sub-Group A now had to replace the revenue brought in by SET, could not use a wealth tax, knew also that a payroll tax would not do anything like enough and had to face up to the fact that Roy Jenkins as Chancellor had dipped into their own new preference, indirect tax, by major increases – over a billion pounds in two budgets – in duties and purchase tax. According to Cockfield, Maudling would have been happy to resile in slow motion from the promise saying that 'abolition need not necessarily have a very high priority in the Party's programme for the reduction and reform of taxation'. In other words, 'Use the tax for as long as you can.' There were times when Maudling's want of keenness and ethical deficit could be very endearing. The Tory Opposition was striving to reform tax and cut direct tax at a time when North Sea oil revenue, which would make all things possible in the eighties (as well as protecting the Government from runs in the financial markets), was not in sight.

The effect of all this was to make VAT, which as a European requirement already had Heath's seal of approval, bulk larger. It also became necessary for his conference rhetoric to move rather quickly. At Blackpool in 1967 Macleod spoke of having examined 48 taxation packages, broken expenditure into 22 headings, examined 28 different households as examples, and used a computer (a more impressive announcement 30 years ago than now) before deciding to announce a major new tax on goods. A great deal of work had indeed been done, but the 48 taxation systems were reached by counting all sorts of minor variations. However, VAT there would be and, with rejection of the wealth tax removing a progressive correction to the shift away from direct taxation, there was a real risk of Conservative tax plans tipping all too crudely towards a class interest. When Ash Wheatcroft, the VAT specialist, had made his heavy input into Sub-Group A's deliberations, it would be faced with the choice between a French system which fell more heavily on the average consumer and a more progressive German model.

Since, unlike Mrs Thatcher, neither Macleod nor Heath was a class warrior, they opted eventually for the German system.

They also made plans to spend £500 million in benefits to offset the burden of regression, and Macleod settled firmly for the exclusion of food. VAT, which he sold so brilliantly to conference, has been accepted remarkably easily by the public. Were it to come in now, the militant anti-Europeans would be affecting a social conscience and spelling out its comparative regressiveness. For, even after the exclusion of food and other categories of essentials (one of which, domestic heating, was restored by Mr Lamont), it is steps away from the Gladstonian system. But broadly VAT has done its job and avoided giving offence. Though the private view of Lord Cockfield today is that old-fashioned purchase tax before it was muddled in response to pressure groups was a better tax.

There were other activities for this diligent committee, including thoughts on Save as You Earn. But another ambitious and socially progressive scheme – the use of tax credits or negative income tax, a scheme dear to Barney Hayhoe, who had written an ardent pamphlet 'Must the Children Suffer?' – also went to the wall. The scheme would have discriminated against superfluous allowances made to the middle classes and pointed more than £200 million at the 250,000 most needful. Macleod wanted to introduce this and set Terence Higgins to make a study of it. Hayhoe's full idea was not realised and fear of offending middle-class Conservatism played its part in that. But the idea of a credit calling itself a benefit while integrating part of the old allowance would later emerge.

Although there were disappointments, including Macleod's own preferred idea of a payroll tax, Sub-Group A achieved a great deal. For a committee of politicians, academics and businessmen discussing hypotheses, at first in a desultory way, it became a major force for change. It determined thinking towards the practical means for the shift from direct to indirect taxation. (Macleod was at one stage thinking about a 15 per cent tax; his successors would start at 10 but eventually get past him.) Tax and benefits have not yet been integrated and the elaborations of the Borrie Committee for Labour leave that matter very tentative. But politically, the work was done which would let indirect taxation take the weight previously borne by income tax and politically, the effect has been irreversible. In 1997 a Labour Opposition seeking to return to office effectively undertook not to increase a rate of income tax standing at 23 per cent. Rab Butler was deemed (wrongly) to be electioneering when he reduced it from the equivalent of

47¹⁄₂ per cent to 45. The volume of tax taken has not fallen significantly but it falls upon just and unjust in ways which, only in the late nineties, push indirect taxation to the level which annoys the voters and creates the sort of strain of which Arthur Cockfield spoke.

Most of the sub-group's work would be adopted, though VAT came in a year late because after Macleod's death his successor, Anthony Barber, took it upon himself to repeat the elaborate process of consultation that Macleod had already carried out. Barber, a painstaking man without much talent for direct courses of action, saw hundreds of representatives compared with the 30 with which Macleod, determined not to have his thinking amended by interest groups, contented himself.

Macleod as Shadow Chancellor had worked hard and with concentration in a highly technical field, despite having no native taste or interest in economics itself. Politically he had reasserted himself. The walk-out of 1963 and the *Spectator* article of 1964 were water under the bridge. His command in the Commons and his ability to charm and a little bamboozle conference gave much pleasure. He knocked Labour about, choosing his victims according to his own temperament. To James Callaghan, an ex-naval petty officer and though very able, a non-intellectual, he was affectionate: 'By a long chalk the best of them.' With the overcool and formal Roy Jenkins he felt no affinity: 'He makes speeches to the House of Commons, good speeches, but has no dialogue with the House.' Wilson he actively and unilaterally detested. He was ungenerous here. Given to too much heat in partisan matters, he once, close to the 1970 election, shouted 'Swine!' at the Prime Minister. Unlike Jenkins and like Michael Foot and his old friend Enoch Powell, Macleod was a House of Commons man, gregarious, eloquent, enjoying public argument. But after Enoch Powell had spoken in 1968 of black immigration in those famous terms intimating street war and inter-community violence, their friendship was at an end.

Powell and Macleod, together with Maudling, were the exceptional products of Conservative entry in 1950. Both were brilliant speakers, both had reacted in the same disgusted way to Macmillan's chicanery. They were starting to differ on economics, Powell coming to the view that money in circulation rather than wages paid was the driving force of inflation. Macleod used to speak of travelling with Enoch some of the way but getting off a few stations before the train hit the terminus or the buffers. If Macleod had lived and if Powell had not been driven to conclusions which delighted Smithfield meat porters, one might imagine the thinking of the eighties being reached through a filter unclogged by class feeling, triumphalism and central-command politics. The Macleod who flung himself and all his energies into the charity Crisis at Christmas, who intervened against all etiquette on an adjournment to speak against compulsory treatment of meths-drinkers and argue that the problem was greater and more urgent than realised, was a different order of human being from Margaret Thatcher. His views on the role of monetary aggregates in determining the rate of inflation or the optimum size of the private sector might well have changed, but the idea of there being no such thing as society belongs in a galactic system unimaginably remote from the one he inhabited.

Robert Carr describes Powell's relationship with the Shadow Cabinet in which he served, dealing with defence, as one of wide tolerance beyond normal rules, with Powell making speeches on other territory and at odds with official policy. (As much might be said for Macleod, who had enjoyed the free-range approach encouraged by Churchill and who, on Callaghan's Immigration Bill as it affected Kenyan Asians, voted with a bloc of all-party dissidents.) When Powell, on 20 April 1968, made the speech – River Tiber, excreta through letterbox, the fears of ordinary English people – he received the only possible response.

Simon Heffer has described Enoch Powell as 'immensely great'. Powell was in fact saying the sort of things which start riots, give official accommodation to hatred of incomers and other races and translate in the vernacular mind from Horatian allusion to 'The blacks are coming to get us.'

Macleod, Edward Boyle, Quintin Hogg and Robert Carr were, in the view of the Chief Whip, William Whitelaw, ready to quit. But as Edward Heath was as outraged as they were, it was Powell who went, and at once. Macleod had been allowed to break the rules and Powell had not, but only a pedant could object. Putting aside Macleod's former ministerial responsibilities to Kenyan minorities, the Conservative Party was required by Powell's speech to define itself. Heath, whatever his subsequent failings – and he might best be described as a good man without fingertips – did define it. Powell and Macleod, who had been hot and cold, had shared living space and a key and brought their brilliance into politics, were effectively sundered. Macleod had no need to define himself, but when Nigel Fisher was threatened in his Surbiton constituency by a rightist group keen to replace such a liberal with a Powellite, Macleod wrote to *The Times* supporting Fisher and to William Whitelaw saying that if Fisher went, he went.

Macleod should not be projected as an angel. He was an ambitious politician who could be unfair in argument, could calculate and who wanted and enjoyed office. But over Crisis at Christmas, the Kenyan Asians and the whole racial imbroglio, he acted on principle, the sort of principle which comes out in ardent emotional commitment to the non-optional good, Perhaps he did thereby define himself. He was living out a natural morality which didn't stretch and a high politics which justifies public life.

There was very little left to Macleod. He had done the work which related to tax and the economy. He had made his parliamentary contribution to Opposition and at successive conferences had fun and raised morale amid the general nonsense, and also made that memorable oration about other parties scheming their schemes and dreaming their dreams, ending to triumph with the words, 'But we have *work* to do.' There would be very little work, only really the general election in June 1970. It was marked by discouraging polls for the Tories, including one from NOP which gave Labour a 12 per cent lead.

Like most politicians during an election, Macleod managed to give contrary impressions: optimistic ones – including a prophecy of a 35-seat majority very close to the result – and stoical contemplation of defeat. He paced himself lightly, being too much of an old professional to believe that frantic activity achieves anything beyond a virtuous exhaustion. The election went its own way, despite some mischief-making from Powell. It would possibly be affected by a random statistic on the trade deficit, perhaps reflecting a long-matured discontent with Labour stretching back to the July measures of 1966 and the devaluation of 1967. Suddenly, in the last week, polls and feeling changed, Heath seemed to find himself in the campaign and, on the day after the election, 19 June 1970, the Conservatives emerged with a majority just below the number Macleod had lightly flung out, one of 30. Macleod was now Chancellor of the Exchequer, the uncontested second man in government.

He would be there for four weeks, arranging his work on a strict ten-to-five, no receptions, no lunches, no red boxes basis to conserve his energy in the face of mounting, intolerable pain. He would appoint Jenkin, Higgins and Maurice Macmillan as his Treasury team, call up Cockfield to come and advise him, note gloomily some slippage on the wage-front, make one, rather technical, speech to the Commons, point up to his civil servants work to be done on public-spending reductions and the downgrading of statutory control bodies like the Prices and Incomes Board, fall ill, seem to recover and die.

Almost the last thing he did concerned the Deputy Master of the Mint. 'And who is the Master of the Mint?' asked Macleod. 'You are,' was the reply. The falling ill was a sudden burst of new pain suspected of being appendicitis but actually a diverticulum of the pelvis at once successfully operated on. He left hospital (St George's) on 18 July 1970, but stayed in bed at Number 11. Convalescent, he entertained his own doctor to dinner on the evening of Monday 20 July. Having watched some sport on television, he was taken ill at 10.30. There was a delay in a doctor coming from St George's and at 11.35, Iain Macleod was dead. Ted Heath and Willie Whitelaw hastened to comfort Eve; Terence Higgins summoned the undertaker. Calls were put out to colleagues and so Patrick Jenkin, unreachable in the middle of the night because he didn't have a bedside phone, was called next morning and, as he has told, spent a day trying not to collapse into tears.

Macleod's death deprived Edward Heath of someone to argue with him, someone able to say no. It made the Government a one-man affair, removing a Chancellor who would surely have stopped the uncritical reflation of 1972. Equally, Macleod would not, like his successor, Anthony Barber, have let tax changes be so split between two years as to feed the rich separately and make Labour propaganda.

And surely Macleod, equipped to handle the unions as a former Minister of Labour and indeed as a card-player, with the skill that entailed, is unlikely to have been driven into a 'who governs Britain?' election. But if he had been, he would never have delayed it from 7 to 28 February while the actual union claim was visibly being conceded. If Macleod had lived, it is hard to see Heath falling. His talents would almost certainly have foreclosed his succession.

But his loss of the highest post occurred when, driving hard to give black colonies independence, he offended traditional

Tories. And that rejection was underwritten when he opened the dubieties of October 1963 to the people who vote in elections. He always sought to rise, but he had qualities which stood in the way.

---

[1]Churchill, a telephone addict, as one of his exertions for Hailsham had rung Home to discourage his candidacy. The phone was answered by Home himself. Churchill, shocked, put his hand over the speaker and said, 'Goodness, how sad. They live like bloody coolies these days.'

ENVOI

No rules exist for the outcome of races. Endless hope for some and steady profit for others could not flourish on the turf if there were.

But there are pointers as to why, looking for the ablest, most creative, competent or intelligent leader, we quite often get someone else. Macleod had abundant courage and he made enemies who detested his dedicated, unapologetic decolonisation in the teeth of his own party's prejudice. Butler was not a fighter but, having privately judged right over Suez that it was going to hurt us, he made enemies among much the same people for having had the wrong thoughts. Healey had spent much of his political career being, like Butler, the next best thing to a bureaucrat. This was the chap who would sort out defence or the economy and politics would only come into it as an afterthought. But his cuts and economies were political because they hurt and, affronting both ideologues and seat-mindful MPs, they hurt him.

The 'stupid people' of whom Rab Butler complained to his cousin David blocked Macleod's way because the fellow acceptable at Health, admirable at Labour and at getting the party an attractive look for the public, put blacks before kith and kin. And another set of stupid people, Labour leftists blind to economic gravity and the soft Labour middle incapable of resolution, opposed or abandoned Healey.

Gratitude for things done played no part or all would have been chosen. Successfully conducted economies, outstanding education acts, reformed defence structures and home offices

and brilliant demonstration by way of the Health Service that
the Tory Party would not affront the public were water under
the bridge.

Clubbability was esteemed and found wanting. All three of
our near-arrivers were good with their own kind – civil servants
for Butler and Healey; his own warm circle of young,
liberal-minded men for Macleod. Macleod, with his intensifying
physical pain, was short and brisk, except among friends, where
he seems to have been delightful. Healey could be excellent
company, but only if he rated you, and he could be immensely
rude in a way often meant to be joshing but frequently not taken
that way. Butler had no small talk. Lord Denham, later a better
Chief Whip in the Lords than Margaret Thatcher deserved, tells
against himself the story of offering as a young man his opinion
about something to Rab – and Rab's eyes glazing over.

All liked to think of themselves as politicians, but none of
them quite were, though all three actually deserve that
ten-guinea word 'statesman'. Neither Butler nor Healey had an
organised faction; Macleod did, but as his long-term PPS,
Reggie Bennett, remarks, being the leader of one was a fatal
retreat from his strongest position in the late fifties as a *Party*
hero.

Yet all three were party men, good party men – Macleod
sometimes almost tiresomely partisan for someone with
mid-spectrum convictions, Butler to the point of resurrecting his
party in the late forties, Healey in saving Labour from
self-destruction.

All three would have governed better than the chosen
options. Macmillan, Home, Callaghan and Foot had their
qualities, Macmillan and Callaghan especially so. But the idea of
Butler, Macleod and Healey, the cross-party apostolic succession
of best talent, leading Britain lingers regretfully. What a cool
irony of our politics it is that all three were, and would have
called themselves, meritocrats. Politics, after all, is too human
(which may mean too stupid) to be left to merit.

BIBLIOGRAPHY

R. A. BUTLER

Boyd, Francis, *Richard Austen Butler* (Rockcliff Political Monographs, 1956)

Brittan, Samuel, *The Treasury under the Tories 1951–64* (Pelican, 1964)

Butler, Mollie, *August and Rab* (Weidenfeld & Nicolson, 1987)

Butler, R. A., *The Art of the Possible* (Hamish Hamilton, 1982)

Carlton, David, *Anthony Eden* (Blackwell, 1981)

Channon, Henry (Ed. R. Rhodes James), *'Chips': The Diaries of Sir Henry Channon* (Weidenfeld & Nicolson, 1967)

Dell, Edmund, *The Chancellors* (HarperCollins, 1996)

Gaitskell, Hugh (Ed. Philip Williams), *The Gaitskell Diaries* (Jonathan Cape, 1983)

Henderson, Nicholas, *The Private Office* (Weidenfeld & Nicolson, 1984)

Horne, Alistair, *Macmillan 1891–1956* (Macmillan, 1988)

——, *Macmillan 1956–1986* (Macmillan, 1989)

Howard, Anthony, *The Life of R. A. Butler* (Jonathan Cape, 1987)

Jenkins, Roy, *Portraits and Miniatures* (Macmillan, 1993)

Jenkins, Roy (contributor), *The Dictionary of National Biography 1981–85* (Oxford University Press, 1990)

Munch-Petersen, Thomas, *Common Sense Not Bravado* (Scandia, 1986)

Ramsden, John, *A History of the Conservative Party* (Longman, 1978 *et seq.*)

Rhodes James, Robert, *Anthony Eden* (Weidenfeld & Nicolson, 1986)

Shepherd, Robert, *Iain Macleod* (Pimlico, 1995)

Walters, Sir Dennis, *Not Always With the Pack* (Constable, 1989)

Williams, Philip, *Hugh Gaitskell* (Jonathan Cape, 1979)

DENIS HEALEY

Benn, Tony (Ed. Ruth Winstone), *The Benn Diaries 1980–90* (Hutchinson, 1994)

Bullock, Alan, *Ernest Bevin* (Volume III – Foreign Secretary) (OUP, 1985)

Burk and Cairncross, *Goodbye Great Britain* (Yale University Press, 1992)

Callaghan, James, *Time and Chance* (Collins, 1987)

Crossman, Richard (Ed. Anthony Howard), *The Crossman Diaries* (1979)

Dell, Edmund, *The Chancellors* (HarperCollins, 1996)

Healey, Denis, *The Time of My Life* (Michael Joseph, 1989)

——, *My Secret Planet* (Michael Joseph, 1992)

Howard, Michael, 'The Central Organisation of Defence' (Chatham House Pamphlet, 1970)

Pimlott, Ben, *Harold Wilson* (HarperCollins, 1992)

Pliatzky, Leo, *Getting and Spending* (Basil Blackwell, 1982)

IAIN MACLEOD

Campbell, John, *Nye Bevan* (Weidenfeld & Nicolson, 1987)

Churchill, Winston S., *His Father's Son: A Life of Randolph Churchill* (Weidenfeld & Nicolson, 1996)

Cockfield, A., 'A Study of Conservative Preparations (1966–70) for Reform of the Tax System' (unpublished)

Dell, Edmund, *The Chancellors* (HarperCollins, 1996)

Fisher, Sir Nigel, *Iain Macleod* (Deutsch, 1973)

Horne, Alistair, *Macmillan 1956–1986* (Macmillan, 1989)

Jenkins, Roy, *Portraits and Miniatures* (Macmillan, 1993)

Morgan, Charles, *The House of Macmillan* (Macmillan, 1943)

Pimlott, Ben, *Harold Wilson* (HarperCollins, 1992)

Shepherd, Robert, *Iain Macleod* (Pimlico, 1995)

Walters, Sir Dennis, *Not Always With the Pack* (Constable, 1989)

Williams, Philip, *Hugh Gaitskell* (Jonathan Cape, 1979)

INDEX